D0146836

Ohio

The History of a People

Andrew R. L. Cayton

The Ohio State University Press
Columbus

𝒥𝐻

Copyright © 2002 by The Ohio State University.
All rights reserved.

Library of Congress Cataloging-in-Publication Data

Cayton, Andrew R. L., 1954–
   Ohio : the history of a people / Andrew R. L. Cayton.
      p. cm.
   Includes index.
   ISBN 0-8142-0899-1 (cloth : alk. paper)
   1. Ohio—History. I. Title.
   F491 .C39 2002
   977.1
                                        2001007350

Text and jacket design by Dan O'Dair.
Type set in Adobe Garamond by Sans Serif, Inc.
Printed by Thomson-Shore, Inc.

The paper used in this publication meets the minimum requirements of the American
National Standard for Information Sciences—Permanence of Paper for Printed Library
Materials. ANSI Z39.48-1992.

9   8   7   6   5   4   3   2   1

for Mary Kupiec Cayton, a Virginian lost in Ohio

Contents

Preface

﹏

THIS BOOK is a history of the state of Ohio from its creation in 1803 through the beginning of the twenty-first century. It recounts important political events as well as major economic and social developments. But *Ohio: The History of a People* is above all a narrative driven by the stories people have told about life in an American state.

I have drawn on the fiction, art, music, architecture, jokes, petitions, letters, diaries, parades, speeches, organizations, sports, and strikes of a variety of Ohioans in an effort to weave together a larger tale of grand expectations, intense conflicts, and serious disappointments. Despite Ohio's reputation in contemporary American popular culture as a bland, uninteresting place, its citizens have thought a good deal about what it has been and what it might be. Indeed, a significant part of public culture has been about asserting and defending differing interpretations of the state's past and its future.

Taken together, the narratives Ohioans have constructed to make sense of their world trace the rise of a culture of respectability, the resistance it provoked, and its ultimate transformation into a culture of consumerism. In the 1800s, a considerable number of mostly Protestant, middle-class Ohioans came to believe that material and moral glory would grace their state if they devoted themselves to the great cause of human progress. To be respectable was to behave in ways that stressed self-discipline and commitment. Changing the world was not the work of a handful of great men acting decisively on battlefields or in legislative chambers. Only the collective power of multitudes of ordinary people would improve the human condition as a whole. "[T]he growing good of the world is partly dependent on unhistoric acts," explained the English novelist George Eliot in the concluding lines of *Middlemarch,* "and that things are not no so ill with you and me as they might have been, is half owing to the number who lived faithfully a hidden life, and rest in unvisited tombs."

Not everyone appreciated the nobility of such efforts. Indeed, the champions of respectability, who thought they were liberating human beings from centuries of barbarism and servitude, alienated as many people as they inspired. Their critics thought them arrogant, hypocritical, and dangerous prigs who squeezed the joy out of life. Worse, they threatened to restrict the freedom of American citizens to live their lives as they chose. These charges were as powerful as the resistance they engendered, especially in the late 1800s and early 1900s. Ultimately, however, the self-proclaimed respectable citizens of Ohio adapted their vision to changing circumstances. In the twentieth century, the descendants of the apostles of reform became the guardians of the status quo their ancestors had established. As they and their fellow citizens stressed the importance of economic rather than moral progress, they redefined life in Ohio as the pursuit of material comfort and personal satisfaction.

Ohio: The History of a People, then, is a chronicle of tales of American life whose common denominator is their location in the culturally contested landscape we call Ohio. Its major theme is the transformation of a radical imperative to do good into a conservative desire to live well.

The courthouse in Chillicothe served as the capitol of the state of Ohio from 1803 to 1810. (Courtesy of The Ohio Historical Society, Columbus, Ohio)

Prologue
Citizens

⁓

"I . . . NOW CONSIDER myself a Citizen of Ohio," Gideon Granger, postmaster-general of the United States, informed his friend Samuel Huntington in 1804. This simple declaration was an extraordinary statement. Granger had never been to Ohio, nor would he ever set foot within the borders of the new state. He called himself a "citizen" solely because he had decided to "fix [his] residence in the County of Trumbull."[1] Granger's assertion reminds us that Ohio was a state before it was a place, a government before it was a community, an idea before it was a reality. Created primarily for political reasons, it was an awkward construction with arbitrary borders.

The members of the 1802 Constitutional Convention who gathered in Chillicothe to devise a state government described themselves as the representatives of "the people" living in "the eastern division of the territory of the United States northwest of the river Ohio" who had mutually agreed "to form [them]selves into a free and independent State, by the name of the STATE OF OHIO." These men had only slightly more emotional attachment to Ohio than Granger. Most had lived north and west of the Ohio River for a few years at best. As important, they thought they were very different from each other. Few understood, let alone respected, the Wyandot, Miami, Shawnee, and other Indians who lived along the southwestern shores of Lake Erie. Like the Northwest Territory from which it was carved, Ohio was, in the words of a group of Marietta residents, a "mixed mass of people, scattered over an immense wilderness, with scarcely a connecting principle."[2]

Still, if the founders of Ohio knew little about their state's past or present, they cared deeply about its future. They imagined Ohio as a

1

place of limitless possibilities. Ignoring the presence of Indians—and despite the risk to their lives and prospects—they saw their new state as a blank canvass on which they could paint a magnificent future of prosperity and harmony. The creation of Ohio was one of the great acts of the American Enlightenment. Its founders did not consider the state distinctive or romanticize its landscapes and its peoples. Such things did not matter to them because they were not trying to create something unique. Rather, they were making a political community designed to exemplify a larger experiment in universal brotherhood.

True sons of the eighteenth century, Ohio's founders believed in progress, the importance of the triumph of civilization over barbarism, limited democracy, and a vague commitment to social equality for respectable white males. Yet they also took a rather dim view of human nature. People, after all, were at heart passionate beasts who would normally pursue their own interests at the expense of their neighbors. Properly structured, a public culture built around governments, churches, schools, and newspapers could educate people about the importance of overcoming their natural instincts. It could tame human beings by inculcating civility and industry. Ohio was an opportunity to fashion a world that would bring out the best in people.

The political experiment that was Ohio would work only if its residents could be persuaded to behave like citizens. Unlike subjects, who lived at the mercy of their superiors—be they kings, queens, emperors, or aristocrats—citizens actively participated in their government. In a monarchy, power flowed from the top down. The most important political connections were vertical ones; the most important source of loyalty was to the Crown; and, at least in theory, a country was the domain of the its ruler. Eighteenth-century revolutions had overturned this conception of politics. In the United States, as in France, subjects became citizens. Endowed with natural rights and equality before the law, they became "the people." Their primary loyalty was to each other, not to their superiors. Liberty was now a universal right, not an exclusive privilege.

In the minds of its founders, Ohio's success depended above all else on the participation of its citizens, not just through suffrage, juries, or military service, but in the public realm as a whole. Citizens had responsibilities as well as rights, obligations as well as freedoms.

Ohioans had to talk to each other. They had to gather information from newspapers, books, and pamphlets, elevate their sensibilities through exposure to events and peoples throughout the world, and participate in a larger community of free, independent men. Public culture was all about public conversation. It was a ceaseless process of engaging the world and caring about more than local or selfish interests.

Breaking with centuries of European tradition, the founders of Ohio, like the founders of the United States, created no standing armies, no established churches, no entrenched aristocracy to ensure stability. Rather, they imagined that the thousands of ordinary white men who were populating the state would create their own institutions and rely on each other for support and protection. Together, they would demonstrate the capacity of human beings to overcome their fears and prejudices and develop a place of unprecedented material and moral progress. Constitutions could make states, and laws could create borders. But a community was something formed by its members in conversation with each other about common interests. In the end, Ohio could be nothing more or less than what its citizens thought it should be.

Creating a State

In the late eighteenth century, the United States claimed the area that became Ohio as part of the Northwest Territory. Organized by Congress in the Northwest Ordinance of 1787, the territory was made up of federal land to which the states, particularly Virginia, had ceded their claims. It was one of the few places over which the U.S. government had direct authority. Initially governed by a nationally appointed governor and three judges, the territory acquired a weak two-house assembly as it grew, although there were property restrictions on voting and serving. Meanwhile, the powers of the territorial governor remained high: they included the right to veto all legislation and to call and dismiss the assembly at will. The undemocratic character of this government was intentional. The United States Congress wanted to ensure that its officials and friends had established a proper environment before the residents of the Northwest Territory assumed the rights of American citizenship.

Many of the young and ambitious settlers of the Ohio Country in the late 1790s and early 1800s objected to what they saw as an autocratic territorial government. They had no patience with congressional plans for the slow development of the region. Demanding to govern themselves, they increasingly focused their ire on territorial governor Arthur St. Clair. Scottish-born, the pompous and indiscreet St. Clair was a prominent local landowner in western Pennsylvania before he embarked on an undistinguished career as a military officer during the American War for Independence. St. Clair's frontier experience and his dogged support of a strong national government won him appointment as territorial governor in 1788, a post he held until he was dismissed by President Thomas Jefferson in early 1803. St. Clair alienated many people with his incompetence, his lengthy absences, his alleged drunkenness, and his arrogance. The governor had little interest in participating in the public culture of the Northwest Territory. He ignored the opinions of the overwhelming majority of the people he governed, dismissing those citizens as "a multitude of indigent and ignorant people" who were "ill qualified to form a constitution and a government for themselves."[3] No one could take seriously St. Clair's commitment to shaping good citizens when he seemed to have so little concern for them as human beings.

The underlying opposition to St. Clair coalesced with the meetings of the territorial assembly in 1798 and 1799. Immigrants from Virginia and Connecticut found common cause in seeking to bring down the tyrant. By the early 1800s, a coterie of Virginians in the Scioto Valley in alliance with some ambitious merchants in Cincinnati and recently arrived New Englanders in the northeast had emerged as the leaders of the opposition. Principal among them was the earnest Thomas Worthington, a Virginia-born planter who had settled in the Scioto Valley in 1797 and who was in the process of building an estate he called Adena. (Rather, Worthington's African-American "servants" were building it, his Quaker-based opposition to slavery as an institution notwithstanding.) By 1813, Worthington owned over 18,000 acres and lived in a fine Georgian mansion designed by Benjamin Latrobe. Thirty years old in 1803, Worthington was a prickly and reserved man who communicated with others through correspondence and a local newspaper.

Worthington suffered in comparison with his popular brother-in-law. The English-born Virginian Edward Tiffin was a doctor and Methodist lay preacher who would become Ohio's first governor in 1803. Tiffin's easy manner gained him friends throughout the Scioto Valley. As ardent as Worthington was cautious, deeply religious and unashamedly personal, Tiffin relied on his sincerity to win "the affections of the people." Invoking a language of love, he envisioned Ohio as the home of people whose strongest connection was affection for each other. According to Tiffin, even partisan political organizations offered opportunities to join with "good *democratic republican[s]*" (that is, Christian "fathers, brothers, and friends") in order "to connect in the indissoluble bonds of patriotic friendship citizens of known attachment to the political rights of human nature, and the liberties of the country."[4] More than a political act, the creation of an American state would facilitate the flourishing of a society based on choice and affection rather than command and force.

In 1802, the campaign for statehood climaxed in a widespread public discussion. Hundreds of letters, handbills, and public toasts spoke of the need to rid the region of St. Clair and create a more democratic government. Corresponding societies rallied voters. Nothing was more important in this crusade than newspapers. Territorial residents exchanged ideas in long letters to their editors. Widely circulated newspapers made no pretense of objectivity. St. Clair's critics appealed directly to "public opinion," asking citizens to listen, read, discuss, and participate. And they succeeded in dramatically increasing voter turnout.

Overwhelmed, St. Clair and his friends lost everything. By 1802, the area that would become Ohio had more than the sixty thousand residents required to apply for admission to the Union. More important, the new administration of President Thomas Jefferson was eager to dispose of obstructionist Federalist officeholders such as St. Clair. In 1802, a Congress dominated by Jeffersonian Republicans authorized the calling of a Constitutional Convention and then approved both the constitution and the admission of Ohio to equal membership in the United States on February 19, 1803.

Not everyone was happy to leave territorial status behind. Many feared higher taxes; others worried about the motives of Worthington and his friends. But supporters of statehood saw the federal action as inevitable. According to Edward Tiffin, the inhabitants of the Northwest Territory were "free men and have rights which the god of nature and the benign influences of the federal constitution is waiting to confer upon us." Congress was making it possible for them to become legally what they were already were, to move from a government under which "we now *breathe,* to one under which we may *live.*"[5]

If St. Clair and his allies believed that intractable human tendencies had to be regulated by strong institutions dominated by enlightened gentlemen, Ohio's new leaders held that people could become good citizens by learning how to restrain their selfish impulses. While government should not coerce its people, responsible leaders had to help their fellow citizens make themselves into better human beings. The idea was to encourage civility, not impose it.

The members of the Constitutional Convention agreed that "the voice of the people . . . is the voice of god in a republican government." Despite worries that without a strong court system "the whim of the moment would be the law of the land, and there would be no security for the enjoyment of life, liberty, or property," most were eager to put power in the hands of the people's representatives. Accordingly, they made the General Assembly the most powerful branch of government. The people would choose state representatives annually and state senators every two years to consider the general welfare, enact appropriate laws, and appoint judges and administrators. Governors, who would be elected every two years, would facilitate this process but exercise little real power; they could not veto acts of the legislature, for example. Meanwhile, the General Assembly was responsible for appointing all state and county judges, including members of the Ohio Supreme Court. The structure of the state government embodied the contention of Michael Baldwin, one of the most active participants in the Constitutional Convention, that "all power" ought to flow "from the people," for they were "fully competent to govern themselves" and were "the only proper judges of their own interests and their own concerns."[6]

The constitution guaranteed citizens more than it demanded of them. Article 8 affirmed that Ohioans had been "born equally free and independent, and [had] certain natural, inherent and unalienable rights; amongst which are the enjoying and defending [of] life and liberty, acquiring, possessing and protecting property, and pursuing and obtaining happiness and safety." "[F]ounded on their sole authority," Ohio's government was dedicated to protecting the "rights and liberties" and securing the "independence" of its citizens, who alone had the right to "alter, reform or abolish their government, whenever they may deem it necessary."

In Ohio, the rights of the people were supreme. The constitution outlawed slavery and involuntary servitude except as punishment for criminal behavior. Because "no human authority can, in any case whatever, control or interfere with the rights of conscience," no one would be forced to support any religion. No official could search anyone's home or arrest anyone without a warrant. There would no be no hereditary titles. A citizen could "speak, write or print, upon any subject, as he thinks proper, being liable for the abuse of that liberty"; expect expeditious, fair, and public trials by juries of his peers; and assemble peaceably with others to seek redress of grievances.

To be sure, the constitution stressed civic obligations. It restated the Northwest Ordinance of 1787's insistence that because "religion, morality and knowledge" were "necessary to good government and the happiness of mankind," schools were "forever [to] be encouraged by legislative provision not inconsistent with the rights of conscience." It also acknowledged that, on occasion, private property had to be sacrificed "to the public welfare," as long as the owner was compensated. Still, the document was largely an assertion of liberty against the tyranny of power.

Indeed, the founders of Ohio thought it better to deal with an excess of freedom than to lose it altogether. Many envisioned Ohio as a state dominated by men such as themselves, respected local leaders who would meet once a year as the General Assembly. They assumed that the major business of state government would be the progressive development of Ohio and the restraint of human licentiousness. As the state constitution noted with regard to criminals, "the true design of all punishments" was "to reform, not to exterminate, mankind."

The constitution's authors knew that the success of their experiment rested on the commitment of the citizens. They had to participate.

They had to care about public as well as private concerns. They had to identify themselves not just as citizens of the United States but as citizens of Ohio. To become more than a "mixed mass of people" without "a connecting principle," they would have to imagine themselves as a community.

Defining "the People"

Nothing was more central to public conversation in early Ohio than deciding who constituted "the people." Judging by the constitution, the founders of the state saw "the people" as adult white males. In order to determine the number of representatives in the General Assembly, they ordered a census "of all the white male inhabitants, above twenty-one years of age" be taken every four years. To serve in the legislature, a man had to be a citizen of the United States and a resident of the county or district he would represent, as well as an adult of at least twenty-five years (for the House) or thirty years (for the Senate). The rules for elections reinforced the limits of citizenship. White males over twenty-one could vote in early Ohio, according to the constitution, if they had lived in the state for at least a year and who were subject to a state or county tax. Although this provision did not amount to universal white male suffrage, it was remarkably democratic. Merely paying taxes, not owning property, gave a person a stake in the community.

The absence of references to women and the frequent use of the pronoun "he" indicate that women were not members of the body politic, although they were participants in public culture. They influenced their husbands, sons, and brothers and shaped the character of private and public conversation. But women could not vote, serve in the militia, hold office, or participate in jury deliberations. Although some women owned property and paid taxes, they were generally seen as dependent creatures, unable to control their own bodies and emotions, let alone their environments. Women were too immersed in personal relationships, in ties of familial affection, especially to their children and relatives, to qualify for the manly business of citizenship. After all, the primary responsibility of a citizen was to think about the larger interests of the state as a whole.

The same was true of African Americans. "The people" was a brotherhood of equal white men. The constitution's ban on slavery did not equate with a warm welcome for blacks. In the convention, a proposal to give blacks the right to vote was defeated when president Edward Tiffin broke a seventeen-seventeen tie. That vote marked the high point of political rights for blacks in the early nineteenth century. In 1803, the General Assembly passed an act "to regulate black and mulatto persons." Regulation was only the half of it, however. The assembly was intent on keeping African Americans out of Ohio. After June 1, 1804, the people, acting through their representatives, forbade "black and mulatto persons" from residing in the state without a legal certificate of their freedom. Those who qualified under this provision had to register their name and those of all family members) with the county clerk and pay twelve and a half cents for a certificate within two years. Without these certificates, blacks were forbidden to work. Anyone who hired someone without legal documentation was subject to a fine (to be divided between the state and the informer), as was anyone who aided or harbored fugitive slaves. The act also required local officials to cooperate with people seeking the return of enslaved African Americans. It is worth noting that the act referred to black people as "persons" and threatened anyone who illegally tried to seize a black or mulatto person without observing the legal requirements with a thousand-dollar fine. These provisions, however, should not obscure the purpose of the legislation, which was to make it difficult for blacks to live in Ohio.

Three years later, in January 1807, the General Assembly tightened these restrictions. Now blacks and mulattos could not live in Ohio unless they had, within twenty days of their arrival, posted a five-hundred-dollar bond with the clerk of the county court. Such an exorbitant amount of money was to ensure the "good behavior" of the people posting it and to support them if they became indigent, but the underlying purpose was to exclude all but a handful of African Americans. Any resident who helped someone evade the bond faced a fine of up to a hundred dollars. The 1807 act went beyond restricting migration. Section 4 forbade blacks and mulattos from being sworn or giving evidence "in any cause depending, or matter of controversy, where either party to the same is a white person."[7] While these regulations were often ignored in practice, blacks had to contend with discrimination in every aspect of their lives. Most whites deemed them too unruly and too uncivilized to develop the necessary breadth of vision and self-control necessary to become good citizens.

Indians were another matter altogether. They were not mentioned in the constitution. In 1795, the Great Lakes Indians had surrendered their claims to the southern two-thirds of what became Ohio in the Treaty of Greenville. Thousands of Wyandots, Shawnee, Delaware, and others continued to live within the borders of the state, especially in the northwest, where Americans would not venture in large numbers until the 1820s and 1830s. Along the Sandusky and Maumee Rivers were several Indian villages, the homes of African Americans and French Canadians as well as Indians. The Quaker Gerald T. Hopkins was particularly impressed with Browns-Town, a village of two hundred houses inhabited largely by Wyandots located between present-day Toledo and Detroit. The town had a "Civilized appearance." Its residents lived in log houses with bark roofs, erected fences around their fields, cultivated corn, wheat, oats, and fruit, and raised cattle, hogs, and horses.[8]

Most whites, however, were frightened of Indians, coveted their land, and wanted to be rid of them. After the War of 1812 between the U.S. and Great Britain, the major group of Indians remaining within Ohio was encircled with new borders. When the Wyandots signed the Treaty of Fort Meigs on September 29, 1817, they agreed to live on reservations. Fifteen years later, pressure led to another treaty in which the Wyandots, Senecas, and Shawnees were restricted to 146,316 acres near Upper Sandusky. Finally, the Wyandot Treaty of 1842 provided for the removal of the Ohio Indians to 148,000 acres west of the Mississippi River. The federal government paid them an annuity of $17,500, along with $10,000 for their new settlements, and $23,860 to cover their debts. Close to seven hundred people departed on July 12, 1842, traveling south through Cincinnati and west via the Ohio River. Segregated and then removed, Indians never enjoyed the option of considering themselves citizens of Ohio.

The early leaders of Ohio had created a democratic government and announced a commitment to social equality for adult white men. But while they had laid the foundation of a public culture, they had not established a general definition of the meaning of life in their new state. To the contrary, there would be as many stories of Ohio as there were people living within its borders. What made Ohio dynamic were the voices of the diverse peoples pouring into the state in the early nineteenth century, most of whom saw its promise less in terms of citizenship than in the protection of their families.

John F. Mansfield drew this map of the State of Ohio in 1806. (Courtesy of The Western Reserve Historical Society, Cleveland, Ohio)

1

Strangers in Canaan

—

ONE DAY in the summer of 1804, Joseph Gibbons, a young Quaker from Chester County, Pennsylvania, sat on his horse on a piece of land near Steubenville and tried to make up his mind. Should he buy this place and bring his "tender wife and helpless offspring" on "a wearisome Journey to a Strange land?" Or was it just too much trouble, too much of a risk? Gibbons finally decided to purchase the property, reassuring himself that he could always sell it later without any appreciable loss. Besides, approximately thirty acres had been cleared and fenced, and there was "a good Spring near to a suitable place for building." Perhaps it could "be made a hansome agreeable place." But still there were weeds and lice. "[T]he best land" was gone. Farms thirty or more miles from the Ohio River were unlikely to be profitable because of the difficulty of transporting goods to markets. The land was rough and uneven, "which in some places will make unpleasant Plowing & must for a considerable length of time cause bad roads."[1]

None of these problems dissuaded Gibbons. He could not resist the possibilities of life in Ohio. The cost of living was low, and the price of land was going up. Indians were no longer a serious threat. The state's constitution was tolerable, except for the fact that it did not exempt Quakers from military service or marriage requirements, which he thought could safely be ignored. Above all, the prospects for commerce and happiness were high. When Gibbons first saw the Ohio River, which was "the handsomest" he had ever seen, he could not help but contemplate "the future grandeur of this western world—when this Stream should be covered with vessels spreading their canvass to the wind, to convey the produce of this fertile country to New Orleans and across the Atlantick Ocean." Ohio was already a place of "general Contentment" for both men and women. Persuaded that "thousands might be found who were lavish in praise of this New Canaan," Gibbons returned to Pennsylvania, sold his property, collected his wife, Sarah, and their children, and moved to Belmont County.[2] There Sarah gave birth to a daughter named Mary on November 26, 1807. Thirteen years later the Gibbonses were still in Belmont County.

On paper, it sounds so straightforward: travel to Ohio, buy some land, move a family, and live happily ever after. In reality, of course, it was much more complicated. Joseph and Sarah Gibbons had several advantages when they moved, including money and a network of connections through their membership in the Society of Friends. The trek across the Appalachians to the Ohio Country—whether through the Cumberland Gap into Kentucky and north, or via western New York and around the south shores of Lake Erie, or across Pennsylvania— was arduous and dangerous. Travelers contended with impassable roads, terrible inns, and general disorientation. They encountered languages, foods, and customs they had never known. They missed relatives and friends they feared they would never see again. In 1816, Massachusetts native Nathaniel Dike found "the act of taking a final leave of my friends" for life in "a land of strangers" to be "most cruel and distressing."[3] Craving news of the places they had left, settlers were overjoyed when they met someone whose name they knew or who had a tie to their home.

And yet thousands of them went. Like Joseph and Sarah Gibbons, they risked everything for life in the new state. Many traveled together, for as one person argued, "the difficulties and inconveniences of a settlement in a new country are rendered the more easy & tolerable when . . . a number of families by agreement [migrate] from a settlement in the same nei[gh]borhood."[4] Once settlers arrived in Ohio, they overwhelmingly sought to live with people they knew. Just as overwhelmingly, they distrusted those whose ways were unfamiliar. Although idealistic about the possibilities of life in Ohio, they were realistic about its limitations and frightened by its dangers, real and imagined. Living in a place with multitudes of ideas, religions, customs, and dialects, people told different stories about their migration and settlement. To one degree or another, they were all concerned with preserving their way of life and promoting the welfare of their families and friends. They generally were unwilling to imagine a world in which people should and could engage in a larger conversation about the progress of the state as a whole. They identified with their households, their religion, their race, or their places of origins. Ohio was a collection of disparate peoples united by little more than a desire to improve their lives on their own terms.

Creating a Landscape

The population of Ohio exploded in the first half of the nineteenth century. From 45,365 in 1800, it rose to 230,760 in 1810, 581,434 in 1820, and 1,980,329 in 1850. Virtually barren of English-speaking residents in 1790, Ohio was the third largest state in the Union by 1850 and elected close to 9 percent of the members of the U.S. House of Representatives. Forty-eight villages had more than a hundred residents. Cincinnati, the largest of them, was the principal American city west of the Appalachians and north of New Orleans.

Most of Ohio's settlers had been born along the Atlantic seaboard, especially in Virginia, Pennsylvania, and Connecticut. Even before the great migration of Germans and Irish to the U.S. in the 1840s, there were native-born and second-generation Germans (usually called "Dutch"), Scots-Irish, Irish, Swiss, and French. By 1850, there were more than seventy thousand Germans in Ohio, some thirty-two thousand Irish, and thousands of French, Welsh, Canadians, Scottish, and Swiss. African Americans came, too, but in small numbers. Officially, there were only 337 blacks in what would become Ohio in 1800; that number more than quadrupled to 1,890 in 1810, reached 4,723 in 1820, and stood at 9,586 in 1830, roughly 1 percent of the total population of the state. The Indian population, already small in 1800, dwindled after the War of 1812 and was pretty much eradicated by removal in the 1840s. There were plenty of people of Indian ancestry, but fewer and fewer identified themselves as such. Despite the diversity in the origins of its settlers, Ohio in 1830 was a white person's world.

To the extent that anything united Ohioans, it was their belief that their status as American citizens entitled them to live their lives as they saw fit. Most were interested in preserving ethnic or religious traditions. Women in particular sought to preserve and extend social networks and their ties with families and friends back home. Loyal to their language, faithful to their religion, familiar with their food and animals, most men and many women were nonetheless almost always on the lookout for ways to make money. Settlers frequently worried about access to the nearest market. Where could they sell their corn, wheat, whiskey, pork, hides, potash, honey, ginseng, apples, dairy products, and cattle? Where could they buy coffee, tea, salt, sugar, hardware, cloth, books, mirrors, and china?

Within two decades, immigrants had purchased most of the land in Ohio. The U.S. had extinguished the claims of Indians through treaty cessions, most notably the Treaty of Greenville in 1795, an 1817 treaty with the Wyandots, and the St. Mary's Treaty of 1818. Meanwhile, the federal Land Act of 1800 made it possible to buy land (in sections of 360 acres) on credit for $2 an acre; an 1820 act abolished credit but reduced the purchase size to eight acres and the price to $1.25 per acre. Land sold by Congress in the 1780s to the Ohio Company and John Cleves Symmes, as well as the territory reserved for Connecticut (the Western Reserve and Firelands), was also available. By 1821, federal land offices in Marietta, Zanesville, Steubenville, Chillicothe, Cincinnati, Piqua, Wooster, and Delaware had sold two-thirds of all available federal lands, amounting to more than 7 million acres. By 1830, there was little desirable land left in the state. The settlement of Ohio had happened with unprecedented speed and thoroughness. A child born in the sparsely populated Northwest Territory in 1802 faced an impossible task if he wished to find good land to buy when he was twenty-one. Only the northwestern corner of the state, much of which was swampy, remained unimproved.

Buying land was easy compared to the backbreaking labor of clearing it and preparing it for cultivation. A few people could afford to hire others to do the work for them. Others relied on family members and friends. Many did it themselves, often leaving stumps to rot in the middle of fields while they plowed around them. However they accomplished the task, they got it done quickly. Heavily forested

Ohio was stripped bare. By 1900, only about 10 percent of the state was wooded (compared to nearly 40 percent in 2000). Meanwhile, flora and fauna also were transformed. Ohioans hunted deer and squirrels for food and killed wolves that threatened domesticated animals. Counties posted bounties for wolf pelts. In December 1818, more than five hundred men gathered in Medina County to tighten a figurative noose around local animals. In one day, they slaughtered three hundred deer, twenty-one bears, and seventeen wolves.

In a few decades, immigrants completely revised the landscape of Ohio. Dividing and subdividing land, destroying forests, and eradicating animals and plants, they substituted a mixture of old and new crops and animals. As all encompassing as the transformation was, it was far from uniform. Regional variations were pronounced. The citizens of Ohio who lived in the Miami Valley shared much with the citizens of Ohio who lived in the Western Reserve. Most spoke English, most were Protestant, most wanted easy access to markets. But when early settlers suspected that the various regions of the state were very different, they were not wrong.

Terrain and drainage dictated development. Ohio offered settlers a variety of land and soils. Geologists refer to much of the western half of the state as the Till Plains. Shaped by glaciers that advanced from the north more than a million years ago, the area's fertile escarpments and plains to the north and valleys to the south made it prime agricultural land. Around Lake Erie was the Lake Plain, a series of shifting and often wet terraces. Running diagonally from the northeast toward what is now Columbus, glaciation produced a variety of flat and undulating terrain that was of mixed value agriculturally. Least affected by glaciers was the hilly southeast.

Glaciers also rearranged waterways. Water to the north of the Backbone, which crosses Ohio from the west center to the northeast center of the state, flows toward Lake Erie; to the south it drains into the Ohio River. In the early 1800s, everything followed the movement of water. For a hundred-plus miles south of Lake Erie creeks drained into the Tuscarawas, Cuyahoga, Sandusky, and Maumee Rivers and then into the lake itself. All water south of the Backbone flowed into the Muskingum, Hocking, Scioto, Little Miami, and Great Miami Rivers and then into the Ohio, the Mississippi, and eventually the Gulf of Mexico. Not until canals and then trains linked the Ohio River and Lake Erie would the two drainage areas be united—and then only weakly. Even today, Cincinnati arguably has more in common with the river cities of Louisville, Nashville, St. Louis, and Memphis than it does with the lake cities of Cleveland, Toledo, Detroit, and Buffalo.

Paralleling variations in soil and terrain were variations in settlement patterns. Southerners tended to move into the river valleys in the southern third of Ohio, while New Englanders clustered in the northeast and the lower Muskingum Valley. Pennsylvanians and settlers from New Jersey and New York dominated eastern and central Ohio as well as the Miami Valley. They brought with them different words, accents, foods, and building styles. New Englanders tended to build cottages of one and a half stories as well as English-style three-bay barns. In the middle of the state were found simple log houses and I-house homes (one room deep and two stories high). Barns were Pennsylvania Dutch or bank style with a lower level in the side of a hill and an overhanging forebay on the upper level. Southerners dotted the bottom third of Ohio with Virginia I and "saddlebag" houses and transverse frame barns. In central and southern Ohio, settlers tended to speak a Midland dialect. In the northeast, they used a New England–New York dialect. Midland expressions included quarter 'til, blinds (for shades), skillet, and cling peach, while northeasterners introduced pail, swill, Dutch cheese, and johnnycake.

Within regions existed distinctive local communities. Election procedures reinforced the homogeneity of rural neighborhoods. County sheriffs, who supervised elections, announced the time and place of the polling and provided the ballot box. After 1809, township trustees served as election judges. Voting usually occurred at a courthouse, tavern, church, or, occasionally, a private home. Men came from miles around to participate, spending the day entertaining themselves with conversation, food, and drink. There was a lot to see because voting was done in public. Typically, a prospective voter presented the election judges with a paper (usually printed) with the names of the candidates for whom he wished to vote. At this point, another citizen could challenge the qualifications of the voter. If there was no problem, the judges inserted the ballot into the box. At the end of the allotted time, the three judges counted the votes, recorded them, and announced the results.

This public informality favored well-established residents with family connections in the community and discriminated against strangers. Because township judges were the sole determinants of residency, they could deny suffrage if they decided that the person had not resided in the township for at least a year. Until at least the middle of the nineteenth century, new voters were at the mercy of neighbors who, by excluding them from participation in the choice of county commissioners, local officials, and state representatives, effectively excluded them from membership in their community as a whole. Election procedures, in other words, permitted Ohioans to indulge their prejudices against people who were different. Supporters of various candidates lobbied and bullied voters. In 1822, a Dayton newspaper editor watched with disgust as a printed ballot was "thrust into [a voter's] hand, a guard placed over him to attend him to the ballot box and watch to see that he votes the ticket thus palmed upon him."[5]

Because distrust of difference was widespread, people tended to gather together against the world, to congregate in enclaves of familiar people who shared similar customs and values. They also tended to attack those people who made a public fetish of their idiosyncrasies. More often than not, such attacks took the form of jokes, verbal insults, and gossip. Occasionally, however, it was more serious. A particularly egregious example of hostility toward Ohioans who celebrated their uniqueness occurred with the Mormon settlement at Kirtland.

Founded in the early 1820s by Vermonter Joseph Smith, who called himself "the "Prophet," Mormonism grew quickly thanks to the zealousness of its early members, the appeal of its democratic theology, and its call for a return to simple principles. The Book of Mormon told the story of the development of an American branch of Christianity in the earliest days of the church, a branch uncorrupted by the decadence and hierarchy of Europe. Mormons came to Kirtland in the early 1830s, building homes, businesses, schools, and temples, and publishing books. They hoped to strengthen the bonds of their community by improving themselves and presenting a united front to those who opposed them. The centerpiece of their work was the construction of a sandstone temple, which looked like a New England church but with two levels and features peculiar to Mormonism.

Smith was a dreamer, an especially bold version of the town boosters who populated Ohio in the early nineteenth century. With a population of two thousand in the mid-1830s, Kirtland was larger than Cleveland. Smith drew up a plan of an extensive commercial city centered on the new temple. To finance these dreams, he and others founded their own bank, the Kirtland Safety Society Anti-Banking Company, which by 1837 had more than one hundred thousand dollars' worth of notes in circulation. The anti-bank was extra-legal because it lacked a state charter. Worse, the Panic of 1837 put it out of business. Hundreds of investors lost money; the total approached forty thousand dollars.

The anti-bank's failure prompted dozens of lawsuits against Smith and a schism in the Mormon church. Smith left Kirtland for Missouri in January 1838, and somewhere around sixteen hundred Mormons followed him by mid-summer. The few hundred who remained were mostly gone by the early 1840s. The antagonism toward Smith and the Mormons was rooted in deep suspicion of their insistence on restricting personal behavior, including banning alcohol and tobacco, as well as their goals for the development of Kirtland and the surrounding area. There also were rumors of what would become known as "plural marriage," the practice of having multiple wives.

In many ways, the Mormons were typical Ohio settlers: ambitious, eager to improve themselves, looking for ways to make the market work for them. The problem lay in their conspicuous behavior. Their economic success, their huge temple, and their determination to emphasize their differentness from others created fear and resentment almost immediately. In 1832 in Hiram, fifty men stripped, beat, tarred, and feathered Smith and another Mormon missionary. In the aftermath of the anti-bank fiasco, arsonists torched the Mormon printing press and later a Methodist chapel near the temple in Kirtland.

United within their families and religions against a fluctuating and hostile world of strangers, Ohioans remained suspicious of those people who strutted their peculiarities in public. Private idiosyncrasies and local eccentricities were tolerable. But to put them in the public eye and tie them to grandiose plans was to invite serious opposition. Ohioans seemed more comfortable with living in segregated worlds among diverse peoples who had little use for those who intruded into their space.

Cincinnati and the Miami Valley

While Ohio grew phenomenally in the early 1800s, its various regions developed at different rates and in different ways. The Miami Valley was by far the most dynamic. In 1830, one-quarter of Ohioans lived in the southwest. Originally purchased from Congress by the New Jersey speculator John Cleves Symmes in 1787, the Miami Valley attracted people from New Jersey, New York, and Pennsylvania. In 1788, Brigadier General Josiah Harmar established his headquarters at Fort Washington in the new city of Cincinnati. Fort Washington became the departure point for expeditions against the Indians living along the Maumee and Wabash Rivers in the 1790s. The presence of the army and the money that came with it turned Cincinnati into a boom town. Merchants, artisans, prostitutes, and camp followers, and hopeful adventurers literally surrounded the fort. Territorial officials and missionaries were thoroughly disgusted. The Moravian Johann Heckewelder described Cincinnati in 1792 as the home of "plenty of idlers" who, according to "respectable persons," were "a bunch of Sodomites."[6] In any case, there was no denying the fact that many Cincinnatians were young, male, and restless.

With the signing of the Treaty of Greenville in 1795, the military presence declined rapidly. Fort Washington was abandoned. Cincinnati survived the transition and after some stagnant years prospered. The key to its success was its location. Cincinnati sits on a series of plateaus and hills about halfway between Pittsburgh and the Mississippi River at the peak of a northern turn in the Ohio River. Before the arrival of the railroad in the middle of the nineteenth century, rivers were the great highways of North America. Towns, even homes, faced the water. The Ohio River was one of the continental superhighways, "the American Nile," one immigrant called it.[7] Many of the people who rode its current into the interior of the continent stopped in Cincinnati to rest and resupply. Before the completion of the Erie

Canal in 1825, the Ohio River provided the main access to the markets of the world for the farmers of the Ohio Valley. Cincinnati's harbor was full of flatboats and steamboats headed to New Orleans.

Cincinnati's fertile and accessible hinterland fueled its growth. Across from the city is the mouth of the Licking River, which flows deep into the heart of Kentucky. Upstream some dozen miles is the mouth of the Little Miami, and downstream another ten miles is the mouth of the Great Miami River. The Whitewater River also empties into the Ohio just to the west of the Great Miami. North of the city, the terrain is a rolling collection of ridges and slopes with rich bottomland and innumerable creeks, perfect for growing corn and raising hogs, which was what most settlers did in the early nineteenth century. Every fifteen to twenty miles north of Cincinnati, villages appeared around the mills necessary to grind the corn into meal; some were the sites of federal forts. They included Hamilton, Middletown, Dayton, Piqua, Eaton, and Greenville. A man who traversed southern Ohio in 1804 declared that the Miami Valley was "the most beautiful and desirable country we have yet seen. The Country lies in Waves of great regularity & is covered with heavy towering timber and the soil inexhaustible Rich." By 1807, a settler reported that Xenia was "a growing Town" with "a full store of goods."[8]

In 1849, Ohio led the nation in the production of corn with more than fifty-nine thousand bushels. Much of it was transformed into more durable and portable products such as whiskey and hogs. In the 1850s, half of the corn grown in Ohio ultimately became pork or whiskey. Hogs were especially prized because they required little supervision; they were eager scavengers who killed snakes. Every part of their bodies could be made into something of value, whether it was leather or soap. Slaughtering and processing pigs became a big business, especially in Cincinnati. The city gained its first pork packing house in 1818, and had forty-eight of them by the 1840s. More than twelve hundred men worked in what amounted to disassembly lines. The sights and sounds and smells of live and butchered hogs were everywhere in Cincinnati. No wonder people began to call it Porkopolis.

Some travelers found the city repulsive. The most caustic was the Englishwoman Frances Trollope, who in *Domestic Manners of the*

Americans dealt with her failure to establish herself in Cincinnati society by maliciously lampooning the citizens as ignorant, greedy provincials. Dirty and smelly, Cincinnati seemed to Trollope a place in which people were always in a hurry, eager to make money, and blithely unaware of the ridiculousness of their efforts to behave in a genteel way. Even the city boosters agreed that the pursuit of wealth was the chief occupation of Cincinnatians. No matter what it was called, wrote the lawyer James Hall in 1848, "it is still money-making which constitutes the great business of our people—it is the use of money which controls and regulates every thing." In 1830, Timothy Walker, a recent immigrant from Massachusetts who would become Cincinnati's most distinguished lawyer, reported that "business, stirring active unremitted business, is the habit of this place. Refinement begins to make its appearance, but it must gain ground slowly." Walker was not disappointed. To the contrary, he thought it remarkable that such a diverse group of settlers "so soon have laid even the foundations of wealth. My expectations are fully realized with what Cincinnati is; and my imagination hardly sets any bounds to see what it is destined to become. In 20 years more it will be in the center of the U.S. and I see no reason why it may not be the seat of government."[9]

This is the language of the eager, young booster who saw his career and his city intertwined. Yet no one could deny Cincinnati's spectacular growth. The population, which was 16,230 in 1826, rose to 70,409 in 1844 and showed few signs of slowing as it moved to 161,044 in 1860. Huge waves of immigrants in the 1840s and 1850s made the city even more diverse. Germans, Irish Catholics, and the occasional migrant from China, Turkey, Guatemala, and Denmark meant that in 1850, 47.2 percent of Cincinnatians had been born outside the U.S.

Cincinnati did more than process pigs and corn, of course. By the late 1810s, its fledgling industries produced lumber, glass, iron castings, and cloth in growing quantities. Its breweries turned between 40 and up to fifty thousand bushels of barley into beer in 1815. Manufacturers began to take their places beside merchants among the city's elite. Meanwhile, hotels, taverns, and shops sprang up throughout the city. Cincinnati, wrote a pair of boosters in 1826, had a "new population . . . composed of men of commercial habits." "[F]lattered by the immediate prospects of realizing immense profits in their business, which required no preparation, and involved no loss of time, they devoted themselves at once to mercantile pursuits."[10]

Capital was always in short supply. Men needed money or credit to buy land and develop farms, all of which could cost upwards of five hundred dollars. There also were schemes to improve access to markets; adventurers dreamed of canals, bridges, and roads that would make hauling corn and driving hogs easier and cheaper. It is hardly surprising that the first attempt at a bank in Ohio was in Cincinnati in 1803. The Miami Exporting Company, whose stockholders included some of the most prominent men in the area, was the first of many. Over the next few years the General Assembly incorporated banks capitalized at one hundred thousand dollars at Chillicothe, Steubenville, Zanesville, Warren, Cincinnati, and Dayton. There were twenty-eight banks in Ohio by the late 1810s, as well as two branches (in Cincinnati and Chillicothe) of the national Bank of the United States. In addition, dozens of wildcat, unregulated companies loaned money on easy terms to willing Ohioans. Nowhere were men so eager to borrow and invest as in Cincinnati and its environs. And nowhere were people hit harder when the first national economic depression hit in late 1818. The Panic of 1819 was a major setback in the fortunes of many. Traumatic as it was, its impact was short term. By the late 1820s, boom times were back.

Lawyers and merchants reaped the biggest financial rewards in early Cincinnati. New Jersey–born Nicholas Longworth arrived in the city in 1803. Shrewdly accepting land in lieu of money as legal fees, he became one of Cincinnati's wealthiest men. Longworth was pudgy and sloppy in his dress, which was always black. He built one of the city's finest mansions on Fourth Street at the top of the plateau overlooking the Ohio River and dispensed money to reform societies and young artists. Longworth was but one among many men who achieved a comfortable standard of living. The traveler Timothy Flint exclaimed in the mid-1820s that in Cincinnati, "the elegance of the houses, the parade of servants, the display of furniture, and more than all, the luxury of their overloaded tables, would compare with the better houses in the Atlantic."[11]

Cincinnati's gentry—a network of merchants, manufacturers, lawyers, and other professionals—dominated the city's politics and high society. For all their interest in personal profit and fame, they, like Timothy Walker, believed that their lives and that of their city were interdependent. One could not flourish without the other. Cincinnati's intellectual elite relentlessly boosted the city's prospects and sought to refine its character. Chief among them was the New Jersey–born Dr. Daniel Drake, sometimes called the "Franklin of the West" because of his wide range of interests. Drake not only became an expert on the history of the Ohio Valley, he lobbied hard for the founding of educational and cultural institutions in Cincinnati. The fate of his Western Museum, which he helped to found in 1820, was typical. Designed to house relics and artifacts of animal and human life in the Ohio Valley, it was a quick failure. People had no interest in seeing Drake's elaborate collections. They did, however, flock to see the wax figures, deformed animals, and animated version of Hell that filled the museum after its sale in 1823.[12] The short lives of the Western Museums and similar schemes did not deter local do-gooders. Bolstered in the late 1820s and early 1830s by a steady stream of New England immigrants, including the renowned Beecher family, they devoted themselves to finding ways to accommodate democratic materialism and cultural improvements.

Most Cincinnati residents were not as well off as the city's elite. Quite a few worked as laborers at the wharves or in the packinghouses or as domestic servants and cooks. Skilled laborers found employment in the expanding manufacturing centers, which produced steamboats and furniture, among other things. At least in the first few decades of the nineteenth century, many men and some women worked as artisans or craftsmen in small shops or owned their own stores. Because labor was in short supply in early Cincinnati, workers often were well paid. The standard of living for most probably was higher before 1825 than it was afterwards. Food (especially pork) was cheap and plentiful. In 1806, room and board could be found for just over a hundred dollars a year. Dramatic rises in costs in the 1830s and 1840s did not immediately undermine Cincinnati's reputation as a good place to live.

African Americans were a significant presence in Cincinnati. Their numbers grew rapidly, from 433 in 1820 to 3,237 in 1850. About half were mulattoes. Most had been born free. In 1845, only 364 of 2,049 blacks said they had once been enslaved. Partly by choice and partly because of racism, African Americans tended to cluster in "little Africa," an area along the river front, and in "Bucktown," in the East End. Creating their own community within Cincinnati, by the 1830s they had established an African Methodist Episcopal church and a Union Baptist church. Most men worked as boatmen, barbers, cooks, laborers, and waiters, while women overwhelmingly were washerwomen, cooks, and domestic servants. Although the average African American owned only seventy-five dollars' worth of property, some saved money to purchase the freedom of enslaved relatives. In 1834, more than a third had bought their own freedom at an average cost of $450 per person or $215,522 collectively.[13]

Despite the fact that slavery was illegal in Ohio, Cincinnati was an uncongenial place for blacks. The Virginia-born John Malvin, who lived there in the 1820s, recalled that he "found every door closed against the colored man in a free State, excepting the jails and penitentiaries, the doors of which were thrown wide open to receive him." Malvin was surprised. He had supposed that doors would be open to him in "a free State like Ohio . . . but from the treatment I received by the people generally, I found it little better than in Virginia." Sometimes it was worse. In 1829, and again in 1836, hundreds of whites attacked the bodies and homes of the African American citizens of Cincinnati. In 1841, armed black men organized to defend their families against a white mob with a cannon. After a declaration of martial law in the city, three hundred African American men were arrested. Once in custody, many were beaten while their homes were attacked. In the end, the destruction of black property totaled some $150,000.[14]

Much of the white rage originated in economic competition. No less important were black pretensions to citizenship. "White men . . . are naturally indignant," wrote a workingman in 1841, "when they see a set of idle blacks dressed up like ladies and gentlemen, strutting about our streets and flinging the 'rights of petition' and 'discussion' in our faces." As the result of such virulent racism, some Cincinnati blacks dreamed of setting up their own communities in the countryside, although they lacked the capital to finance such arrangements. Others, fearing even tighter enforcement of the Black Codes, planned a colony in Canada. In the end, some 460 people left Ohio. One of them later wrote, "Ohio's not the place for me: . . . slaves had better far be hurled / Into the lion's den. / Farewell, Ohio! / I cannot stop in thee. / I'll travel on to Canada. / Where colored men are free."[15]

Racial tensions were only the worst instances of the distrust that living in a rapidly growing city of diverse peoples engendered. Whether black or white, German or Irish, Protestant or Catholic, rich or poor, residents of Cincinnati epitomized the difficulties early Ohioans had in dealing with each other. Thrown together, unused to the customs of others, eager to get ahead, people often fell into misunderstandings or outright violence. "So rapidly has our city enlarged itself," wrote a correspondent of the *Cincinnati Journal* in 1834, "and such is the migratory character of our citizens, that we are almost strangers to one another."[16]

Outside of Cincinnati, villages such as Hamilton and Dayton replicated the development of the Queen City on a smaller scale. They quickly became regional urban centers with their own complement of lawyers, banks, taverns, stores, and small manufactures. Still, most people in the Miami Valley continued to live on farms. Much as these people shared in common, they also diverged in critical ways. Perhaps the most important was religion. More than a theology or form of worship, religion was the foundation of personal identity. Sharing sacred beliefs and rituals did not guarantee unity, however. Irish Catholics and German Catholics did not exactly see eye to eye. Presbyterians did not trust Methodists, whom they found to be loud, emotional, and unrefined. Baptists and Methodists thought Presbyterians were arrogant and cold. All Protestants distrusted what they saw as the superstitious rituals of Catholics.

Rural communities devoted to one denomination or another flourished in Ohio. Probably the most controversial example in southwestern Ohio was the Shakers. Principally followers of English émigré Ann Lee, the Shakers had existed as a religious community for little more than a generation when the first members of their faith arrived in Turtle Creek, some thirty miles northeast of Cincinnati in the Miami Valley. Many of the residents of Turtle Creek had left the

Presbyterian Church for a more democratic, personal, and spiritual religion that revived the idea of a primitive Christian church rooted in equality and worldly perfection. The first group of Shakers soon converted many of the Christians at Turtle Creek, including Richard McNemar, a prominent figure in both movements. By late April 1805, the Shakers numbered thirty. The appeal of the Shakers, like that of the Christians, lay in their advocacy of free will and the possibility of redemption from sin in the face of the approaching millennium. In the scattered villages of rural Ohio, the certainty and community provided by the Shakers and other religious sects provided people with a foundation of faith and hope.

Under the leadership of David Darrow, the Shakers created their own world at Turtle Creek, or Union Village. They built an elders' house, a mill, a smith shop, and a meetinghouse, creating the well-ordered, straight lines of a Shaker landscape. They claimed to have hundreds of adult members in communities from Kentucky through the Indiana Territory, including Eagle Creek in Adams County and Beulah in Montgomery County. By the early 1820s, there was a fluctuating population of six hundred at Union Village and another hundred at Watervliet.

Leading Shakers traveled frequently in order to convert others. Like Methodists and members of other denominations, they relied on the tenacity of itinerant preachers to spread the word from farmhouse to farmhouse and village to village. Anticipating the imminent return of Jesus Christ, Shakers focused on unity and purity to prepare them for the millennium. They looked to visible signs of God's presence in their lives and preferred personal experience to the words of learned men, although the Ohio leaders published their theology and gave it an intellectual cast. Above all, Shakers made the redemption of women a key part of their belief. Ann Lee, in their view, was appointed by God to function as the female Christ, completing the union of the sexes. By the 1820s, Shakers followed a set of laws designed to encourage simplicity, cleanliness, love, and, most famously, celibacy. Increasingly, Shakers avoided contact with others in order to keep their focus on a simple, spiritual life. Seeking self-sufficiency, they expressed themselves in dances, needlepoints, carpentry, and, occasionally, outbursts of religious ecstasy.

The Shaker settlements of like-minded people who lived in relative isolation from those who were not like them (or would not join them) reflected the clannish quality of early Ohio settlements. Villagers found community in uniting among themselves and against strangers. Nothing was more likely to arouse the wrath of Ohio citizens than their fear that one group or another was making a fetish of its peculiarities or attempting to convert others. No finer illustration of this point exists than the reaction of people in rural southwestern Ohio to the Shakers. The cliquishness of the Shakers disturbed their neighbors. Their practice of celibacy seemed to threaten traditional notions of human relationships. Shakers were too obviously different and too eager to win others to their way of life. Suspicious neighbors sometimes tried to intimidate them with physical violence or verbal harassment. One missionary from Union Village was labeled as a man "who goes about to seduce the people and ravish the women, accumulating property and making disturbance among those who before lived happily."[17]

Few of the early settlers of Ohio gave much thought to the question of citizenship. To be sure, many men participated in elections and served on juries or in militia units, while Shakers and Quakers paid fines to avoid military service. One way or another, most people paid taxes. But the state was not a major factor in their sense of themselves and what was important in their worlds. Much more significant were allegiances to family, church, place of birth, and the siren song of the market. With so many recent arrivals and so much moving around, most people could scarcely imagine Ohio as more than a temporary refuge. It was a place to live, not a place that shaped one's personality or culture. That was done not by public schools or courts but by communities of relatives and friends, people who shared similar prejudices and hopes, people with whom settlers could feel comfortable in a region of unimaginable diversity.

The Western Reserve

Two hundred miles from the Miami Valley, the Western Reserve was another world altogether. The Reserve was land in the northeastern quadrant of the state set aside by Congress in the 1780s to satisfy the claims of Connecticut to lands in the West. The state had sold its holdings of just under 3 million acres in 1795 to the Connecticut Land Company, a group of investors headed by Moses Cleaveland. It had also reserved the western twenty-six miles—called the "Fire Sufferers' Lands" or "Firelands"—for the relief of Connecticut families who had suffered from British raids during the American War for Independence.

In many ways, the early history of the Reserve was the opposite of that of the Miami Valley. While there were settlers from all over the U.S. as well as Germany, Scotland, Ireland, and Wales, most were New Englanders. African Americans were rare, amounting to no more than five hundred as late as 1840. Northeastern Ohio was far more homogeneous in its population than any other part of the state. The Western Reserve lagged behind the Miami Valley in terms of urban and economic development, largely because of its inaccessibility. Until the opening of the Erie Canal in 1825 linked Lake Erie with the Hudson River and the port of New York City, there was no easy way to get in and out of the Reserve. Despite the fact that the land was relatively flat and fertile, the transportation of goods was expensive and time consuming.[18]

In 1820, the village of Cleveland was stagnant. With only six hundred residents, it was smaller than Painesville and Youngstown. Only with the opening of the Erie Canal and the start of construction on the Ohio Canal did Cleveland awaken. Connections to the outside world brought vitality to the city. By 1835, there were 5,080 people in Cleveland. A newspaper reported that "there is not a room to be rented and families have been compelled to take shelter in barns."[19] The population rose to 6,071 in 1840 and 43,417 in 1860. Still well behind Cincinnati, Cleveland began to grow more rapidly than the Queen City. Its population became more diverse as it expanded. In 1846, the 10,135 residents included 1,472 Germans and 632 Irish. There also were two Jewish congregations. The census of 1850 showed that only 27.2 percent of Cleveland's residents had been born in Ohio and a bare majority (52.8 percent) in the U.S.; 18.5 percent were Germans, 14 percent were Irish, and the rest were English, Canadian, Scottish, Welsh, and French.[20] By 1860, nearly one-third of Clevelanders were Catholic and one-half of 1 percent were Jewish.

Cleveland's African American population remained small throughout the nineteenth century; in 1844, there were only 160 blacks, and in 1860 only 779. Of the 160 in 1844, however, twenty owned property, worth $35,000 in total, and many were skilled laborers and professionals. John Malvin found life in Cleveland in the 1830s and 1840s more congenial than life in Cincinnati. He worked as a cook and seaman on Lake Erie and eventually owned his own boat. In 1839, he captained a canal boat with a crew of one white steersman, one black steersman, two white drivers, one black bowman, and one black female cook.[21] Better living conditions and race relations in the Western Reserve reflected the fact that blacks did not constitute a large enough group of people to threaten the economic and social positions of whites.

The abrupt change in Cleveland's fortunes was testimony to the importance of market access. Immigrants to the Western Reserve were desperate for improvements from the beginning. In 1802, future governor Samuel Huntington summarized the experience of many. Heavily in debt, the people of Cleveland were too poor to do anything about their isolation. So "they run to the merchants with what money they can pick up, to buy at an exorbitant price such articles as they had been used to consume in the old countries, without having any way of exporting such commodities as they might manufacture & send to raise money." In 1811, recent Yale graduate Henry Leavitt Ellsworth toured the Reserve with his father, and while he was favorably impressed with the soil and its prospects, he noted the lack of money. "Almost every hut is a tavern," Ellsworth claimed, "as it brings in a *little cash* which is in great demand among the first settlers who, generally speaking, are poor and destitute."[22]

Like many Yankees, Ellsworth was put out by cultural differences he encountered in the Reserve. At Poland he was amused to discover that "the meaning of the word *check* . . . is nothing more than what the Yankeys mean by *lunchon*." At one house he complained that he had "never see[n] so much dirt and filth in any human habitation as in this mans hut." Fleas made sleep impossible. No wonder he felt relieved at his next stop to be in the "good framed house" of a family from Connecticut. Still, roads were so bad that the pair had to use a compass to find their way. Fresh water was so scarce that Ellsworth had to drink whiskey. Most appalling were basic living arrangements. Because houses were small, people often slept wherever they could find a spot on the floor; in the "*same room, man and wife, children, acquaintances, strangers, and servants*" all slept together. The fact that people had to undress and dress in public struck the priggish Ellsworth as "ludicrous."[23]

Traveling from Connecticut to Ohio in 1810, twenty-year-old Margaret Dwight was shocked by the behavior of Germans she encountered in Pennsylvania. Disturbed that so many stared at her, she "concluded that they came to see us *Yankees,* as they would a learned pig." It was "dreadful to see so many people that you cannot speak to or understand." "Nothing vex[ed her] more than to see them set & look at us & talk in dutch and laugh." The Scots-Irish, with their pork and whiskey, were little better. "The people here talk curiously, they all reckon instead of expect—Youns is a word I have heard used several times, but what it means I don't know, they use it so strangely." And then there was the family who said "there has been a *heap* of people moving this fall;—I don't know exactly how many a heap is," Margaret Dwight complained, "or a *sight* either which is another way of measuring people." As she neared Ohio, she was delighted to get back "among people of our own nation & language." When she ran into some people from Connecticut, she "felt as glad to see them & as well acquainted with them in a few minutes, as if we had all our lives been neighbors." Near Youngstown she spent the night at the home of a cousin. "A cousin in this country, is not to be slighted," she exclaimed. "I would give more for one in this country, than for 20 in old Connecticut."[24]

Immigrants arrived with high expectations, even when they knew better. Moses Cleaveland, who gave his misspelled name to the city, visited Ohio only once. Nevertheless, he offered Samuel Huntington a grandiose long-distance welcome when he heard that Huntington and his family had "passed the Jordan and beat down the Walls of Jericho and entered the promised Land." Huntington replied in kind. Rest assured, he wrote to Cleaveland, he had indeed "moved [his] patriarchal Caravan through the Wilderness to this Canaan."[25] The trope of the patriarchal journey was apt. Huntington's retinue consisted of seventeen people, ten oxen, three horses, and seven cows.

Among the people were his wife, Hannah, their six children, Hannah's friend Margaret Cobb, and at least one male servant. Most immigrants did their own labor; gentlemen such as Huntington did not. He hired others to drive his wagons, clear his property, build his homes, and farm his land to free him to devote himself to the business of serving the public interest and his personal ambition.

For most Americans, the household organized both their lives and their identity. A household was something more than a family. It might include parents, children, grandparents, aunts, uncles, friends, servants, and slaves. The household, moreover, was not the place of refuge from the world that it became later in American life. In the early nineteenth century, most people produced what they consumed. Women spun cloth, made clothes, cooked food, and nurtured children. The household perpetuated the family. People rarely went off to work. With few exceptions, much of the business of life was conducted in and around the family home.

Political figures were major exceptions to this rule. Samuel Huntington spent a good deal of time away from the Reserve. Hannah Huntington, on the other hand, lived there without interruption from her arrival in 1801 until her death in 1818. Born in Norwich, Connecticut, in 1770, Hannah married Samuel in 1791 and gave birth to six children. Like many women, Hannah was a reluctant emigrant who had no desire to leave family and friends to settle in Ohio. But she reconciled herself to Samuel's decision, reasoning that her obligation to her immediate family was preeminent. "[T]o say I should not feel a regret in leaving the friends I enjoy in Norwich would be ridiculous," she told Samuel in 1798, "but my husband and children are the dearest objects I can ever know and with them I would go wherever fortune would direct."[26]

Hannah found a finished cabin and servants awaiting her when she got to Cleveland. And she had her children and her friend Margaret Cobb to keep her company. Margaret stayed in Ohio for six years. Together, the friends endured the isolation and privations of frontier life. Hannah worried that Cleveland was "almost beyond the limits of human society." She objected to the fact that Samuel was often away on business. Malaria and other illnesses plagued the family. When Margaret returned to Connecticut, Hannah was devastated. "With her . . . I have borne [Samuel's] repeated absence with fortitude, in sickness and health I have lean'd upon her." Now "I shall have no one attach'd to me but from motives of interest."[27]

Work kept Hannah busy. She supervised the household, including the education of her children and the pregnancies of Patty, the hired girl. She managed the business of the farm, reporting necessary details to her husband. The Huntington household included boarders. Hannah appreciated them more for their sociability than for the money they paid. Agreeable companions were few and far between.

Hannah was fortunate in that she and Samuel genuinely loved each other. As she told him in 1798, they were "one of the (I am afraid) few couples who delight in each other and are happy in each other's company." Supportive and deferential, Hannah could not always understand why Samuel spent more time worrying about his career than his family. After the death of one of their children, she demanded to know whether "honour" was "a compensation for [his] absence[.]" "I love my children, I love my family—but what is that? Children, family and the whole world without you is barren and joyless—they may say I am weak, foolish, even a worshipper of flesh and blood. What care I, it is my glory and happiness that I feel as I do—let your station in life be ever so exalted, little will it gratify me if it must be purchased at so high a price as our separation."[28] Despite these complaints, Hannah never seriously challenged her husband or her position. To the contrary, she sought a familiar world. While she coveted refined society and treasured affectionate friendships, her primary loyalty was to her household. Membership in the public community of Ohio mattered only as a means to a greater end. If public office meant a higher standard of living in a more congenial place, then she was all for it. But if the pursuit of office meant that she was relegated to loneliness, she was not.

Although Samuel Huntington became governor of Ohio in 1808, he never achieved the prominence of which he dreamed. So too was Hannah's life a mixed blessing. Comforted by her family, her friends, and the occasional presence of her husband, she had to contend with both a wilderness and long periods of depression. Going home was not an option. According to Margaret Dwight, many stayed in the western country not because it was "so good, but because the journey is so bad."[29]

As long as the Western Reserve remained isolated, its social as well as its economic development was stunted. Hannah did not live long enough to see Cleveland rival Cincinnati or Pittsburgh. She never knew what canals and trains would do to increase the level of society in her adopted town. Cleveland for her was always a small, unhealthy, unrefined village buffeted by the cold winds of Lake Erie. The land-locked Western Reserve remained a place of unfulfilled dreams. Households and family ties mattered everywhere in Ohio, but nowhere did they matter more than in the northeast, where people had little to fall back upon but the familiarity of friends and neighbors.

The Scioto Valley

South-central Ohio was as homogeneous demographically as the northeast, but in a different way. Just as Congress had reserved land in the latter region for Connecticut, it had reserved land in the former for Virginia. As part of the deal by which the state of Virginia ceded its claim to the lands northwest of the Ohio River in the early 1780s, the U.S. set aside what became known as the Virginia Military District. Thousands of acres west of the Scioto River were to be made available for Virginia's veterans of the American War for Independence. Each former soldier was given a piece of paper entitling him to a certain number of acres, depending upon his rank. All veterans had to do was locate, survey, and claim their share of the district. Many Virginians did not wish to move and sold their claims to speculators. Meanwhile, Virginia and Kentucky surveyors such as Nathaniel Massie did a brisk business in the 1790s locating land claims; their price was a share of the land. In this way, Massie, his protégés, and other surveyors accumulated huge holdings throughout the new state. In 1810, Massie owned 18,047 acres, making him the twelfth largest landholder in Ohio. The top three (Lucas Sullivant, William Lytle, and Duncan McArthur) had all been surveyors at one time. While there were prominent landowners throughout Ohio, they tended to be concentrated in the area west of the Scioto. By 1850, some one hundred men owned more than two-thirds of the land. Notwithstanding the fact that the median owner of land in early Ohio had 150 acres, a grand farm by European standards, inequality was pronounced in the Virginia Military District.[30]

Among the prominent landowners was Thomas Worthington, the leader of the statehood movement, who owned eighteen thousand acres in 1830. He called his estate Adena. Surrounding a Georgian brick structure designed by the architect Benjamin Latrobe on a hill outside of Chillicothe were hundreds of acres farmed and maintained by a host of former slaves who had been freed when they were brought to Ohio. Worthington's daughter later referred to the servants as members of the family.[31] In reality, they were lifetime servants whose comings and goings were closely monitored. In many ways, Worthington lived like an idealized Virginia gentleman. Not only did he serve in many public offices, he grew corn, wheat, and other products, operated mills, and engaged in commerce with New Orleans.

Worthington was only one of many Virginians who settled in Ohio. Indeed, in 1850, 89 percent of all southern-born Ohioans were from Virginia. The Scioto Valley was like an extension of Virginia, jutting northward into the heart of Ohio from the former Virginia county of Kentucky. Crisscrossed by creeks, often quite hilly, even mountainous, irregularly surveyed, with large farms and small towns, the region seemed to have more in common with western Virginia and Kentucky than it did with the Western Reserve or the Miami Valley. Accents and customs were Virginian. People lived in the I and shotgun houses common to the South, not the salt box houses found in the Western Reserve. Methodists and Baptists dominated the area, not Congregationalists or Presbyterians.

For all the similarities, south-central Ohio was never an exact replica of Virginia. Its uneven landscape and easily flooded valleys made it unsuitable for large-scale farming. Tobacco grew but did not flourish. One unusual business in the area was cattle raising, which required large farms and capital. The most well-known entrepreneur-ranchers were the Virginia-born Renick brothers, George and Felix, who settled near Chillicothe in 1801 and 1802. While they raised hogs and corn, they concentrated on cattle. In 1805, George took sixty-eight head of cattle to Baltimore and sold them for thirty-two dollars a head. His profit encouraged others to follow suit. By the late teens, herds of hundreds of cattle grazed on the large land holdings on the plains between the Scioto and Miami Valleys.[32]

As important in distinguishing the Virginia Military District from Kentucky and Virginia was race. There were more African Americans in this region of Ohio in the early nineteenth century than anywhere else in the state. In part, this had to do with the proximity of Kentucky and the fact that many Virginians brought black servants with them when they migrated across the Ohio River. The attitude of these white Virginians toward African Americans was complicated. On the one hand, many claimed that they migrated to Ohio because slavery was forbidden there. Devout Methodists or Quakers, they abhorred the practice of human beings owning human beings. Their distaste for slavery was sincere and often heartfelt. On the other hand, they had little desire to live among free blacks and were among the strongest supporters of the state's Black Codes.

Groups of free blacks nonetheless migrated to rural communities in south-central Ohio where they could enjoy relative freedom, if only through geographical isolation. In 1819, several hundred blacks, freed under the terms of the will of Samuel Gist, their deceased owner in Virginia, migrated to two Brown County locations purchased by the trustees of Gist's estate. One white Ohioan feared the consequences of such migrations. He reported that people in Richmond, Virginia, considered the blacks freed by Gist as "depraved and ignorant" and "hailed with joy" their departure. While he could never imagine Ohio as a slave state, he also thought that the citizens of the free state "in justice to themselves and their posterity . . . will refuse admittance to such a population." The blacks nonetheless settled in Brown County, persisting in spite of the constant antipathy of some white Ohioans, one of whom proclaimed in an 1835 newspaper that their settlements were a failed "experiment. . . . In all Ohio can any white settlement be found equally wretched, equally unproductive?"[33] Fortunately, the isolation of their settlements meant that black Ohioans did not have to confront their critics directly—at least most of the time.

Another large number of blacks freed by the will of their deceased owner, John Randolph of Roanoke, migrated from Virginia to Mercer County, Ohio, in 1846. They numbered close to four hundred and traveled in sixteen wagons and then a steamboat down the Ohio

River. Again, white Ohioans expressed sympathy for the plight of the blacks but recoiled at the thought of them as neighbors. The Cincinnati *Gazette* attacked slavery and condemned Randolph for failing to prepare the "poor creatures" for freedom. Still, it was "neither our interest, nor our duty, to add to the ignorance of our State in any way. . . . We have already several colored settlements among us." The white citizens of Mercer County were even more alarmed, and a mob forced the blacks to move on to Shelby County, where threats of violence pushed many of them on to Piqua. Most ended up in western Miami County among sympathetic Quakers. The principal settlement was called Hanktown. It soon acquired a church and a schoolhouse. Many descendants of Randolph's slaves still live in Troy and Piqua.[34]

Another Virginia-born African American who settled in Ohio was James Madison Hemings. The son of Sally Hemings, Madison Hemings was freed by Thomas Jefferson when the former president's will was executed in 1826. After he left Virginia in 1836 with his wife, Mary McCoy, and young daughter, he worked as a carpenter and a farmer in Pike County until he died in 1877. Hemings's brother Eston and his wife also lived in Ohio, in Chillicothe, until 1852. In 1873, Madison Hemings asserted in a local newspaper that Jefferson was his father. He remembered Jefferson as an "undemonstrative" man who "was not in the habit of showing partiality or fatherly affection to us children."[35]

White Virginians in south-central Ohio were staunch in their disdain for both slavery and Africans Americans. Virginia-born Methodists were particularly pronounced in their antipathy to slavery. Indeed, their distaste for the institution made them among the most articulate in defining the new state of Ohio. It was a land of liberty, they believed, for everyone. Slavery was pernicious in its effect on whites as well as blacks. The preacher Philip Gatch, who was a member of the Constitutional Convention in 1802, had fled "a land of slavery" for the freedom of Clermont County. Happy to be away from the "Evils" of Virginia, he wrote with a booster's enthusiasm about the possibilities for trade and agriculture. Religion also flourished. In one revival, both one of his "children and "a Black Boy of our Familey got converted." Gatch may have taken pleasure in a young African American's conversion, but he did not feel comfortable with blacks. He and his wife had "been more affraid of the Negroes in Virginia [day] or Night than I have ever been in this Coun[try of the] Poor Indians."[36]

Gatch was certain that slavery had ruined many young Virginians by making them unused to work. Ohio provided the opportunity for them to realize the value of labor. "A Family that is supported in Virginia by a Farm and several Negroes," claimed Gatch, "can be supported by a Farm equally as well without a slave, only they must wait on themselves, which in Idea is more than to reduce it to practice." He "perceive[d] a remarkable temedity in the old Virginians owing to their customs. They dread that. That I have felt a pleasure in." Another Methodist was certain that his family enjoyed working. They "frequently mention[ed] how much better to do their family business of Cooking &c themselves, than to have any black ones about them."[37]

The Methodist minister John Sale seconded Gatch's opinion that Ohio was different. He expected that "this State will be as the Garden of God & it is pleasing to me to live in a Country where there is so much of an Equallity & a Man is not thought to be great here because he possesses a little more of this Worlds rubbish than his Neighbour." Sale and Gatch were overly optimistic. There were more than enough examples of inequality to contradict their statements. To them, however—and to many others—Ohio was unique because slavery was illegal and labor was valued. In many ways, it was more equal than other parts of the country. They believed themselves to live in "a Land of *Liberty*." According to Frederick Bonner, "the Lord provided for the Vertuous sons of the Eastern States in the liberty of State of Ohio." Bonner offered particular thanks that there was "no red Sea in the way; no phar[a]o[h]'s host to pursue us while traveling to the American Canaan & as for our Jordon (I mean the Ohio) it is easy to cross and (what's better) when once planted here our children are saved from the harmful practice of trading on their fellow creatures."[38]

Despite their hosannas about a land of liberty, family and religion were much more central to the lives of these Methodists than political allegiances. Their letters were full of news of relatives; most of their boosting of Ohio was part of their larger effort to persuade brothers and sisters to join them in the new state. Nothing mattered more than religion. They treasured eagerly anticipated revivals and the conversions of their relatives. Methodists reveled in unrestrained expression of affection. Love was a constant theme in their correspondence. They hoped that someday people might deal with each other like brothers and sisters. States were secular constructs made necessary only by the failings of human beings.

Eastern Ohio

From Portsmouth at the mouth of the Scioto River, up the Ohio to Steubenville, then west to Zanesville, was an area that was most directly a demographic and economic extension of Pennsylvania and western Virginia. The major exception was the settlements of the Ohio Company of Associates, a group of New England veterans of the American War for Independence who had purchased more than a million acres from Congress in 1787. Their center was at Marietta at the mouth of the Muskingum River, but villages of New Englanders dotted the landscape throughout the Muskingum and Hocking Valleys. The Ohio Company had had great plans for Marietta. Under the leadership of superintendent Rufus Putnam, the associates designed an elegant city, complete with Latin names and broad avenues, to become the commercial and cultural capital of the Ohio Valley, a portal to the West and an exemplar of balance and harmony. In the 1790s and early 1800s, Marietta was one of the most important cities west of the Appalachians. It enjoyed boom times when its residents constructed ocean-going vessels that sailed the Caribbean and the Atlantic. The arrival of a Marietta-built ship at a port in Italy was a testament to the vision and persistence of the city's founders. The ship-building business, however, never recovered from the embargo of 1807. Subject to devastating floods and often unhealthy, Marietta lacked the location and the hinterland to compete with Cincinnati and Pittsburgh. Moreover, even though the town retained what people called a New England character, its population reflected the proximity of Virginia and Pennsylvania.

With the exception of the Ohio Company settlements, southeastern Ohio was similar to the states across the Ohio River. There was some prosperity along the rivers and their tributaries, where the land was flat and fertile and access to markets convenient. Settlers who lived a few miles from navigable water, however, could not produce enough crops nor get them to market easily enough to sustain the kind of agricultural and urban explosion that characterized the Miami Valley. "The country where we lived is very hilly and rough, and the land generally poor," recalled William Cooper Howells, the son of a Welsh family that lived on several farms around Steubenville in the early nineteenth century. Sandstone fragments covered much of the hillsides, "while the heavier rocks outcrop along the ravines and precipices."[39] Away from frequently flooded bottom lands, people had difficulty making more than a subsistence living. The major towns included Steubenville and St. Clairsville on the Ohio River, and Zanesville on the Muskingum. These were market centers, with artisans, grocery stores, mills, and, later, banks. There also were taverns where great quantities of whiskey were consumed.

Languages were so diverse that the Massachusetts-born lawyer Nathaniel Dike in 1816 suggested that "many of the inhab[itants]" of Steubenville "could not speak [English] at all. I actually seemed to be among foreigners in a foreign country." Dike was a snob. Yet his disgust at the behavior of the Scots-Irish and other low-born, poorly educated people he encountered testifies to the problems all people had dealing with diversity. Dike objected to the popular election of local officials, including sheriffs, and to the fact that the constitution of Ohio did not require towns to support schools. Why, towns were not even towns as they were in New England! A township in Ohio was a town in New England. Good order did not prevail, without education, without regular religion, with excessive drinking. People took their example from slaveholding Virginians whose "whole enjoyment & pride are founded upon an exemption from labor, and a never failing supply of whiskey." At least in Ohio drunks were "obliged to be more industrious."[40]

Most people in eastern Ohio, as elsewhere, lived in rural areas. Howells's family owned or rented a series of farms, none of which proved to be a success, although, as he admitted, their failures may have had more to do with their lack of agricultural aptitude than the quality of the land. Howells's father was a wool manufacturer by training. The land he bought was partially improved; that is, his fields had been cleared, but deadened tree stumps still dotted the landscape.

Like many farmers, he hired others to do much of the labor. The work was seasonal but tedious: wheat had to be cut, cradled, raked, and bound, reaped, housed, threshed, and cleaned—all by hand. Meanwhile, Howells's mother and other women cooked large meals over open fires. Howells's father also tried raising sheep and cows but found that they cost more than they brought in.[41]

Barter compensated for the lack of cash. Howells was "struck with the scarcity of money, and the difficulty of getting it, and the expedients of barter that were resorted to." People generally paid each other in wheat, although certain items—tea, coffee, iron, powder, lead—could not be gotten without cash. Whatever profit the Howellses might have made from wheat was eaten up in transporting the crop to the Ohio River, a distance of thirty-five miles from their farm. In any case, cash had to be reserved for necessary items, and for taxes.

Religion preoccupied the people. There were endless disputes among the various denominations over issues such as free will. Nothing accentuates the extent to which early Ohioans were strangers to each others than their religious practices. Methodists, who worshiped with great fervor, singing and praying loudly, unnerved those unfamiliar with them. Methodist meetings terrified Howells, who had been raised as a Quaker, so much that he prayed for their speedy conclusion.[42]

Howells went to Methodist meetings because his mother was a Methodist. For the most part, people stayed within the confines of the denomination in which they were raised or that they had chosen. Religion was something more than a sacred matter. Beyond the household, churches were sources of support in a world of strangers. They were the basis of social networks on which people could depend; they were something familiar in a world that was largely unfamiliar.

Joseph Gibbons, the young Pennsylvania farmer who visited eastern Ohio in 1804 when considering moving his family there, was aided immeasurably by his contacts with other Quakers. Like New Englanders going to the Western Reserve, Gibbons was often put out by the filth and rowdiness of the people in whose homes he stayed during his trip. Methodists were particularly loud and obnoxious.[43] He was much relieved when he encountered Quakers. Whether he knew them or not was immaterial. They shared similar values and prejudices. Not surprisingly, he looked for a farm around the Quaker settlement at Short Creek, not far from St. Clairsville, where he attended the meeting of Friends and where Quakers housed and advised him. By 1826, more than eight thousand Quakers lived in eastern Ohio. From 1815, the bustling town of Mount Pleasant hosted the yearly meeting of Ohio Quakers in its massive, two-story meeting house with a seating capacity of two thousand.

The caustic New Englander, Nathaniel Dike commented in 1818 that "the spirit of emigration pervades the world. It has loosened the foundations of society, severed the ties of the kindred, and set mankind afloat as it were, upon a tumultuous sea, without any settled destination." The people of Ohio were a mixed bunch, he believed. They were "for the most part . . . strangers to each other, and want of confidence, & jealousy embitter all social intercourse. . . . They are only birds of passage."[44] Dike exaggerated—but only to a degree.

Longing to improve their circumstances while clutching tightly to the familiar, thousands of settlers transformed Ohio into one of the most populous states in the Union in a remarkably short time. But they had not developed any sense of themselves as members of a larger political community. Ohioans identified with their household, with their religion, with their desire to market what they grew. Quakers, Methodists, Mormons, Yankees, Virginians, Germans, Scots-Irish, African Americans—all were citizens of Ohio in name only. A pleasing prospect with seemingly endless possibilities, early-nineteenth-century Ohio was a collection of separate communities and distinct regions without a transcendent public culture of the kind its founders had believed was critical to the realization of its enormous potential.

This representation of the Dayton Aqueduct over the Miami and Erie Canal evokes the pervasive sense of the possibilities of progress in early-nineteenth-century Ohio. (Courtesy of the Ohio Historical Society, Columbus, Ohio)

2

Improving Ohio

⸺

In 1838, THE General Assembly voted to construct a new state-house. Only two decades old, the federal-style, two-story brick building in Columbus was obsolete. The people of Ohio needed a structure whose grandeur reflected the power and possibilities of the young state. Completed in 1861, the new capitol was a massive rectangular stone edifice in the popular Greek Revival style with a shallow dome that rose 158 feet above the floor of the rotunda that separated the legislative chambers. Long flights of stairs led through rows of columns to the four entrances. Inside the legislative chambers were huge windows with elaborate decoration. At the bottom of the House dais was a bronze version of the state seal with the sun rising above plains and mountains stacked with wheat and arrows.

The capitol was not the only elaborate public building erected in Ohio in the middle of the nineteenth century. Courthouses, churches, and college halls, many in the Greek Revival style, suddenly dotted the landscape. The Montgomery County courthouse in Dayton, fashioned mainly from local limestone in the late 1840s, had Doric pilasters on all of its facades except for the front, which featured a six-columned portico. Inside was a huge oval courtroom with a Roman Pantheon–like domed ceiling. St. Peter in Chains Catholic cathedral in Cincinnati was more eclectic in appearance. Modeled on an Italian basilica, it was a limestone, Greek Revival structure topped with a 211-foot spire. In Cleveland, perhaps the most impressive church was First Presbyterian, sometimes called Old Stone. Romanesque in appearance, with two towers, it had a high, wooden vaulted ceiling.

These and a multitude of other new structures were part of an effort to revise Ohio's ragged and disconnected landscape, to seize control of its development by laying the foundations of a public culture. The goal was to encourage citizens to contemplate something larger than their local and personal interests. The transformation of Ohio was incredible: unprecedented change occurred at unprecedented speed. The world in the 1860s, replete with railroads, telegraphs, great cities, and industry, was almost unimaginably different from the world in 1803. Not everyone celebrated this dramatic change. Some even resisted it, worried that the development of a public world would undermine local autonomy and the power of households and churches. Indeed, the people who acted to improve Ohio, to unite it into something more than the sum of its parts, constituted a relatively small group. Usually, they were members of families who had settled permanently in Ohio and done relatively well. Because they saw their personal interests intertwined with those of the state, they cared about its future. Merchants, professionals, shopkeepers, artisans, and their wives, they were overwhelmingly Protestant. Whether Congregationalist or Methodist, Ohio's persister families explicitly linked material progress with moral progress. "[W]ealth is power," exclaimed the prominent Cleveland Presbyterian minister Samuel Aiken in 1851, "and when properly used, is a source of unspeakable good."[1]

An exemplary Ohioan in this regard was John A. Foote. The son of a U.S. senator and governor, Foote was born in New Haven, Connecticut, in 1803. After graduating from Yale, he came to the small town at the mouth of the Cuyahoga River to establish a law practice. He achieved success professionally and became one of Cleveland's most distinguished lawyers. Elected to city council in the late 1830s and to both houses of the Ohio General Assembly as a member of the Whig Party, Foote was also a member of the boards of a bank and a railroad corporation. Foote valued his membership in the First Presbyterian Church, which he joined shortly after his arrival. A sense of public responsibility suffused his life. He was a member of countless local improvement organizations, including the Cleveland City Temperance Society, the Cuyahoga County Anti-Slavery Society, the Cleveland Anti-Gambling Society, and the Children's Aid Society. A trustee of the Ohio Boy's Industrial School from 1854 to 1875, he adopted a boy from the Cleveland Industrial Society. Each of his wives was Presbyterian, although, unusually, neither belonged to any reform organizations.

So strong was Foote's reputation that the man he defeated in an 1851 campaign for Congress complained that Foote won because people thought he "was the better temperance man, because he did not allow his wife to put brandy in her mince pies, and pickles, too." The humor underscored Foote's earnestness. Subtlety did not come naturally to him. In writing about temperance reform in 1843, he claimed that "our cause is literally the means in the hands of a gracious God of administering to the wants of the needy—of restoring reason to the maniac—domestic happiness to the family circle—of diminishing crime, pauperism, and death—and of preparing the soul for the high and holy duties and privileges of religion."[2]

As admirable as Foote may have been, he did not speak for everyone in Cleveland, let alone Ohio. Not everyone agreed with his vision of the state's future. Not everyone put such a high premium on elaborate public buildings, transportation networks, public schools, prisons, and temperance. Not everyone saw life as an opportunity to improve one's self and one's neighbors. Most people in early Ohio were too busy trying to survive or get ahead to worry about grand projects of social improvement. For many, especially those who were not evangelical Protestants, religion was a source of spiritual sustenance and community rather than a call to moral arms.

Ohio's emerging middle class worked hard to overcome apathy and resistance to the construction of a great state. To a large extent, the creation of public space and institutions designed to overcome local differences—buildings, roads, canals, schools, and reform societies—was a work of collective will. Reformers imagined an Ohio transformed from a fragmented collection of isolated and distrustful local communities into a larger community of respectable citizens. They did not always win; on more than one occasion they had to compromise and take what they could get. Nonetheless, their achievement in promoting their vision of Ohio was considerable. They laid the foundation of a public culture that, for better or worse, reflected their values more than anyone else's.

Public Transportation

In September 1851, twenty-nine-year-old Rutherford B. Hayes, an ambitious Cincinnati lawyer, wrote a newsy letter to his fiancée, Lucy Webb, about his recent doings. Buried in the middle was a paragraph about a trip Hayes took about fifty miles north of Cincinnati. "I went to Dayton yesterday and back," he wrote, "celebrating the completion of the railroad which makes Dayton a suburb of Cincinnati. Only two hours and a half to Dayton! Shades of departed coaches, 'buses,' and canal-boats, hide forever your diminished heads! The 'iron-horse' has taken away your occupation, to keep it until aerial ships take away his!"[3] Hayes's excitement was understandable. When he was born in 1822, it had taken days to get from Cincinnati to Dayton.

Nothing was more likely to inspire middle-class Ohioans than improvements in transportation. Equally important, nothing was more likely to inspire controversy than questions about how to build and pay for them.

Few people objected to better roads, bridges, canals, and eventually, railroads. Most everyone welcomed easier ways to travel and transport goods. Ohioans generally wanted to sell what they could not use and buy goods from markets in the northeastern U.S. and Europe. Still, many of the same people who took advantage of the opportunities presented by steamboats and canals fretted about their impact on their lives and those of their children. Improvements in transportation were fine as long as they enhanced their worlds rather than destroyed them. Most people's frame of reference remained their town, their family, their church, or their county. With little money, they were reluctant to pay taxes to support improvements that would benefit other parts of the state but not their own. Ohioans shared the general American willingness to accept what government could do if they were sure that they were getting more than their fair share. In other words, people in Dayton who were willing to pay for a canal that went through Dayton were unwilling to pay for a canal that went through Chillicothe. Why should the people of Piqua support a state system of roads or canals if none of them came to Piqua?

A coterie of boosters and politicians devoted themselves to overcoming such fragmentation and regional jealousies. Among their leaders were Governor Ethan Allen Brown, Micajah T. Williams of Cincinnati, Alfred Kelley of Cleveland, and Ephraim Cutler of Marietta. In the 1820s, their agenda included getting the General Assembly to create statewide systems of canals and of public education. According to Harry N. Scheiber, they shared "a distinctive vision that transcended local concerns and embraced a view of statewide and regional possibilities." While they "did not fail to seize the main chance for themselves . . . they also devoted their efforts to seizing the opportunities for the community by mobilizing its government."[4]

Boosters, claimed that canals and schools would encourage each citizen "to connect his own good with that of society, and to enjoy his own rights in a manner that will not injure his neighbors." Isolation fostered a provincialism in which people considered "themselves the center of perfection, the arbiters of right and wrong." Improvements counteracted these tendencies and produced "a uniformity of interests," a sense of shared purpose. Governor Brown asserted that "[r]oads and canals are veins and arteries to the body politic," diffusing "supplies, health, vigor and animation to the whole system." As much as they made markets accessible and helped increase population, they would help the citizens of Ohio imagine themselves as a whole. Canal advocates in the early 1820s warned that without such a spirit of patriotism—"the secret chain, which binds together in one great family, the numerous individuals of which a state or nation is composed"—a state is made up of "a multitude of uncongenial spirits" and filled with "clashing interests [and] personal animosities." The great value of "the canal spirit" was that it would force Ohioans to promote "a common interest."[5]

Men such as Brown, Williams, and Kelley assumed that only governments could accomplish such a grand goal. An effective canal system required coordination. Canals dug by private corporations working solely for profit would create a haphazard collection of waterways. Traditionally in British North America, improvement projects had been carried out by private companies or individuals designated by governments to serve the public interest. Small and poor, governments farmed out most of their responsibilities—from caring for the impoverished to building roads to settling the West—and allowed individuals or groups of men to make money off of their offices or contracts.

By the 1820s, this blurring of public and private interests struck many Americans interested in open competition in the marketplace as favoritism and corruption. Nonetheless, the federal government had been an important player in the development of Ohio since the formation of the Northwest Territory in 1787. When Congress created Ohio, it had allocated 3 percent of the proceeds from the sale of federal land within the state to finance roads. Another 2 percent went toward the cost of the National Road, a project intended to link the Potomac and Mississippi Valleys from Cumberland, Maryland, to Vandalia, Illinois.

Little progress was made on these projects before the 1820s. If at all possible, people traveled by water. Roads, which were little more than muddy trails, were the responsibility of county governments. With little income (in 1815, the 3 percent fund produced $170,000; in 1820, Ohio collected only $200,000 in tax revenue), the General Assembly left transportation in the hands of local officials.[6] The state government gave money to counties to spend as they saw fit. Meanwhile, the legislature encouraged the occasional development of roads, bridges, and ferries in time-honored fashion by granting charters to private companies. Incorporation permitted them to function as legal bodies, to sell shares, and to enjoy certain privileges, such as collecting tolls.

In the 1820s, not even improvements in the quality of some roads could stem mounting enthusiasm for canals as the cheapest way to make markets more accessible to isolated Ohioans. Inspired by the success of the Erie Canal in New York, which linked Lake Erie with the Hudson River, the General Assembly on February 4, 1825, authorized the construction of two canals. The Miami Canal would unite Cincinnati and Dayton, and the Ohio Canal would connect the Ohio River and Lake Erie via the Scioto and Muskingum Rivers. To pay for these huge man-made channels, the legislature created a system of taxation to ensure that the people who would benefit most from the canals would pay the most to support their construction, and authorized the borrowing of money, up to six hundred thousand dollars in 1826 and 1827. Ohioans were so desperate for improved transportation that there was surprisingly little opposition to the scheme.[7]

Still, we should not construe acceptance of a statewide system of canals as acceptance of a statewide public culture. Canal commissioners argued that "sectional jealousies" were "degrading" and hoped that no one "would be envious of an immense benefit to a portion of their fellow citizens, procured without expense to themselves, by an operation which cannot fail to enrich the whole community, and place at their disposal most ample resources for education and for every kind of internal improvements."[8] But the reality was that Ohioans were intensely jealous of each other. To win approval of the canal projects, advocates had to persuade legislators that their constituents would not be paying for something they would not use.

Two years after the official ground-breaking ceremony on July 4, 1825, the section of the Ohio Canal connecting the elevated terrain of the Portage Summit to Cleveland was completed. With the 1832 opening of the entire canal, people could travel from the Ohio River to Lake Erie in about eighty hours (at a speed of four miles an hour) for five dollars. By 1845, the Miami Canal had been extended to unite the Great Miami River with Lake Erie at Toledo. Other feeder lines linked various parts of the state into the two main canals. All in all, the Ohio canals were a magnificent achievement. The French traveler Michel Chevalier observed that rural Ohio had "with the aid of some second-rate engineers borrowed from New York, constructed a canal longer than any in France."[9]

The grand public enterprise was a material success. Farmers could get crops to market more quickly, efficiently, and profitably. The price of a bushel of wheat in the area around Akron more than doubled. Cleveland benefitted enormously from the combination of the Erie and Ohio Canals. No longer isolated, it became the axis of an exploding commerce that spread into the Ohio Valley. Goods flooded into Ohio, including hardware, textiles, clothing, and machinery, in exchange for the processed crops from farms throughout the region.

The potential of improved transportation awed Englishman James Martin, who settled with his family in Crawford County in the early 1820s. He reveled in the knowledge that when the road that ran by his house was finished and the Erie Canal was opened, there would be only forty-two miles of "land travel from my house to New York." The people of nearby Bucyrus lived in anticipation of the possibilities in trade. They were not disappointed. By 1833, a daily stage coach passed Martin's house on the "excellent" turnpike. Three years later, he marveled at the "astonishing" migration to Ohio and the fact that "altho' 14 years ago I sat down in a complete wilderness I am now surrounded with a very dense population."[10]

Bucyrus grew because of a road. Towns fortunate enough to be along the canals expanded even more dramatically. Among them were Massillon, Newark, Hamilton, Middletown, and Piqua. Founded on the Portage Summit in 1825, Akron grew with the canal. By the mid-1830s, it had sixteen hundred inhabitants and many retail stores. Its manufacturers produced mirrors, maps, chairs, carding machines, woolen goods, and clocks. Akron also had two blast furnaces, a flour mill, a distillery, six warehouses, two sawmills, a printing office, and five taverns. The canal erased the location's greatest liability—its inaccessibility. Meanwhile, the opening of the Miami Canal turned sleepy Dayton into something of a boomtown. In 1840, in addition to stores and professional offices, it boasted six cotton-spinning establishments (with six hundred employees) and one weaving mill. Dayton's greatest asset was the fact that it was on navigable water at the center of a fertile region. Commerce and industry combined to elevate the burgeoning city above its local rivals.

Toledo, which in 1840 only the most optimistic of boosters could have called a town, let alone a city, became by 1850 "the great meeting-place and mart" of northwestern Ohio. In four years the value of its trade rose from $8 million to $31 million. Irish immigrants who came to work on the canals swelled the population, as did other people eager to cash in on the improvements. In six northern Ohio canal counties, the value of urban property rose by 360 percent (or almost $2 million) between 1832 and 1840. Toledo grew, wrote one contemporary, because canals had "pierced the forests and brought . . . from afar the richest harvests of the West."[11]

While the canals encouraged economic development, their cultural impact was not what their advocates had imagined it would be. On the one hand, they did bring Ohioans together. They literally linked parts of the state and broke down the isolation that had so frustrated early residents, especially in the northeastern and central sections. Many people now traveled the length and breadth of the state and met others whose interests and values were similar to theirs.

The canals also demonstrated the power of collective enterprise. Built by the people acting as a state, they were a model of government direction of state development.

On the other hand, canals intensified the heterogeneity of Ohio's population in ways that long-time residents did not appreciate. Irish Catholic and German immigrants as well as African Americans flocked to Ohio to work on the canals, canal boats, and locks, bringing with them even more distinctive linguistic and religious diversity. Villages on or near canals were no longer the relatively homogeneous networks of religious and household connections that they once had been. Even as the canals brought Ohioans into more regular contact with each other, they helped to fray the well-defined borders of what it meant to be an Ohioan. The admittedly difficult Englishman James Martin complained bitterly in 1833 about the "envy and jealousy" that his efforts to proselytize produced in the village of Bucyrus. "Everyone here is afraid that his neighbour should be greater than he is in politics. This principle they carry into religious controversies."[12] Neither roads nor canals would destroy local cultures or parochial interests.

Nor were the canals a blessing for everyone. The laborers who constructed them endured long hours of back-breaking work, for they literally dug the canals with picks and shovels. Disease, including cholera and typhus, raged periodically. Food and shelter were usually deplorable, even by the standards of the time. Immigrants and local farm boys nonetheless showed up eager, at least initially, to make enough money to buy some land. Often, contractors proved to be incompetent or deceptive. One man lost three hundred dollars in pay when a contractor skipped town, thereby ending his dream "of making some money to helpe myself to a small farm to make a home." As early as 1826, canal commissioners lamented that dishonest contractors had not only cheated workers and suppliers, they had "tended in some degree, to bring the work into disrepute, and to destroy the confidence of the laboring community in the certainty of receiving their wages." While efforts were made to check such behavior, the board insisted that it was the responsibility of the laborers themselves to make sure their employers were reliable and that they made regular payments. "He who will take *promises* instead of *payment*, should be contented with promises; and not grumble if he gets nothing at all."[13] These difficulties, and the high prices of crops in the early 1830s, reduced the number of young locals willing to work on the canals. Increasingly, contractors turned to Irish immigrants, and, on at least one occasion, convicts.

The Panic of 1837 and a subsequent economic depression did not devastate Ohio. Hard times, however, did call the role of government into question. Many voters, especially those in counties located some distance from the canals and who, therefore, were not basking in their economic glow, demanded an end to state-supported improvement projects. Mainly Jacksonian Democrats, they echoed the national party's objection to government involvement in public works. Meanwhile, voters in those areas that were reaping the benefits of the canals and becoming more commercialized tended to support Whig candidates at the state and national levels. Whigs supported the idea that state and federal governments should undertake projects that would serve the public good.

Far more controversial than canals in this regard were banks. Democratic voters demanded reform of Ohio's lax banking system. In 1842 and 1843, the General Assembly required all banks to pay their capital stock in specie (not paper notes) and to hold all officers and stockholders individually liable for losses suffered by the banks' creditors and debtors. Originally, the Ohio legislature had seen banks as instruments of development and incorporated them to serve the public interest, often with little oversight and few restrictions. When Ohioans suffered from the economic depression of the late 1830s, many demanded more accountability, if not the outright abolition of banks. The actions of the General Assembly in the early 1840s left only eight banks in the state. Fifteen others had lost their charters when they applied for renewal because they could not meet the new requirements.

Angry Democrats, however, could not sustain such a strong anti-bank policy for long in a state so committed to economic development. Defections by soft-money Democrats, who favored banks, led to the passage of the Kelley Bank Bill of 1845. In addition to state-chartered banks, it established a State Bank made up of a consortium of independent banks in twelve districts, all with a representative on the State Bank's governing board. The Ohio banking system had achieved a measure of stability with a balance of private initiative and public regulation.

The partisan squabble over banks in the aftermath of the Panic of 1837 was not so much a question of the value of market capitalism as it was one of government involvement. More and more Ohioans saw government not as a disinterested umpire, the voice of the people acting in the best interests of their common wealth, but as a corrupt and corrupting source of favoritism that compromised basic democratic principles.[14]

With the rise of the railroad in the 1830s and 1840s, the idea of state enterprise as the best way to encourage development was further discredited. The Ohio General Assembly never attempted to micromanage a state railway system as it had with canals. It chartered some nineteen railroad corporations in the early 1830s and a total of seventy-seven by 1840. While the state retained language that ensured its regulatory powers, in practice the companies did pretty much as they pleased. The railroad companies were incorporated, which meant, among other things, that the stockholders had limited liability. They also were entitled to exercise the right of eminent domain, which they did with little or no warning and at cheap prices. Finally, the companies received grants of tax exemption. All of these provisions, intended to encourage private corporations to take risks in the interest of the public good, cemented the essentially private nature of railroad development. "It is our duty to foster and promote such enterprises," wrote one Ohio judge in upholding the sweeping eminent domain rights of the companies. "We cannot and ought not to be indifferent to the imperative demand made by the rapid progress of the age."[15]

Private corporations rushed to build railroads in the middle of the nineteenth century. Demand was high, costs were relatively low, the state offered powerful inducements, capital from the East was usually available, and local towns and counties were willing to bear some of the costs, except during depression years. A few local railroads were built in the 1830s, but it took another decade for railroads to become serious competition for the canals. In 1851, three major lines began operation: the Sandusky, Mansfield, and

Newark; the Cincinnati, Hamilton, and Dayton (on which Hayes made his day trip); and a line linking Cincinnati and Cleveland. Later in the decade, Ohio railways connected with expanding Eastern lines, such as the Pennsylvania and the Baltimore and Ohio. By 1860, when Ohio led the nation with almost three thousand miles of railroads, the state-supported canal system was in a precipitous decline from which it would never recover. A year later, the state leased the system to a syndicate of six private operators for ten years. Although the state regained control of the canals in 1877, from then on they were never much more than a curiosity.

Railroads dominated transportation for more than a century. Trains brought new goods and new peoples to Ohio, transforming the possibilities of urban areas distant from water. In fewer than sixty years, the problems of inaccessibility and isolation that had confronted early settlers were largely overcome. Railroads also created new problems and highlighted old ones. They made the population of the state more diverse, and they became giant private corporations that seemed to serve their own interests more than public ones. With the rise of the railroads, the river city of Cincinnati began to lose its preeminence in the state. Cleveland and Toledo, located directly on lines that linked the huge western metropolis of Chicago and its extensive hinterland with the ports of the Atlantic seaboard, began to expand dramatically.

The world had become smaller. The dreams of many a wide-eyed traveler who commented on the possibilities of Ohio in the early 1800s had been fulfilled. In 1853, a person could board a train in Cleveland and travel to Columbus in about five hours, all for four dollars. As important as travel within the state was, the lure of places beyond Ohio became even stronger. Now, Boston and Philadelphia, Chicago and Denver, were not so far away. A train could carry a traveler from Cleveland to the heart of Manhattan in twenty-four hours at the cost of ten dollars. Physically and economically, Ohio was drastically different from the wilderness that had confronted its first white settlers. Whether it had become a community of citizens who saw the public interest as paramount in their lives, however, remained an open question.

Public Education

As with canals, public education was largely the cause of a few people interested in training citizens who would, when necessary, subordinate personal interests to public ones. From the start, some Ohioans argued that happiness would not be found in "ambition, avarice, or sensuality, or in the indulgence of licentious passions." Good order would not result from "a people making money their god, intent alone upon its acquisition—forgetful of their own proper good, and by a sordid insensibility to the real honors and pleasures of intelligent beings." Without public education, wrote a correspondent of the *Western Spy* in 1817, "our lives and property are insecure, government precarious, and social and political happiness at an end. And it is relatively thus, in proportion as the means of education is not within the control of the poorer class of society." In asking the legislature to create a state public school system, Governor Thomas Worthington warned that an ignorant "poorer class" would be "unable to manage with propriety, their private concerns, much less to take any part in the management of public affairs; and what is still more to be lamented, unacquainted with those religious and moral precepts and principles, without which they cannot be good citizens."[16]

This melodramatic rhetoric reflected the prejudices of its speakers. Most Ohioans were too busy or too cash poor to think much about education. Many believed, moreover, that schools should generally reflect the values of those who supported them. Where schools existed, as in Marietta or the towns of the Western Reserve, they were the result of local enterprise. A group of citizens, usually from the same Protestant denomination, raised some money, found a suitable building, and hired someone to serve as the teacher. Some of these schools flourished; others quickly disappeared. Attendance often was spotty. Despite the best of intentions, these early academies rarely fulfilled their potential.

William Cooper Howells recalled that he made as much "progress" in his studies "at home as at school." In total, Howells attended schools in and around Steubenville in the 1810s for about nine months. "Whatever else of education I received at home with my mother as my teacher." While his father did not offer formal instruction, he spent time talking with his son. Howells later believed that he "learned the half or more of all I did learn when a boy, in the course of conversations with men."[17] He claimed to have asked questions and to have read books on his own. All in all, Howells did not seem dissatisfied with his education. But his experience indicates the degree to which education in early Ohio was haphazard.

Ambitious young men and women with one or more interested parents sometimes did well. The young Rutherford B. Hayes was sent away from his home in Delaware to attend private academies, first the Norwalk Seminary when he was fourteen, and then Isaac Webb's school in Middletown, Connecticut. He and his sister Fanny briefly attended a district school but were so frightened by the Yankee schoolmaster (who silenced a loquacious pupil by throwing a "large jack-knife" in his general direction) that they did not learn much. Fanny thrived at home, where she read history and Shakespeare and studied Latin and Greek with her brother and his tutor. Eventually, she graduated from a seminary in Putnam.[18]

Their experience was not typical, however. Many Ohioans were indifferent to education. In 1825, Howells learned this lesson the hard way when he tried to start a grammar school. He failed, in no small part because the "young men and women" who attended saw school largely as a social occasion. Grammar was boring; courtship was fun. If you wanted to open a school, you might as well make it a singing school, advised Howells, for it taught something people found enjoyable.[19] In any case, education beyond the basic necessities of reading, writing, and arithmetic was a luxury few could afford. Household work was unrelenting, and what free time people had was better spent with family and neighbors.

Advocates of a general system of public education nonetheless pressed forward. In 1821, the General Assembly permitted local districts to raise taxes for the maintenance of schools. An 1825 act, passed in conjunction with the canal bill, required people to pay a property tax to support local schools. But all control was local. Township trustees allocated resources and hired and fired teachers. Despite the efforts of professionals such as Samuel Lewis, superintendent of common schools in the late 1830s, progress in education largely took place at the local level. In 1847, the General Assembly passed the

Akron School Law. It provided for one district for Akron with the modern system of grades, local grade schools, and (eventually) a central high school. Its managers was a board of education that was to be elected by voters; all real property would be taxed to support the operations of the school district. This system was institutionalized in the Ohio School Law of 1849 and modified in the Ohio School Law of 1853. The state government optimistically estimated in 1850 that 500,000 students attended Ohio's 11,661 public schools and another 15,000 were in 200 private academies.

These changes established the basic characteristics of public education in the state, one of which was the tradition of strict local autonomy. Because voters in each district established how much they would pay and who would run their schools, the quality of education varied widely from community to community. What a student learned was largely an accident of birth. Coupled with localism was the problem of indifference. Nearly everyone could see the value of learning basic skills, but few understood the need to go beyond that. Why spend money for young people to think about ideas that they would never need when they could be usefully employed in the field or the kitchens?

To advocates of public education, the answer was obvious. A broad education would create bonds between people. Uniting citizens of Ohio in a common endeavor in their youth, education would foster the self-control and disinterestedness necessary for the survival of a republican form of government. Advocates fretted that a state whose citizens thought of no one and nothing beyond the borders of their household, town, or county was no state at all. From the beginning, the diversity of Ohio's population worried them. How could a multitude of different people, strangers to each other, cohere into a whole? How could they unite in the cause of progress and development? The perception of fragmentation was critical to the movement for public education. The migration of thousands of Germans, Irish, and other Europeans into Ohio in the 1830s and 1840s intensified these fears, especially when many resisted having their children educated in public schools so obviously committed to destroying all vestiges of family, ethnicity, and even religion.

The future schoolteacher John M. Roberts, a resident of Madison County (just west of Columbus), welcomed the appearance of a railroad linking the county seat of London with the state capital. Roberts was especially pleased that it went "right strait through our place near the creek. We will make something by that operation," he wrote. Roberts was an ambitious and sensual man. He loved a good time, devoted much of his diary to recording his dismal efforts at courtship, and was always on the lookout for ways to improve himself, both materially and intellectually. At the same time, he decried the universal cry for "a little more. A little more fun, a little more money, a little more land, a little more time, a little more power, a little more wind or a little more calm, a little more war, a little more peace, a little more of everything. A mans soul is never satisfied in this world. He always wants something more than he has got."[20]

Roberts worried that "with the influx of foreigners we also have to put up with a great deal of the refuse portion of Uropes population." He got along well with individual Irishmen but he disliked their drinking. "The Irish are getting to be pretty thick in this country lately, & I am afraid we will have hot times with them before many years will have passed over our heads. . . . [T]he Irish are beginning to get discontented with the Americans & want to have all the government in their hands." In other words, "the Catholics are getting to be very saucy[.]"[21] Roberts was not about to let them have their way in Ohio.

At times, Roberts found the number of foreigners overwhelming. In the spring of 1857, he bought a German grammar book for a dollar in Findlay. He had decided to learn the German language because "[t]here are any amount of Dutch in this country, and they just gabble away at me as if I understood it." His good intentions did not last long. A few days later he had decided that "Germany must have taken a puke in to this part of the moral vineyard." In his opinion Germans were "perfect clodheads" who knew only enough to plow and eat "sour krout. Heaven deliver me from the Dutch and all their kin."[22]

Catholics by and large resisted efforts to require them to send their children to public schools. Whether Irish or German, parents wanted children to grow up with their values. Catholics were not against education. They simply wanted to control what their children learned, much as rural Ohioans had done for years. After trying to work out an accommodation in Cincinnati, Catholics recognized that the purpose of public education was to inculcate a Protestant version of moral literacy. Instead, they formed parochial schools under the leadership of Bishop John Baptist Purcell.

Leaders of the public school movement believed in the importance of their ways of doing things. Many of the values they proscribed were superficially innocuous, including such noncontroversial notions as punctuality, cleanliness, and honesty. The textbooks of William Holmes McGuffey, who taught at Miami University and Ohio University in the 1830s and 1840s, were the most influential expressions of this approach. But Catholics and Jews found the Protestant tone and content of some of the teachings offensive. While few objected to their children's becoming good citizens, many worried that putting civic identity above their religious identity—making being an American or an Ohioan more important than being a Catholic or a Jew—left the immortal souls of their children at risk. Why surrender the ways of their ancestors, especially in the midst of such hostility? And why did Catholics have to pay taxes to support public schools that they did not use?

Catholics deliberately excluded themselves from the public school system. Blacks were a different matter. Although Germans and Irish could be raised from the depths of ignorance, blacks seemed to many whites to be permanently degraded. It was illegal for African American children to attend public schools until the 1840s. Because their parents were not considered citizens, they did not have to pay taxes to support schools. In 1848, the General Assembly, responding to growing antislavery agitation, created separate black schools where there were twenty or more African American children, to be supported by taxes paid by their parents. Where there were fewer than twenty children, blacks students could attend public schools if there was no objection from the local community. Ohio's black schools were appalling. With shoddy buildings and poorly qualified teachers, they attracted few students.[23]

Advocates made the case for black education on several occasions. Their argument was straightforward. If whites feared blacks as members of "a degraded and inferior race," then what better way to elevate them? "Educate them, and they become useful members of the community that has cared for them," exclaimed a member of the 1851

Ohio Constitutional Convention. The state commissioner of common schools made the same point in his 1860 report. "[I]s it not better that their [African Americans'] children should be so taught that they will be intelligent, respectable and useful, rather than be left to grow up in ignorance, and become degraded and dangerous members of society? The fact that many of these people are of low and worthless character, is, to a great extent, the result of their defective and vicious education." The commissioner hastened to add that he believed in segregation. He simply thought that these "rational and immortal beings" should receive a proper education. How could whites as good Christians and republicans do otherwise?[24]

The answer was simple. According to another member of the 1851 convention, the problem was not equal rights but residency. He opposed public education for African Americans because he "would strenuously oppose every proposition which, in its practical effect, will tend to encourage the emigration of blacks into the State." Giving blacks an education would encourage them to think of themselves as citizens. The delegate had to "look first, to the interests of the white race." The best solution was for blacks to migrate to Liberia or somewhere else in Africa. There they could exercise all the rights and privileges of citizenship. They could vote, hold office, even become president of a republic. But not "in this country," which was dominated "by a different and a higher race. I am willing that [they] shall enjoy all these rights and privileges in [their] native country." By themselves, they could enjoy the quality and liberty extolled in "the language of our sublime Declaration of Independence."[25]

Not all Ohioans shared this view. In the 1830s, African Americans in Cleveland organized their own school in a room in a mill with a succession of teachers. In 1835, a meeting of African Americans in Columbus led to the formation of the School Fund Society, "the object of which," according to John Malvin, "was to establish schools in different parts of the States for colored children." This they did in Cincinnati, Columbus, Springfield, and Cleveland, although the schools lasted only for a couple of years. In 1843, the Cleveland city council began to subsidize black schools. In the 1850s, the city abolished segregated schools altogether. African American children not only went to the same schools as whites, a black person even taught in white schools. This development was not uncommon in northern Ohio, where the African American population was small and did not seem likely to grow.[26]

In Cincinnati, on the other hand, African Americans had to fight for what the historian Joe William Trotter described as "the establishment of separate schools for black children, paid for by black taxpayers and governed by black boards of directors elected by blacks." It happened in 1858 only as the result of an Ohio Supreme Court decision. Peter Clark had led the movement to open a school earlier in the decade. African Americans united in the Colored Education Society ran three schools in Cincinnati in the 1850s and paid completely for two of them. Whites also supported schools for blacks, most notably Gilmore High School. Established by the English minister Hiram S. Gilmore in 1844, it employed five teachers to teach three hundred black students Latin, Greek, art, and music, among other subjects. All these efforts notwithstanding, only 38 percent of black children attended school in the late 1850s, compared with 72 percent of whites.[27]

No matter how much they worried about citizenship or feared blacks and foreigners, little could jolt many Ohioans into a great passion about education. In 1836, Superintendent Samuel Lewis traveled throughout the state on a generally anonymous mission "to visit many schools in the country, and to converse with teachers, children, school officers, and parents." Lewis rode his horse more than twelve hundred miles and saw some three hundred schools. His trip was disheartening. Outside of Cincinnati, there were "very few places in the State, where common school instruction proper, is furnished, approaching near the grade we have supposed; that is, where the means of proper instruction *are free to all, rich and poor, on equal terms.*"[28]

In language that remains familiar more than a century and a half later, Lewis described overcrowded classrooms, short school terms, and overworked teachers. Despairing of reform, parents with any means withdrew their children, giving their local school "the name of a school for the poor, and its usefulness is destroyed." The result was catastrophe. "[T]he poor, whose conscientiousness of poverty always makes them jealous and watchful, detect the smallest partiality, and leave the school in disgust, or stay to scatter the seeds of discontent and insubordination."[29]

To make matters worse, "many of our common, as well as private school teachers, are unqualified for the task they assume. . . . The most general defect is want of learning and energy." If Ohioans wanted good teachers, Lewis argued, they would have to pay for them.

"We may speculate as much as we please, pass resolutions, mourn over the defect, establish schools for teachers, and invent an hundred other plans," Lewis wrote. Still, "the more we teach the candidates, the less number of teachers we shall have; for men of learning and talent will not teach, unless the compensation and respectability of the business, are both greatly increased. Men are, and will be, as a general rule, governed by self-interest, and while so wide a field is open for enterprise and learning in other departments, they will not engage in this, unless we make the emoluments in some proportion equal with other professions."[30]

Higher salaries alone would not be enough, according to Lewis. State and local officials had to work together to improve schools. A "passive assent in favor of education will not answer; the same course in reference to internal improvement would never have made our canals and other public works." Well-intentioned parents could help their children, but Lewis doubted that most possessed the expertise to teach them. Church schools might also provide quality instruction, but their "influence" was limited to their own "sect." Better that the General Assembly act to "preserve a universal, liberal, republican, christian education" among "a people so varied in their origins, habits, and prejudices." Still, Lewis knew that any legislative attempt "to prescribe rules for the internal regulations of the schools" would fail without the cooperation of local officials. All he could do was hope that in spite of local variations, every student would "learn to *read, and write, and cypher.*" He was far less sanguine that they would be taught that "real patriotism consists in a proper cultivation of those arts and principles that adorn society, and make in practice, what we claim in theory, viz: the cottage equal to the palace. The natural impetuosity of unrestricted liberty, is to be tempered by a well-grounded conviction that obedience to the law is real liberty."[31]

In the meantime, Lewis could take comfort in the fact that some Ohioans were staunchly committed to public education. In 1858, young John M. Roberts began what would be a half-century career as a teacher in a one-room school near Mount Sterling and Palestine in Madison County. Roberts settled for twenty-five dollars a month in pay, which he knew was too low. (A friend was earning thirty-eight dollars a month in Preble County.) His pupils were few and irregular in their attendance, a problem he blamed on parental apathy; they averaged just over seventeen a day out of a total enrollment of thirty-three. Roberts particularly regretted the neglect of women's education. Farmers did "not cultivate [their daughters] half as much as they do their corn fields." If only they knew rhetoric, logic, and arithmetic and could "strengthen the mind and make it able to think," things would be much better for everyone.[32]

Roberts's employers were simultaneously strict and uninterested. Jacob Oglesbee gave Roberts his "orders" when he got the "the key to the temple." Roberts was to hold no evening classes, nor was he to allow meetings of any kind in the schoolhouse. Two weeks later, Oglesbee dropped by with a pail and a cup but neglected to bring a broom. Roberts concluded that "they do not take an interest in their school here that they ought." His neighborhood was charming but lacked "excitement." Things were so "dull," he even missed "family quarrels," "drunken Irishmen & Dutchmen," and "gamblers."[33]

None of these complaints, which were commonplace and familiar to the likes of Lewis, wore down Roberts's enthusiasm for teaching. It was "a glorious occupation." He loved his "school room and its appurtenances." He loved "to see the minds of children expanding, growing, & refining . . . and although I am not as well qualified to give them the right kind of ideas as I should be, yet I feel like devoting my one talent to that noblest of professions, the training of the immortal mind."[34] While Roberts chose education in part because he could not think of anything else to do with his life, he also did so because he found teaching meaningful.

The controversy over public education was passionate because it went to the heart of the relationship between civic and private identities. People who might compromise to improve transportation were far more tenacious when it came to schools. Parents wanted their children to be like them. As long as education consisted of basic skills, it was fine. But when questions of character and culture arose, it was something else again. The debate over who should be educated, how it should be paid for, what it should consist of, and who would control it had just begun. Indeed, these questions would be at the heart of some of the most divisive and persistent public conversations in the history of Ohio.

Deviance

If some Ohioans believed that the state had an obligation to supervise the training of future citizens, what was its role in dealing with incorrigible members of the body politic, those people who were either unable or unwilling to improve themselves? Could they be rehabilitated? What about the poor and the sick? Like other northern states, Ohio constructed institutions to deal with the indigent, the mentally ill, and criminals. Traditionally, local governments had handled such matters. When households could not care for people, counties or towns did, often by locking them up in jails. The grim buildings constructed in the 1800s—horrible as they were—reflected an assumption by the state of responsibility for the mentally ill, the blind, the deaf, and criminals. No longer treated as permanently lost to society, they were considered capable of improvement.

Institutions designed to help people with physical problems proliferated in the 1820s and 1830s. They brought citizens with similar challenges together, isolating them in a more regular and supportive environment. The deaf could go to an institution in Columbus as early as 1827; by the 1850s it had room for four hundred people. Facilities for the blind opened in Columbus a decade later. The mentally ill also received attention. A state hospital opened on the outskirts of Columbus in 1838, as did local hospitals for the insane in Cincinnati, Dayton, and Cleveland. Conditions were generally miserable, patient care often impersonal and inadequate.

Yet hope remained, certainly more so than had been the case before the late eighteenth century, when anyone with such problems would have been judged permanently incompetent. Further evidence of the trend was the opening in 1857 of a small school to educate "idiotic and imbecile youth." By treating the mentally ill in an ordered environment with regular rules, the directors of the institutions hoped to return them to a normal status as citizens. So strict were they in insisting that patients be isolated from the rest of the world that they forbade all correspondence. "Long and tender letters, containing some ill-timed news, or the melancholy tidings of sickness and death . . . may destroy weeks and months of favorable progress," wrote Superintendent William Awl in his annual report for 1840.[35]

More pressing was the problem of criminals, people who had violated the basic code of society and lost the right of membership in the community. Ohio had its fair share of murderers, rapists, and thieves. In 1867, W. L. DeBeck published a lurid collection detailing Cincinnati's many violent murders. One man had stamped his wife to death. Another had crushed his victim's skull. Some criminals were sentenced to long terms in local jails; others were executed. In keeping with time-honored tradition, executions were festive occasions. Crowds gathered to hear confessions and witness the deaths. The 1829 hanging of African American Philip Lewis drew an estimated ten thousand people. In 1832, when a last-minute reprieve saved the life of John Birdsell, a throng of fifteen thousand was sorely disappointed. Some people had come from miles away; others had waited for days. Cincinnati had essentially shut down for the occasion. Scientists who planned to experiment on the body of the accused had sold tickets to interested spectators.[36]

By the 1830s, men convicted of grand larceny or a crime of violence increasingly were sentenced to terms in the Ohio Penitentiary in Columbus. The prisoners were hardly respectable. Most were from other states, and many were unskilled. Their average terms varied from life for the crime of murder to six years for assault and four years for counterfeiting.[37]

Built in the 1830s, the Ohio Penitentiary in Columbus was a state-of-the-art facility. Prisoners were put to work in more than forty shops or on projects such as canals. They lived in a regular environment with a prescribed daily routine. Removed from the corruption of society, they were, in theory, made susceptible to moral improvement. Prison was like a school. Its purpose was to elevate the soul and discipline the mind, to teach people how to behave like proper citizens. "Never, no never shall we see the triumph of peace, of right, of Christianity, until the daily habits of mankind shall undergo a thorough revolution," wrote chaplain James B. Finley. "Could we all be put on prison fare, for the space of two or three generations, the world would ultimately be the better for it. Indeed, . . . society [should] change places with the prisoners, so far as habits are concerned, taking to itself the regularity, and temperance, and sobriety of a good prison."[38]

In practice, things did not work out as the good chaplain hoped. According to the directors, "The whole system of discipline depends upon non-intercourse between convicts." A large building and separate cells were not enough to keep prisoners from talking with each other. In fact, the prisoners seemed to one warden to control the operations of the prison. He complained in the early 1850s that when he took up his duties, "nearly all convicts were clamorous for what *they* claimed were their rights. . . . They acted as though they were martyrs. . . . Indeed the prison seemed a perfect bedlam."[39] Despite their multiple problems, asylums and prisons reflected a larger commitment to the spirit of improvement. All white human beings, it seemed, enjoyed the possibility of being rehabilitated for renewed participation in the body politic. No one, unless black, was lost entirely.

When reformers reflected on why penitentiaries were necessary in a free society, they frequently harped on failures within households. In a mirror image of the arguments of education advocates, prison reformers quoted the aphorism that trees grew as twigs were bent. Prisons were monuments to the failures of homes and local communities. "Unhappy orphanage," observed the warden of the Ohio Penitentiary in the early 1850s, "leaves the susceptible youth without those restraints and safeguards which conduct to a life of probity."[40]

Weak families and communities were, perhaps, to be expected in a rapidly fluctuating population. Yet most people had no trouble pinpointing an even more deleterious cause of criminality—intemperance. It was a truism that imbibing alcohol made it impossible for people to control their passions. If education was the means to self-discipline, alcohol was the shortest path to self-indulgence. By the 1840s, large numbers of Ohioans had identified drunkenness as the root of all social evils. It destroyed the sense of social and political obligation by undermining families, keeping men from schools and churches, and leading citizens into the licentiousness of saloons and city streets.

Like all Americans, Ohioans consumed vast amounts of alcoholic beverages in the early nineteenth century. Whiskey and beer were big business in Cincinnati. The Queen City had 223 saloons and taverns in 1834; together, they paid $9,682 in annual license fees, amounting to some 18 percent of the city's revenue.[41] Licking County had thirty-eight stills producing ninety-seven thousand gallons of whiskey in 1820. Men and women everywhere relied on whiskey, fruit brandies, and beer for both medicinal and social purposes. It was rare to find a store or inn without a barrel of whiskey open for visitors. Often, whiskey was a form of payment. For Irish and German immigrants, drinking alcoholic beverages was central to their culture. Many Germans could not imagine a meal without beer.

William Cooper Howells remembered three stills within two miles of his farm in eastern Ohio, each capable of producing twenty-five to forty gallons at a time, perhaps even a barrel a day. "The custom was for every man to drink it, on all occasions that offered; and the women would take it sweetened and reduced to toddy." So prevalent was whiskey that Howells's father, who abstained completely, gave in and furnished it to his neighbors when they had performed some service for him.[42] Thirty years later, the future Madison County schoolmaster John Roberts complained about the prevalence of alcohol and the vices that accompanied its consumption. The problem went well beyond the Irish and the Germans who were the usual objects of his scorn.

In December 1853, Roberts noted the appearance of neighbor Valentine Wilson, Jr. at the family farm. Wilson was looking for his wife. Roberts thought Wilson "a real brute" who had "thumped his wife most unmercifully in times past, & it is my opinion that he will do so again." Yet Roberts was certain that Wilson's wife would come back to him. She clung "to him with a constancy that is truly wonderful." He was not sure why. Wilson was neither "beautiful" nor "virtuous. He wont work and will get drunk. The fact is, he is good for nothing." Roberts hoped that Wilson would serve as "a warning to others not to let whiskey reign over their reason and make beasts of them [in] every sense of the word." He could not imagine anything worse than being "a slave to my passions & especially to the love of strong drink."[43] Roberts had pretty much summarized the dangers of intemperance. Men who would be slaves could not be republican citizens or respectable husbands. To eliminate drunkenness would be to eliminate a host of social problems.

Such beliefs were the foundations of the powerful temperance movement that swept Ohio and other northern states in the middle of the nineteenth century. At the core of the movement were women who were especially sensitive to the impact of whiskey on families. The abuse of wives and children as well as the neglect of work as often as not had their roots in excessive drinking. A drunk could not be a good father, let alone a good citizen, although the two roles were inextricably related.

In Cincinnati, the temperance movement mushroomed in the 1840s. The most successful organization was the Order of the Sons of Temperance. Its membership nationally was made up of artisans, merchants, and professionals. Ohio was no different. By 1847, there were some seventy-four chapters in sixty-five Ohio towns, the vast majority of them rapidly growing communities on canals, roads, railroads, or near large cities. Membership peaked the next year at 21,566. An independent parallel organization, the Daughters of Temperance, proved equally popular. The Cincinnati chapter had more than two hundred members in 1848. Originally, these organizations dedicated themselves to so-called "outside work," that is, to converting people to abstinence, sponsoring lectures, and publishing pamphlets.[44] But they soon became more important as fraternal organizations where like-minded strangers could get together and enjoy each other's company without alcohol.

As with education, an important spur to the growth of temperance reform in Cincinnati (and other Ohio cities) was concern about the arrival of tens of thousands of Germans and Irish. The city's population more than doubled in the 1840s from 46,000 to 115,000. By 1850, 44 percent of Cincinnatians were foreign-born, including 26 percent German and 12 percent Irish. Some of these newcomers were poor. Many were young males who had a tendency to become involved in criminal activities. Whether or not the immigrants were law-breaking vagabonds was immaterial to many native-born Ohioans. They thought they were, and that was all that mattered.

In Cleveland, an interlocked network of Protestant ministers and business leaders pushed hard for temperance in no small part to retain some degree of control over a community that was increasingly foreign-born and Catholic. Drinking became the central issue in a cultural war. If Ohio's Protestant, native-born temperance advocates could convince a young Irish Catholic man or a German Protestant to give up alcohol, they thought they were well on the way to transforming him into a useful citizen.

By midcentury, reliance on moral suasion in Cincinnati, Cleveland, and points between had given way to calls for government intervention. Desperate temperance advocates demanded a provision in the revised Ohio Constitution of 1851 to end the licensing of taverns. Members of the Constitutional Convention, fearful that the controversial issue would doom the document as a whole, refused. Instead, the General Assembly made it a separate issue in a statewide referendum. Not only did the proposal fail statewide, it lost in Cleveland by a vote of 672 to 579. Reduced to recommending political candidates on the basis of their single issue, temperance supporters took consolation in local victories, such as the prohibition of sales of liquor in hotels and bars and on Sunday in the city of Cleveland.

The 1859 death of prominent Clevelander Elisha Sterling illustrated the difficulties inherent in any crusade to reform human nature. President of the Cuyahoga County Steam Furnace Company and a founder and member of the vestry of St. Paul's Episcopal Church, Sterling was discovered lying unconscious on Bank Street and died shortly thereafter. The coroner's jury determined that a fractured skull had caused Sterling's death and that it was improbable that it had happened as a result of an accident. Sterling had spent much of the night of his death playing cards. His death allegedly occurred in a drunken brawl prompted by gambling debts. True or not, the story gave Cleveland's ministers the opportunity to point out the invisible depths of human misery in their city. Strong drink inevitably dragged "a man down to the level of a brute," thundered Sterling's pastor, R. B. Claxton. Not even the rich and powerful could escape. The lesson was clear: Clevelanders had to become more vigilant. They could not be fooled by appearances. Who knew what evil lurked behind a respectable demeanor?[45]

The Sterling tragedy also demonstrated the scale of the challenge that Ohio's reformers faced. Internal improvements, schools, public institutions, and reform societies could not manufacture ideal citizens. Exposure to noble civic ideals did not ensure their acceptance. Many Ohioans would defy them and offer alternatives of their own. Yet it would be folly to ignore the impact of reform efforts on the landscape. Even if advocates of progress had not brought unity to Ohio, if they had not convinced everyone of the value of education or the evils of alcohol, they had constructed the framework of a public culture that would dominate the state well into the twentieth century.

The wedding portrait of Rutherford and Lucy Webb Hayes, taken in Cincinnati, December 30, 1852. (Courtesy of Rutherford B. Hayes Presidential Center, Fremont, Ohio)

3

Considering Ohio

━

"IF THERE BE a matter of fact people on the earth, look at Ohio, and you shall see them," the young Harvard graduate Isaac Appleton Jewett confided to a friend in his home state of Massachusetts in 1831. "No visions here—no poetry here—all tabernacles of the flesh—all stern realities." Jewett's complaint about "the soulless utilitarianism of this Western World" was not unusual. Travelers and immigrants, especially from New England, often remarked on the degree to which Ohioans concentrated on making money and ignored making art. The most infamous critic was Frances Trollope, whose *Domestic Manners of the Americans* lampooned the pretensions of Cincinnati's supposedly narrow-minded elite. The city's leading citizens came across as nouveau riche—people with money and power but without taste or refinement. According to one journalist, Cincinnati in the 1830s "seemed too much disposed to look at her pork, and let poetry go to heaven the way it might think best."[1]

How, then, do we explain the fact that hundreds, if not thousands, of Ohioans insisted on exercising their minds as much as their bodies in the pursuit of progress? By the 1830s, nearly every village had at least a handful of residents who made reading and writing a major part of their lives. Men and women were scribbling furiously in diaries and journals, reading newspapers and magazines, listening to sermons and public lectures, composing poems and short stories, painting and designing, and attending public meetings and parties. Romantic and sentimental, they emphasized emotion as much as reason, feelings as much as logic. Describing rivers and forests, lamenting the passing of Indians, detailing the deaths of children, cataloguing the vagaries of love, they were often melodramatic. "Mawkish" and "maudlin" are words critics frequently use to describe this work; most of it was in a generic romantic style that flourished everywhere from Vienna to Edinburgh, Rome to Paris, Boston to Mexico City.[2]

Nineteenth-century Ohioans never intended their poems, stories, histories, paintings, buildings, and songs to be strictly ornamental. Their creativity was always in the cause of something larger than aesthetic satisfaction. Their devotion to the life of the mind ran deeper than provincial boosterism. A flourishing of art, literature, and music, many believed, was one of the key markers of all great civilizations. Without an indigenous culture of its own, Ohio would never achieve the position for which its citizens insisted it was destined. Culture was an essential part of progress. As important, the creation of art was an extension of the education of a useful citizen. Writing, reading, and talking were ways of improving one's self. While a poem might not make its author famous, the act of expressing oneself within an established form made him or her a better person.

More than anything else, cultural life was an unending conversation about the rules of existence, about the ways in which the world worked and the ways in which people imagined it ought to work. "The pervading bias of the present age," wrote Cincinnatian Benjamin Drake in the 1830s, "is an inquisitive and enlightened spirit of research. . . . Nothing is now taken upon trust." The printing press, canals, railroads were wonderful things that had liberated mankind. Human beings were no longer passive. "Animated by the opulence of human power," people were now working to "free the human mind from its mental and moral bondage."[3]

Mid-nineteenth-century Ohio was as dynamic intellectually as it was economically. Progress was not simply a matter of connecting and educating people, of reminding them of their larger responsibilities as citizens. It was also about liberating them to create stories about themselves and their world. If Ohioans were rarely original, they were full of ideas. Their conversation about the past, present, and future of their state was as lively as any thing else they did.

Conversing with Oneself

Rutherford B. Hayes—who grew up in Delaware, Ohio, attended Kenyon College and Harvard Law School, and opened a law practice first in Fremont and then in Cincinnati—embodied the peculiar mixture of contentment and anxiety, ambition and insecurity that characterized growing numbers of Ohioans. Calling them middle class does not do them justice; the term connotes economic status when what really mattered to people such as Hayes was the cultivation of their character, what we might call an attitude. These were men who sought careers in law and politics or who devoted themselves to owning or managing a store, a bank, or a small business. These were women who moved beyond their households to participate in public conversation as writers, teachers, and members of churches and reform societies.

Like Lucy Webb, the woman Rud Hayes married in December 1852, the professionals and businessmen and their wives and daughters who became the leading citizens of towns such as Delaware and Chillicothe believed fervently that in order to make the world a better place, they had to make themselves into better people. For all their commitment to improving human society—for all their devotion to the causes of education, temperance, and morality, which others would find self-righteous and repressive—the foundation of their lives was the notion that before they could reform others, they had to reform themselves. Their point of departure in the cause of self-improvement was usually a diary. Filling page after page with records of their daily doings, they gave their lives meaning by turning them into stories. Their diaries were like friends to whom they could narrate the events of their lives in confidence.

In June 1841, Hayes began a journal that he would keep for the rest of his life. During his twenties and thirties, he obsessed about his courtships, certain that his life would be incomplete until he found a wife. But he also wrote at length about books, lectures, and conversations as well as friends, trips, and the fits and starts of a his career as a lawyer. Nothing, however, preoccupied Hayes more than the development of his own character. In one of his first entries, he discussed "some of the traits of character for which the hero of these etchings is most particularly remarkable." Writing about himself in the third person, he praised his self-confidence, which he thought important to a successful life. At the same time, Hayes worried that his self-esteem might prove injurious because people might misunderstand it. So "no one [was] more anxious to conceal it than he[.]" Moreover, his self-confidence indicated that "he thinks himself possessed of a good share of common sense, by which is meant a sound practical judgment of what is correct in the common affairs of life." Ambitious for fame, the young Hayes wanted above all "to preserve a reputation for honesty and benevolence." "[I]f ever I am a public man I will never do anything inconsistent with the character of a true friend and good citizen."[4]

Naive as Hayes's words may sound, they were heartfelt. Shaping his character was the great work of his life. Yes, he wanted material comfort; yes, he wanted high public office. But nothing mattered more than the good opinion of the respectable men and women of Ohio. Like him, they knew how hard it was to tame impulses even as they asserted over and over again that "the affections [were] within their own control," that they did not have to yield "to *any* passion." They knew that study and practice were critical to molding a good person. They knew that they had to analyze themselves constantly and devote themselves to making self-control a habit. In 1842, Hayes criticized himself for not showing enough "improvement"; he had progressed, but he could have "done much more had the *strenuous will* not been wanting." In other words, he could have done better if he had wanted to do better. He should remember that the "life of a truly great lawyer must be one of severe and intense application . . . it is not by sudden, vigorous efforts that he is to succeed, but by patient, enduring energy, which never hesitates, never falters, but pushes on to the last."[5]

A decade later, when he was setting up a law practice in Cincinnati, Hayes sounded the same theme to his fiancée, Lucy Webb. He asked her to point out his "deficiencies and faults." Marriage was a partnership in improvement as well as affection. "Some faults and imperfections we all have which cannot be got rid of; and with such, sensible people will always cheerfully bear in those they love," he explained. "[B]ut I cannot help feeling surprise every day that friends and lovers are not more true to their duties in aiding each other in cultivating the graces of character and life which depend more on education and habit than on the natural constitution. Within certain limits the formation of character and manners, tastes and dispositions, is within our control. If we do but try—try heartily and cheerfully—we *can* be, for all the purposes of every-day happiness, precisely what *we would wish to be.*"[6] Such faith in the power of people to improve themselves dominated Ohio in the nineteenth century.

Lucy Webb was the ideal partner for Rud Hayes. A native of Chillicothe, Lucy was twenty-one when she married the thirty-year-old Hayes. As a child she had admired her New England–born grandfather, Isaac Cook, who was an ardent supporter of temperance as well as a local judge and politician. When the Webb family moved to Delaware, she met Hayes and his mother and sister. In the late 1840s, she enrolled as a student in the Cincinnati Wesleyan Female College. While Lucy lacked the self-esteem her future husband possessed, she was interested in the same things, especially the improvement of self and society. She wrote essays with titles such as "The Importance of Refined Taste" and "Is the Advancement of Civil Society More Indebted to Intellectual Culture than Physical Suffering?" In "Is America Advancing in Mental and Moral Improvement?" Lucy argued that "it is acknowledged by most persons that [a woman's] mind is as strong as man's. . . . Instead of being considered a slave of man, she is considered his equal in all things, and his superior in some."[7]

These sentiments did not deter Lucy's instinctive deference to Hayes, however. They renewed their acquaintance in the early 1850s in Cincinnati. When Rud impulsively proposed in June 1851, she took her time in replying. Finally, she confessed "I like you very well" in a soft voice that thrilled Hayes but may have indicated some reluctance. Lucy did not believe herself worthy of him. She thought she was "too light and trifling." Later, she was embarrassed to write to Hayes for fear that her letters would not be good enough. When she did, she reassured him of both her love and his devotion. In the summer of 1852, Lucy told her fiancé that he was "more frequently in my thoughts than I ever imagined possible." "If only [you] knew," she added, "what a great man you are."[8]

The seriousness with which Rutherford and Lucy embraced the spirit of improvement should not obscure the pleasure they shared in each other's company. He was as playful as he was analytical, and their marriage was by all accounts happy. Still, no matter where they went or what they did, at some point they always returned to the question of whether they were behaving as good people should.

The couple's lifelong quest for respectability paralleled that of thousands of other middle-class people in Ohio. The obsession with personal as well as public improvement, indeed, the belief that the latter depended on the former, undermined to a significant extent the fragmentation of the state. While most Ohioans remained divided by religion and custom—divisions that would intensify in the second half of the nineteenth century—some of the generation of native-born Ohioans who came of age in the 1840s and 1850s were identifying themselves as something more than members of a particular household, church, or town. They were, in a fashion that their parents could never have imagined, citizens of Ohio. They did not just reside there; they had a strong sense of attachment to the state as their home. Ohio had made them distinctive in ways they devoted their lives to trying to understand.

If nothing else, they knew that a citizen was something more than a political being. A citizen was also a respectable person. His (and increasingly her) identity was not simply a matter of residency and participation but of character. A citizen did not just vote, serve on juries, pay taxes, and participate in the defense of the state, if necessary. A citizen devoted himself or herself to the glorious cause of improvement. Nowhere was this attitude legally spelled out. Indeed, to require respectability was to defeat its social purpose. The impulse for self-control, for progress, had to be voluntary. Political institutions and improved landscapes—both built and natural—did not make good citizens as much as good citizens made political institutions and better landscapes. The middle-class ideal of improvement would offend many people and imprison the grandchildren of the Hayeses' generation in a culture many would find repressive. But in the middle of the nineteenth century, the spirit of improvement was novel and exciting. The progress of the individual and the progress of the state had become one and the same. To be a citizen of Ohio was to entangle private and public identities to such a degree that they could never be fully separated.

Like others, Hayes wrote occasionally about being from Ohio. He referred to himself as a Buckeye, a nickname for Ohioans adopted because of the ubiquity of the buckeye (horse chestnut) tree within the state's borders. The Cincinnati physician, naturalist, and historian Daniel Drake proclaimed in 1833 that Buckeyes drew their character in part from the tree. Speaking at a public dinner in honor of Cincinnati's forty-fifth birthday, Drake insisted that "[u]nlike many of its loftier associates, [the buckeye tree] did not bow its head and wave its arms at a haughty distance, but it might be said to have held out the *right hand of fellowship;* for all of the trees of our forest it is the only one with five leaflets arranged on one stem—an expressive symbol of the human hand."[9]

When Rud Hayes spent a year in school in Connecticut from 1837 to 1838, he proudly stated his "aversion to the Yankees." He delighted in finding a young man who "was a real Buckeye in every sense of the word, and thinks as much of the Queen of the west as I do." He was happy that on a long walk, three of his companions were "Buckeyes and the other an Alabamian." Although he liked "divers things in this blue country . . . better than Ohio" (Thanksgiving dinner among them), he preferred to "go to college at the West, of course." When he was courting Lucy Webb, he remarked that he liked "Kentucky and Southern girls when they are not too haughty and idle—aristocrats, *amusees,* or flirts, wasps, or butterflies. They are warmer of heart, more cordial in their manners, apt to be pretty, quick, and graceful."[10]

The future schoolmaster John Roberts in Madison County did not have the advantages enjoyed by Hayes and Webb. He could not afford to go to college. Yet he too believed in "the spirit of improvement which ought to animate every one . . . to the highest degree." Roberts, like Hayes, kept a regular diary. He knew he would derive "pleasure" from it; he also hoped that he would get "some benefit from it" as well. He had purchased the book "for the Ciceronian Society to use, but they did not want so large a one, so thought I would just keep it myself." In it, he confided that his chief goal was to make himself into a better person, to avoid becoming "a slave to my passions." Roberts struggled to give up alcohol and tobacco. Still, as he noted in one entry, "I go in for all the new improvements that are beneficial to the public." It was not a choice; it was his responsibility as a citizen to do so: "every one ought to feel as if he was a pillar of the state & do all he can to promulgate true principles & promote the happiness of others."[11]

Whatever the outcome, Roberts was sure that there was no better place to make the effort than Ohio. He took some satisfaction in 1853 in knowing that an uncle who had moved on was not doing "as well as he might have done had of staid here." Admitting that he might someday "leave the bonnie Buckeye state," he thought "Ohio is large enough for me" at present. Roberts believed that "Ohio is as good a place as I want to live. Perhaps it is not the garden of the world, yet I think it comes the next thing to it." After all, it possessed "great and inexhaustible resources." Railroads were opening up markets everywhere. Roberts was jingoistic about his home state within the larger context of his pride at being an American citizen. "Ohio will be the first state in the Union yet," he exclaimed on one occasion. "She has the advantage of almost every other one in a natural way, and then she is fast outgrowing them in the artificial."[12]

Roberts's attachment, like Hayes's, however, went beyond the economic and civic prospects of Ohio. He felt an emotional bond to the landscape—both natural and artificial, what settlers had found and what had been created—that would have been unimaginable to Ohioans a generation earlier. "Madison Co. against Ohio & Ohio against the world for pleasant recreation & profitable instruction. Whew!" he exclaimed. "Nothing like this place for big babies & corn dodgers."[13] It was land and food and family and familiarity that made Ohio difficult to leave. None of these things—not big babies or cornbread or railroads—was distinctively Ohioan. Rather, it was the meaning that people such as Roberts and Hayes attached to them, the ways in which they imagined them as emblems of place and community, which mattered.

Such expressions of state pride reflected a larger romantic interest in the particularities of peoples and environments. Like some Germans, Scots, Mexicans, and others throughout the Western world, many Ohioans became more sensitive to the idiosyncrasies of the place in which they lived. Unlike the state's founders, who had stressed the universalism of their experiment in democratic citizenship, middle-class people in the middle of the nineteenth century were willing to celebrate their uniqueness. Whether or not Ohio was actually different from Massachusetts or Alabama, or Indiana or Pennsylvania, mattered less than the fact that many of its citizens began to believe that it was.

Conversing with Others

Like Rud Hayes and Lucy Webb, thousands of young Ohioans flocked to cities in the 1840s and 1850s. Cincinnati was easily the most popular destination. It was a rough environment, teeming with tens of thousands of Germans and Irish immigrants, most of them male, looking for dependable jobs and cheap housing. Assaults and robberies were frequent. A newspaper claimed that the city had around three thousand professional criminals. Even Dr. Daniel Drake, one of Cincinnati's most prominent citizens, was mugged in front of his home. The Hayeses lived in the center of the city. Affluent and native-born families, however, were moving to the new suburbs of Clifton, Walnut Hills, Mount Adams, and Mount Auburn, to the north and east of the crowded downtown. Cincinnati was noisy and dirty, its air thick with the smoke of coal fires and the stench of raw sewage and hog carcasses. Still, a city of more than a hundred thousand people was a new and wondrous sight to any American in the 1850s, unlike anything most of its new residents had ever known. Some were so overwhelmed that they left as soon as they could. John Roberts ventured to "the great Queen City of the West" in the spring of 1853. Impressed by "the mighty hum of business and the incessant turmoil of city life," he nonetheless could not wait to return to the country. Crowded and gloomy, Cincinnati made him feel "a kind of loneliness." He felt "as though I was such a small atom in such a mass that I was glad when I heard the bell ring for the [train] engine to start."[14]

For all its problems, which were hardly unique in the nineteenth century, Porkopolis had much to offer the young men and women who could overcome its crowds, odors, and noise. In addition to thriving manufactures and bustling commerce, Cincinnati boasted such architectural wonders as Pike Opera House and St. Peter in Chains Catholic cathedral. An innovator in the development of urban services, in 1851 the city had forty-five miles of pipes delivering water to its residents and five hundred gas lamps lighting its streets. The centerpiece was the domed Burnet House with elegant rooms and restaurants to serve the growing number of visitors.

Public conversation in Cincinnati started with attendance at lectures. Prominent speakers made Cincinnati a regular stop on their American tours. The most frequent was Ralph Waldo Emerson, who visited five times. Others included Yankee reformers and ministers such as Bronson Alcott, Theodore Parker, Henry Ward Beecher, Horace Mann, Wendell Phillips, Fanny Wright (who was buried in the city), and the German Carl Schurz, as well as the New England poet Oliver Wendell Holmes, Sr., the English novelist William Makepeace Thackeray, the Swedish writer Fredrika Bremer, and the actress Fanny Kemble. Rud Hayes commented at length on Emerson's rambling style. He also attended lectures by the Harvard scientist Louis Agassiz and a concert by the singer Jenny Lind.

More important than lectures was the production of books. Cincinnati's most prominent booster, Charles Cist, claimed in 1854 that the total value of the city's publishing industry made it the fourth largest publishing center in the U.S. Some people dubbed Cincinnati the "Literary Emporium of the West." Names such as H. W. Derby and Company, W. B. Smith and Company, and the Western Methodist Book Concern, W. B. Smith and Company became well known throughout the United States. They and other firms printed schoolbooks, including the famous McGuffey Readers, and a host of travel accounts, religious tomes, and histories. Cincinnati publishers also put out journals. Some, such as the *Western Literary Journal and Monthly Review,* were intellectual and did not last long. Much more popular were the *Great West* (soon renamed the *Columbian and Great West*), which provided its seven thousand subscribers with romantic frontier tales, and the *Ladies Repository and Gatherings of the West,* which attracted a primarily female audience with its many illustrations and sentimental stories.

Art thrived in mid-century Cincinnati. Wealthy lawyer Nicholas Longworth spent much of his life looking for artists of "genius," several of whom he supported financially. The most famous was the sculptor Hiram Powers, who was discovered making wax figures for a chamber of horrors. Impressed with his talent, Longworth paid for Powers to travel to Italy. While he never returned to Cincinnati, his example was constantly held up as a measure of what the possibilities of life in Ohio. "I scarcely meet a vagrant boy in the streets who has not a piece of clay in his hands, moulding it into the human faced divine," exclaimed the enthusiastic Longworth. Landscape and portrait painters, including the African American Robert S. Duncanson, also lived in Cincinnati. For a brief time in 1850, Cincinnati even had an organization dedicated to encouraging art. The Western Art Union was "to render the city a school for art, a mart for the elegant productions of the pencil, the burin, and the chisel—a center for the concentration of the patronage of the arts of our country."[15]

The cultural veneer of Cincinnati was thin. Much of the support of the arts and architecture was boosterism, part of a general effort to elevate the city to the status of Boston or New York. Most artists who achieved any kind of success soon departed for the East or Europe. The foundation of the publishing industry in the city was the production of school books, not works of high literature. Longworth exercised tight control over the work of his young geniuses. The generic murals Duncanson painted for Longworth's mansion (now the Taft Museum) exemplified the blandness that often resulted from a desire to please patrons rather than express individuality. No one can insist that Cincinnati was a world-class cultural center or that its artists were as important as its bankers. Still, the city possessed an enormous vitality in the middle of the nineteenth century. For people who had grown up on farms or in small villages, Cincinnati was a place of marvels and possibilities.

No wonder that young men and women flocked to the educational institutions and job prospects in Cincinnati. There they could improve themselves and entertain themselves at the same time. Exposed to constant intellectual stimulation (Hayes attended lectures or parties nearly every night of the week), they also made important professional and personal connections. The popularity of temperance and other reform societies was in no small part related to the fact they were a good way to meet people with similar attitudes. All kinds of clubs proliferated. Men's organizations sponsored lectures (by members as well as guests), suppers, picnics, and parties that nurtured both character and friendship. Women's clubs occasionally had lectures but mainly devoted themselves to social occasions. These formal societies and informal groups built around boarding houses and jobs were the foundation of middle-class life.

The most prestigious organization was the Semi-Colon Club. Founded in the 1830s, it met at the home of a wealthy merchant on Third Street. Recent arrivals from New England attended the meetings, as did Cincinnati luminaries Daniel Drake and Timothy Flint. Because the club welcomed both men and women, the lawyer William Greene read all the papers to mask the gender of their authors. In 1849, New Hampshire–born bookseller Ainsworth Rand Spofford and eleven of his friends organized the Literary Club. Like the Semi-Colon Club, which had stopped meeting, the Literary Club mixed fellowship and education. Regular papers were presented at the weekly meetings, a tradition that continues today. Spofford was the driving force behind much of Cincinnati's intellectual life until he moved to Washington, D.C., in 1861 to become the Librarian of Congress.[16]

Everywhere a young man such as Rud Hayes turned there was a club to join, a lecture to attend, a concert to hear, or an issue to be discussed. Hayes flourished in Cincinnati, lamenting only the five years he thought he had wasted trying to practice law in the small town of Fremont. Rud and Lucy chatted about novels and national news. He particularly enjoyed comparing Lucy to characters in Charles Dickens's *David Copperfield.* Hayes did not merely listen to Emerson and Agassiz. He spent pages in his diary mulling over the style and content of their lectures. He, too, seized opportunities to lecture before his temperance society and other organizations. Hayes prided himself on his ability to speak extemporaneously. In the lively whirl of Cincinnati life in the 1850s, he was improving himself—and having a good time, too. He enjoyed a profound sense of personal and public progress.

As exciting as life in the big city was, it was not as great a break with the worlds of their youths as Hayes and others thought. As children in small towns, he and Lucy had read widely and discussed serious issues with family members and friends. Rud had traveled to New England several times and had spent a year at Harvard Law School, where he meticulously summarized the lectures of the legendary Supreme Court justice Joseph Story in his diary. Hayes did not have to go to Cincinnati to discover the culture of self-improvement.

That culture embodied growing class distinctions. Middle-class citizens such as the Hayeses had grown up in villages where divisions between self-defined "respectable" and ordinary people were becoming more pronounced. "Decent" people lived in bigger and better houses set off from others on larger lots. Glendower, a home built by the attorney John M. Williams in Lebanon in the late 1830s and 1840s, was so impressive that his sister-in-law had a slightly larger replica of it constructed on an adjacent lot. Visitors entered the typical stately Ohio home through a porch with columns and decorative facades painted white to conjure up images of ancient Greece. Inside, they passed through large entry hallways into public rooms, or parlors, where families gathered to present themselves to the world. Beds and evidence of private life had long since been banished to the second floor or the rear of the house. By the 1850s, parlors were lavishly decorated with portraits and then photographs of family members as well as books (especially Bibles), lamps, and pieces of furniture that reflected affluence and refinement. Parlors were more than theaters of display; they were theaters of expression. Their decorations—the needlepoint works, the open books, the piano also were evidence that refined people lived there.

Within villages, residents who identified themselves as respectable increasingly segregated themselves. They went to church services and temperance meetings, not to taverns or dirty stores. They drank water, not whiskey. They took care with their clothes and their personal appearance in general. They did not idle away their time playing cards or staring at the sky. They read books, practiced the piano, sang, wrote in their diaries, and talked with other decent people.

Beneath their homogeneous facades, many Ohio towns were divided by class and religion. In the 1850s, New Englanders dominated Claridon Township in Geauga County; by 1870, two-thirds of the township's population had been born in Ohio. In 1850, 70 percent of laborers worked on farms, while the rest supported a farm economy that revolved around dairying. Claridon was the model of a stable rural community but below its surface was a burgeoning split between the original settlement at Claridon Center and a newer one at East Claridon. The former was the home of Congregationalists from Connecticut who were almost all relatively affluent farmers. East Claridon, the commercial center of the village, was the home of Methodists, many of whom were recent arrivals and less likely to be farmers.[17] Residents of the distinctive parts of the township rarely interacted.

A small but growing number of respectable people differentiated themselves from their neighbors by sending their sons away to college. The idea was not only to prepare them for a career but to continue the inculcation of habits of self-control and self-education. Ohio's burgeoning colleges eagerly accepted the challenge of training citizens. The Scottish-born Presbyterian minister, Robert Hamilton Bishop, whom the trustees of Miami University elected president of their struggling institution in 1824, saw higher education as a moral responsibility. Not for nothing was Miami's motto "Prodesse Quam Conspici" ("To Accomplish Rather Than to Be Conspicuous"). Anticipating organizations they would join as full citizens, students at Miami in the 1820s formed the Eurodelphian Literary Society and the Union Literary Society.

Bishop regularly lectured students on the importance of self-discipline and their mission to serve purposes greater than selfish or local ones. Miami might be "one of *the outposts*" of the United States but it would soon be at its "centre." "The states on this side of the Ohio River are to be filled up with a hardy and industrious race of men" who will not be "ashamed" of "honest and daily labor." They must know that education served "the real good of the community." Just as Miami's history was intertwined with "the religion of the Bible," so, too, "its interests must, in the very nature of things, be inseparably connected with the best interests of the state of Ohio, and with the best interests of the western country."[18]

Bishop believed in the inevitability of progress. However, he repeatedly warned that success, either individually or collectively, would not come to the "indolent or stubborn or self-willed" but to those who "acquired . . . habits" of "application and self-government." It would take perhaps a decade after graduation, Bishop told students, "to determine the important question, whether you are to be a blessing, or a curse to the community." So it was with the state as a whole. The "free men and free women" of Ohio were determined "not only to clear and to cultivate the soil, but to cherish and to perfect plants of a noble kind—plants of immortality." These would include libraries, printing presses, newspapers, mail, anything and everything that would ensure the wide availability of a "liberal education" and help "the enlightened, the wise, and the good" to fight the "mass of ignorance and corruption."[19]

Institutions and teachers could only point students in the right direction. To achieve their destiny, students had to take control of themselves and their lives. Thomas Ewing told the members of the Union Literary Society that they "must continue to be close students" and "bring into exercise still farther and farther, your intellectual and moral powers." Bishop wanted Miami students to avoid the provincial, to understand that reasonable people would sometimes differ, and to learn that demagogues would have short-term success in a democracy. But "the man who has the most complete command of his own temper and disposition, will, all other things beings equal, be the best patriot, and the best statesmen, and the best citizen, and will, ultimately, bear away, through life and through succeeding generations, the largest shares of a nation's glory." Good citizens, said the Reverend William Gray, lived "not exclusively for [them]selves, but to profit others, and to promote the common interests of mankind."[20]

Lectures were not the sum of the collegiate experience. Like cities, colleges brought like-minded people together in ways that could never have happened in small towns. Young men and women met people who seemed to be like them, people with similar habits and ambitions, people who understood what it was to covet respectability. Lifelong friendships were forged in college. Some young women found the ties of affection formed at Oberlin College gave them the strength to forgo or delay marriage and to embrace the causes of woman's rights and abolitionism. Lucy Stone and Antoinette Brown became like sisters in college and corresponded regularly with each other for decades. They encouraged each other to "stand alone in the great moral battlefield with none but God for a supporter." Brown and

Stone would demonstrate that "woman can take care of herself & act independently without the encouragement & sympathy of her 'lord and master,' that she can think & talk as a moral agent is priveledged to."[21]

Like many others, male and female, Brown and Stone took comfort in each other's company. Only a year after they graduated, Brown was nostalgic for "the time when we used to sit with our arms around each other at the sunset hour & talk & talk of our friends & our homes & and of ten thousand subjects of mutual interest till both our hearts felt warmer & lighter for the pure communion of spirit."[22] In the 1850s, the two women married brothers, adding a new depth to a relationship that endured until Lucy's death.

In these and other ways, college life was an important precursor to the urban world. The years spent at the many institutions of higher education that dotted the Ohio landscape by the 1850s were like more carefree versions of the Cincinnati world. With the exceptions of Ohio University in Athens and Miami University in Oxford, all of the colleges were supported by Protestant denominations. More than twenty received charters in the second quarter of the nineteenth century. The schools were initially a happy marriage of local boosterism and religious zeal. Congregationalists, Methodists, and other sects needed to train ministers and establish bases; small towns needed something with the cachet of a college to put them on the map. The union of church and town in a college formed the quintessential "respectable" Ohio institution, mixing secular and sacred purposes in the larger cause of progress.

The most famous college in Ohio was Oberlin, which was founded by Congregationalists in 1833. Notorious for its practice of coeducation and its abolitionist sympathies, Oberlin attracted students from all over the country, not all of whom came because of its affiliation with the Congregational Church. Other schools, with the exception of Cincinnati's Lane Seminary, were not so controversial. Most were quiet places closely identified with their founding church. Congregationalists also had Marietta and Defiance Colleges. Denison College was a Baptist school. The Lutherans had Wittenberg and Capital; the Disciples of Christ, Hiram; Roman Catholics, Xavier; Methodists, Ohio Wesleyan, Baldwin, and Mount Union. Wilberforce College in Greene County was purchased by members of the

African Methodist Episcopal Church in the 1860s and became the first college in the U.S. dedicated exclusively to black students.

Rud Hayes attended Kenyon College in Gambier, an Episcopal school started in 1824. He was one of several hundred students who spent their years there reading Latin and Greek and thinking about philosophy and history. Kenyon was where Hayes began the diary that he would keep throughout his life. It was where he became serious about a career and marriage. College life confirmed his propensity for self-analysis and his obsession with improvement. He also become more sociable. Hayes treasured the friendships he made at Kenyon for the rest of his life.

Students studied together, partied together, and rebelled against college rules in the manner of nineteenth-century American college students, who were forever disrupting the prescribed regime of the institutions they attended. Then as now, groups of young males, no matter how much they devoted themselves to their diaries, were occasionally rowdy bunches who were anything but temperate. At Miami, President Bishop complained that shopkeepers in Oxford were selling hard liquor to impressionable young men. In January 1835, Bishop dismissed a student from Alabama for intoxication, idleness, and riot. He expelled another student in March for insulting a professor. Shortly thereafter, he did the same with a student who had attacked one of his peers with a "cowhide and dirk" and another who wounded the attacker with his pistol. By the end of 1835, Bishop had expelled eleven students. Despite the popularity of Miami University (in 1839, it was the third largest college in the U.S. with 250 students), faculty divisions, religious controversies, and continued student misbehavior led to Bishop's demotion in 1840 and his dismissal in 1844. The trustees were particularly offended by the dirty and dilapidated condition of the college building and the "habit indulged in by the Students of *Urinating* out the College windows."[23]

If the college experience was neither as inspirational as Bishop's rhetoric nor as vulgar as the behavior of some Miami students, it did cement friendships that cut across the borders of localism. Hayes's years at Kenyon, like his years in Cincinnati, expanded his network of acquaintances and friends far beyond what he would have known had he stayed in Delaware. At college, Hayes found that he had a good deal in common with other young men. It was as if the colleges were doing for affluent young men what canals and public schools were supposed to have done for all Ohioans. They were encouraging a group of like-minded people who imagined themselves as a community. Wherever he went, Hayes knew what to expect and how to behave because of what he had learned in college. When he and his classmates left Kenyon, they promised that they would see each other again on the floor of Congress.

School life had a similar impact on the handful of women who were able to enjoy it. Like men, women were prepared for a life of self-control, moral reform, material comfort, and companionship with other respectable people who shared their attitudes about life. The career of Betsey Mix Cowles exemplified this development. She was the eighth child of a Congregational minister and his wife, who migrated to Austinburg in the Western Reserve in 1810, the year of Betsey's birth. Betsey attended a subscription academy organized by her father and his friends. She quickly found that she enjoyed reading and learning and decided to make a career as a teacher, writing that she wished that "there was no such thing as marrying."[24]

Cowles believed that "God hath created all, with the evident design, that his rational creatures should improve every faculty; in contemplating his character; as exhibited in his works of creation." Education was a religious obligation, a sacred responsibility to contemplate the workings of God in this world. It was also a realm in which women could excel. In 1838, Betsy entered Oberlin College. She was thrilled that the college took women seriously and offered them "a *full* and thorough course."[25] Cowles was certain that God had intended women for a higher purpose than they had realized thus far in human history.

After two years at Oberlin, Betsey's family could no longer afford to send her to college. After a brief stint as an instructor at the new Portsmouth Female Seminary, she was hired as the first female principal of the Grand River Institute's Women's Department in Austinburg. Founded as a Congregational college, the institute was more than a decade old when Cowles took over in 1843 and had begun admitting women three years earlier. In addition to working with about thirty female students, Cowles devoted enormous amounts of

energy to attending antislavery meetings and writing newspaper essays about Ohio's history. Cowles, like many of her peers, believed
strongly in the importance of a public commitment to something
larger than herself: "If we are only doing something which will benefit the world, something which will make people happier and better; this every little child can do. Let us make somebody happier
every day we live; then we shall not live in vain, or look back upon
with sorrow."[26] Cowles honored this philosophy until her death in
1876. Through a succession of jobs as a teacher in northeastern
Ohio, she remained an advocate of education and of women's rights.
Like Rud Hayes and Lucy Webb, Betsey Cowles identified herself
less in terms of region or family than in her commitment to respectable behavior and moral progress.

Conversing in Print

In 1848, a Cincinnati critic asked: "Is the majestic forest which
stretches to the West . . . devoid of interest? . . . Hath the empire West
of the Alleghanies [*sic*] . . . nothing worthy of the pencil in her history?" The answer to the second question was "it certainly does," according to the editors of *The Genius of the West*. A speaker had dared
to state that "[t]he West has no literature." He was wrong, the editors
wrote. "The West HAS a literature—a literature of her own—fresh,
bold, vigorous, and beautiful—not refined into stupidity—not degenerated into obscenity—but looming up like her own mountains—
fertile as her rich soil—attractive as her blooming prairies."[27]

Few people read this literature. The vast majority of journals that
contained brief essays and histories sold only a few hundred copies.
Such setbacks did not dampen the enthusiasm of Ohio authors, however. They were eager to explain why their state was the home of
growing numbers of respectable people like themselves. Whether they
were writing fiction or history, they celebrated the progress of humanity from savagery to civilization and the peculiar role of the Ohio Valley in the realization of that development. More often than not, the
stories went something like this: Remarkable was the speed with
which civilization had come to Ohio. Heavy was the responsibility its
citizens bore in refining and extending it. In contemplating their

world and their positions in it, Ohioans would do well to follow the examples of their parents and grandparents who had created civilization out of wilderness, not to mention those of the noble savages who had accepted their fates with grace. The triumph of civilization was not necessarily inevitable. God's plan unfolded through the choices of individuals. Development was contingent upon human character. God had given Ohioans a fertile environment. What they did with it was up to them. The important thing was to have a great cause, to care about something nobler than selfish or local interests.

William Davis Gallagher was an editor and poet who lived almost the entire nineteenth century in Cincinnati. Born to Irish parents in Philadelphia in 1808, he arrived with his mother and siblings in Mount Healthy, outside Cincinnati, in 1814. Gallagher was nothing if not garrulous. His 1850 presidential address to the floundering Historical and Philosophical Society of Ohio exemplified the florid style of the times. Like many nineteenth-century writers, Ohioans never used one word when a dozen would do. Gallagher said that the "primary object" of the society, recently reformed and relocated from Columbus to Cincinnati, was "research in every department of local history; the collection, preservation, and diffusion of whatever may relate to the History, Biography, Literature, Philosophy, and Antiquities of America—more especially of the State of Ohio, of the West, and of the United States."[28]

Gallagher's overheated talk harped on "progress" and "civilization."[29] The essence of both was respect for all human beings. Like his peers, Gallagher believed that people had been liberated from ignorance and presented with unprecedented opportunities. While ancient civilizations had constructed palaces and pyramids and established empires and "rich cities," "the modern civilization builds the common school, the christian church, the lunatic asylum, the institution for the blind, the school for the deaf and dumb, the hospital, and the almshouse." While ancient civilizations had built walls to protect their cities, "the modern civilization connects its cities by good roads and canals, to invite visits from one another, and constructs railways from state to state, and across continents from ocean to ocean, to facilitate intercommunication, and this brings and binds people together, instead of walling them apart." Ancient civilizations had indulged in militaristic arts; "the modern civilization fills its private residences and public halls with paintings and statues that awaken the purer associations, call into activity the higher sentiments, and fill the mind and heart with images of beauty, truth, holiness, and love." Ancient conquerors were soldiers; modern conquerors were "the schoolmaster and the missionary."[30]

Where would modern civilization reach its apogee? The Ohio Valley, of course. Progressing from savagery to civilization in less than a century, the region had an astonishing history. Christianity and representative government had made the place so special that many people chose to live in the Old Northwest even when there was more land south of the Ohio River. Gallagher proclaimed that "an Experiment in Humanity, higher in its character and sublimer in its results" than any attempted elsewhere was happening in Ohio. Here there would be "the freest forms of social development and the highest order of human civilization." All signs pointed to "a Day . . . dawning upon this North-Western region" that would awaken all "to a just sense of their real dignity and importance in the social scale, by proclaiming to them that they are neither slaves nor nonentities, but true men and women." Here would Anglo-Saxons find their manifest destiny realized. Here would "Truth, Justice, Mercy, and Love" flourish.[31]

Gallagher was not alone in his energetic faith. The members of the Historical and Philosophical Society of Ohio were committed to overcoming the "great indifference" of so many "citizens" to the state's history. They were determined to preserve sources and record oral traditions ensure that "[t]he history of our state" would not be lost. That history, after all, was "of romantic interest, without a parallel in the history of mankind." In the words of Mariettan Samuel Prescott Hildreth, one of the most industrious of Ohio's early historians, "There is nothing more noble than to feel a deep interest in the honor of our country, our state, or the community in which we mingle."[32]

Gallagher's interest in the progress of the Ohio Valley echoed the subtler writings of Daniel Drake, the so-called "Franklin of the West." Born in New Jersey in 1785, Drake grew up in northern Kentucky, attended the University of Pennsylvania, and settled in Cincinnati, where he became one of its leading citizens. Drake devoted his life to the study and improvement of the Ohio Valley. Devoted to the causes of education and temperance, he worked to establish civic and literary institutions. His most persistent and significant campaign was to accumulate information about the Ohio Valley. Over the years, his publications ranged from detailed treatises on diseases to pamphlets listing vital statistics about the city of Cincinnati to his memoir of his youth, *Pioneer Life in Kentucky.* When he died in 1852, Drake's greatest achievement was the life he had led. If his fellow citizens admired him more than they imitated him, it was in part because Drake's genteel sensibilities were out of step with the rollicking atmosphere of life in nineteenth-century Cincinnati.

Gallagher was one of several men and women who took up the challenge laid down by Drake. If they were more romantic than he was, they were just as committed to the business of collecting information about their state and region. In the pamphlet containing Gallagher's speech were several pages of advertisements from H. W. Derby and Company. The publishing house listed among its recent books James Hall's *The West: Its Commerce and Navigation* and Jacob Burnet's *Notes on the Early Settlement of the North-Western Territory.* A well-respected, longtime citizen of Cincinnati, Burnet combined history and autobiography in a book biased in favor of the efforts of Northwest Territory governor Arthur St. Clair and his allies to create strong political and legal institutions. Also advertised was Samuel Prescott Hildreth's *Pioneer History,* which was the first book supported by the Historical and Philosophical Society.

Hildreth was one of the oldest residents of Marietta in Washington County. A medical doctor, he devoted seven years to compiling the information in *Pioneer History.* His "tedious" research included recording the memories of dozens of old men, sifting through newspapers at the American Antiquarian Society in Worcester, Massachusetts, and reading diaries and official papers.[33] While Hildreth dealt generally with the history of the Ohio Valley in the eighteenth century, he focused particularly on the Ohio Company settlements in Washington County from 1788 to 1803. Hildreth's painstaking research dominated his text. Loath to express opinions, Hildreth was as careful as Gallagher was exuberant.

Style aside, Hildreth told the same basic story as Gallagher. The Ohio Company settlers (whom he later memorialized in *Biographical and Historical Memoirs of the Early Pioneer Settlers of Ohio*) were a truly heroic band. Enduring great privations and dangers, they persisted not only in building settlements but in promoting education and religion. Unlike "the ignorant, the vulgar, and the rude," they (women as well as men) were the pioneers of civilization. Like Greeks, they brought science and art into a "howling wilderness." Hildreth sympathized with the plight of the Indians, now that they were no longer a threat to Ohioans. He even admired the resistance of the "savages." "Who . . . shall condemn them for trying to put off the evil day that boded their destruction?" Nonetheless, his heroes were the New England–born founders of Marietta who had been "obliged to work in their fields as the Israelites did at the rebuilding of the walls of Jerusalem, every man with a weapon in his hand." With the help of God, they had triumphed. Now they enjoyed their reward. "The lights of science and of art have removed the long reign of darkness, and the simple aborigines of the forest have been supplanted by civilization and the cultivation of the white man; and although we may deplore their misfortunes and pity their calamities in their removal from the land of their fathers, yet who shall say that the hand of God hath not directed it?"[34]

Hildreth and Burnet ended their histories in 1803 when Ohio became a state. Caleb Atwater, a native of Circleville, did not. His *History of the State of Ohio, Natural and Civil* appeared in 1838. Atwater was particularly proud of the physical appearance of his book because it showed "what is daily doing in Cincinnati, in the arts of book making. It is an Ohio production, in all parts, fairly representing the views and feelings of a large majority of the reading people of this state." The content of the book was predictable. Atwater celebrated progress, material and spiritual. Blessed with a healthy climate, good rivers, and rapidly improving roads and canals, which will increase "our numbers, our wealth, and our moral powers," Ohio and its neighboring states were obviously "intended" by God to dominate the U.S. "Thus far we have been mere 'hewers of wood, and drawers of water' for the east. As the wheel of time revolves, we, who are now at the bottom, shall be on its summit."[35]

Atwater believed that Ohio had not yet reached the peak of commercial and moral perfection. He worried that the Ohio Constitution had been written by "young men, who had been little engaged in legislation." It created a legislature with "too much power" and a governor with too little. What was need was a government more committed to directing the progress of Ohio. "[G]overnment," Atwater proclaimed, "is nothing more than a bundle of habits; . . . Good government, consists, not so much in laying down good rules, as, in constantly practising, on those rules, until good habits are firmly fixed, and invariably adhered to, by the people." The state government, according to Atwater, should be building schools and encouraging religion. Ohio had made considerable progress, "but our exertions to improve our condition, are by no means to be relaxed." "[I]t will be our own fault if we are not the happiest people in the Union."[36]

The themes of progress from savagery to civilization and the merging of public and private identities permeated the histories and memoirs that poured forth from Cincinnati publishers at mid-century. James Finley's *Sketches of Western Methodism* did for religious leaders what Hildreth did for secular ones: it presented the lives of pioneer itinerants as model characters for present and future generations. The early pioneers had not achieved perfection. But what mattered was that they had tried. Their sons and daughters should not abandon all that they had struggled to accomplish. Building Ohio—creating an ideal commonwealth—was not the work of a year, a decade, or a generation. It was a long-term process requiring the collective wills of tens of thousands of people. Finley hoped that "[t]he noble examples furnished in these sketches, of untiring labor and self-sacrificing devotion of those who cheerfully gave up all for Christ and the advancement of his cause" would "stir up every impulse of our nature to emulate their virtues and strive to imitate their truly-heroic deeds."[37]

These books used the past to anticipate and justify the values of their authors. Yet for all their flaws, they had undeniable power. Taken together, they reiterated that realizing the possibilities of life in Ohio would require individuals to discipline themselves and to put public interests above private ones. Even Henry Howe's immensely popular *Historical Collections of Ohio,* a detailed compendium of information about the state in a simple style, made the same point. Howe promised his readers that his book would illustrate "the cus-

toms, the fortitude, the bravery, and the privations of its early settlers" that had made possible "the rise and unexampled progress of a
powerful state."[38]

The fiction written and published in mid-nineteenth-century
Ohio tended to deal with the same themes as the histories. The most
popular genres were poetry and the short story. In 1860, William T.
Coggeshall collected poems from well over a hundred writers in the
Ohio Valley, including close to three dozen women. The majority of
the poems had previously appeared in Cincinnati literary magazines.
Most are clumsy odes to nature or love or death in innumerable
stanzas of relentless iambic pentameter. Still, the content is occasionally intriguing, as in Gallagher's "The Mothers of the West" or
"Song of the Pioneers," hymns to the self-sacrificing characters of
early settlers.[39]

When poets wrote directly about Ohio, they tended to focus on
stories about its past. Charles A. Jones mourned the passing of Indians. Lewis J. Cist admired "Ohio's Pilgrim Band" who had conquered
the Indians and established "an Eden fair." The people of Ohio should
be proud to "trace our Buckeye blood" from them. Most of the poetry
was generic. William Dana Emerson's "To the Ohio River" could be
about any river in North America. Similarly, Edward A. McLaughlin's
"To Cincinnati" promises a bright future for the Queen City of the
West but suggests almost nothing distinctive about the city. In the
Western Reserve, the Vermont-born Sullivan D. Harris conjured up
"A Song for Ohio" in which he spoke of God's favor and human labor
in "rear[ing] up such a State, as the gem of the nation."[40] Sullivan
Harris mentioned rivers and praised farmers, but he could not make
Ohio sound like a real place. It existed in his imagination, the fulfill-
ment of a vague dream of progress.

Writers of fiction were more successful not only in evoking place
but in discussing the meaning of Ohio's progress. Their stories were
melodramatic and sentimental, full of coincidences, virtuous young
women, dastardly villains, and lots of implicit sex and violence
wrapped around the travails and eventual triumph of a young romantic couple. The stories did more than entertain their readers; they offered cautionary tales about human nature and society. They were the
kinds of tales one would have read throughout the Western world in

the 1800s. What was different about the Ohio Valley was the setting, both natural and man-made, and the fact that authors seemed to believe that it was not only unique, but more conducive to the achievement of a great civilization. In 1852, the prolific newspaperman Emerson Bennett published a hundred-page tale called *Mike Fink; Legend of the Ohio*. Like Davy Crockett, Fink was popular because he allowed young boys—the target audience for these tales—to enjoy Fink's wild high jinks while they learned the costs of such unrestrained behavior.

While most male authors asserted the triumph of progress, many female writers worried that moral improvement was not keeping pace with technological improvement. Accepting the fact of change, women often questioned its impact. Julia Louise Cory Dumont was born in Waterford in Washington County in 1794 and grew up in New York. In 1813, she and her husband, John Dumont, moved to Cincinnati and then to Vevay, Indiana, downriver from Cincinnati. In addition to her work as a wife and mother, Julia Dumont taught school and wrote fiction. Her published legacy is a collection of short stories called *Life Sketches from Common Paths,* many of which had previously appeared in Cincinnati literary journals.

Dumont's stories are more morally complicated than the histories of the time. To be sure, her context was almost always the wake "of the mighty car of improvement." But Dumont was most interested in promoting "the bonds of friendship, of domestic affection, and human trust" and in showing young people "the existence and reality of goodness in our bad world."[41] The last phrase is the key one. Dumont hoped for good but she believed in evil. The world she lived in was not an altogether happy place. In tales such as "Ashton Grey" and "The Picture," Dumont addressed the common theme of progress with a healthy dose of skepticism.

"Ashton Grey" chronicles the love affair of the title character and Annabel Hampton. Raised by Indians, Grey is Annabel's "beau-ideal of the fearless and self-sustained backwoodsman." The young couple persist in their relationship despite prejudice and a false murder charge. All ends happily when it is discovered that Annabel and Ashton are both children of Virginia gentry. While Dumont reassures readers that Ashton and Annabel violated neither class nor racial boundaries, she also affirms their love. They are innocent. The world around them makes their lives difficult. Only happenstance saves them from misery. Dumont suggests that white society in the Ohio Valley is not necessarily an improvement over Indian society. Ashton's unreliable father explains at one point that he would not have minded if the young man had chosen to live his entire life among the Potawatomi. "But natur is natur, and one must larn what cursed villains there are among *white* men, before he can make up his mind to be satisfied with Indian life."[42]

The hero and heroine of "The Picture" are Roswell Carr and his adopted step-sister, Edith Lennox, the children of migrants from the East to Kentucky. Separated at a young age, they are reunited in Cincinnati in the 1790s as an American army prepares to advance against the Indians. Roswell is now a noble backwoodsman. Strongly attracted to Roswell, Edith remains loyal to her officer suitor because of Roswell's "semi-barbarism." She cannot marry someone who is so uncivilized, even if he is handsome and intelligent. Roswell has to save the life of the officer and nearly die from a wound suffered in the process before Edith can acknowledge her love for him. Following their hearts and enduring unremitting toil, they build a respectable life for themselves in a "splendid mansion." But it is not acquired refinement that makes them good citizens. If Roswell knows "little of literary refinements or classic sentiment," he has "an original strength in his mind and character." He is courteous, with a "disregard of self."[43]

Pamilla W. Ball, a Virginia-born writer who lived in Zanesville, published similar stories in the 1830s. "The Maid of Muskingum" tells of two cousins who end up finding happiness in the late eighteenth century on the banks of the Muskingum River. The Ohio frontier is less a savage borderland than a place of refuge from white civilization. Ball makes a similar point in a "A Tale of Early Times." Three young Virginians—Charles and, Horatio, and Horatio's sister, Margaret—migrate to Ohio. Charles is proud (like a Virginian), but Horatio shows all the promise of becoming "a real Buckeye"—that is, he works hard and he believes in equality.[44] In fact, he marries Nance, the beautiful hired girl he meets one night in a family cabin. A friend urges the marriage so that they will not have to drink any more of

Margaret's wretched coffee. Nance can learn respectability more easily than Horatio's refined Virginia-born sister can master the art of cooking.

As the frontier faded in memory, the idealization of its supposedly straightforward inhabitants as the antithesis of selfishness and deception became commonplace in American literature. The classic example is James Fenimore Cooper's Natty Bumppo. More than wistfulness permeates Dumont's and Ball's portraits of noble people in a simpler past. The stories are also social criticism. Dumont and Ball were questioning the extent to which the citizens of Ohio were better off in the mid-1800s than they had been in the late 1700s. Population growth, transportation improvements, and burgeoning cities cannot hide the fact that life is often cruel. Human relationships need nurturing. Progress is not progress if it undermines basic human kindness. Dumont wants her readers to remember that the mark of a respectable person is "that entire abandonment of self . . . that must have been the perfection of ancient chivalry." They need to learn "that a warm, rich, confiding nature . . . sheds a thousand times brighter light than the cold, moonshine glitter of intellectual refinements." "[W]e are none of us sufficient to ourselves," one of Dumont's characters says. We need love as much as we need bread.[45]

Nothing demonstrates this point more than Dumont's "Aunt Hetty," the story of a German immigrant woman whose neighbors admired her as "a superior woman of her class—gentle, cheerful, active, self-sacrificing, true and kind." But her handsome and dissipated son idles away his life until he reportedly is hanged in New Orleans. Later, a widowed Aunt Hetty is summoned to nurse a dying cholera victim. The narrator describes her as "scarcely forty," yet filled with an "intense sorrow that was the fixed expression of every lineament and motion."[46] Of course, Aunt Hetty recognizes the corpse as that of her son. Breaking down momentarily, she recovers herself and arranges his funeral. Superficially, the story warns of the dangers of a dissolute life. It is also a tribute to the strength of a woman whose life is as painful as that of any pioneer woman.

Even more complex are the more realistic, if still indifferently plotted, stories of Alice Cary. She was born in 1820 to New England immigrants who had settled in Mount Healthy, near Cincinnati. After her father remarried in 1837, two years following her mother's death, he built a new house and left Alice to care for four younger siblings in the first home. Alice and her sister Phoebe worked very hard, devoting their days to scrubbing, milking, washing, and sweeping and their nights to reading and writing. Soon they were publishing in Cincinnati periodicals and expanding a network of influential friends. With the number of their male patrons multiplying, they moved to New York in 1850. Finding support in a community of female writers, Alice Cary published several books, the most important of which dealt with the hamlet of Clovernook, a fictional version of Mount Healthy.[47]

Life in Alice Cary's stories is difficult. Cary agreed with historians that Ohio "was a wilderness when my father first went to it" and that it was "now crowned with a dense and prosperous population." She accepted the basic plot of Ohio's development into a unique place. Her problem was the cost of that achievement. "Change" may be "the order of nature," but it is not always improvement. Change means growing old, dying, seeing the "hands that reached eagerly for the roses . . . drawn back bleeding and full of thorns," and "saddest of all," it means broken hearts. Progress in a Cary story was "striking out from a wilderness of dew-wet blossoms where the shimmer of light is lovely as the wings of a thousand bees, into an open plain where the clear day strips things to their natural truth—we go from young visions to the realities of life!" Cary was a gloomy person. No matter how cheerfully she began a tale, a friend noted, she usually ended with "a tombstone."[48]

Cary's pessimism helped her to write more realistic stories that function to some extent as social criticism. While her convoluted plots were full of melodramatic contrivances, she managed to convey a sense of the texture of life in and around Cincinnati better than any of her contemporaries. Internal improvements and intellectual conversation could not obscure the existence of poor people. Cary romanticized poverty as a trial that nurtured "the sweetest humanities" in people. Sentiment aside, she boldly argued that in a country where "all men are not 'created equal,'" the "log cabin" was as important as "the marble mansion."[49]

"Mrs. Wetherbe's Party" illustrates the themes of Cary's best work. She begins by portraying the idyllic lives of Jenny Mitchel and her husband, the blacksmith Helph Randall. Although they embody contentment, Cary wants us to understand that they did not achieve happiness easily. Their story is one of struggle and misunderstanding. Helph had grown up with his aunt, Mrs. Wetherbe, and her husband in Clovernook because his middle-class family in Cincinnati had treated him abysmally. Indeed, the Randalls, who live in a fine house, abuse everyone, including their adopted daughter and servant Jenny and their other servant, the once enslaved Aunt Kitty. When Mrs. Randall attends a party at Mrs. Wetherbe's, she makes a fool of herself trying to transform it into "a fashionable party." Unlike her sister, Mrs. Wetherbe is a simple woman. Because she has "not been at all exclusive" in her invitations, all kinds of people have attended, some rich, some poor, some in fine clothes, others more rudely dressed, some standing on ceremony, others ignoring it.[50]

During the party, Helph goes to his parents' home in Cincinnati in search of Jenny. Scorned by his drunken father, he finds his adopted sister with help from "[p]oor kind-hearted" Aunt Kitty. Jenny is distraught about being unable to attend Mrs. Wetherbe's party because Mrs. Randall has taken her only decent dress. Jenny is then called to care for a sick boy, who, we learn later, is her younger brother. Jenny and Helph find the boy in a five-story, brick building "on an unpaved alley, and opposite a ruinous graveyard." Cheaply built and crowded, "it was a perfect hive of misery." Soap suds, coffee grounds, bones, and trash lie all around. Men are "smoking and jesting, or quarreling and swearing," while women are yelling and "half naked" children are taunting each other.[51] In the midst of filth, Jenny and Helph watch the sick boy die. Horrified, they resolve to marry and lead a better life. But the Randalls abruptly leave for England, forcing Jenny to go with them and abandoning Aunt Kitty to misery and an early death.

Helph refuses to give up, even when he learns that Jenny has married an Englishman. He works hard, builds a fine house, and waits. When after fifteen years Helph learns that Jenny's husband has deserted her, he arranges for her to return to Clovernook, where they live "with such graces and accomplishments as should make her the wonder and him the envy all of who had contrived or wished their separation."[52]

The happy ending of "Mrs. Wetherbe's Party" does not erase the serious questions Cary raises about life in Ohio. Where is the much vaunted progress in the tenement in which Jenny's brother dies? Even respectable people such as the Randalls are not what they pretended to be. Jenny and Helph achieve happiness without a formal education. Their success happens in spite of the social and cultural landscape of Ohio, not because of it. Offering a fictional counterpoint to the male histories of progress that flooded the public culture of mid-nineteenth-century Ohio, Cary constructs an ambiguous landscape. True progress, she suggests, must be more than a matter of prosperity and improvement for a privileged few.

The literary culture that thrived in Cincinnati at mid-century gradually dissipated as many of the city's foremost writers and artists left to seek fame and fortune in the East or in Europe. Grappling with serious themes, they had been unable to escape existing genres. Most had described the progress of the Old Northwest without establishing it as a distinctive place. Nevertheless, the struggles of many Ohioans to express a sense of who they were and to define the kind of world that had emerged since the founding of the state were significant. Acting like citizens, they had initiated a great public conversation about issues that transcended local communities. In discussing the question of slavery, and especially in making sense of the bloody Civil War, they would at last find a collective voice. Contrasting themselves with Southerners, they would begin to consider Ohio as something more than an area defined by arbitrary political borders inhabited by people who were strangers to each other. Indeed, they would begin to imagine Ohio as something much more important than the sum of its parts.

John Mercer Langston in a daguerrotype taken in 1853. (Courtesy of The Oberlin College Archives, Oberlin, Ohio)

4

Defining Ohio

—

TRAVELING through the "magnificent" Ohio Valley in the early
1830s afforded the Frenchman Alexis de Tocqueville the opportunity
to reflect on the impact of slavery on the development of the United
States. If the Ohio River was a great artery into the interior of North
America, it was also a border "between freedom and slavery." Tocqueville contrasted the sparse population and general idleness of
Kentuckians with the "fine crops" and "elegant dwellings" of
Ohioans. He concluded that divergent white attitudes toward work
explained the difference between the two states. North of the river,
where labor was "honorable" and associated with "progress," "man
appears rich and contented." South of the river, where labor was
"connected with the idea of slavery," it was considered degrading. In
Ohio, people could "profit by [their] industry, and do so without
shame."[1] Not so in Kentucky.

Two decades later, Harriet Beecher Stowe, a New England woman
who had lived in Cincinnati for nearly two decades, affirmed the differences between Kentucky and Ohio in her enormously successful
novel, *Uncle Tom's Cabin.* In one of the most indelible scenes in American literature—the young slave Eliza's escape across the Ohio River in
the dead of winter—Stowe vividly dramatized the chasm between the
two states. Such were the attractions of Ohio that enslaved African
Americans would literally jump across ice floes to reach its soil.

A pervasive trope, the imagined contrast between Ohio and Kentucky went to the heart of an emerging popular image of Ohio that
would become extraordinarily influential. Kentucky made Ohio look
good. Middle-class Ohioans thought that their material progress was

directly related to their superior moral progress. The fact that slavery was illegal in Ohio made all the difference in its development. Victory in the Civil War confirmed the belief that Ohio was a better place than Kentucky (and other Southern states). "If Kentucky allowed equal political rights to all her people," remarked one Cincinnatian in 1847, "she would not be dragging behind Ohio, as she now does, in the march of improvement, prosperity, and population."[2] Slavery, in short, inhibited progress. Freedom created possibilities.

African American Citizens

African Americans did not need whites to tell them that Ohio was a promised land. In songs, oral traditions, and published memoirs, black people called the Ohio River the American Jordan, separating a land of bondage from a land of freedom. Former slave John P. Parker knew that the Ohio Valley was a "Borderland." He had purchased his freedom for eighteen hundred dollars and endured many a travail in order to build a home in Ripley, on the north bank of the Ohio River, from which he could help other African Americans escape from slavery. A husband and wife arrived at Parker's door one night "wet and exhausted." Not knowing how to swim, they had traversed the Ohio with the wife "astride a log" and the husband holding on to it. He had "literally kicked his way across that deep and dangerous river." Between 1845 and 1865, Parker claimed he aided some 440 runaway slaves.[3]

Parker was part of the Underground Railroad, one of the most enduring symbols in Ohio history. Popular images of whites and blacks working together to smuggle thousands of slaves out of bondage rest heavily on embroidered romantic tales written by whites later in the nineteenth century. Just as the number of people who resisted Hitler and Mussolini increased dramatically after their defeat in World War II, so too did the numbers of whites involved in antislavery activities burgeon in the aftermath of the Civil War. Still, if the size and scope of the Underground Railroad has been exaggerated, many people did work hard to help fugitive slaves get across the Ohio River into Ohio and, in many cases, Canada.[4] While whites such as Levi Coffin, a Quaker who lived in southern Indiana and then in Cincinnati, were actively involved in these activities, more often than not, the Underground Railroad was the work of courageous African Americans such as Parker who risked everything to help others.

Ironically, they did so with the knowledge that Ohio was a promised land for blacks only in the sense that slavery was illegal. Racism and discrimination were pervasive in the free state. John Malvin, a free young black man, left Virginia in the late 1820s and made his way to Cincinnati and then to Cleveland. Writing in the 1870s, Malvin claimed he had never been idealistic about Ohio. From the beginning, he found "the treatment [he] received by the people generally . . . little better than in Virginia." Malvin nonetheless remained optimistic about the possibilities of Ohio and devoted his life to winning recognition as an equal citizen. As an old man, he took considerable satisfaction in believing that he and others had "demonstrated that an intelligent colored man can be as good a citizen as an intelligent white man."[5] His memoir was a story of the triumph of class over race as well as freedom over slavery. Malvin was confident that by behaving like respectable middle-class citizens, black men would prove that they were worthy of full membership in the body politic. Class would trump race.

Malvin was not alone. While African Americans were few in number (36,673 in 1860, or roughly 1.6 percent of Ohio's population), they were disproportionately involved in public conversations about the meanings of citizenship. African Americans took the rhetoric of the American Revolution seriously. In demanding that they be accorded the rights of citizens, they affirmed the legitimacy of the American political order. The problem with Ohio lay not in the content of its ideals and institutions but in their exclusivity. The message of African Americans was simple: open up Ohio's schools and elections, erase the border of race, and affirm the meanings of American freedom. Make Ohio the promised land in reality as well as fact. If African Americans were given access to equal public education as well as the ballot box, they would model the character of respectable citizens. Black Ohioans would strengthen, not threaten, the emerging middle-class status quo.

Black men called public meetings, wrote petitions, and published newspapers articles. They also held conventions in Columbus almost every year from the late 1840s through the Civil War. Dozens of men representing all parts of Ohio assembled for the avowed purpose of achieving equal rights as citizens. Over and over, they insisted that because they "were born in the United States, and reside in Ohio, [they were] citizens of Ohio." Residency and age were the only legitimate determinants of citizenship. "[N]o accidental circumstance, like the color of the hair or the shape of the nose, has any power in reference to their rights." Black men paid taxes and fought for their country; therefore, they were entitled to the rights and privileges of citizenship. To give them the vote did not require any major change in the state constitution; all the convention had to do was strike the word "white."[6]

Many whites, however, saw removing color as a marker of political identity as nothing less than a revolutionary redefinition of what it meant to be an Ohioan. Under pressure from blacks and white abolitionists, the General Assembly in 1849 repealed a few of the legal restrictions on African Americans, including the generally ignored but symbolically potent requirement to post a bond and secure white recommendations before taking up residence in an Ohio county. Blacks also were allowed to testify in court. But white legislators refused to grant them the right to vote. Delegates to the 1850–51 state Constitutional Convention similarly rejected a proposal to extend the suffrage to black men by a margin of sixty-six to twelve.

Some African Americans discussed leaving the country altogether. In 1849, the majority of delegates to a state convention agreed to consider the possibility of colonization in Africa. George Williams of Ross County argued that blacks "must have [a] nationality." He was "for going any where, so we can be an independent people." Even talk of leaving the United States, however, affirmed its basic principles and institutions. The convention adopted a resolution that accepted the idea of colonization only if slavery were abolished in the U.S. as a whole. Then, "prompted by the spirit of the fathers of '76, and following the light of liberty yet flickering in our minds, we are willing, it being optional, to draw out from the American government, and form a separate and independent one, enacting our own laws and regulations, trusting for success only in the God of Liberty and the Controller of human destiny."[7]

Mostly, the convention addressed itself to the condition of blacks in Ohio. In their Declaration of Sentiments, the delegates promised opposition to "every form of oppression or proscription attempted to be imposed upon us, in consequence of our condition or color." As important, they advocated the advancement of the people of their race through conventional, middle-class means. They would give their "earnest attention" to education and the cause of temperance as well as Christianity itself. And they would "leave what are called menial occupations, and aspire to mechanical, agricultural and professional pursuits."[8] They called for a newspaper operated by and for African Americans.

The painter Robert S. Duncanson epitomized the middle-class attitudes of many blacks. The son of free African Americans who had migrated from New York to Monroe, Michigan, Duncanson learned the family trade of housepainting. Ambitious and naturally talented, he taught himself how to paint landscapes and portraits. Duncanson settled in the Cincinnati area in 1840, working as an itinerant artist, acquiring powerful white patrons such as Nicholas Longworth, and becoming one of the most important painters in the Ohio Valley until he moved to Europe in 1861. In the middle of the 1850s, he collaborated with James Pressley Ball, a black artisan who operated a daguerreotype gallery, in the making of retouched or tinted photographs.

Duncanson's work reflected the tastes of his patrons, which perhaps explains why he was so conventional in style and content. His specialty was grand romantic landscapes in the manner of Thomas Cole. The most accomplished was *Blue Hole, Flood Waters, Little Miami,* which depicted three fishermen dwarfed by an imposing natural scene. More impressive in size and scope were the Belmont murals Duncanson painted on the walls of Longworth's mansion. Because Duncanson's scenes are generically romantic, we must be cautious about reading meanings into them. Nevertheless, he commented on the development of Ohio. His *View of Cincinnati* showed the barely developed, wild rural landscape of Kentucky, inhabited by black slaves, giving way in the distance to the great city of Cincinnati with its busy wharves and factories. Virtually all of the subjects of his somber, earnest portraits were well-known white abolitionists. And in his only direct representation of slavery, *Uncle Tom and Little Eva*, Duncanson chose to offer his largely white audience a reassuring picture of black passivity and innocence.[9]

John Mercer Langston also sought acceptance within the emerging middle-class public culture of Ohio. Born in Virginia in 1829, Langston was the son of his white owner and an enslaved African Indian woman. When his father died in 1834, Langston was freed under the terms of his will and entrusted to a family friend in Chillicothe. After attending schools in both Chillicothe and Cincinnati, Langston was admitted to Oberlin College in 1844. He worked for a time as a teacher while he prepared himself for a career in the law.

In some respects, Langston's life was similar to that of Rutherford B. Hayes. Thoroughly bourgeois in his attitudes toward work and morality, Langston devoted himself to the great cause of improvement. As he noted in the dedication to his third-person autobiography, "manly and self-reliant effort" was the key to success in America. "God and Destiny shall prove themselves the sure supporters of such person, bearing him to victory in every contest."[10] With good reason, Langston considered his later appointment as U.S. ambassador to Haiti and his election to Congress from a Virginia district as evidence of his success.

In his smug memoir, Langston, like Malvin, presented his life, somewhat unconvincingly, as a triumph of character over color. Much as he tried to ignore racism, discrimination followed him everywhere. One night in 1845, while traveling from Chillicothe to Oberlin, Langston tried to get a room in the Neil House, the "chief hotel" in Columbus. Turned away at the door by "a person seemingly in authority" who was "gruff, coarse, and vulgar," he was told that the hotel did "not entertain *niggers!* You must find some nigger boardinghouse."[11] Fortunately for the stunned Langston, a black man took the young student under his wing and gave him shelter with his family for the night.

The next morning, the same man who had prevented Langston's entrance into the Neil House tried to force him to ride the rest of the way to Oberlin with the driver of the coach. Another passenger intervened, and the passengers were seated inside the coach in the order in which they were listed on the bill. Nowhere else on this journey,

Langston noted, did "his color figure in the matter of his treatment." The incident at the Neil House "made an indelible impression upon his mind, and although he has been a thousand times since entertained, being well and considerately accommodated, he has never forgotten his first experience there."[12]

Langston, writing as an old man, represented the incident as unusual because his story of his life turned on the degree to which such virulent racism did not really matter in the long run. Seeing the color of his skin as unimportant in determining who he was, he considered himself a good citizen because he had a good character. But to us the events at the Neil House reveal the fragility of his faith in the power of class. At any moment, a white person could decide to rob a black man of his humanity. Like other African Americans, Langston had no legal recourse. Dependent on the kindness of strangers, he remains largely passive in his account of the incident.

Langston went out of his way to deny his color. After receiving an M.A. in theology from Oberlin, Langston read law with Judge Philemon Bliss. In 1854, when he applied for admission to the Ohio bar, a three-member committee examined and recommended him. But his race made admission a moot point; a black man could not legally practice law in Ohio. So the resourceful Bliss arranged to present the light-skinned Langston to a court as a white man. Calling Langston forward, the presiding judge saw that he was a white and the court approved his admission to the bar. Whether the judge evaded the restriction or really thought Langston was white is unclear. According to Langston, he had to "be construed into a *'white man,'* as he was at once upon sight."[13] This charade took place within a growing legal consensus in Ohio that the definition of "white" was a local issue. Local officials could determine race based on local custom. Since people treated Langston as if he were white, the court decided to deal with him as a white man. Race mattered more than Langston was willing to admit.

Langston went on to buy land, marry Caroline M. Wall, the mulatto daughter of a North Carolina planter and a black woman, win election as a township clerk in 1855, and enjoy a successful legal career built, ironically, on a clientele of white Democrats dealing with charges of intemperance. In 1856, he moved his family to a home "in the most desirable part of the village of Oberlin." He was particularly pleased with the elegance of his new house and its many improvements. He took pride in succeeding in a profession in which many young white men failed. Never mind that none of the black residents of Oberlin sought his counsel. All evidence to the contrary, Langston argued that race was immaterial. After all, "when one goes upon the market with an article for sale at reasonable rates which is in demand, it matters very little as a rule whether the vendor be Jew or Gentile, white or black. . . . The question . . . as an able and prudent man will always find in life of whatsoever profession he may be, is, can he put upon the market to answer popular demand something superior and individual."[14]

Despite his acute sensitivity to any comment rooted in race, Langston received the approbation of his neighbors, including repeated election to the Oberlin city council and board of education, until he and his family left for Washington, D.C., at the end of the Civil War. He earnestly participated in the antislavery movement. It had "brought to the colored people of the North the opportunities of developing themselves intellectually and morally." Now they could attend schools, which meant they had become "comparatively intelligent, industrious, energetic and thrifty." They had "moral and pecuniary strength."[15]

Langston was hardly representative of Ohio's African American population in the 1850s. Few blacks lived in nice homes or practiced law. For most, life was a mixture of poverty and discrimination relieved only by the support of their neighbors. Perhaps little more than one-quarter of black households owned property. Overwhelmingly illiterate, Ohio's African Americans were probably less affluent than free blacks in the upper South. And freedom was a relative term. The passage of the federal Fugitive Slave Law in 1850, which deprived blacks of any legal recourse, left them vulnerable to what amounted to kidnapping. Children were especially at risk. But everyone had to deal with the insults of ordinary daily life.

Racism was so pronounced in the Old Northwest in the 1850s that around twenty thousand African Americans emigrated to Canada. Those who stayed dealt with discrimination by living in largely black rural communities or by demanding full citizenship. Almost no one proposed an alternative construction of society. Blacks demanded integration into the story of Ohio, not a change in its basic plot. The solution lay in inclusion, in making race invisible, in asserting that class was more important. Male or female, they sought sustenance in organizations, struggled to adapt to northern notions of respectability, and looked to education and information as solutions to the ills of American society. Their faith was that citizenship was a panacea as well as a right.

Women Citizens

African Americans were not the only people conscious of their exclusion from the public world. Growing numbers of middle-class women were beginning to demand their rights as citizens. The political status of women in this period was ambiguous at best. Most people agreed that women were citizens (after all, citizenship was voluntary and based on residence) without rights. They could not serve on juries, vote, or fight for their country. Legally, women were subject to the protection of their fathers or husbands, much as a child was, because of their alleged physical and emotional weaknesses.

The May 1850 meeting of a convention of white men called to consider revisions to the Ohio Constitution of 1802 provided an occasion for a spirited conversation about the role of women as well as African Americans in Ohio's public life. A month earlier, on April 19 and 20, a large group of women had gathered in Salem to discuss their political status. The Salem convention was not the first meeting of woman's rights advocates in the U.S. That had occurred in Seneca Falls, New York, in 1848. But it was extraordinary in the extent to which delegates discussed the American political system. In terms of gender, the meeting was literally a world turned upside down. Seated in the gallery of the Hicksite Friends Meeting House, men watched perhaps two hundred female delegates debate and vote on the floor below them.

The participants did not mince words. In the spring of 1850, dozens of Ohio women had signed a call for a convention in Salem "to concert measures to secure to all persons the recognition of Equal Rights, and the extension of the privileges of Government, without distinction of sex and color." A writer in the *Anti-Slavery Bugle,* applauding the meeting, specifically hoped "that no patronizing *male* orators" would "control its proceedings." For many, race and gender were a common cause. Some supporters wanted to extend "EQUAL SUFFRAGE to adults, without regard to sex, COLOR, or CONDITION of the members of society." In their view, "The *free white men* of this State have, by the laws they have enacted, become the virtual robbers of those who have the same natural rights."[16]

The convention passed resolutions demanding equal rights. They were, after all, "*human* rights, and pertain to human beings, without distinction of sex." As citizens, women should be able to vote and control their own property and persons. Otherwise, they were little more than slaves. The delegates objected to "all distinctions between men and woman in regard to social, literary, pecuniary, religious or political customs and institutions" as well as "the practice of holding women amenable to a different standard of propriety and morality from that to which men are held amenable." Women, they continued, could not escape political oppression until they were able to labor as they wished. Moreover, the success of the cause depended on women learning how to assert themselves. Women had to renounce "idle, aimless" lives for lives of courage in the face of subjugation.[17]

When a woman is "subject to the control and dependent on the will of man," proclaimed the formal memorial of the convention delegates, she "loses her self-dependence, and no human being can be deprived of this without a sense of degradation." Laws should make all people independent, not dependent. States should empower their citizens, not enslave and degrade them. Therefore, the women asked the Constitutional Convention to make sure that "women shall be secured not only the Right of Suffrage, but all the political and legal rights that are guaranteed to men." Like black men, women demanded entry into the system more than they sought reform of it. The problem with citizenship was its exclusivity. Because women wanted to function as "responsible, intelligent, self-controlling members of society," the delegates to the Salem convention called upon their "sisters of Ohio to arise from the lethargy of ages" and "assert their rights as independent human beings."[18]

Reacting in horror at the thought of blacks and women sharing their status, the white male delegates to the Ohio Constitutional Convention rejected calls to delete the words "white" and "male" from the state's constitution. The convention adjusted but did not radically alter the 1802 constitution. The legislature remained strong and the governor weak, although all other state officers and judges were now to be elected. Suffrage was restricted to white men who had lived in the state for one year. The delegates denied the vote to blacks by a margin of sixty-six to twelve and to women by a vote of seventy-two to seven. (They also agreed to delete the discussion of women's suffrage from the record of their proceedings because of its delicate nature.) The white male citizens of Ohio approved the new constitution in June 1851.

Supporters of expanding the electorate to include blacks and women took some consolation in the fact that the delegates at least discussed their petitions. One member asked why, if "ladies can accompany their husbands or fathers or brothers to church, or public lectures, or entertainments," they could "not as safely accompany the same persons to the ballot box."[19] After the defeat in the Constitutional Convention, the Ohio Woman's Rights Association, organized in 1852, sponsored annual conventions and petitioned the legislature (occasionally accumulating thousands of signatures) to reform married women's property law and to hold a statewide referendum on suffrage. But there were no substantive legal changes in the status of women in Ohio.

Indeed, a proposal to ban blacks from Ohio proved far more popular at the convention. Although the idea was defeated by a fifty-eight to thirty-nine margin, its supporters far outnumbered those of black and female suffrage. The most extreme opponent of black suffrage was William Sawyer, a forty-five-year-old blacksmith from Auglaize County, who objected to accepting petitions calling for African Americans to be allowed to vote. "These United States," he believed, "were designed by the God of Heaven to be governed and inhabited by the Anglo-Saxon race and by them alone." Opposed to slavery in Ohio because it was "a curse to the white race," Sawyer believed that it had been "productive of good to the negro" because contact with whites improved blacks. On their own, they "were very little removed from the condition of dumb beasts—they wallowed in the mire like hogs, and there was nothing of civilization in their aboriginal condition."[20]

Antislavery and the Emergence of Ohio

Most whites wanted neither slavery nor African Americans in Ohio, believing that both threatened their growing sense of their state as a land of freedom, industry, and morality. They rallied to the cause of antislavery only in the 1850s when white Southerners appeared to threaten what they imagined to be the distinctive features of the Old Northwest. In the first half of the nineteenth century, the free blacks and white evangelical Christians, mainly in the Western Reserve, who demanded the immediate abolition of slavery in the U.S. aroused more hostility than sympathy.

Racial tensions were particularly strong in Cincinnati. The number of blacks grew so rapidly in the late 1820s that they constituted 10 percent of the city's population. Meanwhile, white people from New England and New York also moved to Cincinnati. Among the latter were students and professors at Lane Seminary, a school devoted to training Congregational ministers whose new president in 1832 was the renowned revivalist, the Reverend Lyman Beecher of Connecticut. By early 1834, thirty-eight of Lane's ninety-two students were from New York. Only eighteen were from Ohio. Eight came from the South and five more were from other states in the Old Northwest. In 1834, Lane's students formally debated the merits of immediate emancipation. Most agreed that slavery was a sin and an abomination and should end now. Zealously embracing the abolitionist cause, many began to work with blacks in Cincinnati. They taught reading and writing and organized lectures. As one of the students, Theodore Weld, explained, "We believe that faith without *works* is dead."[21]

This attitude frightened white Cincinnatians, some of whom had rioted against the surge in the black population in the 1820s. When city officials announced in 1829 that they were going to enforce the state's black laws, whites began to harass blacks. In August, a mob rampaged through an African American neighborhood. Their campaign of terror was so successful that almost half of Cincinnati's black residents migrated elsewhere. African Americans would not again exceed 5 percent of the city's total population until well after the Civil War.

Responding to community pressure, Lane's anxious trustees banned antislavery activities. Seventy-five students, refusing to back down from their principles, left the seminary. Most of the "rebels," as they were called, continued to work for abolition over the ensuing decades. They believed that they had a responsibility to attack slavery. They agreed with Weld that it was "the business of theological seminaries to educate the *heart,* as well as the head."[22]

Although the Lane controversy eventually cooled, white Cincinnatians' fears of African Americans persisted. The former saw the latter as sexual and economic threats. So strong was the fear of miscegenation in a city with a large population of mulattoes, that abolitionists felt compelled to protest that they were not sexual "*amalgamationists.*" Their words fell on deaf ears. Serious riots against blacks convulsed the city in 1836, 1841, and 1843. Opponents of abolitionists, who comprised the majority of people, insisted that antislavery agitation threatened commerce with the South. Respectable Cincinnatians occasionally encouraged the actions that led to violence against African Americans and abolitionists. Typically, they justified their behavior as a defense of their city against outside influences. In 1836, a handbill warned of the dangers of an abolitionist newspaper recently established by James G. Birney. "The Citizens of Cincinnati" were ready to stop abolitionist agitators from pursuing a course which would give "the business of the place . . . a vital stab." They had "to eradicate an evil which every citizen feels is undermining his business and property."[23]

Two hundred miles to the northeast, growing numbers of Ohioans disagreed. The Western Reserve produced a plethora of abolitionist leaders, from John Brown to Joshua Giddings, and was a reliable bastion of support for antislavery political parties in the 1840s and 1850s. Its residents were primarily New Englanders or their children who had little respect for Southerners and a life style built on black labor. Religious conviction reinforced cultural prejudice. Congregationalists, who dominated the Western Reserve, saw slavery as an unequivocal sin. Holding other human beings in bondage was not merely immoral, it was an affront to God. No less important in encouraging the antislavery sentiment of the region was its relatively small number of black residents. African Americans were not serious competitors for jobs, nor was the area's commerce tied to the South.

In the mid-nineteenth century, Oberlin was a national center of abolitionist sentiment and radical reform movements. Some of the Lane rebels helped establish a Congregational college there in 1833. Oberlin College, with the famous revivalist Charles Grandison Finney as its president in the 1850s, became what the Lane Seminary had aspired to be. Dependent on manual labor, it focused not just on intellectual life but on moral improvement. It trained its students to go out and do God's business in perfecting the world. They were to live simply, dress plainly, and refrain from tobacco, alcohol, and caffeine. The idea, as the original town covenant put it, was to "strive to maintain deep-toned and elevated personal piety, to 'provoke each other to love and good works,' to live together in all things as brethren, and to glorify God in our bodies and spirits which are His." As the son of a professor remembered: "The law of our household was first religion; second, work; and third study. With us law meant not only submission and obedience, but regularity and order, system and method, both in religion, work and study."[24] Oberlin College eventually admitted women and blacks, although only one hundred blacks attended the college before 1865. According to the 1860 census, 416, or just under 20 percent, of the 2,114 free residents of Oberlin were black. Most were laborers.

White or black, the citizens of Oberlin were eager to invoke both the Bible and the U.S. Constitution in the defense of human freedom. Overwhelmingly Free Soil and then Republican voters, they held the balance of power in Lorain County. In the fall of 1858, several dozen citizens, including college professors, rallied to the defense of a black man about to be returned to the South as a fugitive slave and spent several weeks in prison in Cleveland because of their defiance of secular law. This action was in keeping with the commitment of most of the Western Reserve's population to the general reform of American society.

Opposition to slavery became more popular when it focused on a critique of the South that explicitly congratulated residents of the Old

Northwest on their cultural superiority. In speeches and ordinary conversation, Ohioans participated in the creation of a "South" that was the antithesis of the "North." When the *Ohio State Journal* characterized a Southerner as an "idle, pleasure seeking, heedless, improvident and extravagant" person "who scarce moves hand or foot without the assistance of crouching, abject slaves," it was articulating an emerging consensus about state and regional identity.[25]

Whether such stereotypes were true or false hardly mattered. Increasing numbers of Ohioans believed in them in the 1840s and 1850s. The power of *Uncle Tom's Cabin* lay in no small part in the ways in which Stowe's characters and plot confirmed the essential differences in character between the North and South. The latter not only denied blacks their God-given independence, it discouraged whites from fighting their passions and welcomed men such as the Vermont-born Simon Legree who were unmarried, unrefined, and devoted to profit and lust. These perceptions informed Ohioans' sense of the significance of their state and its rapid progress from wilderness to civilization. Disparaging others not only made them feel better about themselves, it helped them think about who they were more concretely.

In the 1840s, antislavery agitation became politically important out of proportion to its numerical strength. Because most abolitionists were Whigs, their support for antislavery third parties hurt the Whigs more than the Democrats. Whigs usually won the governorship in the 1840s but their margin of victory was razor thin. In 1848, the Whig candidate won with 148,766 votes to 148,452 for his Democratic opponent. With the rise of the Free Soil Party, based on opposition to slavery in any of the territory acquired from the Mexican War, the Whigs no longer won at all. The Free Soilers increased their vote percentage from 5.1 percent in 1850 to 17.5 percent in 1853. When national political events inflamed anti-Southern feelings even more, a new party, dedicated to the restriction of slavery within its existing limits, succeeded in winning the governorship of Ohio. Members of the party were called Republicans, and their candidate was Salmon P. Chase.

Chase was the most important political figure in Ohio in the mid-nineteenth century. Born in New Hampshire in 1808, he had arrived in Worthington in 1820 when his widowed mother sent him to live with his uncle, Philander, an Episcopal minister. Three years later, Chase returned to New Hampshire, where he graduated from Dartmouth College in 1826. After a sojourn in Washington, D.C., he settled in Cincinnati in 1830 and became a successful attorney. Well-educated and deeply religious, Chase was ponderous, pompous, and adept at self-deception. According to Rutherford B. Hayes, "political intrigue, love of power and boundless ambition were striking features of his life and character."[26]

In the late 1830s, deeply affected by attacks on blacks and abolitionists in Cincinnati, Chase became an ardent opponent of slavery. Because he craved power, he was willing to compromise in order to win elections. Above all, he wanted to make antislavery a respectable cause that would not frighten Ohio's burgeoning middle class. Drawing on the ideas of James G. Birney, Chase developed a constitutional argument designed to win widespread support for an antislavery movement in the name of law and order. He argued that the founders of the American republic were generally opposed to slavery and had hoped to see it disappear from the new nation. Their United States was to be an empire of freedom. No federal document offered a positive support for slavery, and some, most notably the Northwest Ordinance of 1787, condemned it. In their desire to limit the powers of the federal government, the founders had essentially avoided the issue of slavery. Therefore, Chase concluded, slavery was "a State institution—the creature and dependent of State law—wholly local in its existence and character." Freedom was the natural state of residents of the U.S. "The very moment a slave passes beyond the jurisdiction of the state . . . he ceases to be a slave; not because of any law or regulation or the state which he enters confers freedom upon him, but because he *continues* to be a man and *leaves* behind him the law of force, which made him a slave."[27] The significance of this argument was clear: since slavery was created by the states, it could be destroyed by the states. The federal government had no obligation to defend the institution at all.

In the early 1840s, Chase brought these ideas to the Liberty Party, which was having trouble rallying support beyond a core group of Congregationalists in the Western Reserve, and wrote most of the party's public documents. Chase transformed antislavery, at least superficially, from a moral crusade to a legal contest. This approach differentiated him from Liberty leaders in the East who looked upon his strategy as something of a sell-out. But Chase persisted, and his ideas flourished with the emergence of the Free Soil Party in the aftermath of the Mexican War and his election to the U.S. Senate in 1848. The contention that "Freedom is national; slavery only is local and sectional" would become a mainstay of the Republican Party in the 1850s. As governor of Ohio from 1856 to 1860, Chase gave antislavery the face of a lawyer rather than a minister, a sober citizen rather than a radical agitator.

In so doing, Chase helped to define the significance of Ohio's story. His ideology was as much anti-South as it was pro-black. While he supported black suffrage, he hoped that the abolition of slavery would lead to more distance between the races. By identifying freedom as the national and natural state of Americans, Chase pushed Ohio to the forefront of American politics. The first state created from the Northwest Ordinance of 1787, which outlawed slavery, was the national ideal. The values of Virginia or the Carolinas were local. The values of Ohio were national. When Southerners demanded that the federal government protect slavery, when they dominated Congress, the presidency, and the Supreme Court, they were essentially imposing local views on the nation as a whole. They were usurping the definition of the United States from those who knew it best, that is, from Ohioans and other citizens of the Old Northwest.

Attacking slavery was not just a matter of defining Ohio against a barbarous and backward South. It was a matter of rescuing the republic from those who would betray and pervert it in the interests of their selfish, local world. To refuse to fight was to accept the position of slave. Ohio senator Thomas Morris had sounded the alarm in 1839. Morris felt compelled to defend "the institutions of my own State, the persons and firesides of her citizens, from the insatiable grasp of the slaveholding power as being used and felt in the free States." Ohio had nurtured his instinct for freedom. "A free State was the place of my birth," he told the Senate. "Ohio is my country, endeared to me by every fond recollection. She gave me political existence and taught me in her political school; and I should be worse than an unnatural son did I forget or disobey her precepts." Therefore, he had no choice but to fight the "Slave power," which was "seeking to establish itself in every State, in defiance of the constitution and laws of the States within which it is prohibited."[28]

By the 1850s, as Southern members of Congress demanded repeal of the Missouri Compromise and the return of fugitive slaves, many Ohioans had had enough. They agreed with the Cincinnati *Gazette* in 1854 that it was "impossible to satisfy the South." As future Republican John M. Butler said in the same year: "We have submitted to slavery long enough, and must not stand it any longer. . . . I am done catching negroes for the South." By 1856, the *Ohio State Journal* put the case directly: "The slave drivers seek to make our country a great slave empire: to make slave breeding, slave selling, slave labor, slave extension, slave policy, and slave domination, FOREVER THE CONTROLLING ELEMENTS OF OUR GOVERNMENT. They say so, and they mean it."[29]

When Congress effectively repealed the Missouri Compromise of 1820 with the adoption of the Kansas-Nebraska Act in 1854 (whereby referenda among territorial voters would determine whether a state was free or slave), these ideas caught fire. Outraged Northerners organized the Republican Party, which elected Chase as governor in 1855. The victory, however, was not exactly what African Americans had in mind. The triumph of Republicanism had less to do with ending slavery for black men than it did with preventing slavery for white men. Antislavery was as much about saving Ohio as it was about saving enslaved African Americans. In 1854, Chase's newspaper asked succinctly whether "the people of Ohio were the enemies of Slavery or the friends of Oppression." "[E]very man who is in favor of Equal Rights, Northern Manhood and National Honor" would rally to the cause, proclaimed the *Cincinnati Gazette*.[30]

Complicating the cause of antislavery was the fact that many white Ohioans were more worried about immigrants, many of them Catholic, then they were about Southerners. In the 1850s, more than 40 percent of Cincinnati's population had been born outside of the United States, the highest percentage of any of the ten largest cities in the country. Native-born citizens of Ohio simply did not like the new arrivals. Not only did immigrants threaten to take jobs and undercut wages, they did not seem to subscribe to middle-class notions of respectable behavior and social improvement. Many Catholics wanted to create their own schools. Most wanted to no part of temperance crusades. Some Ohioans considered immigrants little more than pawns of the Vatican, people who had no appreciation for the workings of a democratic republic.

Resentment toward the foreign-born became a volatile political issue in Ohio in the early 1850s, especially in Cincinnati, where controversy centered on the issues of temperance and public education. Archbishop John Purcell's February 1853 request that the state government offer financial support to parochial schools made the race for mayor that year livelier than usual. A Democrat sympathetic to the Catholic Church won only because three opponents of funding for parochial schools split the majority of the vote.

Ohio nativists believed that if immigrants were to stay in the United States, they had to transform themselves, or at least allow their children to be transformed, into American citizens, even if the price of that transformation was the loss of their language and customs. Not surprisingly, many German and Irish immigrants refused to cooperate. They had not come to the U.S. to surrender key components of their identity. Such resistance fueled the suspicions of the native-born that the foreigners were opposed to the basic principles of republican government, that they were slaves to the power of the Vatican and its many minions. Members of the Order of the Star Spangled Banner, nicknamed Know Nothings, called for immigration restriction and a longer naturalization period. "How people do hate Catholics," wrote Rud Hayes in 1854, "and what a happiness it was to thousands to have a chance to show it in what seemed a lawful and patriotic manner."[31]

Ohioans, like many Americans, were deeply anxious in the 1850s. Their state seemed to be under siege by people who refused to cooperate with their version of the development of Ohio. The People's Party, which combined antipathy to the Kansas-Nebraska Act and the Catholic Church, swept to victory throughout Ohio in the mid-1850s. Sick of politics as usual, many Northern voters turned to insurgent groups as more responsive and less corrupt than traditional parties. By the fall of 1856, the Republican Party had become the most likely major alternative to the Democrats. Led by Chase, Republicans sought the middle ground of reform. They were opposed to the extension of slavery but did not support radical abolitionism. Against the power of the Catholic Church, they did not object to foreign immigrants of the right type, particularly German Protestants whose votes they occasionally won.

Like Hayes and Chase, Republicans tended to be middle-class voters: independent farmers, professionals, and merchants in small towns and cities who were Protestant, native-born men devoted to the cause of progress. They were citizens eager to preserve and extend their notions of what Ohio should be like. Negative in their attacks on white Southerners, Catholic immigrants, and blacks in general, they were positive in their assertion of the benefits of self-improvement and honest labor. The Republican Party in many ways spoke for middle-class Ohioans' sense of their state as a coherent community of like-minded citizens.

When in March 1857 the U.S. Supreme Court, dominated by Southerners, ruled in the Dred Scott case that African Americans were not citizens of the United States and that slave owners could take their property anywhere they wished, even those Ohioans who were hostile to blacks reacted angrily. A committee of the Ohio Senate declared that the "case had no parallel in wickedness in the history of the world." The entire history of Ohio was overturned. "We learn that our own Ohio, instead of being, in fact, a free, is in effect, a slave State." The issue had gone beyond black slavery. Suddenly, many citizens saw themselves as Ohioans in ways that they never had before. Their borders made sense. They could define themselves with a lyricism that had been unimaginable in 1803. Should anyone attempt to enforce the Dred Scott decision "in our State, and from the blue waters of Lake Erie on the North, to the beautiful Ohio on the South, from the hills of Pennsylvania on the East, to the plains of Indiana on the West, but one voice will be heard echoing, and re-echoing, the war cry of the revolution, 'Give me Liberty, or give me Death.'"[32]

The Civil War and the Significance of Ohio

On April 12, 1861, the Ohio Senate was conducting business as usual. Acutely aware of the tensions produced by Republican Abra-

ham Lincoln's election as president of the United States the preceding
November and the subsequent secession of several Southern states, the
senators were blissfully unaware that a war that would last four years
and take the lives of more than five hundred thousand Americans had
already begun. The previous evening, troops of the recently formed
Confederate States of America had commenced a bombardment of a
federal fort in the harbor of Charleston, South Carolina. Without
warning, a senator, telegram in hand, entered the chamber. "Mr. President," he said, "the telegraph announces that the secessionists are
bombarding Fort Sumter!" The stunned Ohioans sat in silence, ab-
sorbing the news, until a woman in the gallery shouted: "Glory to
God! Glory to God!"[33]

The incident demonstrated several things. First, progress had indeed swept the United States. Now information traveled across wires
in a matter of minutes. In 1775, it had taken weeks for news of the
Battle of Lexington and Concord to reach all corners of the future nation; news of Fort Sumter took a matter of hours. Second, the
woman's comment suggested the extent to which the war would become a moral crusade, an effort not only to defeat the Slave Power
and preserve the freedom of Northern white men but to punish evil
and cleanse the nation of its sins. To a remarkable degree, the abolition of black slavery would eventually become part of that crusade.

In the spring of 1861, the prospect of military glory thrilled young
Ohioans because they had no idea of the cost of extended warfare.
The Civil War was the first conflict to involve large numbers of men
in forty-five years. The exception was the Mexican War (1846–48),
which had reinforced the appeal of military service as relatively short,
not too dangerous, and potentially transcendent. Eager to defend
their way of life against Southern tyrants, more than thirty thousand
Ohioans, including German and Irish immigrants, answered Lincoln's
call for volunteers in the wake of Fort Sumter. Chaos reigned, especially in Columbus, where facilities were make-shift and equipment in
short supply. Governor William Dennison persisted, however. By late
April the First and Second Regiments of Ohio Volunteers were traveling by train to Washington, D.C., to protect the nation's capital.

Even the defeat of Union troops in the first major battle of the war
at Bull Run, Virginia, on July 21, 1861, did not dampen the ardor of

Ohio's citizens. When Lincoln called for more volunteers, another seventy-seven thousand stepped forward, exceeding the state's quota by ten thousand. Although enlistment slowed considerably as the war dragged on, 346,326 Ohioans were reported in service as of December 1, 1864. In proportion to its population, Ohio sent more men into battle than any other Northern state. Governor Dennison's desire that Ohio "lead the Union" was largely realized. Not only did the state provide more than its share of ordinary soldiers, it produced a disproportionate share of military leaders. Among the most famous generals associated with Ohio by 1865 were Ulysses Simpson Grant and William Tecumseh Sherman.

The ragged appearance and checkered personal history of Grant, a native of Point Pleasant who had grown up in Brown County, obscured a sporadic strategic genius and a stubborn refusal to accept defeat that would serve him well as he rode victories in the Mississippi Valley to the overall command of Union armies in 1864. When General Robert E. Lee surrendered the Army of Northern Virginia at Appomattox Court House in April 1865, he did so to an Ohioan, the plainly dressed, alcoholic, cigar-smoking Grant, son of a tanner and the husband of the daughter of a Missouri slave holder. A few days later, General Joseph E. Johnston, Jr. surrendered the only other major Confederate army to General William Tecumseh Sherman. Born in Lancaster, Sherman grew up in the prominent Ewing family and, like Grant, attended West Point. Like Grant, Sherman was saved by the Civil War from an obscure life, in his case as a failed banker and mediocre teacher. Also like Grant, Sherman as a commander was most noteworthy for his tenacity and his single-minded devotion to finding some way to win.

Neither Grant nor Sherman saw war as glorious. They considered it a horror to be used only to achieve one's objectives. Victory meant not only the surrender of the enemy but his complete acceptance of the significance of his defeat. In the fall of 1864, Sherman led tens of thousands of Ohioans and other Union troops in a devastating march from Atlanta to Savannah, Georgia, that embodied the unforgiving qualities of total war. For Sherman, war had a logic all its own, and once they started it, human beings were as much in its control as they were in control of it. In late February 1865, Sherman's army sacked

Columbia, South Carolina, capital of the first state to secede from the Union, aiding and abetting fires that destroyed the city. General Sherman had no sympathy for the South Carolinians. "They had brought it on themselves," he said. Years later, his attitude had not changed. "I deliberately put myself and army where if not absolutely destroyed and overwhelmed, the existence of a Southern Independent Confederacy was an impossibility," he recalled. "From the moment my army passed Columbia S.C. the war was ended."[34]

Grant and Sherman were recognizably from the Old Northwest, and they represented the rise of a new kind of leader in the country. Undistinguished men, they dressed like common soldiers and scorned pomp and ceremony. Whatever their virtues as officers, they were most notable for their unrelenting commitment to their assignments. Neither had intellectual pretensions, yet their memoirs are classics of their kind, marked by lean and direct prose. They approached writing in the same way they approached fighting: straightforward and pragmatic.

Not every Ohioan devoted himself to the great cause of punishing the South and saving the Union. More than eighteen thousand Ohioans reportedly deserted during the course of the Civil War. But close to thirty-five thousand died (a third of those from wounds and the remainder from disease), and some thirty thousand carried battle scars with them for the rest of their lives. Indeed, military service was the high point of many of their lives. For half a century after the Confederates surrendered, these men would on regular occasions gather as members of the Grand Army of the Republic in halls and homes across Ohio to reminisce about battles in Tennessee and Mississippi, camps and games in western Virginia, and long stretches of monotony throughout the South.

With one major exception, war took Ohio men (and the women who followed them) away from the state. Despite frequent rumors, the only serious Confederate raid into Ohio occurred in July 1863, just days after the decisive battles of Gettysburg and Vicksburg. General John Hunt Morgan led just under twenty-five hundred cavalry troops in a wild ride from Harrison on the Indiana border eastward through Batavia and Jackson to the Ohio River at Buffington Island. After a skirmish, Morgan and half of his troops continued north to McConnelsville and Old Washington, until they were cornered and captured in Columbiana County. Later, Morgan and six of his officers completed the only successful nineteenth-century escape from the Ohio Penitentiary in Columbus. Morgan's raid did little serious damage beyond frightening people.

Confederates hoped to get Ohioans to give up the cause. They knew that support for the war was far from unanimous. There was sympathy for the Confederacy especially in isolated counties and those with large numbers of people of Southern ancestry. Some Ohioans fought for the Confederacy, including seven men who became generals. Among those who remained loyal to the Union, many protested the length and cost of the war. The Lincoln administration's employment of a draft to raise troops, its restrictions on newspapers, and its endorsement of emancipation in late 1862, fueled political opposition. Critics of the war supported Democratic candidates, who did well, especially in 1862, although Republicans and War Democrats controlled the state government throughout the conflict.

Clement Vallandigham was the most prominent Copperhead, a name given to opponents of the war. An Ohio native, he was a son of Southerners who nonetheless behaved like a Yankee in his commitment to hard work and an ascetic life. Vallandigham demonstrated Sherman-like stubbornness in his support of the Democratic Party. A lawyer and newspaper editor in Dayton, he was thrice defeated in campaigns for the seat from Ohio's Third Congressional District (Montgomery, Preble, and Butler Counties), a fate he blamed in the third instance on illegal African American voters. He won election to the U.S. House of Representatives in 1858 and again in 1860. No fan of secession, Vallandigham nonetheless opposed the war and criticized Lincoln's conduct. The congressman's zealous dissent and difficult personality polarized Ohioans. Barely defeated for re-election in 1862, Vallandigham responded with a public address in which he urged peace. Even some Democrats thought he had gone too far. When he decided to run for governor of Ohio in 1863, he faced an uphill battle.

Vallandigham did not stand alone. A considerable number of Ohioans opposed the war or had serious doubts about it. Historians have generally ascribed their feelings to racism, their fears of miscegenation and of blacks competing for jobs. Without question, racism was rampant in Ohio, and not all of it on the part of Southerners.

The Irish-born Hugh Anderson of St. Clairsville, a man in his late sixties, believed that "the Negro race" was "unfit for freedom." Anderson blamed the impending war on abolitionists. How could one live in a place "governed by the *laws, made by a set of red mouthed abolitionists disunionists nigger elevators, nigger lovers or men* who make laws making my children only *equal to be raised up educated at the same school and associated with,* a race perhaps two removes from a baboon[?]"[35]

There was more to Copperheadism than racism, however. In many ways, Democratic critics of the war were simply holding true to Jacksonian principles. They were asserting local autonomy and individual rights in the face of a suddenly powerful federal government, which was running rampant over its citizens, suspending the writ of habeas corpus, restricting freedom of speech and freedom of the press. When General Ambrose E. Burnside, commander of the Department of the Ohio, issued General Order No. 38 on April 13, 1863, authorizing the arrest of Southern sympathizers by the military, he simply confirmed a pattern of power eating away at liberty.[36]

In traditionally Democratic counties, criticism of prosecution of the war grew more vitriolic as the number of deaths mounted and it became clear that the Republicans were moving toward freedom for enslaved Africans. A Democratic newspaper in Crawford County charged in March 1862 that the Republican administration had "trampled the Constitution under foot . . . enfranchised negroes and mulattoes . . . brought about civil war . . . made widows and orphans . . . prostrated business . . . plundered the people, cheated the soldiers . . . muzzled the press, denied the right of free speech . . . [and] suspended the privilege of the writ of habeas corpus." Later that year, a group of reluctant draftees shouted that they were for "the Constitution as it is, and the Union as it was" and that they would not "fight to free the nigger."[37]

Republicans fought back, most famously with satire. The New York–born printer and editor David Ross Locke, who took over the *Bucyrus Journal* in 1856, invented a figure he called Petroleum Vesuvius Nasby, a charmingly incompetent and unscrupulous local political operator. In a series of letters to a Hancock newspaper, which he edited during the war, Locke, writing as Nasby, satirized the Democrats of Crawford County as petty, self-interested, and provincial. A mock ordinance of secession, supposedly drawn up by local citizens, noted that they had "too long submitted to the imperious dictates uv a tyranikle goverment," including a refusal to relocate the state capital in their village, not to mention the State Fair and the penitentiary, or to build a canal nearby. "It hex compelled us, yeer after yeer, to pay our share uv the taxes" and had "never appointed any citizen uv the place to any offis wher theft wuz possible, thus wilfully keepin capital away from us." No longer willing to "endoor sich outrajes," they declared their independence from the state of Ohio and promised to defend themselves "with arms, if need be."[38]

Whether because of racism, Southern ties, distrust of powerful government, exhaustion with a long and bloody war, or all of the above, thousands of Ohioans supported Clement Vallandigham. Their fervor mounted after General Burnside had the former congressman arrested at his home in Dayton on May 5, 1863. Refusing to go quietly, Vallandigham was "taken from his wife's bedroom amidst a perfect torrent of tears and heart-rending sobs." Angry citizens of Dayton denounced the action as "kidnapping" and destroyed the property of Republicans, including a newspaper office, in retaliation. Mary Ladley, a young woman in Yellow Springs anxious to become a schoolteacher, was pleased. Vallandigham, she thought, had "done more mischief or at least as much as any Rebel."[39] A military tribunal tried Vallandigham and sentenced him to prison for the rest of the war. Lincoln intervened and ordered the Copperhead turned over to the Confederates. The exiled Democrat did not stay long in the South. Traveling by ship, he took up residence in a hotel in Windsor, Ontario. Now a martyr to the cause of freedom, he won the Peace Democrats' nomination for governor in July 1863 and campaigned by mail while he entertained a string of sympathetic visitors from Ohio.

In October, War Democrat John Brough smashed Vallandigham at the polls by a margin of more than 100,000 votes. Crucial, although not decisive, were the votes of tens of thousands of soldiers. Among the troops, Brough won by 41,467 to 2,298. Intimidation and corruption were widespread. Still, there was little support for Vallandigham and Peace Democrats among the soldiers. Typical was a man who wondered why anyone thought "the soldiers will vote for a man that they hate worse than they do the rebels? . . . for we know that just such men as Vallandingham [*sic*] is keeping up this war" and "causing all this misery."[40]

Fighting seemed to radicalize many Ohio troops. The traumas of battle and exposure to the South, which struck many of them as an exotic and backward place, left few with any sympathy for white Southerners or slavery. Ohio was superior to the South in virtually every way, they decided. To be from Ohio meant to stand up for the Union, for labor, for education, for progress, and for liberty.

In early 1861, the lives of Lucy and Rud Hayes were flourishing. They had three sons and a recently expanded home on Cincinnati's Sixth Street, complete with two servants. Rud had become a successful lawyer (with a salary of thirty-five hundred dollars) and a locally prominent Republican. Both continued to emphasize the importance of personal improvement. Rud wrote about the impending crisis of the Union calmly but firmly. For once in his life, he disdained compromise. If the South left the Union, he was sure that "the free States alone . . . will make a glorious nation" whose citizens would be "full of vigor, industry, inventive genius, educated, and moral; increasing by immigration rapidly, and, above all, free—all free." Nonetheless, Hayes wanted no part of a "war of conquest" against the South; he was sure it would be an expensive failure.[41] Besides, freedom and slavery probably could not coexist under the same flag.

Like many Ohioans, Hayes warmed slowly to the idea of war. After Fort Sumter, he concluded that "the war is forced on us. We cannot escape it." He wrote to a friend from Kenyon who was living in Texas that he supported a war only "for the maintenance of the authority of the Government and the rights of the United States." As ever, Hayes was acutely aware that people would differ on this subject. Perhaps the war would be short and he and his correspondent would "remain friends." After all, wars had "good points. . . . People forget self. The virtues of magnanimity, courage, patriotism, etc., etc., are called into life. People are more generous, more sympathetic, better, than when engaged in the more selfish pursuits of peace." Sure that Southerners would behave as well as Ohioans, he noted in a postscript his son's confusion about how God could support both sides.[42]

Characteristically seeing the war as an opportunity for moral improvement, Hayes volunteered. He was dispatched to (West) Virginia, where he reconciled himself to the tedious routine of military life. Within a few months, Hayes was weary of the "forced marches without shelter, food, or blankets over mountain bridle-paths, in the night and rain." The Confederates turned out to be more persistent foes than he had anticipated. They had better artillery and leadership, and their troops were superior to the Union ones, except for those from the West, that is, Ohio. By the fall of 1862, Hayes, now a colonel in the Twenty-third Ohio Regiment, had long since realized that the war was going to take much longer than expected and that it would test everyone's patience. He could do nothing more than his duty.[43]

While in Maryland in the maneuvering that led to the battle of Antietam, Hayes was wounded in his left arm. He continued to give orders while lying behind his men. He found himself close to a wounded Confederate with whom he had "considerable talk . . . I gave him messages for my wife and friends in case I should not get up. We were right jolly and friendly; it was by no means an unpleasant experience." Three days later, Hayes listened to the sounds of the armies clashing at Antietam Creek. All told, he informed his mother, close to half of the Twenty-third Ohio was wounded or killed in one of the bloodiest battles of the Civil War.[44]

Within days, Lucy was at Rud's side to nurse him back to health. For the next several years, Rud saw no serious action. He rejoiced in the victory of Brough over Vallandigham, particularly the unanimous support of his regiment and brigade. Hayes and his colleagues wanted the chance to finish what they had begun. In the fall of 1864, Hayes was elected to Congress from Ohio's First District while serving in Virginia. He was still in the thick of things—hearing bullets whiz around him, having his horse killed, getting hit in the head by a spent ball—but now he was sure of victory. "[The] rebels fight poorly," he confided to his diary. "Awfully whipped.—Cannon and spoils on our side. Glorious!"[45]

When Robert E. Lee surrendered in April 1865, Hayes was relieved to see the end of "this cruel war." Reflecting on the Union victory, he was proud but anxious to get on with his life. Lincoln's assassination filled him with sorrow and determination. "Now," he told Lucy, "the march of events can't be stayed, probably can't be much changed. It is possible that a greater degree of severity in dealing with the Rebellion may be ordered, and *that* may be for the best."[46] The Civil War had in duration and distress exceeded anything Rud could have imagined in 1861. If it had brought out the best in some of the people some of the time, it had also brought out the worst. Rud Hayes remained what he had trained himself to be: a man of the middle way.

Others, however, got angry. College professor and state senator James A. Garfield of Hiram was a staunch Republican in the late 1850s. Opposed to the Slave Power and ready for war, he harbored no illusions. Although he lacked both military experience and physical fitness, Garfield was appointed an officer in the Forty-second Ohio. Like Hayes, he saw close combat and acquitted himself well. Garfield's reaction to war was ambivalent. On the one hand, it was a horror. Long after it was over, he said that "at the sight of these dead men whom other men had killed, something went out of [me], the habit of [my] lifetime, that never came back again; the sense of the sacredness of life and the impossibility of destroying it." On the other hand, a horrible war was better than a horrible peace. Like many Ohioans, Garfield was conscious of the extraordinary era in which he lived. "The young men of the present day never saw or read of a time as grand as this. They never had such opportunities of doing great and noble actions."[47]

Moreover, the war was a holy crusade both to save the Union and end slavery. The evangelical Garfield increasingly resented the emphasis on the former at the expense of the latter. He was "coming nearer and nearer to downright Abolitionism." Why was it taking so long? Why did so many Northerners oppose ending slavery? Garfield took refuge in the mysterious operations of God. He assumed that it was His plan "to lengthen out this war till our whole army has been sufficiently outraged by the haughty tyranny of proslavery officers and the spirit of slavery and slaveholders with whom they come in contact that they can bring back into civil life a healthy and vigorous sentiment that shall make itself felt at the ballot box and in social life for the glory of humanity and the honor of the country."[48] In other words, they would learn to vote for antislavery Republicans such as Garfield.

Garfield wanted the war prosecuted with vigor. He had no patience with West Point training. "[O]ur real objective point is not any place or district," he wrote in language with which Grant and Sherman would have agreed, "but the rebel army wherever we find it. We must crush and pulverize them, and then all places and territories fall into our hands as a consequence."[49] Not for Garfield the fears of Copperheads about government power. He wanted plantations confiscated. He wanted equal rights for African Americans. Lincoln's emancipation policies were too little, too late. The Civil War did not change Garfield's basic opinions so much as they intensified them.

George Wise, a young native of Bellaire and a member of the Forty-third Ohio, shared Garfield's anger. In July 1862, Wise knew that if Great Britain and France allied themselves with the Confederacy, the United States would become "a nation of soldiers. And even then I believe we would be successful and that the infamous league of Despots and traitors would be overpowered by the desperate valor of the American republic strug[g]ling for its liberty and the liberties of the world." Wise, like Garfield, wanted the Union to fight energetically. There was no reason to hold back. Why should soldiers suffer bad food and lousy conditions in unpleasant Dixie? Why not get it over with quickly? As he fought near Kennesaw Mountain, Georgia, in June 1864, Wise anticipated "the most glorious fourth" of July in the history of the republic. The soldiers might miss the comforts of home, but they were proud to be parts of "the mightiest energies for the preservation of true liberty & self government that any nation has ever put forth in any cause."[50]

As bad as conditions were, nothing could compare to the dangers of battle. Oscar Ladley described a few minutes of his life on July 2, 1863, in Gettysburg, Pennsylvania. "I was standing behind the wall when they came over," he wrote to his mother and sisters. "A Rebel officer made at me with a revolver with his colors by his side[.] I had no pistol nothing but my sword. Just as I was getting ready to strike him one of our boys run him through the body so saved me. There was a good man killed in that way."[51]

Was the cause worth it? Many soldiers thought so, even though their loved ones disagreed. Some struggled to make wives and children understand that their futures depended on the sacrifices their husbands and fathers made now. "Why denounce the war when the interest at stake is so vital?" wrote a lieutenant to his frustrated wife. "Without Union & peace our freedom is worthless . . . our children would have no warrant of liberty. . . . [If] our Country be numbered among the things that were but are not, of what value will be house, family, and friends?" Another man praised his son for writing him a letter. "It tells me that while I am absent from home, fighting the battels of our country, trying to restore law and order, to our once peaceful & prosperous nation, and endeavoring to secure for each and every American citizen of every race, the rights garenteed to us in the Declaration of Independence . . . I have children growing up that will be worthy of the rights that I trust will be left for them."[52]

Being in the South convinced many Ohioans of the justice of their cause. To many, the region seemed backward and stagnant. One man noted in Tennessee "how far behind the North they are in improvements of every kind." The South lacked "all enterprise and prosperity. School houses are a rare sight." Colonel Marcus Spiegel, the highest ranking Jewish officer in the U.S. Army, began the war as a Democrat; in January 1863, he staunchly opposed Lincoln's Emancipation Proclamation. But seeing the effects of slavery changed his mind. In January 1864, while in Louisiana, he announced his conversion to antislavery. "[S]ince I [came] here," he told his wife, "I have learned and seen more of what the horrors of Slavery was than I ever knew before . . . . I am [now] a strong abolitionist."[53] A few months later, Spiegel gave what Lincoln at Gettysburg called "the last full measure of devotion" to a cause for which he had never intended to fight.

When George Wise marched with Sherman's army through South Carolina, he came to see the war as a morality play. Southerners had sinned. "South Carolina: poor, proud, aristocratic, ignorant South Carolina, began the war—most terribly has she been punished. Our march over that devoted State has been like an awful storm, but it has passed, and her black ruins will stand as a warning of more terrible things to come if it ever becomes necessary to pass over her territory again." South Carolina was not a land of progress; it was not Ohio. Its people were "mostly very poor & ignorant." The haughty rich thought they should govern everyone. "Their cant about aristocracy is perfectly sickening."[54]

Lincoln's assassination in April 1865 hardened already hard hearts. The news literally sickened Connecticut-born Holiday Ames, a blacksmith from Ashland and a lieutenant in the 102nd Ohio Volunteer Infantry. He wrote to his wife that he would stay in the army and fight "for reveng, yes fighting until every Cursed Rebble is exterminated. . . . I say hang every one of them from Jeff Davis down." Ames could not believe that "this unholy Rebellin" could end with the death of the president. If he "had all the Rebbles in my power for one day they would not be so pleanty at night I would hang every one of them without judge or jury."[55]

Ames's reaction was extreme but his sentiments were not. Hostility to white slave holders led Ohio soldiers to embrace things they would never have contemplated a few years earlier. In 1863, Ohio, following the lead of Massachusetts, allowed African Americans to enroll in the 127th Ohio Volunteers. Paid at half the going rate and organized in segregated units with white officers, black soldiers suffered a series of indignities. For the most part, arming black men resulted from necessity, not ideology; by that time, it was hard to raise troops. Most Ohioans would have endorsed the comments of a state legislative committee assigned to investigate black migration in to the state during the war. The members wrote that "the Negro race is looked upon by the people of Ohio as a class to be kept by themselves; . . . The colored man will not in all future time that he may remain an inhabitant . . . attain any material improvement in the social and political rights over that which he now enjoys."[56]

Still, more than five thousand black men served with Ohio units and hundreds of others fought with troops from other states. On occasion, white troops were very happy to see African Americans with rifles, even if they could not contain their racism. Private William James Smith of Morrow County was fighting in the Battle of the Wilderness in May 1864 when he and his colleagues found themselves in need of reinforcements. Suddenly to their right, they "saw a VERY DARK CLOUD," a division of "COLORED TROOPS." When "the DARKIES gave them a VOLLEY," the Confederates "didn't wait to say goodby." Later, Smith learned that the black troops had run four miles to save him and his comrades. He did not talk about the incident much, but there can be no doubt what these white Ohioans thought about black troops, at least temporarily.[57] Smith voted for the reelection of President Lincoln later in 1864 with enthusiasm, even though he was not quite twenty-one.

Some Ohioans hoped that there was "a brighter day coming for the colored man," believing that the sacrifice of "home comforts, and his blood, if necessary" would "speed the coming of that glorious day." Republicans generally supported suffrage for African American men. In 1867, when Congressman Rutherford B. Hayes was elected governor by a three-thousand-vote margin, he boldly noted "the plain and monstrous inconsistency and injustice of excluding one seventh of our population from all participation in a Government founded on the consent of the governed in this land of free discussion. . . . No such absurdity and wrong can be permanent."[58] Enough voters agreed with Hayes to reelect him governor in 1869, albeit barely, and to help him take the presidency in the disputed election of 1876.

More significant was Ohio's ratification of the Thirteenth, Fourteenth, and Fifteenth Amendments to the U.S. Constitution, which abolished slavery and guaranteed suffrage and due process to all without regard to race. Yet Ohioans could not bring themselves to change their own constitution. A referendum to allow African Americans to vote lost in 1867 by a margin of fifty thousand. Enlightened in so many ways, John Roberts of Madison County could not accept African Americans as his equal. In the summer of 1864, he was outraged that black men were being used as soldiers. Before the war started, he had hoped that "they may clear every wooly head out of the country and not allow another one to come in here for forty years." Now as the war neared its end, Roberts still believed that "Negroes wont make good soldiers nor good, substantial citizens."[59]

There were too many people who shared these sentiments to support any major change in political rights or social relationships. Blacks could now vote in Ohio, even if the state constitution refused to acknowledge a right extended by the U.S. Constitution and won by the efforts of hundreds of thousands of white and black men on battlefields from Missouri to Georgia. The antislavery crusade and the Civil War had defined the state as a community of white, native-born, Protestant citizens committed to moral and material progress.

One of a series of eight daguerrotypes of Cincinnati taken by Charles Fontayne and William S. Porter in September 1848 from a rooftop in Newport, Kentucky. (Courtesy of The Public Library of Cincinnati and Hamilton County)

5

Alternative Ohios

—

IN THE SECOND quarter of the nineteenth century, thousands of people from Cardiganshire, Wales, arrived in Jackson, Meigs, and Gallia Counties. Making enough money to purchase some land, most settled in as farm families who supplemented their income with industrial work. The Welsh settlers built an ethnic enclave within the larger landscape of Ohio. Religion especially united them. They organized neighborhood seiats (essentially cells of worshipers) within the Methodist Church. Then they erected chapels, which became community centers and "repositories of Welsh culture, both architecturally and spiritually."[1] Within the chapels, the immigrants and their children observed liturgical practices that remained unchanged from what they had known in Wales. Especially distinctive were the ty capels (or chapel houses), which were used to house visitors. The Cadw y Mis, or keeping of the month, maintained the ty capels, making each family responsible for caring for the building and guests for a month. Welsh songs reinforced allegiance to the world the immigrants had left behind in Europe. The traditions of Gymanfa ganu, or gatherings of people to sing sacred songs, and Cwrdd Mawr, great meetings for preaching and singing, persist in southeastern Ohio, even though they now occur in English rather than Welsh.

Despite their commitment to preserving their customs, the Welsh were eager to take advantage of the potential of the expanding market economy. In 1854, they pooled their resources to participate in the local charcoal iron industry on their own terms. Organizing their own corporations was a way of taking control of their lives. Eager to make money, the Welsh had little interest in engaging a broader public world. To the contrary, their money-making efforts were designed to make it possible for them to maintain their segregation from others. Like most settlers, the Welsh valued an identity constructed around religion, language, family, and custom rather than class-based notions of progress. They were interested in local conversations, not trans-local ones. Isolated in the hills of southeastern Ohio, the Welsh, according to the Methodist minister Daniel Jenkins Williams, "had but little contact with the outside world and what contact they had was forced upon them by circumstances."[2]

The Welsh preference for associating with familiar people and maintaining familiar customs was not unusual. Like earlier settlers, many European immigrants built cultural enclaves in both rural and urban areas in which they tried to blend the best of Ohio with their own traditions. Their efforts were a perpetuation of the localism that middle-class proponents of improvement had sought to overcome with everything from canals and roads to books and reform societies. Reformers found European immigrants more of a challenge because their diversity was so pronounced. Catholicism and Judaism were not Protestant denominations. German and Italian were not dialects of the English language. Moreover, European immigrants arrived too late to influence the formation of political institutions and public culture. Inevitably, they found themselves on the defensive. Asked to send their children to public schools whose teachers spoke English and advocated values different from their own, immigrants faced enormous pressure to assimilate themselves into "respectable" behavior as white, middle-class Protestant Ohioans defined it.

Many resisted doing so, largely by insisting on autonomy over the ways in which they lived their lives. Catholics asserted their right to send their children to parochial schools where they were certain to receive a Catholic education. Germans demanded the right to frequent beer gardens despite calls for temperance. Yet, as much as immigrants contested the meanings of Ohio and persisted in celebrating ethnic and religious identities, few directly challenged the dominant public culture of the state. Most wanted to be left alone to become materially comfortable and morally respectable on their own terms. In so doing, they complicated but did not compromise the essential middle-class vision of Ohio's many possibilities.

German Ohioans

"German" is a generic and anachronistic term covering a whole range of peoples who shared a common language. Describing someone as German is as meaningful as describing someone as Southern. Immigrants from different German states came to Ohio at different times for different reasons. They brought different religions, different customs, and different goals. Some were farm families. Some were artisans. Others were intellectuals. Some were Catholic, others were Protestant. The construction of a generic German identity was as much a reaction to the hostile reception immigrants received, forcing them to band together in common cause, as it was something they brought with them from Europe.

Despite their differences, German immigrants were committed to achieving respectability. They quickly acquired a reputation for neat homes and orderly farms. German influence does not stand out today because it is the norm. No one fought harder for the development of a public culture in Ohio than Germans. In many ways, the attitudes of most overlapped with those of native-born, middle-class Ohioans. Unlike many immigrants, German speakers did not want to live in isolation. They wanted to engage and improve the world around them. Proud of their heritage, they also wanted to integrate themselves within a revised public culture. Not surprisingly, Germans were the immigrants most likely to vote for Republicans.

Germans were the most important immigrant group in Ohio from the 1830s through the early 1900s. Close to half of all immigrants in 1850 and half of all foreign-born residents in 1870s were Germans. From 111,257 at mid-century, the number of German Ohioans reached 235,668 in 1890. Germans were everywhere, in rural areas, in Cleveland, and in Columbus, where a "Little Germany" flourished on the south side of town. In thirty-seven of Ohio's eighty-eight counties, Germans were the dominant ethnic group in 1850 and again in 1950. Nowhere were Germans more of a presence than in Cincinnati, where 41 percent of the population in 1900 was German.

Among the early arrivals in the 1830s was a group of well-educated and prosperous political liberals (later called the Dreissigers). Karl Reemelin, Heinrich Rodter, Stephen Molitor, and Johann Stallo became leading citizens of Cincinnati and staunch advocates of a democratic society in which institutions such as the church, aristocracy, and government would be eliminated or weakened. Reemelin arrived in Cincinnati in 1833. He made a fortune as a merchant and won election as a Democrat to the Ohio legislature and the 1850 state Constitutional Convention. Rodter and Molitor edited a Democratic newspaper, and the latter served in the legislature. A professor and a lawyer, Stallo was the author of *The General Principles of the Philosophy of Nature,* an elaboration of Georg Wilhelm Friedrich Hegel's ideas about nature as an evolutionary process involving a constant dialectic among all things. These men and others formed societies dedicated to principles of equality and justice and helping Germans improve themselves and the world around them. Conservative Catholics, who made up perhaps two-thirds of Cincinnati's German population, were uncomfortable with the activism of the liberals.

Another group of Germans appeared in the wake of the great migration of the late 1840s and early 1850s. Spurred by the revolutions of 1848 in Europe, these immigrants (called "forty-eighters") were fleeing deteriorating living standards for laborers in both urban and rural areas. They came to North America in search of social justice and freedom from economic dependency. Unlike the Dreissigers, the forty-eighters wanted strong governments to redress the balance between the rich and the poor and to protect labor. More far-reaching in their radicalism than earlier immigrants, they formed their own improvement societies and labor organizations. In the words of a national paper, they were committed to "a democratic-republican constitution that guarantees everyone prosperity, free quality education to maximize personal capabilities, and the elimination of all sources of hierarchical and privileged power."[3] While critics condemned such rhetoric as socialism, no one was calling for redistribution of property. The goals of the forty-eighters, in fact, were similar to those of many native-born Ohioans.

As early as the 1850s, Cincinnati struck many visitors as a German town. An Englishman noted that the German language "is seen inscribed on doorways, and so frequently heard spoken, that one almost feels as if he were in Hamburg."[4] Settling in large numbers north of the Miami and Erie Canal, a couple of miles from the river front where housing was cheaper, Germans were creating a distinctive community. Since Germans called the canal the Rhine, the district became known as Over-the-Rhine. The residents held concerts along the canal and, on Sundays, gathered to drink beer and socialize. They organized a Saengerfest, a festival of competitive singing, in 1849, as well as a theater and schools.

German speakers of all backgrounds rushed to join societies for their intellectual, moral, and physical improvement. The German Reading and Cultural Society was organized in 1844. Soon thereafter appeared the Turngemeinde, a branch of a German movement in support of democracy; it claimed 330 members in 1854. The Verein fur geistige Aufklarung und sociale Reform (Society for Spiritual Enlightenment and Social Reform, later abbreviated to the Freeman's Society) had five hundred to a thousand members who attended public lectures, discussed issues, exercised, and championed culture. Both organizations combined physical and moral improvement with opportunities to build community.

Germans participated enthusiastically in public debates over the great issues of the era, including labor organization, anti-Catholicism, and antislavery. They never presented a united front. The relatively affluent Dreissiger immigrants tended to be cautious when it came to direct attacks on powerful institutions. The skilled craftsmen who were the core of the forty-eighters, on the other hand, were more direct in their demands, taking a staunch stand against the Papal and Slave Powers. For their part, German Catholics stood up for their religion and their more conservative values.

The most dramatic episode in Cincinnati's mid-century cultural wars divided Germans as well as nativists. In 1853, there was a large protest against the visit of the papal nuncio Gaetano Bedini. Recent immigrants objected not just to Bedini's position in the Vatican but to his alleged role in the suppression of the Italian Revolution of 1848. On December 26, six hundred to twelve hundred men, women, and children marched on the archbishop's house, where Bedini was staying, and hanged him in effigy. Cincinnati police, some of whom probably were Irish Catholics, interrupted the procession. They fired at the crowd, beat participants, and arrested more than sixty people. One man died and around twenty were wounded. The action of the police caused a surge in support for the protestors. Some of the men arrested pressed charges against the police. The incident revealed both the depth of anti-Catholic feelings and the folly of trying to reduce Germans into one homogeneous group.

The diversity of Germans did not reassure native-born Americans. Worried about jobs and their way of life, they felt overwhelmed by the huge tide of German immigrants. Some attacked them, mocking them as "sauerkrauts" and perpetuating cultural stereotypes. A woman at Wielert's restaurant in October 1870 appreciated the music more than the meal, which "was good but a little heavy." Too many sausages! The woman was "amazed at the quantity of beer some of these people can absorb." Her husband said he had heard of men drinking "fifty to sixty steins daily." "They look jolly and well, but no wonder so many of them have not seen their feet for years."[5]

Native-born Cincinnatians tended to associate Germans with crime. They suspected that the roots of the city's thriving underworld lay in a preoccupation with alcohol and conviviality, which Germans seemed to relish. By the 1880s, saloons, restaurants, dance halls, burlesque houses, and gambling dens lined Vine Street, the city's central north-south artery in the heart of Over-the-Rhine. Near the canal, neighborhood beer gardens catering to families predominated. Further north the atmosphere was less respectable. Vine Street became notorious as a district where enforcement of ordinances and licenses was lax at best. Some Cincinnatians insisted on blaming the German working class for the moral squalor of Vine Street. "The morality of the whole city," wrote one, has been "so vitiated by the German proletarian view of things that freedom in a free country means the license to be as crooked, as injurious to society and disgusting in personal habits as the most immoral and reckless persons may choose to be. . . . [U]nless freedom makes an improvement in men and women, unless it gives Cincinnati a better, more intelligent race of human beings then this experiment in free government has failed." Dangerous and clannish "proletarians" have "made vice rampant and unblushing. There are few more licentious cities of its size in the world than Cincinnati. . . . Vienna is hardly worse."[6]

The attacks on Germans were largely misguided. Whether they were Catholics or Freethinkers, conservatives or liberals, the vast majority of Germans were committed to industry, improvement, and progress. In many ways, their "crime" was simply their ethnicity. In 1854, the editor of the *Cincinnati Enquirer* objected to a meeting of Ohio Germans in part because their "European" notions of democracy "borders on anarchy and unbridled license." What really inflamed him, however, was the "idea of men banding together, according [to] the place of their nativity or the language which they speak." "It should be the object of all foreigners who arrived in this country to become American citizens as soon as possible, and not to perpetuate their nationalities by acting together as Germans, or Irish, in political matters."[7] The more German leaders functioned within the confines of political parties, the more they toned down their rhetoric, the more acceptable they became. And it was not difficult to assimilate Germans because they were espousing what amounted to variations on the themes of democracy and development so cherished by middle-class, Protestant Ohioans. It is hardly surprising that many German immigrants quickly became prominent Cincinnatians, whether they were Reemelin in politics, Elias Kahn in meat marketing, or Frederick Rauh in insurance.

However large the number of respectable Germans, nothing could shake the reputation of Over-the-Rhine as a German enclave dedicated to licentiousness. William C. Smith, who was born in 1872, recalled accompanying his grandfather in the 1880s on weekly visits to a wine house to meet informally with a group of friends. They talked in German about "the old way of life in Germany compared to conditions in America, tales of the Schwartswald (Black Forest), ghost stories, and Old World superstitions—with a heavy seasoning of American politics." Smith witnessed the complexity of the German experience in the mixture of dialects. His grandfather "spoke the Wurtemburg dialect naturally" but had trouble with "high German."[8] Smith's German relatives impressed him with both their industry and their enjoyment of beer, cider, and sausages.

Some of Smith's fondest memories were of Cincinnati's innumerable saloons. While patrons could get mixed drinks in downtown bars, beer was the refreshment of choice in "the German quarter." Indeed, saloons in the latter area were "consecrated to the sale of beer." Catering primarily to neighborhood residents, they were packed on

Saturday nights. With an abundance of free or cheap food—spreads of cheeses, sausages, pretzels, pickles, sauerkraut, hot dogs, and sandwiches prepared by the wife or daughter of the saloon keeper—a person could relax amid good company for as little as fifteen or twenty cents. Germans knew how to enjoy the evenings, according to Smith. They tended to linger "a long time over a glass of beer, whereas Americans tossed it down and yelled for a refill."[9]

Saloons functioned as the center of social life in Over-the-Rhine and other parts of Cincinnati. Some had family rooms. They were homes away from home where people could talk with their neighbors. Not exclusively German, saloons were the antithesis of the ideal environment of middle-class Ohioans who had dedicated their lives to mastering the fine art of self-control. Germans took recreation seriously. They considered spending a day at a beer garden or a music festival a necessary part of life, essential to one's well-being. As the German visitor Franz von Loher noted in the 1840s, "The contrast between the lower-class German section and the English is especially apparent on Sunday. In the English, everything is quiet; while in the German, people crowd into beerhalls and coffeehouses on nearby hills."[10]

Germans were far more than happy beer drinkers. Many were deeply committed to revising the middle-class vision of life in Ohio, to making it more inclusive and less austere. Sensual pleasures, Germans contended, were a crucial aspect of any great civilization. Progress was more than a question of moral improvement and material development. It had to have an aesthetic dimension as well. Some influential Germans offered a romantic variation on middle-class notions, particularly in asserting the importance of art and music in fulfilling the possibilities of Ohio. In forcing changes in the nature of public culture, Germans decisively shaped Cincinnati's physical and cultural landscapes.

One of the most impressive explorations of a German alternative to the meaning of Ohio was *Cincinnati, Oder Geheimnisse Des Westens* (Cincinnati, or The Mysteries of the West), a novel by Emil Klauprecht (1815–96). Published in 1854 and 1855 by C. F. Schmidt and Company of Cincinnati, the book was an imitation of urban crime novels that had been popular in western Europe in the 1840s.

Klauprecht was a lithographer and journalist who had lived in Cincinnati since 1837. In 1864, he was appointed American consul at Stuttgart and remained there after his tour of duty was over.

The plot of *Cincinnati* revolves around a conspiracy of local businessmen and Jesuit priests to steal the inheritance of a naive young white man named Washington Filson, whose grandfather John Filson was one of the original founders of Cincinnati. Secret documents show that young Filson is the rightful owner of the land on which the city sits. Trying to get rid of Filson, the conspirators have him arrested on a charge of murder brought by a Shawnee masquerading as a German and thrown into a hellish city jail. The disgraced Filson cannot marry beautiful Johanna Steigerwald. Her father, Guenther, insists upon her engagement to John Stevens, one of the confidence men trying to ruin Filson. After hundreds of pages of clandestine meetings among a cast of characters that includes mulattoes, a Creole couple from Louisiana with a missing illegitimate child, a befuddled German Democratic newspaper editor, and the real-life former Missouri senator Thomas Hart Benton, Filson learns the truth, virtuously renounces his claim in order to spare the citizens of Cincinnati, marries Johanna, and moves with her and her family to rural Iowa.

Writing in the wake of the enormous success of Harriet Beecher Stowe's *Uncle Tom's Cabin,* Klauprecht addresses the major political questions of the 1850s, slavery and Catholicism, and denounces them. Both are institutions that inhibit the free will of human beings; both prevent people from achieving happiness; both are corrupt and degenerate and prey on innocent people in the dark. *Cincinnati* is thoroughly conventional. It reinforces the essential narrative of Ohio found in histories and novels by non-Germans: the state is a land of limitless opportunity because it is free of slavery, blacks, and, until recently, Catholics. When the Creole couple travel to the Cincinnati suburb of Mount Auburn, they find that "the very absence of Negroes had a positive effect on their mood," for they were now in a "blessed landscape cared for by happy, white country people."[11]

Senator Benton reveals the truth to Washington Filson and readers in a conclusion set on Mount Adams, a hill overlooking Cincinnati from the east. Klauprecht sets the scene by telling us, as he has before, that the city is a miracle of rapid progress. Its "fabulous history" is the "sudden transition from the savage isolation of the primeval forest to the noisy bustle of a populous metropolis." The view from Mount Adams shows the stages of human development, from the log cabins and clearings in distant rural Kentucky to the more substantial houses of Covington to Cincinnati herself, "the daughter of free labor, [which] emerged from the forehead of the giant of the primeval forest, armed at the outset with railroads and canals, with her hundreds of steamers, factories and shops for their greater service."[12]

Filson has been saved by a drifter by the name of Alligator, a man who has lived a long time without achieving much. "[H]e had accompanied [Cincinnati] through all the stages of its growth. Gradually, he had seen the red man give way to the white, the log cabins to the palaces, the keel boat to the steamer, the freight car to the locomotive, the thick primeval forest from the river to the foot of the hills give way to a broad sea of houses, he had seen the first poor settlers, whose measure of value was kept in skins of otter and deer, give way to nabobs of trade and manufacture." If Alligator represented the past, like "one of the rotten, collapsing log cabins, which remain [as] . . . relics of the old days of the first settlement," Filson "was more in harmony with the newer, stately, elegant luxury buildings of the metropolis whose heir he was."[13]

This trope of development was well worn. What is different in the German novel is the ambiguous view of the Queen City. Material success has come at the price of moral failure. Cincinnati is a bustling place full of criminals, thieves, and pork aristocrats who plot to cheat each other. The facade of the elegant Burnet House, the city's finest hotel, is a metaphor for the city as a whole. Pull backs the curtains of progress and behold a world of poverty, racism, and duplicity. No wonder Klauprecht begins his novel with a description of "Rat Town," the collection of bars and businesses near the river front that forms "the dirty seam of the splendid garment of the Queen of the West." Cincinnati is the home of a menagerie of people living amidst a "prevailing confusion of tongues."[14]

Confusion is one thing; crass materialism is another. The German characters lament the fact that Ohio is a "land of selfishness" whose most prominent inhabitants are relentlessly focused on business. Making money transcends all else for affluent, native-born whites.

By contrast, what unites "different" people in the city—that is, those who are not white Anglo-Saxons—is their concern with spirituality and morality. While praising the Dumas Hotel as the center of Cincinnati's black population and the local Underground Railroad, Klauprecht remarks that "the most attractive characteristic of the free Negro [is] that his compassion for his brothers pining in servitude does not die out in the materialistic self-gratification of his white context."[15]

Creoles and women are similarly blessed. With the notable exception of Washington Filson, it is white men who have lost their souls. At a ball, Filson defends the glories of German music against American philistines who prefer "Yankee Doodle" and African American songs to the works of Beethoven. Alas, Americans "are still a mercantile people," mired in nationalistic provincialism and bereft of aesthetic appreciation. As Johanna, full of the spirit of German romanticism, later tells Filson, American men are "so preoccupied with their plots and plans that the feeling for love, such as a German experiences, has no time for full, sensual ripeness."[16]

Cincinnati, in short, offers Germans imagining themselves as sensual romantics whose contribution to Ohio is saving native-born Americans from cold materialism and repression. Proud of his ethnic origins, Klauprecht is intent on participating in the development of the United States. He does not argue that Europe is better than North America. He still believes in the possibilities of a New World. If native-born, white males have developed Cincinnati and Ohio into a paragon of commercial progress, Germans will now refine their work, demonstrating the social value of art and music. Ambition and self-discipline alone do not make good citizens; Ohioans must fill their souls as well as their pockets.

Prime evidence in support of this thesis is Carl Steigerwald, Johanna's older brother, who has become "utterly Americanized in his customs and outlook. The endless pursuit of business in this country, in a life without any rest for the soul, without any recreation other than a fashionable concert, or a Sunday sermon alongside his [American] wife, has bestowed on his once-handsome oval face a vague, blase, indifferent expression." Becoming a "Yankee" has meant giving up singing, playing music, and drinking. Carl has lost his "fine sense" for "the beauties of art, which ennobles life." Meanwhile, his brother Wilhelm refuses to Americanize. He is a painter, of course, not a businessman, whose "principal characteristics were the love of art and friendliness." What differentiates him from Carl is "his bright soul . . . . One was the amalgamated residence of business calculation and hypocrisy; in the other, happiness and goodness of heart extended its laughter toward us."[17]

Much more than a celebration of progress, *Cincinnati* is at once a revision and an elaboration of the middle-class construction of the possibilities of Ohio. Worried that Ohio is moving beyond salvation, Klauprecht puts his faith in the marriage of Washington and Johanna, which apparently can only prosper far away from the sordid city in the pastoral plains of Iowa.

To be German and American was not to live torn between two worlds but to build connections between them. Far more than their native-born counterparts, middle- and upper-class Germans in Cincinnati sought to create public spaces, such as parks, where people could appreciate nature and feed their souls. Germans interested in target shooting organized in 1866 to purchase a hill to the west of the city which became known as Schuetzenbuckel (shooting hump or knob). In 1868, the members created a park company, which renovated a seminary building on the grounds and built bowling alleys, picnic areas, swings, and a dance pavilion. Problems of accessibility doomed the project, and the property was leased in the early 1870s and sold in the 1880s. But the Schuetzenbuckel indicated the distinctive kind of plans Germans had for Cincinnati.

As early as the 1850s, leading Cincinnatians were eager to put Germans to work improving their city. They hustled to employ a Prussian landscape designer, Adolph Strauch, who was stuck in Cincinnati because of a missed train connection. They offered him work planning the grounds of their suburban estates in Clifton, a suburb at the crest of the hill that rose north of Over-the-Rhine. Accentuating views of the Ohio River and eliminating fences, Strauch gave Clifton a pastoral feel. His local reputation secured, Strauch was hired to redesign Cincinnati's Spring Grove Cemetery. He created lakes, a promenade, and woods, making the cemetery the largest in the world and a model of its kind. Like other rural cemeteries, Spring Grove en-

couraged visitors to meditate on life and death in an aesthetically uplifting setting. According to Strauch, "A rural Cemetery should form
the most interesting of all places for contemplative recreation; and
everything in it should be tasteful, classical, and poetical."[18]

Strauch had less success when called upon to create public parks in
the years after the Civil War. Cincinnati had lagged behind in the creation of parks, partly because it was topographically compact and
partly because its citizens were more interested in commercial than
aesthetic development. In 1870, proponents called for public parks
with a now timeworn formula. Parks would make Cincinnati famous,
"enhance the value of real estate," and contribute to "the [general]
prosperity of the place." As important, they would "enlarge the ideas
of the people to develop within them a broader and higher compre-
hension of the beauties" of the world around them.[19] In short, parks
were the antithesis of Vine Street. In 1870, the movement achieved its
first success with the opening of Eden Park on Mount Adams, more
than two hundred acres overlooking the Ohio River. Strauch
smoothed out the terrain and planned a stone shelter and a Victorian
band pavilion. The most controversial feature was the lack of side-
walks. Strauch wanted visitors to walk on the grass. Unfortunately,
Eden Park, Cincinnati's only major public park, was a considerable
distance from the downtown area.

Perhaps the finest example of German influence on Cincinnati's
landscape is the city's signature image, the Tyler Davidson fountain
representing "the Genius of Water." Donated by Henry Probasco and
placed in a cleared area on Fifth Street between Vine and Main that
became known as Fountain Square, the fountain was another merger
of native-born money and German talent. Probasco was a successful
hardware merchant with a fondness for European art. When in the
late 1860s, he decided to pay for a fountain, he had it cast by a
foundry owned by Ferdinand von Mueller. The design was the work
of August von Kreling, a young artist committed to realism who had
conceived the idea in von Mueller's home in the 1840s.

A similar fusion of cultures took place in music. In the late 1850s,
Germans transformed Cincinnati's fledgling musical world into one
of the most important in the United States. So strong was the demand
for music that teacher Dwight Hamilton Baldwin started a piano

company. In 1870, some Germans organized a Saengerfest. Everywhere, it seemed, Germans were establishing singing societies and public festivals. Germans in Chillicothe supported two singing societies, the Eintracht and the Teutonia, in the late 1850s. The Eintracht survived into the 1900s, by which time, most of the singers no longer understood the German words.

The 1870 Saengerfest in Cincinnati was monumental in scale. The city constructed a two-story hall, lined with portraits of German composers, on the edge of Over-the-Rhine to accommodate three thousand singers and musicians and an audience of ten thousand. Beer and food were available on the first floor. The Saengerfest was so successful that, two years later, Theodore Thomas, a German immigrant who led an orchestra on concert tours of the United States, accepted an invitation from Maria Longworth Nichols to conduct a major musical festival in Cincinnati. Intended to be more sober than a Saengerfest, the festival did not include beer in its plans and won only moderate support among Germans. Nevertheless, the first May Festival was a smashing success. Boosters liked the festival for the same reason they liked Eden Park. It put Cincinnati on the map and elevated the tastes of its citizens. In 1875, businessman Reuben Springer donated more than half the cost of a building to house the festival. Opened three years later, the mammoth red-brick Music Hall had a spacious foyer, two balconies, and a seating capacity of four thousand.

While native-born citizens initiated and paid for the May Festival and the Music Hall, the tone and content of the events were largely German. Germans conducted the orchestra and the choruses in performances of largely German compositions. Other Cincinnati music institutions were more directly linked to Germans. In 1867, Clara Baur, who had migrated from Stuttgart in the early 1850s, established the Cincinnati Conservatory of Music, now the College-Conservatory of Music. Baur insisted on a broad, liberal education for her students. Music, she believed, could be understood only in conjunction with other arts. By the 1880s Cincinnati had an annual opera festival, and in 1895 it acquired a permanent orchestra.

German immigration to Cincinnati continued into the twentieth century, bringing wave after wave of people in search of a better life. The high point came in 1890 when Germans and their descendants constituted 57.4 percent of the city's total population. In 1917, some 127,000 people, or 34.9 percent, spoke German. In the words of a French visitor in the 1890s, "five thousand miles from the Rhine a Germany was ever and overwhelmingly present; here she drank, danced, sang, dreamt, struggled, plotted, worked, and prayed."[20]

In the process of participating in the public culture of Ohio, some Germans struggled to keep connections with their birthplaces. A coherent community was difficult to maintain, however. Proud as they were of "Deutschthum," or the sum of Germanness, it became increasingly vague. Germans were too diverse in terms of religion and politics. "Wherever four Germans gathered," observed the *Deutsche Pionier* in 1879, "they will find four different ideas." Only devotion to a common language held them together. "The German language is to the German in America what the ceremonial ritual is to the church," wrote the *Volksblatt* in 1898. "It is the outward and visible sign of recognition for all those sharing in the endeavor of bringing to bear on this country the best qualities of Germandom."[21]

Fifteen years later, the paper insisted that "whosoever abandons the German language abandons *Deutschthum.*"[22] German was offered in most Cincinnati public and parochial schools in what amounted to a bilingual language program that had originated in the 1840s. In 1900, there were around 175 German teachers in elementary schools working with 18,000 students. In some schools, students had the option of alternating half of their days between German and English teachers. This "parallel-class system" became widely known as the Cincinnati Plan. As long as children learned German, a sense of ethnic community remained alive.

In the early twentieth century, some Germans became more assertive about their contributions to the development of the United States. They wished to be recognized as critical people in the building of communities. In part, this new assertiveness reflected a more general nationalism associated with the rising power of Germany. But it was also a response to efforts to prohibit the consumption of beer and other alcoholic beverages. The foundations had been laid in the 1880s by A. H. Rattermann, the editor of the *Deutsche Pionier,* who insisted that Germans would not be second-class citizens. If they had "not come as masters, . . . neither do we wish to be serfs." Rattermann

claimed that Germans were the original pioneers of Ohio. They "before all other whites are entitled to the rights of primogeniture."[23] Rattermann's extreme views gained credence in the early 1900s.

Several Germans devoted themselves to writing histories that argued that Germans had been indispensable in the progress of Cincinnati and Ohio. In addition to Rattermann, who edited the paper and
wrote dozens of monographs until his death in 1923, they included
Heinrich H. Fick, a German teacher in the public schools, Max
Burgheim, and Gustav Bruehl. They specialized in school books and
German American histories. Fick wrote occasional poems about Germans Americans and a national textbook, *Neu und Alt,* a synthesis of
writings by Schiller, Goethe, Franklin, Lincoln, Washington, and
German Americans.

At the turn of the twentieth century, Cleveland Germans were
similarly insistent on the significance of Germans in the origins and
history of Ohio. The author of one compendium of information,
"The Significance of Germans for the Flourishing of Cleveland," insisted that "German energy and entrepreneurial spirit has done the
most to make Cleveland what it is today." He also lamented the German propensity for "envious localistic pettiness." Germans "have divided themselves" into a multitude of associations. Better to be united
in their refusal "to be robbed of their language, their customs and us-
ages," and their wish "to be good Americans while keeping their German way of life." More specifically, that two-dimensional identity
amounted to mixing high culture with the Ohio obsession with development. Industrious Germans were also committed to art and music,
to the nourishment of hearts and souls, to bringing "some light,
warmth, and joy into a meaningless effort and striving[.]" One could
be German and American simultaneously. The goal of all was to make
"the community of Cleveland . . . a place of intellectual freedom, in
the noble fulfillment of the welfare of citizens."[24]

Even in small towns, German societies highlighted the German
American heritage. Leaders of the Chillicothe club insisted that "we
must tell our children that the German people, the very mention of
whose name elicits respect from all and fright from their enemies,
have contributed enormously to culture, civilization and freedom in
America."[25] Germans in Seneca County celebrated the German vic-

tory in the Franco-Prussian War in the 1870s as they had the centennial of the birth of Friedrich Schiller in 1859. But they also marked the Fourth of July and saw no conflict between honoring their German origins and their American citizenship. They were eager to bring Christmas trees and other German customs into their middle-class homes.

World War I initially intensified this resurgence in German pride. When the U.S. went to war with Germany in 1917, German citizens found themselves on the defensive in the face of mounting attacks on their patriotism as Americans. The weekly *Freie Press* proudly declared in April 1917: "We shall not become Englishmen, and we shall continue to cherish our memories but with steadfast devotion we shall stand by our country which will need us now more than ever. We shall watch over her internal peace, and we shall make every sacrifice which is demanded of us." But the war destroyed any public sense of a community. Literally forced to demonstrate their loyalty to the U.S., German Ohioans had to move any evidence of their ethnicity from the public into the private realm. Wrote the *Christliche Apologete* emphatically: *"[H]enceforth all discussion of the war and its justification must stop. Every American owes his government loyalty and obedience."*[26]

Germans' efforts to prove their loyalty, however, did not stem a flood of hostility. Insisting on complete Americanization, nativists were no longer willing to tolerate the existence of parallel loyalties within their larger community. The Cincinnati school board stopped the bilingual program; the public library removed all German books; the city council changed German street names to English ones; and there was a general intimidation of all peoples associated with the "Huns." The conductor of the Cincinnati Symphony Orchestra, Ernst Kunwald, an Austrian citizen whose sympathies lay with the Central Powers, was arrested as an alien and imprisoned near Dayton. Two decades later, when Kunwald emigrated from Nazi Germany, he lamented that "I got into trouble in Cincinnati for being too German, but I got into trouble in Berlin for not being German enough."[27]

Fearful Germans stopped speaking their language in public, changed names, signs, and labels into English, broke up ethnic organizations, and discontinued German newspapers. Many offered public testimonials to their patriotism. The pressures of war removed the German stamp on the public culture of Cincinnati in the late 1910s and 1920s. The circulation of the *Freie Press,* the only survivor among Cincinnati's many German general-interest newspapers, dropped from 23,342 in 1919 to 12,318 in 1930. The number of German-language periodicals fell from fifteen to six in the same period. Without the means of exchanging ideas in print, German Ohioans could no longer participate in the public sphere as Germans.

In the early 1920s, people continued to think of Over-the-Rhine as a German enclave. At the huge outdoor Findlay Market, customers heard German accents and bought cabbages, pickles, sausages, cheeses, and meat for sauerbraten and wiener schnitzel. But the era of self-conscious, public ethnic identification was over. Teachers, barbers, businessmen, and vendors stopped speaking German. Organizations withered and died. Above all, German families were moving out of the downtown area into suburbs such as Price Hill and Cheviot. In the second half of the twentieth century, Over-the-Rhine was a neighborhood of new immigrants, white and black migrants from the South. Only the name and Music Hall remain as tangible symbols of the extent to which from the 1850s until the 1910s, Cincinnati was a German city.

Jewish Ohioans

Isaac Meyer Wise arrived in Cincinnati in 1854. A native of Steingrub in Bohemia, he was thirty-five years old and had been in the United States since 1846. Ambitious, confident, and vain, Wise had accepted the position of rabbi of Bene Yeshurun, a Jewish congregation that had been struggling for more than a decade. Wise had been living in Albany, New York, where his efforts to make Jewish rituals more respectable had led one congregation to fire him and another to organize in support of him. When Cincinnati Jews asked Wise to consider becoming their rabbi, he demanded a unanimous election, a lifetime contract at a high salary, and six months to move. When the congregation of Bene Yeshurun agreed to pay him fifteen hundred dollars per year during "good behavior," Wise accepted and inaugurated a tenure in Cincinnati that would have a profound impact on all American Jews.

Wise agreed to the offer in part because he knew that the people were "young and aspiring and not yet cast into a fixed mold." He would "go to Cincinnati, start a new weekly journal, give Judaism a new and powerful impetus, and avenge myself for the good of humanity on the narrow religious bigots, so that they will think of me for a century."[28] And that is exactly what he did. When Wise took over Bene Yeshurun, the congregation consisted of 180 members worshiping in a traditional fashion with little pomp or ceremony. When he died in 1900, there were close to 400 Jews in an elaborate temple with a fine choir and organ. Cincinnati's Plum Street synagogue opened in August 1866. Built at a cost of $263,525, it had thirteen domes and two minarets that gave it a Middle Eastern flavor. More important, its congregation was thoroughly reformed. The men worshiped with their heads uncovered, the ritual was American, and the services were held primarily in English rather than German.

Wise was one of the founders of Reform Judaism, an effort to Americanize the religion by making it respectable and decorous. In 1873, a convention of more than thirty Jewish congregations established the Union of American Hebrew Congregations with the purpose of encouraging an American Judaism; its headquarters would remain in Cincinnati until after World War II. One of the organization's first major projects was the founding of Hebrew Union College in 1875, which became the premier Jewish institution of higher learning in the United States. By the 1880s, when Wise began ordaining graduates as Reform rabbis, Cincinnati was the most important city in American Judaism, the center of education and publishing.

With Max Lilienthal, elected rabbi of Bene Israel in 1855, Wise immersed himself in local affairs, especially those relating to education and social welfare. Proud of their religious and ethnic heritage, the two men had no desire to emphasize that heritage at the expense of setting themselves apart from respectable citizens. To the contrary, they wished to highlight the extent to which Judaism qualified them to be part of a larger community dedicated to material progress and moral improvement. The *Israelite* was delighted in 1869 to describe the intersection of Eighth and Plum Streets as "the most striking monument of civil and religious liberty in this or any other country." With four houses of worship—a Catholic cathedral, a Unitarian church, a Presbyterian church, and a Jewish synagogue—on its four corners, it was a place "to which the world at large can offer no parallel, no precedent, no comparison."[29] The Plum Street synagogue was a tribute to Cincinnati as well as Judaism.

Wise and Lilienthal achieved such success in forming a kind of middle way for Jews in large part because they shared the ambitions of the members of their congregations. No German speakers were more eager to integrate themselves into Ohio than Jews. In 1850, Jews numbered 2,800, or about 2.43 percent of Cincinnati's total population. By 1900, there were 16,000, or 4.9 percent; and by 1910, 28,000, or 7.7 percent. A similar pattern emerged in Cleveland and Columbus. In 1880, about 3,500 of Cleveland's population of 159,404 were Jewish, mainly German; by 1920, 75,000 of 796,841 were Jewish, an increase reflecting a huge influx of eastern Europeans in the last decades of the nineteenth century and the first decade of the twentieth century.

Whatever the city, German Jews found employment in a variety of occupations. Some worked as peddlers and clerks. Others became successful merchants. In Cleveland, Jews such as Jacob Landesman, Felix Hirschheimer, Kaufman Koch, Moritz Joseph, Alex Printz, and Joe Biederman dominated the clothing trade, while others worked in tobacco, liquor, and dry goods. Jews made up a substantial portion of the laborers in the clothing trade. They also owned banks and managed public utility corporations. German Jews in Cleveland formed voluntary societies and fraternal organizations whose purposes were friendship, mutual aid, and the preservation of cultural traditions. While few Jews showed up on the boards of prominent Cleveland organizations, some were well-known members of the community as a whole. As in Cincinnati and Columbus, German Jews worked hard to fit in.

Martin A. Marks exemplified this ambition. A Cleveland banker and insurance executive, Marks was active in his temple as well as in several local organizations, most especially the chamber of commerce. He seemed to have struck a balance between his religious and civic identities. Like many of his peers, Marks wanted to show the world that Jews were respectable people. He admired Cleveland rabbi Moses J. Gries, a graduate of Hebrew Union College who would become his brother-in-law, for improving relations between Jews and Gentiles. Gries was committed to Americanizing Tifereth Israel, making it less

German and orthodox. He intended a new ninety-nine-thousand-dollar temple to demonstrate the congregation's choice "to omit symbols which proclaim the oriental and the foreign." While the "temple is none the less Jewish," Gries wanted its "appearance . . . [to] proclaim to all, that we are not a people in the midst of the nation, that we are not foreigners, nor children of the East, but that we are Americans . . . and all our hopes and happiness are in the occident." Thanks to the rabbi's efforts, Marks believed, "a more exalted opinion is held of the Jews and Judaism." A Christian-Jewish meeting at the new temple showed that "the difference between the Jew and Gentile is not so great after all," something that was "worth to our people the price that our Temple has cost."[30]

Anti-Semitism was less intense in Ohio than in other parts of the United States—or at least it rarely was public. As late as the 1870s, Jews in Cleveland seemed not to notice much in the way of prejudice against them. That changed in the next few decades, as eastern Europeans flooded into the city. Well-established German Jews were often appalled by the behavior of the new immigrants, whose religious orthodoxy as much as their customs seemed to accentuate their differentness. The premium among Germans throughout Ohio had been on what they shared with other Americans. Now, German Jews worried that the behavior of immigrants would stigmatize them. Martin Marks spoke for many when he complained that "no matter what one Jew does all Jews are blamed for it" and urged new arrivals "to overcome this prejudice . . . by becoming part of the country itself."[31]

Historians attribute the relative acceptance of German Jews in nineteenth-century Ohio to their eagerness to become part of the larger public community. The Jewish vision of Ohio as a promised land rested on four basic ideas, according to Jonathan Sarna: economic success; free and equal interaction with non-Jews; an obligation to work for improvement "as good citizens and as good Jews"; and a mission to "develop a new kind of Judaism, . . . one better suited than traditional Judaism to the new American milieu." They believed, in the words of an early Jewish settler, the Englishman Joseph Jonas, that "the Almighty will give his people favour in the eyes of all nations, if they only conduct themselves as good citizens in a moral and religious point of view."[32] Few people more enthusiastically embraced a larger vision of Ohio as a place where economic and moral progress met than German Jews. Reform Jews were not only contributing to the greater glory of their religion in establishing beautiful temples, schools, and colleges and in reforming their rituals, they were adding to the reputation of Ohio and its major cities. Reform Judaism and boosterism had a symbiotic relationship. They both reinforced the cause of respectability.

The appearance of thousands of ragged eastern Europeans, speaking foreign languages and worshiping in orthodox fashions, was embarrassing to Ohio's German Jews. The immigrants' adherence to old ways amounted to a reversal in the history of both their people and their state. Well-established Jews zealously sought to assimilate the newcomers. Sympathetic to the plight of eastern European Jews, who were fleeing not only economic hardship but waves of pogroms, established Jewish leaders raised money for their support. Rabbi Wise famously threw his wallet on the floor of the temple as a visible symbol of his commitment.

The new immigrants, according to the *American Israelite* in 1881, were without decent clothes or any idea of how to proceed in their new country. They were "queer-looking people" who naturally aroused the resentment of potential neighbors in Cincinnati's tenements. They had to "become good citizens of this country . . . or we have no use for them." They had to be progressive or they would "do considerable damage to the good reputation" of other Jews. Ideally, they were intelligent people who could be remade by public schools. "Let every immigrant at once declare his intention to become a citizen of the United States and take out papers to that effect, to impress him at once with the idea that he is in America to be an American and a free man, and that for the rest of his life his interest and his prosperity are closely connected with the American people and government."[33]

In Cleveland, eastern European Jews benefitted greatly from networks and organizations established by their predecessors. Congregating in the Haymarket and near Broadway Avenue, they often found work as peddlers, tailors, carpenters, and grocers. But their class set them apart from many Cleveland Jews. Their behavior was less respectable, and they did not seem to care about what Americans thought of them. Orthodox in their religious practices, many found Zionism (the effort to found a Jewish state) and socialism appealing. By 1913, Cleveland had two chapters of Doale Zion (Workers of Zion), a fact that caused considerable alarm among Jews and Gentiles who considered themselves respectable. Middle- and upper-class Jews in Ohio cities had no interest in radical reform of the American system, let alone the establishment of a Jewish state. They had committed themselves to the U.S., to Ohio in particular, as the place for the fulfillment of their spiritual and material ambitions. Zionism and socialism were alien concepts.

This conflict among Jews was not limited to the big cities of Cleveland and Cincinnati. Columbus's population increased dramatically at the turn of twentieth century, reaching 181,511 by 1910. Columbus was unusual in that it had a relatively small immigrant population; only 9 percent of its citizens in 1910 had been born outside the United States. Still, the same split developed between German Jews who were well established by the 1880s and newer Jewish immigrants from eastern Europe. The former, including the family of Simon Lazarus, whose men's clothing store was thriving by the time of the Civil War, were interested in Reform Judaism and in adjusting themselves to a social life that paralleled the middle-class existence of their Gentile neighbors. The latter, however, many of whom were peddlers and their families, wanted little to do with assimilation, at least in the first generation. Rejecting Reform, in the words of one historian, they "huddled close together and sought to recreate in their New World neighborhood—even in the heart of the midwestern United States—as much of the Old World as possible."[34]

The emergence of eastern European Jews in Ohio cities in the 1880s, 1890s, and early 1900s was a substantial challenge to the dominance of middle-class expectations. Like their Catholic counterparts, eastern European Jews were not as interested in assimilation as they were in the preservation and extension of the way of life they had brought with them. Ohio had not had such a huge influx of people with less commitment to public culture since its first decades. For many of the new immigrants, their identity as Americans, let alone Ohioans, was not nearly as important as their religious and ethnic identities. They would contest the meanings of life in the state in ways that went well beyond anything imagined by the vast majority of German speakers, whether they were Catholic, Protestant, Jewish, or atheist.

The New Immigrants

The rapid emergence of the United States as the most powerful industrialized nation in the world in the late nineteenth century attracted hundreds of thousands of people from all over Europe and Asia to North America. Many headed for the cities and prairies of the American Midwest. By 1900, immigrants from Scandinavia and southern and eastern Europe had made states such as Wisconsin and Minnesota and cities such as Chicago and Pittsburgh more profoundly multicultural than at any other time in their history. While Ohio received more than its share of these new immigrants, they were disproportionately clustered in the northeastern part of the state.

Cleveland, by 1910 the sixth largest city in the country, was in the middle of an astounding period of growth. Its population increased at a rate of roughly 40 percent per decade. In many ways, Cleveland had surpassed Cincinnati as Ohio's most important city. The abundance of nearby natural resources such as coal, iron, and oil and its location on the main railroad route from Chicago and the West to New York City and the Atlantic fueled Cleveland's expansion. The construction of steel mills and other factories, especially in the 1860s and 1870s, transformed the city from a commercial to an industrial center and created a large number of jobs for both unskilled and skilled workers.

It was the possibility of work that brought immigrants to Cleveland and other northern Ohio cities such as Youngstown, Akron, and Toledo. They sought security and stability far from the dislocations of economic and social change in Europe. Coming to America was rooted in a desire to improve their standard of living; few, however, saw migration as a rejection of their way of life.[35] As was the case throughout the northern United States, most of the immigrants who arrived in Cleveland and its environs between the Civil War and the adoption of strenuous federal restrictions on immigration in 1924 were from central, southern, and eastern Europe. Far less familiar with the Protestant, mostly British values of Ohio's most influential citizens, far less interested in assimilating than most Germans, these new immigrants did not quickly blend into the state's population and tended to resist any efforts to force them to change culturally. They did not fit into an existing place called Ohio as well as most Germans did. Indeed, by the early 1900s, the German predilection for beer and revelry that alarmed some Cincinnatians in the 1850s would seem tame by comparison with the behavior of the new immigrants.

As in Cincinnati, Cleveland's mostly Protestant middle-class citizens were congregating in new neighborhoods some distance from industry and commerce. The wealthiest, or at least the most ostentatious, lived in the great mansions that lined Euclid, Superior, and Prospect Streets, the boulevards of Cleveland's East Side. Immigrants, meanwhile, lived in the far less opulent neighborhoods that grew up around the factories in which the men worked. There they formed organizations that not only perpetuated their way of life but were sometimes modeled on the villages in which they had grown up. Churches, clubs, saloons, coffeehouses, and aid societies were centers of cultural life. Providing more than entertainment, they offered places to gather away from cramped apartments. Three out of four people in Cleveland had been born outside of the United States or were the children of immigrants. More than forty different languages were spoken in the city in the early twentieth century. No wonder people craved the familiar.

In the late 1800s, there were three Polish neighborhoods in Cleveland: Warszawa, centered on Tod and Forman Avenues; Krakowa, at Marcelline and Grant; and Jackowa, near Tod and Francis. In these neighborhoods, the key figures were the priests, saloon keepers, and politicians who mediated between the city government and immigrants. Croatians such as Paul and Peter Kekic and Janko Popovic and Poles such as Michael Kniola combined ownership of local cafes and businesses with work as interpreters and advisers about jobs and homes.

In 1881, the Slovene Joseph Turk settled near the Newburgh steel mills. He and other Slovenes lived in a neighborhood they called Chicken Yard on Marble Avenue. They saved money and built houses in the east eighties. Turk did especially well. In the 1890s, he owned a grocery store and three boardinghouses. He opened a saloon and a boarding house near the Otis Steel Company, around which a Slovene community was flourishing. Turk was able to give saloons to his children and expand into the restaurant business. He survived the depression of 1893, moved to Euclid, grew grapes, sold wine, and opened yet another saloon. Slovenes arriving in Cleveland were sent directly to his saloon, where he often lent them money, helped them get settled, and urged them to become citizens so that they could vote for candidates who would help their community.

Consumed with survival, few immigrants thought much about being citizens of Ohio. The state was part of America, a place they thought of largely in terms of its economic potential and local autonomy. The most important government in their lives was the city government because it directly impinged on their lives, for good or ill. Many had no intention of residing permanently in the U.S.; they had come only to earn money. They did not necessarily identify themselves as Americans, let alone as Ohioans. Religion was much more important. Immigrants committed themselves deeply to local churches because they were community centers, familiar places of refuge in a strange environment. In the early 1900s, a Roman Catholic church, the Sacred Heart of Jesus, was owned by Polish families and offered a mass in Polish. Priests such as the Croatian Nicholas Grskovic urged immigrants to remain loyal to their traditions. Grskovic organized a school in 1910 that was dedicated to the preservation of the Croatian language and traditions. Meanwhile, newspapers in a variety of languages and dozens of social organizations proliferated.

One of the largest ethnic communities in Cleveland was Slavic. It included at least a dozen distinct nationalities, each with its own permutations. Historians have placed Cleveland's Slavs into three categories: East Slavs (Great Russians, Carpatho-Russians, Byelorussians, and Ukranians), West Slavs (Poles, Czechs, Moravians, Slovaks, and Lustian Sorbs), and South Slavs (Bulgarians, Serbs, Slovenes, Croatians, Macedonians, and Montenegrins).[36] Where East Slavs were mostly members of the Orthodox Church who wrote in the Cyrillic alphabet, West Slavs and many of the South Slavs were Roman Catholics who used the Latin alphabet. Culturally, the former were heavily influenced by the Byzantine Empire, while the latter had lived in the Austro-Hungarian Empire. Because of these differences, Slavs tended to live in small enclaves of like-minded people who were often deeply hostile toward other Slavs. Poles and Ukranians, for example, were not the best of friends. Nonetheless, taken as a whole, Slavs were the largest group of new immigrants in Cleveland. In 1918, 46,296 Czechs, 6,000 Croatians, 19,000 Slovenes, 18,977 Slovaks, and 49,000 Poles lived in the city.

Six Hungarian neighborhoods flourished in Cleveland by 1920. One of the earliest was on the West Side. Theodor Kuntz, a native of Metzenseten, worked in the 1870s for a company that made cabinets for sewing machines until he bought the company and hired around twenty-five hundred skilled craftsmen, largely from his home area. They and their families built a community centered on Lorain and Abbey Avenues. By the early 1900s, both a Protestant and a Catholic congregation were in the area as well as the Hungarian Self-Culture Society. The residents read Hungarian-language newspapers and socialized together near their workplace. The only city in the world with a larger concentration of Hungarians was Budapest.

Throughout the twentieth century, Hungarians retained a strong sense of ethnic identity. Even as they adjusted to life in Cleveland, participating as citizens, they also continued to honor cultural traditions. The community of Buckeye on the East Side was an insular one. Hungarians were relatively content with a "parallel existence." They understood life in Ohio through "a powerful ethnic prism" in which "families, relatives, and friends" were the dominant models of behavior. And thus they were able to thwart the process of assimilation and keep "Hungarian ethnic values, preferences, and needs . . . preeminent."[37]

The other great immigrant community in Cleveland at the turn of the twentieth century consisted of Italians. Half of the Italian immigrants came from ten villages in southern Italy and found work in fruit and vegetable markets or restaurants. The focal point of Italian life in Cleveland was the parish of Saint Anthony of Padua. Established in 1887, it acquired a church on Carnegie Avenue in 1904, which housed not only religious services but fraternal and sororal organizations. More than fifty such societies flourished in Cleveland in the early 1900s. The heart of the Italian neighborhoods was Little Italy, located between 199th and East 125th Streets. Its residents worked in the clothing and construction industries. The more than twenty thousand Italians who lived in Cleveland in 1918 were the most segregated people in the city—by choice. According to one woman, language, poverty, and "the desire to escape the well of misunderstanding" were responsible for their isolation. "We Italians like to live with people from our own province who speak our own dialect, and will help us if we get into trouble," explained another resident.[38]

Immigrants in Cleveland and other industrial cities emphasized their ties with the world they had abandoned for life in the United States. Their neighborhoods were bastions of nationalism. "All the progress which our Slovak people have enjoyed originated in the diligent work of the faithful," proclaimed one broadside from a congregation linking religion and ethnicity. "Slovaks! You must realize that the founding of a church advances the Slovak name and the cultural progress of the Slovak people, and thus should thrill the heart of every true Slovak."[39]

While researching a book on Slavic migration to the United States, Emily Greene Balch encountered an unnamed Polish priest who bristled at Balch's use of the word "Americans": "You English constantly speak as if you were the only Americans, or more Americans than others. . . . There is no reason for the English to usurp the name of American. They should be called Yankees if anything. That is the name of English-Americans. There is no such thing as an American nation. Poles form a nation, but the United States is a country, under one government, inhabited by representatives of different nations." The priest rejected the idea that the U.S. would experience "amalgamation, one race composed of many. The Poles, Bohemians, and so forth, remain such, generation after generation." He did favor one language, "*either English or some other*," but saw no reason "why people should not also have another language."[40]

Immigrants tended to be advocates of what is now called diversity, or multiculturalism, because they were on the defensive. Middle-class Protestants had defined the possibilities of Ohio on their own terms. For them, personal and public identities overlapped in a close relationship between the values of their religion and the values of their state. To be a good citizen was to be a good Protestant, and vice versa. In order to preserve their values, Catholics and members of other religions—coming after a quasi-official story of Ohio was in place, outnumbered except within their own enclaves—had to insist on separate private and public identities and a high degree of local control over schools, law enforcement, moral regulations, and culture in general. If being a good citizen meant sharing the values of good Protestants, they had either to become good Protestants or argue for Ohio as a collection of different communities. The latter entailed complicating public conversation with multiple perspectives.

Nothing focused the tension between personal and public identities more than religion. German Jews who arrived in the state before the 1870s resolved the dilemma, although imperfectly, by reforming their religion to reflect middle-class values. Patriotism and piety were two sides of the same coin. Being Jewish and being American were utterly compatible to Isaac Wise. Questions about the use of alcohol and religious education could be accommodated by people of good faith. The important thing was to emphasize what Ohioans had in common, which was a commitment to the material and moral development of mankind.

The new immigrants were not so sanguine about blending religious and civic values. They recognized the existence of fundamental differences between most Protestant denominations and Roman Catholicism, Judaism, and Orthodox religions. The latter groups tended to emphasize ritual more than language. The essence of Catholicism lay in the sacraments and the performance of holy obligations. Organized hierarchically rather than democratically, from the pope down through bishops and parish priests, Catholicism revolved around the rituals of the mass celebrated within a community that united people all over the world. For many Protestants, on the other hand, religion centered on individual conversion. Faith proceeded from within, from a personal decision to accept Christ. They reached this point through reading the Bible, listening to sermons, talking with others, and wrestling with their consciences. With conversion came a responsibility to spread the good news to others and to work tirelessly to reform one's own behavior and that of others.

Immigrant Catholics were hardly against improvement. And they were perfectly capable of reading and thinking on their own. Their world, however, stressed not the perfectibility of human beings but their integration into an interdependent Christian community. Part of the power of Catholicism was that it accepted human failure and offered forgiveness for sin.

Some Protestants believed that Roman Catholicism, with its priests, Latin mass, and more ambiguous attitude toward sin, was fundamentally anti-American. How could people pledged to obey an Italian pope behave like republican citizens? The divergence in church architecture reflected a divergence in values. As soon as possible, Catholics built elaborate churches, replete with elegant stained-glass windows, richly decorated altars, and dramatic heights and columns. While many Protestant congregations spared little expense in the construction of their churches, they tended to prefer less ornate buildings. They believed that architecture should not divert members from their primary focus on their own souls. Catholic churches, on the other hand, created sacred space that humbled human beings in the presence of God and brought them together to share communion, baptism, confirmation, marriage, and death.

"The Americans looked upon us with distrust or rather aversion," recalled a Czech woman years after her arrival. "Later I learned it was only our customs—our bare feet and handkerchiefs over our heads—that they objected to."[41] Her comment suggests a romanticization of the reaction, that at some level American hostility extended only to superficial details. Not only did she not think of herself as an "American," she did not comprehend the importance of those outward signs. The clothes she wore, the smell of her food, the language she spoke, the way she worshiped were the stuff of her identity. By the last third of the nineteenth century, nothing was more critical in the public conversation Ohioans had about who they were and what they were becoming than the extent to which difference was a good thing. While Germans had sought mainly to revise the middle-class vision of the many possibilities of Ohio, later immigrants seemed to ignore it altogether. Arguments about details quickly escalated into major contests over the power to define what it meant to live in Ohio.

Standard Oil Company's No. 1 Refinery in Cleveland in 1889. (Courtesy of The Western Reserve Historical Society, Cleveland, Ohio)

6

Contesting Ohio

—

SOME PEOPLE were nostalgic about rural life between the Civil War and World War I. In his memoir of growing up in northwestern Ohio, Howard E. Good recalled the impact of improvements in transportation and communication. No sooner had his family acquired a Rural Free Delivery address, which meant that mail arrived at their home instead of a post office, than they got a telephone. Overall, however, it was the continuity of life that Good remembered. The rhythms of the seasons dictated the nature of life. Sarah Flynn Penfield and her sister Martha claimed that they had been nearly self-sufficient on their farm in southeastern Ohio. They raised hogs, cattle, and sheep, as well as acres of sorghum, corn, and vegetables, and used the money they got in rent or payment for wool or meat to buy cloth, sugar, tobacco, coffee, and cheese at a general store or from peddlers.

Farm life was hard but rewarding. Women bore children, tended them, prepared food, and cared for the house. Washing clothes involved bringing water in from a pump and heating it over the stove. They made butter, supervised chickens, and collected eggs. In addition, they grew vegetables, canned them, and made pickles and relishes. They prepared their own soap and sewed their own clothes. In 1888, Margaret Dow Gebby, a farm woman in Logan County, sold $130.41 worth of eggs and butter, or 21 percent of her household's cash expenditures for the year of $615.51.[1] Meanwhile, men planted, tended, and harvested crops, dealt with the larger animals, repaired buildings and machinery, and handled most of the outside business of the household. From an early age, men also enjoyed much greater physical freedom than women because their business took them away

from home. Wheeler McMillen, a journalist and proponent of agricultural reform who grew up near Ada, remembered his father as "always neat, modestly dignified, companionable but never effusive," a
representative of "the independent, fair-minded, and intelligent
American of his time who was then making a living tilling the soil."[2]

Rural life was more than labor. Sarah Penfield recalled many diversions, including dances and parties at schools and churches. Martha
described "entertainment" as "mostly walking, climbing hills, berry-
ing, things like that." "'Company' at our house and in a good many
other farm homes was almost commonplace," wrote Good. "Company meant deluxe meals, with ham or chicken—often both—and a
bewildering array of vegetables, fruits, relishes, and desserts."[3] Nothing was more important than a sense of neighborhood defined by relationships built around family. People depended on each other. Their
goals were simple: to marry, have children, and maintain their own
household.[4]

While the texture of rural life stressed continuity, people were very
much aware of the world beyond their farms and villages. They pe-
rused newspapers, books, and catalogs. A few read more widely, including Frank Spurrier, one of the hired men at the McMillen farm,
who gave Wheeler a copy of *Paradise Lost* by John Milton for his
eighth birthday.[5] Some rural people joined the Patrons of Husbandry,
or the Grange. Organized in 1867, the Grange became something of
a social and educational institution. Its meetings and publications
kept people current with developments in technology, politics, and
culture. The Grange welcomed women as well as men as members. In
1875, there were at least nine hundred local chapters in Ohio. Not
everyone valued the Grange. Neither Sarah Penfield nor Howard
Good remembered it as being particularly important in the lives of
their families.[6] On the other hand, Wheeler McMillen's parents were
"faithful members of Pleasant Hill Grange Number 598 at
Huntersville." Thirty families, constituting half the neighborhood,
gathered most Tuesday nights to hear lectures on a range of issues, including political matters.[7] McMillen roundly dismissed the notion
that farm families were isolated. Indeed, all the memoirs of farm life
in this period indicate a strong degree of public conversation, whether
at Grange meetings, school events, church services, or via the phone.

Although these stories were idealized tales told by older people about their youths, they testify to the importance of family and local relationships in helping people deal with one of the most difficult and divisive periods in the history of the state. The memoirs stressed continuity while all around was change. Even though nine of ten farm families owned their land, children increasingly left home to find work in cities. The number of rural Ohioans fell from 83 percent in 1860 to 52 percent in 1900. Rural or urban, most Ohioans in the late nineteenth and early twentieth centuries believed that their world was reconfiguring itself overnight. Cities were becoming more complicated. Industry was becoming more powerful. Governments were becoming more activist. National organizations, such as labor unions and professional societies, were becoming more prominent. Individuals seemed less important. Producing things mattered less than consuming things. A person born in Ohio in the 1850s who lived into her eighties died in a world filled with things she never could have imagined as a child, from refrigerators and telephones to radios and cars.

Such overwhelming change inspired reactions ranging from pride to alienation. It also raised a question of justice. Not all Americans benefited from the transformation of their society, and those who did experienced its impact unequally. Public disagreements over issues such as education, temperance, collective bargaining, and corporate regulation allowed Americans to address a larger question of fairness. Personal considerations rooted in ethnicity, class, race, and religion dictated the kinds of tales people told about the significance of change. Many criticized change and blamed it on corporations and greed. Whatever story they told, Ohioans wanted to define the possibilities of life in the state and the nation on their own terms.

Celebrating Change

On January 10, 1910, the Ohio Society of New York honored Wilbur and Orville Wright for their contributions to aviation history. After dinner, Wilbur spoke briefly and with tongue in cheek about the dominance of Ohio men in the United States. He noted that "it is an old story that any time in the last forty years a man might go down to Washington and have at least three chances out of five at finding an

Ohio man living in the White House. It has got to be such an old story to have an Ohio man as one of the candidates in our Presidential elections, that such elections have lost some of their thrill, and the people are beginning to demand something more exciting." The same story prevailed "all over the world." Ohio men were everywhere. They were dependable; they were a blend of the best features of the different sections of the country. "Ohio stands at the gateway between the East and the West," Wright said, "and her sons possess the boundless energy and enthusiasm of the West, and combine it with the salt of conservatism of the East. The result is a combination that carries Ohio men to victory everywhere." Ohioans were both progressive and respectable. "If I were giving a young man advice as to how he might succeed in life," concluded Wright, "I would say to him, pick out a good father and mother, and begin life in Ohio."[8]

Wright was semi-serious, but many of his contemporaries actually believed that there was something peculiar about Ohio. Look at the great inventors the state has produced, they would say. Never mind that Thomas Edison, who was born in Milan, moved to Michigan when he a child and worked most of his adult life in New Jersey. Or that Wilbur Wright was born in Indiana. Or that when New York–born John D. Rockefeller's family moved to Cleveland in the 1850s, he was old enough to look for a job. Or that Charles Kettering lived mostly in laboratories that could have been almost anywhere in the U.S. The point was that Ohio was fertile ground for the production of a peculiarly American form of genius.

Ohio's success stories were democratic heroes who proved that with the right upbringing and the right attitude, anyone could make it in the United States. Eminently practical, they tackled everyday problems. Their inventions benefited ordinary people. Edison, "the wizard of Menlo Park," was supposedly responsible for electric light, phonographs, motion pictures, and a host of other improvements. His laboratory was a model of American technology: a group of often slovenly men working raucously but purposefully to make life richer and easier. Edison once famously remarked to an assistant who was easily sidetracked into interesting intellectual problems: *"We can't be spending time that way!* We have got to keep working up things of commercial value—that is what this laboratory is for. We can't be like the old German professor who as long as he can get his black bread and beer is content to spend his whole life studying the fuzz on a bee!"[9]

Ohio's inventors were difficult people whose achievements often were collaborative. Yet the image of the untutored solitary tinkerer, dependent not on theory but on determination, committed not to intellectual achievements but to practical inventions, sustained the power of the middle-class vision of Ohio's progress in an era that saw the triumph of corporations and consumerism. The notions of hard work, self-control, and the symbiosis of moral and material progress that had seemed so liberating in the 1830s and 1840s were now described as old-fashioned. Ohio's inventors were both spokesmen for and symbols of an old order. Despite the fact that they participated in the corporate and consumer revolutions, they represented the idea that individual producers were still relevant in a world of national organizations. It is the utilitarian dimension of their ambition that resonates most strongly a century later in a much more cynical era, the conviction that individual progress led inevitably to collective progress. Ohio did not nurture Mozarts and Michelangelos or Shakespeares and Rembrandts. Rather, its glory lay in the ordinariness of its citizens, its pride in the fact that it was typically American. Look for the golden age of Ohio not in museums or palaces but in the stuff of everyday life: in light bulbs and automobiles, in airplanes and steel.

Charles Kettering, who was born in 1876 in Loudonville, about seventy miles northeast of Columbus, graduated from The Ohio State University and settled in Dayton, working, in succession, for the National Cash Register Company, the Dayton Electric Laboratories Company (Delco), which he helped found, and General Motors Corporation. His inventions, which often resulted from collaborations in corporate laboratories, included the self-starter, the high-compression engine, and four-wheel brakes, all of which made operating a car simple and convenient. Renowned for his pragmatism, staunchly defending free enterprise until his death in 1958, Kettering stood for what had become traditional values. Kettering made a fetish of hard work. He liked to call cost the "first dimension" of engineering. He thought experts never accomplished much because they knew too much and were too cautious. No one ever achieved anything who did not risk failure, he observed. Success was less a matter of intelligence than persistence. "If Thomas A. Edison, the Wright brothers, and Henry Ford had taken I.Q. tests, they wouldn't have gotten in the bleachers," he once remarked. Good inventors were "pliers and screwdriver [men], not . . . theory [men]." They also responded to people's desires. They gave customers what they wanted. The prosperity of the automobile industry was "due alone to the fact that an American is never satisfied."[10]

Wilbur and Orville Wright appeared to be everything Kettering admired: supremely practical men blessed with common sense. The sons of Milton Wright, a bishop of the United Brethren Church, and his wife, Susan Koerner Wright, Wilbur was born in Indiana in 1867 and Orville in Dayton in 1871. Early success as bicycle manufacturers allowed the brothers to devote themselves to their growing interest in flight. Starting in the late 1890s, they experimented with gliders, first on the shores of Lake Michigan and then at the Outer Banks of North Carolina. Years of work climaxed on December 17, 1903, when Orville piloted a rudimentary airplane over a distance of 120 feet in twelve seconds. Three attempts later, Wilbur stayed aloft for almost a minute and covered 853 yards. The brothers announced their achievement to their father in a terse telegram: "Success," wrote Orville, "inform press. [H]ome Christmas."[11] Although the Wright brothers became world famous, they were difficult, litigious men who had trouble accepting the fact that their considerable achievement occurred within a larger context of international improvements in flight.

In 1931, a memorial dedicated in North Carolina attributed Orville and Wilbur's "conquest of the air" to their "genius" and "dauntless resolution and unconquerable faith." The Wrights were single-minded in their devotion to their work. Neither married. Neither drank alcohol. Neither used tobacco, except for Orville briefly in his teens. Orville was generally more relaxed and effusive than his older brother; Wilbur was very quiet. A friend described Wilbur as "a man who lives largely in a world of his own." While their bicycle business guaranteed them a comfortable income, on some level they were willing to sacrifice everything in order to achieve something socially useful. Insatiable ambition fueled relentless determination. Rather than "playing with the problem of flying" and "avoiding . . . [the] expenditure of considerable sums of money," Wilbur recalled of the months before their initial flight, they chose "the risk of devoting our entire time and financial resources" to "conquer[ing] the difficulties in the path to success."[12] Like others, they assumed that their character, forged in the promised land of Ohio, a place that elevated determination and discipline to an art, was the foundation of their success.

Thomas Edison's brief sojourn in Ohio supposedly put him on the path to greatness. Sleepy as Milan was in the mid-1800s, its people were "wide-awake and progressive," as their dedication to building a canal to link their village with Lake Erie demonstrated. When the canal opened in 1839, Milan attracted farmers with crops to sell who patronized local shops and taverns.

Meanwhile, Edison's middle-class parents taught him to restrain his free spirit. He credited his mother, Nancy, a devout Presbyterian, with saving him. "I was always a careless boy," he remembered, "and with a mother of different mental caliber I should have turned out badly. But her firmness, her sweetness, her goodness, were potent powers to keep me in the right path." Nancy Edison also instilled in her son a need to please, an obligation to do well in order to justify her selfless devotion to her family. Because "my mother was the making of me," because she "was so true, so sure of me . . . I felt I have someone to live for, someone I must not disappoint."[13] Wilbur Wright felt the same way about his mother, who apparently had great faith in his potential.

The idea of success rooted in an environment that exuded the gospel of material progress, and in parents, especially mothers, who inculcated in their sons the importance of discipline and ambition, was irresistible to many people. No person associated with Ohio better exemplified or more fully believed this story of success built on individual character put in the service of social good than the most famous American businessman of the era, John D. Rockefeller.

While Rockefeller's name is synonymous with wealth, it is also synonymous with wealth earned at the expense of others, as the result of ruthless and sometimes shady deals, wealth made possible by the formation of monopolistic corporations such as Standard Oil of Ohio, which was incorporated as a joint-stock company in 1870. In the late nineteenth century, Rockefeller amassed one of the largest private fortunes in the history of the world by seducing, cajoling, and bullying his major competitors in the oil industry into submission. He ignored the wishes of workers in the oil fields of northwestern Pennsylvania, manipulated railroads with rebates and drawbacks, and defied the sporadic efforts of the governments of Pennsylvania and Ohio to reign him in. Rockefeller skillfully exploited Cleveland's location along the major northern east-west railway lines and between the oil fields and the Great Lakes. He mastered the process of vertical integration, by which he controlled everything from drilling oil to transporting, refining, and delivering it. When the Ohio Supreme Court in 1892 agreed with the state attorney general's characterization of Rockefeller's organization as a monopoly, he simply reorganized his business in New Jersey. Until the U.S. Supreme Court ordered its dissolution in 1911, Standard Oil of New Jersey controlled around 90 percent of refining in the country.

Standard Oil's success was part of the emergence of Ohio as one of the great industrial centers of the world. Throughout the middle of the nineteenth century, the economy of the state centered on the exportation of grains, beef, pork, and related products, as well as the development of a commercial infrastructure around towns with banks. Ohio was a rural world dotted with farmhouses and villages. In the late 1800s, all that was changing. By the turn of the century, just over half of Ohioans continued to live on farms and agriculture was barely clinging to its place as the state's largest economic activity.

With or without Rockefeller, Ohio was well positioned to thrive in an international industrial economy. Centrally located in the United States, it had invaluable natural resources, such as salt, iron ore, timber, limestone, and coal as well as oil and natural gas. In the 1880s, the discovery of oil around Lima and Findlay proved to be an economic boon to all of northwestern Ohio, including the port city of Toledo. Even more significant was the discovery of natural gas, after which the population of Findlay increased from four thousand to eighteen thousand in the 1880s. Nothing was more important to the industrialization of the state, however, than the railroads. By 1908, Ohio had 9,581 miles of track linking coal mines, oil fields, and industries with the rest of North America and the world. Industrial development peaked in the first decades of the twentieth century with the emergence of the automobile industry. Centered in Detroit, a scant forty miles north of the Ohio border in Michigan, the production of cars depended heavily on Ohio factories. Tires came from the Goodyear and Firestone companies in Akron and electric components from Dayton. In the 1910s, the automotive and tire industries grew at the staggering rates of 878 and 923 percent, respectively.

All these details point to the same thing: the transformation of a world of commercialized agriculture and small towns into one dominated by heavy industry located in densely populated urban areas. It was all a bit overwhelming, happening as it did in the space of a lifetime. Edison was born before the Civil War in a town where people gambled on canals and died in one where cars and planes set the pace of development. Wilbur Wright was born two years after the end of the Civil War, and Orville Wright died two years after the end of World War II.

John D. Rockefeller became the richest man in the country through sheer naked ambition. Unwilling to accept the idea of failure, he did whatever was required to achieve what he thought necessary. His innovations were matters of organization, most notably a desire to control every aspect of the business in which he was involved. Like Edison, Kettering, and the Wright brothers, Rockefeller had a hard time sharing success with others.

Whatever demons drove Rockefeller—pleasing his mother or showing up his inconstant father—they drove him with an intensity so palpable that we can feel it a century and a half later. He was born in New York in 1839 to Baptist parents who like many Americans were migrants in search of a better life. Fourteen years later, his father brought the family to the Cleveland area and finally into the city itself. In the summer of 1855, young John D., as he styled himself, embarked on a legendary job search. Rockefeller worked six full days a week for six hot weeks knocking on doors. He later claimed he went only to the biggest firms and always asked to speak to the boss. "I understand bookkeeping," he'd announce to everyone, "and I'd like to get to work."[14] The day he got a job—September 26—was a day he celebrated for the rest of his life. John D. did not exaggerate his capacity for work. He took pleasure in being busy. Managing details and accumulating money were strangely liberating for him. He was relentless, almost monomaniacal, working with a gritty determination that would make sense only to contemporaries such as Thomas Edison and Wilbur Wright.

Making money, moreover, was more than work: it was a means to an end, a glorious cause. Rockefeller did not labor all the time. He took naps, enjoyed the spiritual and social attractions of the Baptist Church, and delighted in his role as a husband and father. Fervently antislavery and committed to temperance, Rockefeller was the model of the respectable middle-class businessman. By the late 1860s, he had married Laura Celestia (Cettie) Spelman, started a family, purchased a house on Cleveland's Euclid Avenue, and become thoroughly domestic. He was as affectionate at home as he was ruthless in business. The Rockefellers centered their life on family and church, avoiding parties, clubs, the opera, and the theater as decadent diversions. While John D. prided himself on not working all the time, he lived a highly regimented life in which every moment was justified in some kind of utilitarian fashion. It was imperative to rest, to get away from work, he argued, because leisure kept men fresh and ambitious. If he worked too hard, he would not be able to work well.

Nothing was more important to the Rockefellers than the Euclid Avenue Baptist Church. With the members of the congregation, John D. enjoyed the most satisfying social activities of his life. He was a stalwart member, both financially and in terms of his time. Rockefeller, like many of his contemporaries, believed that religion was a social as well as a spiritual matter. The Bible and Christianity in general offered men and women invaluable lessons in how to live their lives. As much as anything, the Baptist Church affirmed his sense of mission and humanized his ambition. "It has seemed as if I was favored," he later recalled, "and got increase because the Lord knew that I was going to turn around and give it back."[15] And give it back he did, becoming one of America's greatest philanthropists. He helped finance the African American Spelman College and in the early 1900s started the Rockefeller Foundation to manage the great work of benevolence. When he died in 1937, John D. had given away most of his money, although he still had a tidy estate worth $26.4 million in the middle of the Great Depression.

Rockefeller lived in Cleveland for three decades. In 1883, the family moved to the center of American business, New York City. They returned to Cleveland regularly for visits and vacations. And the mortal remains of America's most famous tycoon lie between those of his mother and his wife in the Rockefeller plot in the city's Lake View Cemetery. John D. Rockefeller helped transform Ohio from a place dominated by commercial agriculture to a landscape of heavy industry. His cultural contributions were just as profound. For both in his telling and that of others, Rockefeller's quickly mythologized life became a tribute to the possibilities of hard work and good character. Like Edison, Kettering, the Wrights, and B. F. Goodrich and his son, Charles, Rockefeller was prima facie evidence of what a community that imagined itself as citizens tireless in the cause of human betterment could achieve. It was an immensely appealing story, even if it made no sense to many Ohioans.

Contesting the Workplace

The righteousness of Rockefeller and others left them intolerant of their critics. Self-discipline and intense labor had worked for them. Those people who would rather idle life away in dissipation and decadence had no right to expect success. Such a dismissive attitude exposed their story of success as parochial, rooted in Protestantism and middle-class pieties. Tens of thousands of Ohioans could testify that hard work alone did not bring fame or fortune.

Industrial workers found life difficult, occasionally dangerous, and generally unfair. The miracles of technological progress disrupted well-established patterns of family and community life. The towering smokestacks that outlined the urban landscapes of northwestern Ohio brought smoke and pollution into homes. The elaborate machinery of steel mills and factories ruined lives and maimed bodies. The success of Rockefeller and Edison, men rising from relatively humble beginnings to affluence, was real but rare.

In retrospect, we know that the Industrial Revolution brought opportunities and material improvements to a great many Ohioans. In fact, real wages rose faster than the cost of living in the late nineteenth century. At the time, however, people often experienced rapid change as a loss of control. A volatile economy plunged into major depressions in the 1870s and 1890s, resulting in massive layoffs and wage cuts. As disconcerting was the impact of change on daily lives. In the factories of the new age, men and some women increasingly worked at repetitious tasks that required little or no skill. Strictly supervised, operating under the tyranny of the clock, they had no incentive to take pride or pleasure in their work. Hours were long and working conditions miserable, and there was little in the way of comfort to expect at home. The kinds of safety nets we now take for granted— insurance, retirement plans, welfare for those out of work, regulation of prices and hours—did not exist. Immigrants from Europe and rural Ohio who poured into Cleveland, Toledo, and Youngstown in search of work in mills ended up with irregular work at minimal pay.

Not surprisingly, industrial workers and farmers told different stories of Ohio's development than did the residents of Cleveland's exclusive Euclid Avenue. Few of the latter questioned the value of capitalism; few sought to reverse direction and expel industry and innovation from the state. The divergence in narratives had less to do with the trajectory of progress than with its equity. The benefits of development were concentrated, or appeared to be concentrated, in the hands of a few. Especially in hard times, when jobs were eliminated and wages cut, injustices were unbearable. Workers wanted to exercise some measure of control over their lives so that they too could realize the possibilities of life in Ohio.

Like many parts of the United States, Ohio was swept with strikes in the 1880s and 1890s as workers sought redress of their grievances and improvements in wages and working conditions. While industrialists organized trusts and corporations, workers organized unions. In newspapers, strikes, speeches, and general calls for reform, laborers sought a reinvigoration of public culture and a revival of an idealized image of an early-nineteenth-century notion of a commonwealth of independent citizens sharing more or less equally in the material and moral progress of the state. The challenge was to revive the image of Ohio as a place of possibilities, restore a sense of justice, and make it more inclusive and tolerant.

More than anything else, what distinguished working-class from middle-class citizens was the former's perception that Ohio was retrogressing morally by becoming a promised land for a smaller and smaller number of detached, ridiculously rich plutocrats. Evidence of the growing class divide was the residential segregation of cities. In Cincinnati, wealthy families were moving to the suburbs of Clifton and Mount Auburn where they could live in Victorian mansions with broad porches, ample lawns, wrought-iron fences, and elaborate window decoration. No city in Ohio by the 1870s was without its version of Cleveland's Euclid Avenue.

Working people in Cincinnati saw development as the sum of the efforts of independent producers, relatively autonomous shop owners, and skilled artisans who enjoyed some measure of control over their lives and work. The expanding scale of corporations made this early-nineteenth-century vision untenable. Large companies such as Procter and Gamble dominated the city's economy by the 1870s. Often, they employed hundreds of workers who were limited to routinized labor. No longer divided by their trades into carriage makers, cigar makers, soap makers, whiskey distillers, and the like, they were now simply laborers engaged in a process of manufacturing with multiple stages. Few men or women or children saw the making of a shoe through from beginning to end; now they did only their part. The journeymen and masters who had supervised the hiring and training of apprentices lost both status and influence. Official Cincinnati tended to celebrate buildings and machines rather than individual artisans. The glory of Ohio lay in its physical things, not its people. The annual Cincinnati Industrial Exposition, which attracted visitors in the hundreds of thousands, was a paean to glorious machinery and redesigned brick factories.

Economic crisis intensified workers' sense of alienation from their jobs. As wages declined or evaporated, families experienced hunger, poverty, and deep frustration. In 1876, Cincinnati was "the poorest and most uncertain place" the shoemaker Joseph Glenn had ever worked. The city's superintendent of streets, Larkin McHugh, lamented that he had never seen "the evidence of suffering I see now. . . . The shops and mills that employ thousands are still—have been for months, and thousands of little mouths cry daily for bread and get none, because those whose place it is to provide them with bread can not get it for work, they have not the where with to buy."[16] Even when times were better, close to 90 percent of average family income went to paying for food, shelter, and clothes. As women and children entered the labor market in skyrocketing numbers in the 1870s and 1880s, the stress in working-class households was enormous. Strikes occurred with increasing frequency (there were 107 between 1873 and 1884), especially when wages were cut, as in the great national strike by railroad workers in 1877, which was put down in part by federal troops ordered into action by President Rutherford B. Hayes.

It seemed clear to many that industrialists had hijacked the history of Ohio for their own use. Despite the stories of inventors rising from humble origins, virtue, honesty, and useful labor rarely led to success. Now the greedy "money power" was dominating the federal government, much as the Slave Power had done in the 1850s.[17] In response to their perception of change controlled by and for the benefit of a few, Cincinnati laborers experimented with new forms of collective action in the 1880s. Some turned to socialism, advocating government intervention in order to restore some degree of equity. Others found hope in trade unionism, including the American Federation of Labor and the United Mine Workers.

Most popular in the 1880s was the Knights of Labor. Founded in Philadelphia in 1869, the Knights accepted industrialization within a world in which labor would once again be honored and producers would live in cooperative harmony. Workers would be independent producers, not "wage slaves." The Knights looked to improve life beyond the factory, arguing for "civic responsibility, education, a wholesome family life, temperance, and self-improvement."[18] In the early 1880s, membership in the Knights increased to more than eight hundred. By 1885, the organization had opened its own hall in Cincinnati.

The 1880s was a tense decade in the Queen City. In March 1884, a protest against light sentences given to two murderers led to a march by several thousand people. They proceeded to burn down the Hamilton County jail and the courthouse. The governor dispatched seven thousand militia to quell the disturbance. Over the next two nights, confrontations became violent. When it was over, thirty-five people were dead and another two hundred wounded. Not all workers supported the initial attack on the county buildings. But almost all were outraged by the mere appearance of the militia, who one group claimed was sent "for the sole object of intimidating the working classes when compelled to strike to secure their just rights."[19]

This exchange was a prelude to the May Day Strikes of 1886. Some thirty-two thousand men and women (35 percent of Cincinnati's labor force) came together to restore a sense of law and justice to a rapidly changing city. They demanded implementation of the Haley Act, legislation passed by the General Assembly in April that supported the idea of an eight-hour workday. Accusing industrialists of trying to evade the Haley Act, the strikers insisted that they were acting only in the name of law and order. One participant explained to a local reporter: "The law says eight hours is a day's work, and we will see that it is a day's work and that we are paid for it. If the law said twelve hours was a day's work, the bosses would make us work that long, and you may be very sure that they would pay us for what we are getting now, a day's pay for a legal day's work."[20]

When the strikers returned to work in June, more than two thousand workers had been given an eight-hour day without any loss of pay, while more than ten thousand had received an increase in pay, although they worked the same number of hours. As important, the May Day Strikes increased the political consciousness of Cincinnati's workers, at least temporarily. Membership in the Knights of Labor swelled to close to seventeen thousand in 1887, and a United Labor Party flourished briefly in 1886 and 1887 as an effort to institutionalize the energy unleashed in the May Day Strikes.

Significant labor unrest also occurred in Cleveland, where by 1900 two-thirds of laborers worked in factories with sixty or more employees. Long-standing grievances about loss of control over the workplace, declining wages, and massive layoffs exploded in the 1880s. The Cleveland Rolling Mill Company was the oldest and largest steel corporation in the city. In 1882 and again in 1885, its workers struck to secure the role of unions and to improve wages and working conditions. The vast majority of the five thousand employees belonged to either the Amalgamated Association or the Knights of Labor. In 1882, the company won because the workers could not afford to hold out for long. In 1885, workers again shut down the mill to protest wage cuts amounting to nearly half their annual income. According to a reporter for the *Cleveland Plain Dealer,* the area of ten acres around the mills "probably contains more misery and squalor than can be found in all the rest of Cleveland. The people living there are gaunt, hollow-cheeked and famine-stricken, but their talk is bold and threatening." One woman promised that if the police interfered with the strike, "[t]he women will charge first, and then the men will come and kill every policeman that comes out here."[21] After several months of escalating hostility, the strikers got the company to rescind some of the wage reductions. The impact was electrifying—but temporary.

Divisions among workers were as important as the hostility of industrialists and governments in breaking strikes and undermining unions. Large numbers of immigrants were eager to fill jobs vacated by strikers. The need to eat prevailed over the urge for solidarity. Antagonism among workers was cultural as well as economic. Native-born workers were often suspicious of immigrants, and vice versa. Immigrants represented a variety of ethnic communities that distrusted each other. One labor leader complained that organization lagged because "our people are not yet a homogeneous American people." Ethnic identity was stronger than occupational identity. A labor newspaper lamented the holding of three or four Fourth of July celebrations in 1879 in the Newburgh section of Cleveland because there was "an almost endless ill-feeling between people of different nationalities, and in these picnics there was a division on that question as usual. How much more sensible it would have been had the different nationalities united in one grand celebration on the birthday of their adopted country." But that was impossible as long as so many diverse peoples needed work so badly. "Cleveland is overrun with people in search of employment," wrote a journalist. "They come from the east, they come from the west, from the north and the south. . . . The like was never before seen in this land." According to an angry Bohemian newspaper editor, "the European workers . . . help defeat the strikers" because they were unwilling to sacrifice wages in order to "show the swelled headed rich, in the interest of all workers, that they are men who deserve humane treatment."[22]

By the early 1890s, most workers had rejected the model of universal producer cooperation across ethnic and craft lines offered by the Knights of Labor. Rent by differences over cultural issues as well as strategies for dealing with wage cuts and layoffs, laborers interested in collective action turned to organizations that recognized differences among workers and protected their autonomy. The American Federation of Labor, founded in Columbus in 1886 by dissident members of the Knights, brought together unions organized by craft into a loose coalition that fought for basic improvements in wages and working conditions rather than a general reform of society as a whole. Similarly, activist miners founded the United Mine Workers of America in Columbus in 1890.

Outside of large cities, labor actions sometimes met with wider community support, if not success. In southeastern Ohio, where mining was usually the most important industry, local citizens often identified more with miners than with their employers. During the depression of 1873, severe competition forced Ohio Valley ironmasters to cut the wages of the heaters and rollers in their mills. When workers went on strike, mill owners struggled to keep their factories open. Unlike urban industrialists, however, they had to confront not just workers but their neighbors and friends. Because most people in relatively homogeneous and compact river towns sympathized with the strikers, the mill owners eventually had to compromise. Even immigrants received a warmer reception than they did in big cities. Ohio National Guardsmen sent into Newark to preserve order and protect property during the Great Railroad Strike of 1877 discovered that they faced a more or less united community. Stopping just short of violence on a couple of occasions, the guardsmen soon found themselves on relatively friendly terms with some of the strikers. They returned home happy that they had behaved like "citizen soldiers."[23]

Race was, as always, more complicated than ethnicity. Whatever their origins, white workers were invariably more hostile to strikebreakers and competitors who were African American. Nonetheless, in the upper Ohio Valley in the 1890s, some twenty thousand blacks belonged to the United Mine Workers. One of them, Virginia-born Richard L. Davis, was elected to the National Executive Board in 1896 and 1897, apparently with white as well as black votes. Davis was an ardent supporter of the union and worked tirelessly to mobilize workers, regardless of race, in response to unemployment and reduced wages.

Like most African Americans, Davis wanted only to be treated equally. "I have got it fixed in my brain," he wrote to a labor periodical in July 1892, "that a man is a man, no matter what the color of his skin is." When someone called him a "nigger," he simply called him a "fool." If unions would ignore the color line, "we, as workingmen," could "turn our attention to fighting monopoly in land and money" and "accomplish a great deal more than we will by fighting among ourselves on account of race, creed, color or nationality."[24]

The mine workers' union was one of a handful of organizations that made any effort to recognize the dignity of black men. Yet prejudice remained strong among white workers, whether they were born in the United States or Europe. Of the latter, Davis complained in 1895: "I, an American citizen by birth, and many of them not yet dry from crossing the salt water pond, and yet they have the unlimited gall to say that an American citizen shall not take part in an American institution because of the color of his skin."[25] Until his death in 1900, Davis fought against such prejudice.

What most workers shared was a desire for regular, safe employment at a reasonable wage, along with a measure of respect from both employers and their fellow workers. No matter how powerful and imaginative, labor movements rarely offered a truly different vision of the possibilities of Ohio. Most workers did not want to overthrow government or reorganize industry; they simply wanted to be treated as more than replaceable components in a machine. Like most people, they tended to see life in the midst of rapid change as a zero-sum game: one group's gain was another group's loss.

Contesting Public Space

In the late nineteenth century, Ohioans were also seriously at odds about how they should live their lives away from work. Whether they lived in cities or small towns, they enjoyed a greater range of options when it came to diversion than ever before. Except in rural areas, all citizens were experiencing a stricter separation between labor and leisure. Growing numbers now left home to go to work, even if the factory, store, or office was only a few hundred feet away. They began to think of their time away from work as "free" time when they could do as they pleased. Entrepreneurs rushed in to help them with everything from shops to nickelodeons and dance halls, from penny arcades and amusement parks to sporting and theatrical events, from restaurants and beer gardens to brothels and gambling dens. Vine Street in Cincinnati was the model of what historians call commercialized leisure.

Many Ohioans found in commercialized leisure a way to express themselves in a part of their lives that was not regulated by employers, teachers, or parents. Young women might spend money they earned in factories or sometimes on the streets on colorful clothes, makeup, and accessories. Respectable people could not fathom this behavior. Why not save the money? Why waste it? But young women were gratified both by their expenditure of money on what made them feel good and by their power to spend money as they saw fit. One of the critical ways in which working-class Ohioans differentiated themselves from middle-class Ohioans was their tendency to focus on self-fulfillment rather than self-control, on diversion rather than respectability.

Nothing revealed these developments better than commercialized sport. Baseball, which had been around in one form or another for decades, flourished among Union soldiers during the Civil War, and its popularity grew by leaps and bounds in the Midwest when they returned home. Ohio boasted several amateur and semiprofessional teams. But its claim to fame was the Cincinnati Red Stockings. Formed in 1869, the team (only one member of which was from Ohio) defeated opponents locally and on tours of New York and California. The Red Stockings were a phenomenon. Around 200,000 people saw them play during the 1869 season. They traveled some 12,000 miles, scored 2,396 runs, had an average margin of victory of 40 to 10, and barely broke even financially. The highlight of their extraordinary season was a sweep of the three major baseball clubs in New York City in June. According to the *Spirit of the Times,* the Red Stockings were "the only true exponents of the game today. Full of courage, free from intemperance, they have conducted themselves in every city they visited in a manner to challenge admiration, and their exhibitions of skill in the art of handling both ball and bat call for unexampled praise."[26]

This comment went to the heart of the tensions that surrounded the growth of baseball. Most of the players were from working-class backgrounds (native-born, German, and Irish in the early years), while many of those watching them play were middle-class men who could afford to do so. Meanwhile, the growing number of professional clubs were owned by affluent men who imitated industrial organization in order to control the players and police the game. In going from a club sport of middle-class amateurs to an entertainment business with owners and employees, baseball epitomized both the changes in Ohio and the ambiguity of responses to them.

Some people lamented the loss of amateur status. Others welcomed increased regulation. Many worried about the desultory character of baseball, involving, as it did, a large number of men stealing away from work on sunny afternoons to smoke, gamble, drink, and watch other men play. It was a recipe for offending even the mildest of respectable sensibilities. Ironically, however, from the beginning, baseball was celebrated (and marketed) as reinforcing middle-class virtues such as hard work and self-discipline. Supporters claimed the game built character by teaching both players and spectators the value of sportsmanship and mutual respect. The tension between baseball as a diversion and baseball as a morality play was as powerful as the tension between baseball as a game and baseball as a business. No matter that the players often drank, that gambling on games was rife, that owners exploited players financially.

Americans imagined baseball as a peculiarly American game that legitimized both a way of life and a particular place. Middle-class men could enjoy watching baseball because it supposedly reflected the values of their world. If a team from Cincinnati won, it was because of a combination of skill and environment. In 1869 nearly five thousand people greeted the Red Stockings' return from their successful tour of the northeastern U.S. with banners, firecrackers, songs, and parades. Even people who did not care about baseball were proud of a team that had done "something to add to the glory of our city." One man was as enthusiastic as he was cynical: "Glory, they've advertised the city—advertised us, sir, and helped our business, sir." Financial woes meant that the original Red Stockings lasted only a couple of seasons. But it was a long time before people forgot the victories over the New York teams. Shortly after the Red Stockings' third victory, a telegram from "all the citizens of Cincinnati" informed the players that "the streets are full of people, who give cheer after cheer for their pet club. Go on with the noble work. Our expectations have been met."[27]

Baseball promoters understood that for middle-class audiences fun for the sake of fun was not permissible. To be socially acceptable, baseball had to be socially useful. This was true in small towns as well as big cities. In villages in the Miami Valley, the performance and popularity of a fluctuating group of amateur baseball teams were seen as indicators of personal and public character. Baseball players were representatives of their hometowns. One editor proclaimed that the Germantown team carried "its banner through the valley to victory and to good repute for our little village."[28] The onus was on more than the players; the size and conduct of crowds also reflected on the character of a town and its citizens. Baseball did not divide Ohioans along class lines as much as it obscured the existence of such lines.

Professional sports, on the other hand, tended to highlight gender divisions. They represented the pervasiveness of an aggressively masculine culture in the years after the Civil War. Like all military veterans, Ohio's victorious soldiers were not eager to abandon the fraternal milieu of the army. Their assertiveness sparked a response among women who saw a male culture centered on drinking and socializing as dangerous, let alone unrespectable. In the 1870s, large numbers of middle-class, deeply Protestant women seemed bent on reminding men of their roles as citizens. Ohio could hardly expect to survive if its citizens publicly gave themselves over to the business of satisfying their basest desires. Built on a foundation of education and morality, a healthy public culture required men who could see beyond what they wanted right now. In reviving a crusade for temperance, middle-class women in small towns reinforced the ties between public and personal identities. Good citizens were first and foremost good husbands and fathers. For many of the women involved in temperance reform, the problems created by excessive drinking were anything but abstractions.

In late December 1873, fifty-year-old Diocletian Lewis, a physician and educator from Boston, gave lectures titled "Our Girls" and "The Duty of Christian Women" to largely female audiences in Hillsboro and Washington Court House, Ohio. In both places, as well as at his stops in New York, Lewis energized those who heard him. Two days after his appearance in Hillsboro, seventy-five women marched against the town's four liquor-selling drugstores and its nine saloons. Three of the drugstore owners signed a pledge to drop alcohol. The women of Washington Court House met with greater success. In a little more than a week, their public marches resulted in the closing of all eleven local saloons and pledges from the three drugstores. These events launched a national crusade that became one of the largest reform movements of the nineteenth century and spawned one of its most influential political organizations, the Woman's Christian Temperance Union.

No state was more central to the initial Woman's Temperance Crusade in the 1870s than Ohio. Of 847 crusades to rid the world of liquor, 307 took place in Ohio; of the 54,218 women who participated in the movement, 32,422 were from Ohio. Temperance reform mobilized women in a massive political action. They met together, marched together, drafted petitions, got pledges, and lobbied politicians. During their protests, church bells rang and some local businesses closed in solidarity. Newspapers carried reports of the temperance crusade far beyond village borders. Women were participating in a public conversation about what Ohio was and what it should become.

The crusaders' tactics were melodramatic but effective, at least initially. A critic described the cornering of a man behind his bar in Morrow, Ohio. The women cajoled and cried. They complimented the man's looks and intelligence. They told him they "loved him," even though they had probably never spoken to him before, and assured him that if he would sign their pledge, he would find his reward in heaven. Participants freely admitted that they were doing everything to manipulate their quarry. What seemed ridiculous to male observers profoundly empowered the women. "It is easy enough to conquer a man, if you only know how," one woman said. "I wish you could see me talking to some of these saloon men that I would never have spoken to before; I employ my sweetest accents; I exhaust all the argument I am possessed of; I look into their eyes and grow pathetic; I shed tears, and I joke with them—but all in terrible earnest. And they surrender."[29]

Obviously, many men were less than enthused by the crusade. Even the husbands of leaders were skeptical. And the protests completely disoriented those who sold alcohol. How did they respond without making a public spectacle of themselves? The owner of a beer garden in Washington Court House instructed his attorney to warn singing crusaders away from his "legitimate business." They were "trespassers on his property and right." But what to do with the intruders? He could not put them out forcibly, "as that would be unmanly," and he could not act "rudely," so all he could do was ask them "to desist from any further annoyance."[30]

In the long run, men such as this generally got what they wanted. But in the short term, they had to endure considerable irritation. In New London, or Paddy's Run, now known as Shandon, men "treated [the women] with respect," although a few mocked their efforts. It was difficult to resist the sincerity and determination of dozens of suddenly empowered women. Only the rare saloon keeper or drugstore proprietor could turn down their entreaties. Most "surrendered" only for the duration of the crusade. Ohioans could still get alcohol, albeit surreptitiously. But the crusade was a major event for women and some men. Paddy's Run crusaders celebrated by ringing school and church bells and firing cannon when the last liquor dealer signed the pledge.[31]

Why was the temperance crusade so popular in Ohio? Probably because there was a noticeable increase in alcohol consumption after the Civil War, accompanied by lax enforcement of liquor laws by the state government. Constitutionally, Ohio had a no-license law. Since 1851, however, it had been illegal to drink in or around the same building where a beverage was purchased or to sell any alcohol to minors or obviously or habitually intoxicated persons. Under the Mc-Connelsville Ordinance, towns could prohibit sales by the drink if they chose to do so. Meanwhile, the Adair Law made property owners and dealers responsible for any damage caused by someone to whom they sold liquor, legally or illegally. But in the early 1870s, Ohio governments were not consistently enforcing any of these laws. Some officials ignored them. Women thus faced a situation where consumption appeared to be growing rapidly while governments were doing little or nothing. In Washington Court House, the number of saloon keepers expanded from zero in 1860 to eight in 1870.[32] Many blamed military service for the rapid growth. A soldier told his wife that "many a poor fellow has been turned to the road to Ruin here in the Army and I have been almost lost[;] thank God I saw my danger in time." Others were not so lucky. A Methodist journal lamented in 1866 that "[o]ur young men have become loose in temperance principles, by the practice of the camp and field" Military metaphors abounded. After helping to destroy a saloon in Perrysville in 1869, a member of the crowd exclaimed: "The people in this part of Ohio honestly think that the next war in this country will be between women and whiskey; and though there may not be much blood shed, you may rest assured rum will flow freely in the gutter. As the women here have taken the matter in hand once before, we claim to have fought Bunker Hill of the new revolution."[33]

Personal experience fueled the fervor of the participants. Either they or friends had been injured by intoxicated men. Indeed, some thought they were fighting for their own safety as well as the security of their families. Allen Thompson, a well-educated Methodist minister from a respectable family, became a public drunk. His mother, Eliza, leader of the Hillsboro crusade, recognizing that moral suasion had failed in this case, was inclined to combat drunkenness in terms of supply as well as demand. "Knowing, as we do, the fearful effects of intoxicating drinks," went one public appeal by a group of women, "we appeal to you to desist from this ruinous traffic, that our husbands, brothers, and especially our sons, be no longer exposed to this terrible temptation. . . . We appeal to the better instincts of your hearts, in the name of desolated homes, blasted hopes, ruined lives, widowed hearts . . . we implore you, to . . . place yourselves in the ranks of those who are striving to elevate and ennoble themselves and their fellow-men."[34]

The temperance crusade, in short, brought women into public culture with the purpose of defending their private interests as wives and mothers. They had their own sense of what Ohio should be. Mrs. Eliza D. "Mother" Stewart, a Methodist and a teacher whose own children had died, was one of the stalwarts of the campaign. A newspaper described her as a small person blessed with "a spirit powerful enough to rouse and inoculate a vast legion of supporters." The roots of the charismatic Stewart's devotion to empowering women to resist "the reign of King Alcohol" lay in her vision of a future of "restored manhood, happy women, glad, shouting, little children, bright, happy homes, where God is reverenced and worshiped."[35]

Immigrants would not have quarreled with such rhetoric. But many had good reason to see the temperance crusade as an attack on their ways of life. After all, Mother Stewart blamed the "curse" of intemperance, "more fearful than southern slavery," on the immigrant as well as the Civil War. She denounced "their ignorance of what 'liberty' means, their disregard for the laws and institutions of the land in which they have found homes, their unscrupulous eagerness for gain, their shrewdness in manipulating politicians, caucuses and elections, intimidating business men, bribing legislatures and courts of justice."[36] Native-born evangelical women such as Stewart worked hard to maintain the momentum of the women's crusade, founding the Woman's Christian Temperance Union in Cleveland in 1874 and the Anti-Saloon League at Oberlin College in 1893. What they saw as a defense of family and citizenship, immigrants saw as an attack on their communities.

Identity Politics

Different kinds of Ohioans told different stories about their lives, whether they were at work, home, or play. Partisan politics embodied these differences. To declare yourself a Republican or a Democrat was to announce who you believed you were. Political campaigns were all about rallying people who thought they had much in common with each other against people with whom they thought they had little or nothing in common. Parties were coalitions of groups defined by ethnicity, race, and class. Novelist Brand Whitlock wrote that native-born, white, middle-class Ohioans in small towns were inevitably Republicans. Not "a matter of intellectual choice, it was a process of biological selection. . . . One became . . . a Republican just as an Eskimo dons fur clothes. It was inconceivable that any self-respecting person should be a Democrat."[37] Because personal and partisan loyalties were intertwined, politics was intense. Winning elections was about acquiring the power to advance one's ideas against those of enemies.

Like other Americans, many ordinary Ohioans complained that there were few real differences between the two major parties other than who would control appointments to federal and state offices. Party leaders supposedly cared only about the opinions of wealthy men. Reluctant to do anything for working people, they would jump into action at the snap of a finger from an industrialist in need of troops to quell a labor uprising.

There was a good deal of truth to these generalizations. Politicians were responsive to the wishes of powerful men. Patronage did affect everything they did. The Republican Party had aged quickly. The energetic newcomer of the 1850s became the standard-bearer of the status quo in the 1880s. Primarily native-born, middle-class Protestants, Republicans tended to argue that governments should promote material and moral progress. They were more likely to support a high national tariff designed to raise the prices on imported goods and spur domestic industry. The most famous example was the federal McKinley Tariff of 1890, named after the Ohio congressman from Canton, who was chairman of the Ways and Means Committee in the House of Representatives. Republicans also sympathized with reform movements intended to improve the character of Americans, including temperance, public education, and on a limited basis, civil rights for African Americans.

Above all, Republicans exuded middle-class respectability. Rutherford and Lucy Hayes were the grand old Republican couple. While Rud served as governor of Ohio in the late 1860s and early 1870s and president of the United States from 1877 to 1881, Lucy was one of the most outspoken first ladies of the nineteenth century. She endeared herself to thousands by refusing to serve alcohol in the White House (thus her nickname, "Lemonade Lucy") and by supporting missionary and reform movements. In 1880, she accepted the presidency of the Woman's Home Missionary Society of the Methodist Episcopal Church. Living in a large house in Spiegel Grove, Ohio, the Hayeses took pride in raising their four sons and a daughter to be decent people. A photograph taken on the porch of their house in 1887, two years before Lucy's death and six years before Rud's, shows the couple sitting in the middle of comfortable affluence surrounded by their children, two of whom had been playing tennis, enjoying all that Ohio had promised to its citizens.

Leading Democrats were no less respectable than the Hayeses. But they tended toward the more culturally laissez-faire views of their most consistent supporters, rural voters of southern ancestry and non-Protestant immigrants in urban areas. Where Republicans were likely to sympathize with moral reform, Democrats were likely to sympathize with immigrant resistance to it. They also generally opposed government intervention, either on the state or federal level, in the lives of citizens. On economic issues, the party tended to favor inflationary policies espoused by Greenbackers and later the Populists. Hardly opposed to progress, Democrats objected to the ways in which Protestant Yankees and Germans defined it.

In late-nineteenth-century Ohio, the two major parties were almost evenly divided. A few thousand votes decided more than one election. Because both Republicans and Democrats could count on relatively consistent support from their core constituencies, swing voters, or groups with particular interests, held the balance of power, exerting influence far beyond their actual support. In the 1870s and 1880s, Republicans had to be sensitive to temperance issues, since supporters of prohibition were more likely to draw voters away from them than the Democrats. Conversely, Democrats had to be wary of desertions on the issue of the money supply.

Temperance was the most controversial issue. In 1874, a Constitutional Convention recommended a new state constitution that would establish annual meetings of the General Assembly, grant the governor veto power, create state circuit courts, and make women eligible for election to school boards. Also on the ballot was a separate proposal to institute a licensing system that would help regulate the sale of liquor. Both proposals were defeated, despite strong support from the recently created Woman's Christian Temperance Union (WCTU). But Republicans kept the issue in public play, in large part because of pressure from temperance organizations. Just over two thousand Ohioans belonged to the WCTU, enough to make Republicans nervous about how their male supporters would vote in the state's relentlessly close elections.

In 1883, a staunchly Republican legislature approved two constitutional amendments and sent them to voters for their approval. They created a local option with regard to the regulation of alcohol, made possible state taxes on liquor, and discussed the possibility of statewide prohibition. The same legislature also passed the Pond

Bill, which taxed alcoholic beverages, and the Scott Law, which taxed retail sales and banned Sunday sales of liquor. Voters defeated the amendments, and the Ohio Supreme Court soon ruled both the Pond and Scott Acts unconstitutional. Even worse for the Republicans, their support of temperance legislation cost them the votes of enough Germans and Irish to allow the Democrats to win the governorship and both houses of the General Assembly in the fall election. Republicans faced an impossible political conundrum: how to maintain the support of an activist element within their party without alienating other voters.

African Americans posed a similar dilemma. Although black voters were few, they overwhelmingly voted for Republicans because of the party's association with antislavery and emancipation. In Cleveland, Republican leaders faced growing numbers of immigrants who seemed to prefer Democratic candidates. In order to win crucial black votes, Mark Hanna and other prominent Republicans cultivated ties with prominent African Americans such as George Myers, the proprietor of a successful barbershop in the Hollenden Hotel. Hanna talked with Myers regularly, sought out his opinion on political matters, and sent a small amount of patronage his way. Meanwhile, Republicans supported the General Assembly's passage in 1887 of a school desegregation law as well as 1884 and 1894 prohibitions on discrimination in public accommodations. They also endorsed the 1887 repeal of an antimiscegenation law. In practice, these acts were sporadically enforced, since local custom dictated white treatment of African Americans. But the fact that Republican leaders supported them demonstrated the degree to which they were sensitive to the interests of a small group of voters who might hold the balance in tight contests.

Democrats behaved the same way. In the late 1880s and early 1890s, the rise of the People's or Populist Party disproportionately took votes from Democrats. Attempting to unite farmers and laborers in a mass democratic movement to regain control over their lives, Populists advocated nationalization of the railroads and industries, a graduated income tax, a cooperative-style federal subtreasury that would store crops in government warehouses until prices rose to acceptable levels, inflationary monetary policies such as the free and unlimited coinage of silver, and direct election of the president, vice president, and U.S. senators.

There was considerable sympathy in Ohio for the Populist program, which identified the greed of industrialists and bankers and the corruption of politicians as major reasons for the persistence of low prices for crops and low wages for workers. The 1890 Declaration of Principles of the Ohio Farmer's Union blamed the plight of farmers on the "corporations, banks, and syndicates" who dominated the political parties. How else to explain layoffs and wage cuts when in the 1880s the total wealth of Ohio increased by close to $275 million? Or the fact that the value of farms had decreased by $27 million? The president of the Ohio Farmer's Union, J. H. Brigham, proclaimed in 1890 that the organization was dedicated to the proposition that "it is possible for us as farmers to do something in the way of influencing state and national legislation." They must overcome "those questions over which we will quarrel and divide and wrangle, and from which no good can come."[38] The most immediate issue for farmers was tax relief. They were tired of paying property taxes on their land when only a fraction of the wealth of industrialists was in property. The rural counties of Butler, Clark, Greene, and Stark paid over $1.7 million more in taxes than Cuyahoga County.

Workers as well as farmers rallied to the Populist banner. An important leader was John McBride, the president of the United Mine Workers of America and later president of the American Federation of Labor. Born in Wayne County in 1854 to an Irish father and an English mother, McBride began laboring in mines at the age of eight. He joined unions, including the Knights of Labor, and helped organize the Ohio Miner's Union. Unlike craft union members, McBride and other miners were convinced that capital and labor were not inevitably at odds with each other. They had faith in the power of negotiation and arbitration to resolve disputes, most of which they saw occurring because of an overabundance of mines and miners. Supply, they believed, was outrunning demand and causing low wages. When negotiation failed, miners went on strike. In the eight years between 1886 and 1894, there were 155 strikes by Ohio miners to raise wages, only nine of which were even remotely successful, and 140 strikes to stop wage reductions, of which only one worked. No wonder McBride and others became Populists.

Once a strong Democrat, McBride concluded by 1890 that there was no serious difference between Democrats and Republicans on economic issues. The "only way to deal a death blow to tyranny and oppression as practiced upon wage workers, and give improved wages and conditions to labor's forces," he told the 1894 convention of the United Mine Workers, "is for the laborers themselves to join in an independent political movement and administer a telling and lasting rebuke to legislative imbecility and administrative corruption. . . . [T]he people must either own or control the means of production and distribution or be subjected to the dictation, as they are now, of those who do own and control these two powerful agencies."[39]

In the early 1890s, Populists wooed voters away from Democrats and to a lesser extent Republicans. Jacob Coxey, a businessman from Massillon who led an 1894 march to Washington, D.C., in a fruitless effort to persuade the federal government to stimulate the economy by giving people public works jobs, was the Populist candidate for governor in 1895. Coxey received fifty-two thousand votes. Still, even though labor protests escalated in the middle of the depression of the 1890s, the Populists were never as successful in Ohio as they were in southern and Plains states.

The fate of the Populists was not surprising given the political history of Ohio. Since the success of the Republicans in the 1850s, third parties had failed to last long. Their low vote totals belie their larger influence on state politics, however. Ohio's close elections meant politicians were forced to make gestures to dissident groups. Democrats and Republicans refrained from direct attacks on third parties and incorporated some of their demands in their platforms. On occasion, they preempted issues altogether, as in April 1891 when the General Assembly passed the Rawlings Bill, which reformed the state's system of taxation in favor of farmers. Trying to recapture voters who had deserted to the Populists, Democratic leaders supported the free coinage of silver and other popular issues. Like the Republicans, Democrats survived because they adapted well and addressed the issues that created third parties. Indeed, as historian Michael Pierce has argued, most Ohioans remained within existing party structures because they had a reasonable faith that the Democrats or Republicans would eventually deal with major issues.

While close state elections led the two major parties to pay attention to special-interest voters, close national elections made the two major parties pay attention to Ohio. Republicans sought to gain an edge by running Ohioans for president. Ohioans were unusually powerful in Washington, D.C. Senators John Sherman and George Pendleton gave their names to some of the most important federal legislation passed in the era. But in the long run the most significant national politician was William McKinley of Canton—governor, congressman, and Civil War veteran. Together with Mark Hanna, McKinley reconfigured the Republican Party. All but abandoning moral crusades, McKinley emphasized the Republicans' commitment to better jobs and a higher standard of living for all Americans. In the presidential election of 1896, McKinley's victory over the evangelical William Jennings Bryan (who alienated core Democratic voters with his pietistic fervor) completed one of the most important political realignments in American history.

Downplaying cultural issues such as temperance, Hanna and McKinley broadened their party and inaugurated an era of Republican dominance both in Ohio and in the U.S. that would persist until the Great Depression of the 1930s. Using lessons learned from business, they organized a national campaign that distributed literature throughout the country and mobilized thousands of voters. The Republican transformation was a matter of substance as well as style. McKinley offered Americans what amounted to multiculturalism on the grand scale. He promised to treat everyone fairly, whatever their occupation or religion. He reassured Catholics and all people who liked to drink alcohol. "We have always practiced the Golden Rule," McKinley said. "The best policy is to 'live and let live.'" The strategy worked especially well with German voters who had supported Democrats in the recent past because of the Republicans' dalliance with temperance. McKinley summarized his new pluralism when he argued that "we are all dependent on each other, no matter what our occupation may be. All of us want good times, good wages, good prices, good markets; and then we want good money always."[40] Avoiding divisive questions of moral development, Americans could come together under the umbrella of material progress.

This Republican reconfiguration offered what would become a popular path out of bitter cultural and economic conflict. At the turn of the twentieth century, many Ohioans were concluding that the future of the state depended on emphasizing what united citizens rather than what divided them. Industrialization, urbanization, and diversity had transformed their world. Rather than concentrate on reforming individuals, some would now focus on reforming the state's landscape. They would create new kinds of public spaces in which people could behave like citizens. They would root out corruption and inefficiencies that hindered the emergence of a larger community. They would return to religion as a source of social harmony rather than discord. And they would look to government, particularly at the local level, as both the engine of change and the arbiter of a new order.

A tintype of Samuel Jones and his second wife, Helen Beach Jones, a schoolteacher in Toledo, made at Put-in-Bay while they were courting. They married in August 1892. (Courtesy of The Toledo-Lucas County Public Library, Toledo, Ohio)

7

Reforming Ohio

—

STARTING IN THE 1890s and lasting through the 1910s, a revitalization movement swept Ohio. Reformers believed that something
was seriously wrong with their state and focused on reforming government in order to reinvigorate public culture. Like similar efforts
throughout the industrializing world, the movement consisted of
many local plans united only by a widespread desire to restore a sense
of common purpose in the midst of rapid change. Consciously seeking an accommodation with a new world created by industrialization, immigration, and urbanization, some wealthy and respectable
Ohioans became even more insistent about the value of a public culture. They feared that the world constructed by their ancestors in the
early nineteenth century, a world that had triumphed in the war
against the South, was fragmenting into a cacophony of competing
voices. So concerned were people with their particular stories that
they rarely thought of a greater good. So obsessed were they with
their own parochial world that they rarely considered the larger political community. Many citizens recognized that the problems were
more complicated than perverse resistance on the part of immigrants
huddled together in neighborhood enclaves. Rapid change had dis-
figured cities and blighted the countryside. Greed had trumped every
other consideration. Material progress had taken precedence over
moral progress.

Particularly in the industrial cities of northern Ohio, some citizens
began to call loudly for reform. Believing that governments, shorn of
corruption and committed to justice, could function as true instruments of the people as a whole, reformers looked to bring order out of

chaos. Municipal governments could own and operate basic public services and see to it that cities functioned efficiently. As important, governments could construct public spaces where citizens could gather to consider their problems as a community and to enjoy each other's company. Civic improvements would draw people out of their neighborhoods and into a wider world. Public parks would provide common ground. Public institutions would provide common information and common services, and public buildings would represent higher purposes than greed and parochialism. Revitalizing public culture would remind Ohioans that there was more to life than immediate gratification and local interests. It would transform the state through constitutional revisions, elaborate legislation, and a host of ornate municipal buildings, elaborate museums, and broad boulevards.

Reformers usually were Protestant, economically well-off citizens who define public culture through the prism of their values. Often, their calls for reform had the character of a religious revival. They seemed to think that shaping an environment designed to encourage people to think beyond themselves would succeed only if Ohioans experienced a conversion to citizenship in their hearts and minds.

The Public Interest

Reforming Ohio began with improving its public institutions. One of their most important functions was to provide citizens with the information they needed to make decisions and to locate themselves within communities beyond their households and neighborhoods. Newspapers, libraries, and schools laid the foundations of citizenship. Without them, Ohioans could not begin to overcome selfishness and parochialism. Happily for reform, the growing professionalization of Americans meant that there were more people committed to achieving some degree of objectivity and balance in the operations of newspapers and schools. Their goal was to provide information dispassionately in ways that would facilitate reasonable discussions of public issues. Many worried that public conversation in the late 1800s had degenerated. What better way to start to reverse that trend than by relying on trained experts who adhered to professional codes of conduct? Were not objective journalists, librarians, scholars, and teachers better equipped to analyze social ills and propose solutions than interested politicians or angry citizens?

In the early 1900s, several Ohio newspapers began to practice was dubbed the "new journalism." "New journalists" dedicated themselves to making newspapers organs of the public interest. Eschewing association with politicians and advertisers, they strove for a combination of objectivity and public advocacy, hoping to increase circulation by convincing their readers that they were reliable sources of information. The pioneer was the *Dayton Daily News.* Under publisher James M. Cox, the paper bought a gasoline-powered press and devised contests to build circulation. Advertising strategies became more aggressive. In addition, Cox strove to expand news coverage. He joined the Associated Press wire service so that his paper could carry the latest in national and international news, and he added a women's editor and a society section. The changes were immediately successful. The *News* drove the Cincinnati papers, which had long dominated the Dayton area, out of the market. Circulation nearly doubled, from 16,305 in 1901 to 30,347 in 1907, and advertising increased dramatically.

The reform of the *Dayton Daily News* was about more than profit. Cox was a Democrat who would become governor of Ohio in the 1910s. Nonetheless, he trumpeted his newspaper's independence: it was a public institution doing the people's business. "When the press takes an independent course, when it opposes wrong and attempts no longer to disguise the facts for political effect," Cox said in 1901, "then will better conditions prevail generally and the press will occupy its proper place as a public benefactor, a blessing to the world, a protection to the people." Being a public servant did not mean passively reporting what others were doing. The *Daily News* sought to improve the world in a nonpartisan fashion. "We do not hope to reform things in a day," Cox proclaimed in 1902. "The evil is too deep-seated to be cured by a newspaper article. But please God, just so long as we have the power to write we shall call attention to the hypocrisy as we find it: just so long as it is a newspaper, the *Dayton Daily News* will denounce the rich criminal in the same terms that it denounces the poor criminal."[1]

Cox's paper combined boosterism and reform in repeated calls for civic improvement. Its journalists advocated parks, a symphony orchestra, a concert hall, a water recreation plant, and Sunday baseball as well as public housing and jobs for the residents of Dayton's slums. Sympathetic to labor, the *Daily News* supported justice for workers within limits: "Every man who works hard should be paid enough to live comfortably, send his children to school, genteely attired if he is frugal." Hardly a radical sentiment, it at least accorded working men some measure of dignity as long as they subscribed to middle-class values. Meanwhile, the paper editorialized, "capital should receive a fair return on its investment and be compensated for the large element of risk attached to its operation." Cox was hostile both to immigrants who refused to assimilate and to African Americans because neither could become good citizens. Arguing that central and eastern Europeans were responsible for the deterioration of public culture, the *Daily News* called for expanded public schools and restrictive voting requirements in order to lessen the influence of immigrants. Announcing that "the Anglo Saxon is the grandest race that evolution has produced," the paper supported de facto segregation in Dayton.[2] In its support of a revitalization of public culture defined by middle-class Protestants, the newspaper embodied the reform impulse in Ohio.

It was far from alone in reimagining itself as a paper of the people. The *Cleveland Plain Dealer* took the same tack. In the early 1900s, professional reporters such as William S. Couch published exposés of corruption, vice, and poverty in Ohio's cities. Meanwhile, the Scripps-McRae League dedicated its chain of papers to the motto: "With a mission and without a muzzle." In addition to the *Cleveland Press* and *Cincinnati Post,* the league acquired the *Toledo News-Bee,* the *Toledo Times,* and the *Columbus Citizen.* Aiming at a working-class readership, the Scripps-McRae papers developed a more colloquial style than the *Daily News* and the *Plain Dealer* but nonetheless described themselves as disinterested public servants.

No institution better epitomized efforts to revive public culture than public libraries. Sometimes with local funds and sometimes through the generosity of industrialist Andrew Carnegie, dozens of Ohio towns constructed symmetrical buildings in a classical style. Housing hundreds of books, newspapers, and journals for the convenience of all citizens, they were monuments to the importance of information in public conversation. While architectural details varied, the libraries normally had a large open room on the first floor where the librarian sat overseeing work like a manager on a factory floor. Often they hosted public lectures or discussion groups in basement rooms. They set aside places for children. In all these ways, libraries housed public conversation. They offered public space in which citizens could gather to read, consider, and discuss the leading issues of the day.

Despite their dedication to democracy, libraries tended to attract mostly middle-class people. (When working-class citizens objected that libraries were elite institutions, they were rewarded with small branches in their neighborhoods.) In practice, librarians, like journalists, advocated middle-class values. Most were professionally trained women intent upon running their buildings with a blend of efficiency and domesticity revealed most fully in their dealings with children. In small towns, middle-class women usually were the driving force behind the creation and maintenance of libraries. Reading was a serious business to be conducted in quiet and with decorum. Where men typically were interested in libraries as symbols of local stability, women focused on their interior space and emphasized morality.

Along with public libraries, public universities promoted a reinvigorated public culture defined by middle-class citizens. While Ohio's many sectarian colleges continued to flourish, the state government committed itself to developing institutions of higher learning that would serve the public, rather than local or religious, interests. With proceeds from the sale of federal lands under the Morrill Land Grant Act of 1862, the General Assembly moved in 1870 to charter the Ohio Agricultural and Mechanical College. Located a couple of miles north of the statehouse in Columbus, it was intended to serve the needs of farmers. The board of trustees adopted a liberal arts curriculum and in 1878 adopted a new name, The Ohio State University.

The mission of Ohio State and other public universities was unambiguous: they were to serve Ohio. Training public school teachers was particularly vital. In 1902, the General Assembly began to subsidize teacher education programs at Ohio and Miami Universities. To ensure that each corner of the state got its share, the legislature created normal schools at Bowling Green and Kent in 1910. It had already established Central State University in Wilberforce in 1887 to train black educators. Meanwhile, cities also started universities to serve the public interest. Cincinnati helped support a local university with taxes in return for outreach programs that emphasized community service and practical training. Toledo and Akron also had municipal universities by the 1920s. Cleveland was the only major city without a university, in part because of the success of the Case School of Applied Science, which merged with Western Reserve University in 1967.

While relatively few Ohioans attended public universities, the emergence of these tax-subsidized institutions represented a larger commitment by governments to the cause of public discourse. The hope was that whatever graduates of the universities did with their lives, they would be better citizens because of their years in college. Although a great deal of students' time was spent in extracurricular activities, their education was essentially utilitarian. It prepared them for specific kinds of jobs. Nonetheless, something momentous had happened. By the early 1900s, higher education was seen as a public responsibility, something that could no longer be left in the hands of churches.

Increasingly professionalized, faculty members devoted a portion of their time to research. The study of history exemplified the change. Throughout the nineteenth century, Ohio's historians were partisan and their stories romanticized. The tendency toward boosterism climaxed in the decades following the Civil War when popular histories were usually unabashed tributes to local communities and their most prominent citizens. Voluminous county histories, which proliferated in the last third of the nineteenth century, offered basic narratives of events broken up with generous quotations from early newspapers and anecdotes derived from questionable oral traditions. At the heart of these books were biographical sketches of local notables and their ancestors as well as notices of important local institutions and businesses. Few said anything that a real estate developer would want to hide from prospective buyers.

Just as journalists, librarians, and government officials prided themselves on their disinterested professionalism, Ohio's historians by the early 1900s became more committed to professional standards in researching and writing balanced monographs whose arguments rested on verifiable evidence. The Ohio Archaeological and Historical Society, the Historical and Philosophical Society of Ohio, and the Western Reserve Historical Society inaugurated annual publications that offered summaries of the organizations' activities along with historical essays and collections of documents. By the 1920s, these had become quarterly journals full of articles written by trained scholars. Historians such as Beverley W. Bond Jr. of the University of Cincinnati, William T. Utter of Denison University, and Randolph C. Downes of the University of Toledo emerged as practitioners of a new kind of history. Supporting their arguments with exhaustive archival research, striving to integrate Ohio's story into a national one, these men reflected the mission of Ohio's universities. They were experts presenting the results of their research as information that would enrich Ohio.

Important as the transformation of higher education was to the revitalization of public culture, the struggle for control of Ohio's public school system was even more significant—and far more intense. Anxious about immigrants, the General Assembly made school attendance compulsory in 1889 and authorized truant officers to enforce the law. In 1902, the legistature made the length of the school year, the content of curriculums, and the number of grades relatively uniform. In 1921, the Bing Law required everyone between the ages of six and eighteen to attend school, unless they had already graduated from a high school.

These changes were only the beginning of educational reform. At the local level, school officials, influenced by experts in education and psychology, moved away from rote memorization and simple moral lessons to more practical curricula. They began to see schools as cities in miniature. Schools' diverse populations made them laboratories in which to test ways to cultivate civic culture. Remodeled or new buildings included public spaces such as auditoriums and gymnasiums, and schools exposed students to the outside world through bulletin boards and community service projects. School boards generally relaxed restrictions on teachers so that they could experiment with different methods.

None of this happened overnight or without conflict. In 1890, the Cleveland school board was responsible for the education of more than ninety thousand students. Influential citizens wanted to deal with changes brought about by rapid urbanization and industrialization by ensuring that education was utilitarian. To enable students to function better in a diverse society, they advocated bringing the lessons of business into the school system. Remarked banker Myron T. Herrick, "Educated and well-to-do people, not only in Cleveland but in a great many towns everywhere, had begun to realize that they had some civic duty besides making a contribution to the campaign funds and paying their taxes."[3]

Reformers sought centralization and professionalization. Overcoming resistance from politicians and Catholics, they achieved many of their goals. Clevelanders started to elect members of the school council at large rather than by wards so that general rather than specific interests would be served. They also chose a school director who, in addition to exercising veto power over the actions of the council, appointed a superintendent. With support from Republicans and hostility from Democrats, reformers won a narrow victory in 1892. They immediately hired Andrew Draper, the superintendent of the New York state school system, who urged teachers to reform their methods and increased the number of students who attended schools. His administration developed kindergartens, promoted vocational education, and eliminated corporal punishment.

Draper was the consummate professional reformer. A Republican in politics, he was a hero to the respectable people of Cleveland. While Draper promised friendship to everyone "who is the friend of the Cleveland public schools," including those who worshiped differently or who spoke indifferent or no English, he was unable to win the confidence of Catholics and other immigrants. They rightly saw his work as an effort to substitute Protestant values for those of their communities. Draper believed his job was to graduate "young men and women" with "intellectual powers so trained that they will have both the ability and desire to acquire more and more; with some moral sense and some love for the good and the beautiful, and with the emotional powers so active that they will continually strengthen; with character set for intelligent, honest, patriotic citizenship."[4] Few quarreled with these notions in general; the devil, as always, lay in the details. The reformers' achievements intensified the commitment of the Catholic Diocese of Cleveland to a private school system that would reflect Catholic parents' values.

Cincinnati school reformers also emphasized the importance of thinking of the city as a whole. More gradually but no less inexorably, power was concentrated in the hands of a superintendent, and teachers were encouraged to adopt more pragmatic pedagogical styles. Cincinnati schools began to stress a broader notion of civic training that incorporated attention to the environment, public health, and respect for the law and for other human beings. Education also became more specialized, focusing on the particular needs of students. More than anything, schools were the means to develop broad-minded citizens who would care about their community and overcome "the unfavorable and antagonistic influences of the home and the street." Public education was an effort to train students to identify primarily with a public community rather than their family, church, and neighborhood. Students participated in clubs and community affairs; made field trips to cultural events and public libraries; learned about "civic operations," the "rights, privileges, and authority of family life," the "service of a rich commercial neighborhood life," and the "advantages of a public control in affairs of great public interest."[5]

Educational reformers, like librarians and journalists, were redefining the idea of the public so as to allow for some degree of pluralism without sacrificing the core values of their class and their faith. Citizens owed more than money and allegiance to the state. They were obliged to devote themselves to the public good above their local worlds. Libraries and universities, newspapers and schools urged a revitalization of public culture that, while theoretically neutral, tended to affirm middle-class, Protestant notions about the possibilities of life in Ohio.

A Christian Commonwealth

Respectable Protestants were aware of the dilemma created by their advocacy of a public culture that reflected their values and silenced alternatives. Recognizing the permanence of the changes wrought by industrialization, immigration, and urbanization, they looked for ways to advance their notions of moral progress in a new context. No longer willing to speak in sectarian terms, and worried about class and religious divisions, they tried to reconcile religion and reform in a general commitment to a broad-based Christian brotherhood. Like the new journalism, new schools, and new libraries, the new Protestantism tried to subsume pluralism under citizenship. Redefining public culture would encourage people to devote themselves to their larger, politically defined community and turn away from supposedly parochial loyalties.

Among the most famous exponents of the relationship between religion and civic life was Washington Gladden. Born in Pennsylvania in 1836, Gladden grew up in Oswego, New York. After graduating from Williams College, he served as a Congregational minister to several churches in New York and Massachusetts as well as the religious editor of a newspaper in New York City in the early 1870s. By the time Gladden accepted the call of the First Congregational Church in Columbus in 1882, he had become a tireless advocate of Christian participation in civic life. "What is assumed by the government is not withdrawn from the sphere of Christian activism, because the Christian is a citizen," he wrote in 1877, "and it is part of his Christian duty to see to it that the government is wisely chosen, and that it performs its duties."[6]

Until his death in 1918, Gladden was one of Columbus's leading citizens, an impressive preacher with a social conscience. Membership in the First Congregational Church grew from 558 in 1885 to 1,214 in 1914. By and large, it was a respectable, white, upper-middle-class group that included professors, teachers, bankers, and industrialists. Shy and reserved, friendly but not familiar, Gladden never compromised the dignity of his position. His popularity as a preacher rested on his sense of humor and the substance of his sermons. A large, relatively short man who sported a full white beard, Gladden was an imposing presence. He lobbied for restrictions on saloons. He also was concerned about immigrants, political corruption, and municipal inefficiency. The proper response to all these challenges, he believed, lay in expanded municipal control over companies that served the public. Elected to city council in 1900, Gladden helped win a reduction in streetcar fares, led a fight for a publicly owed electric plant, and fought a hike in the city's gas rate. These relatively minor battles reflected a profound faith in the power of disinterested local government to protect the public from greedy corporations.

Gladden believed that because the future of America lay in the hands of its citizens, they had to care about their community and participate in their government. "The duty of governing this city is yours," he told the citizens of Columbus in 1885, "and you can do it if you will." And what better example of civic involvement than the pastor of the First Congregational Church? "The pulpit is not the place for partisan politics," Gladden declared in 1895, "but the pulpit is the place for enforcing upon the consciences of citizens the solemnity and sacredness of the obligations which rest upon them, and their duty to discharge these obligations."[7]

Gladden wanted citizens to be sober, disciplined, enlightened, and interested in the development of their character and those of others. But he leavened his righteousness with both an acceptance of change and a tentative accommodation to difference. One of Gladden's great strengths was his ability to deal with new ideas and new challenges. Science did not frighten him; evolution could be subsumed within God's world. Material progress was a good thing if carefully managed. Gladden knew that cities of a size and complexity scarcely imaginable when he was born would not go away. The challenge was not to judge them but to shape their future. If the city was not necessarily a "peril," it was too often rife with vice, crime, poverty, and alienation. "The city ought to be the flower of civilization; by careless or vicious management it may easily become the smut of civilization."[8]

Like others of his class, Gladden denounced the weakness of human beings, especially failures to resist the temptations of alcohol or to ensure that children received a proper education. But Gladden blamed individual failings far less than he blamed the lack of organization in modern urban life. Dealing with social ills had to go beyond haranguing saloon keepers. Good Christian citizens had to go forth and retake power from political bosses and industrialists. Respectable people had to reengage public life and rebuild their communities emotionally as well as structurally. They had to develop "a municipal consciousness." In *Cosmopolis City Club,* a novel published in 1893, Gladden traced the path of good men organizing among themselves in order to save both their community and themselves.[9]

None of this secular work was incompatible with Christianity. To the contrary, civic participation would help establish the Kingdom of God. Reform would produce a world in which "the city that ought to be, the New Columbus, will begin to descend out of heaven from God." Gladden put the matter directly in 1899 when he urged the state legislature to unify and revise municipal codes. "I know of nothing within our power as citizens of Ohio, which would do more to hasten the coming of that Kingdom than the adoption by our legislature of the main feature of this municipal code."[10]

The transformation of a sometimes depraved and generally disordered city into a shining example of civilization depended on the mobilization of all citizens. Only by getting people to feel invested in the larger community could Ohio secure the goodwill of its citizenry. The Kingdom of God would not consist of one group of people restraining all others. It must include "young and old, rich and poor, good and bad, black and white, native born and foreign born, all the people of the city."[11] And the focus of the kingdom would be a popularly controlled city hall, ensuring justice, arbitrating the disputes of labor and capital, regulating city services, and maintaining parks, museums, and buildings.

Gladden spoke to and for many middle-class Ohioans who were seeking a middle way, a path through change that would reaffirm their values without dividing American society even further. His vision, however, was as limited as it was generous. The recipient of an honorary degree from Notre Dame University in 1905 because of his commitment to religious liberty, Gladden spoke often of the failings of Catholic immigrants. His desire to see African Americans become full citizens was undercut by his racism. "To imagine that it was possible, by any political device whatever, to invert the natural order of society, and give to the ignorance of the community the supremacy over its intelligence," he wrote of Reconstruction, "was an infatuation to which rational legislators ought not to have been subject." Guided by sympathetic whites, blacks could become good citizens through education, hard work, and civic devotion. Gladden did not encourage blacks to demand social equality or seek intermarriage with whites. "We stand for no unnatural fusion of races, for no impracticable notions of social intercourse," he said in a 1903 address at Atlanta University, "but we do stand for perfect equality for the Negro before the law, and behind the law."[12]

Gladden's ultimate enemy was selfishness. "Any organization of society which is founded on selfishness will come to grief," he wrote. In addition to living for God, we must have "love for our fellow men . . . such a love as makes us willing to deny ourselves for their welfare and happiness; purity, truthfulness, sincerity of life, these are spiritual things, in contradistinction from which is selfish and worldly and carnal." "How easy it would be to settle all the trouble, if all these men on both sides would only say, 'Come! Let us be friends.' Is that, brother men, a hard thing to say?'" "Friendship" as "Religion" summarized Gladden's thinking.[13]

This naive but appealing philosophy lay behind an explosion of benevolent organizations during Gladden's lifetime. Middle-class women in particular participated in groups dedicated to ameliorating the material conditions of the lives of the unfortunate as well as saving their souls. In Cleveland, five maternity homes for unmarried mothers opened between 1869 and 1936. Increasingly professional in their operations, they were pledged to the reformation and salvation of both mothers and children. So were the Salvation Army, the Young Men's Christian Organization, the Young Women's Christian Organization, the Associated Charities, and the Committee on Cooperation, many of which came under the umbrella of the Welfare Foundation of Cleveland in 1917.

More experimental were the five settlement houses in turn-of-the-century Cleveland. Respectable people went to live in homes in poor neighborhoods on the assumption that their example would lay the foundations for reinvigorated urban villages. The first settlement house was called Hiram House because students from Hiram College opened it in June 1896. Meeting with no success in an Irish Catholic neighborhood, the students moved to a Jewish one. Donations from wealthy Clevelanders allowed Hiram House to survive into the twentieth century.

These well-intentioned efforts amounted to cultural imperialism. Settlement houses were bastions of middle-class respectability designed to rectify the disorder of Catholic and Jewish communities. A spirit of benevolence at best, condescension at worst, permeated the movement. No wonder many immigrants reacted with skepticism. Charity, claimed one, is "the price that House of Privilege pays for the right to continue to steal." Even Protestant L. B. Tuckerman, a doctor and supporter of labor organizations, refused to contribute to the Charity Organization Society because if it was "really interested in charity . . . it would stop the twelve-hour day; it would increase wages, and put an end to the cruel killing and maiming of men. It is interested in getting its own wreckage out of sight. It isn't pleasant to see it begging on the streets." The doctor wanted his "responsibility for poverty . . . kept before [his] eyes[.]" He did not want it out of sight; he did not want to feel better about himself because he gave money to make it invisible.[14]

Tuckerman's criticism went to the heart of what influential people such as Gladden believed was the great work of revising Ohio. Citizens could rearrange space and change laws; they could rebuild cities and sponsor settlement houses. But real change would come only from within individuals. People had to experience a transformation within their hearts that opened them to both God and the larger community. The essential problem with greedy industrialists, corrupt politicians, and parochial immigrants alike was that they had put the gratification of individual desires above their civic responsibilities. The key to reform was an emotional awakening to one's duty to others.

Building New Cities

The political struggle for reform at the turn of the century centered on northern Ohio cities. Samuel M. Jones and Brand Whitlock in Toledo and Tom Johnson and Newton Baker in Cleveland became mayors of those cities in order to do battle with privilege and monopoly. Their issues—the reduction of streetcar fares, municipal ownership of utilities, and home rule for cities—may seem trivial in retrospect. But they were controversial at the time in no small part because they symbolized a struggle for power. More important than specific issues was a wish to expand the level of participation in civic affairs. Jones and Johnson idealistically envisioned a future in which cities boasted broad boulevards, great public buildings, extensive public parks, and government by, of, and for the people.

Pennsylvania-born lawyer Frederick C. Howe, an adviser to Mayor Johnson, dreamed of a more beautiful Cleveland. He was proud that his advocacy had led "an expert commission" to reconfigure a stretch of land along the lakefront. With a mall running down the middle and blessed with gardens and ample parking, the area became home to a city hall, county courthouse, federal building, public library, and auditorium, all in a uniform architectural style intended to create a sense of harmony.[15] Howe's dream was not unique to Ohio or the United States. The notion that well-ordered public space could affirm a sense of community was a worldwide phenomenon.

In the late 1890s, the great political excitement in Ohio was in Toledo. The catalyst was the charismatic businessman Samuel M. Jones, known more widely as "Golden Rule" Jones, whose greatest personal asset was his empathy for other human beings. Born in Wales in 1846 to Methodist parents, Jones had acquired a strong sense of moral responsibility and incredible ambition. Jones was always ashamed of his inability to live up to the high standards he learned as a youth. After prospering in the oil fields of western Pennsylvania, he moved in 1886 to Lima, where he made a fortune during the local oil boom by developing an all-metal version of the sucker rods used to connect pumps in the earth with engines on the surface. He received a patent in 1894 and converted an old factory on Toledo's south side into a manufacturing plant. He divided his time between Lima and Toledo because of his marriage in 1892 to Helen Beach, a schoolteacher who was the daughter of an affluent former mayor of Lima. (Jones's first wife had died several years earlier, leaving him with two sons and a daughter.)

Toledo's problems in the 1890s were similar to those of most major American cities. With twenty-five miles of docks and twenty-three miles of railroad tracks, Toledo sat at one of the major crossroads of the Midwest. In recent decades, the city had become a leader in the refining and shipping of oil and the manufacturing of glass, ships, and bicycles. Economic opportunities brought immigrants. In 1890, 65 percent of the 81,434 residents of Toledo had been born outside the U.S. or were the children of immigrants. Another 10,000 people came to the city in 1891 and 1892. Then catastrophe arrived in the form of the devastating economic depression that swept the nation in 1893 and persisted throughout the decade. Unemployment mounted while businessmen cut the wages of those workers they did not fire.

In the midst of crisis, Jones sailed against the tide. He ran his factory in a fashion that would have been unique in an era of prosperity. Influenced by his personal religious experiences and his wide reading in contemporary social criticism, Jones insisted on the importance of dignity and self-respect for everyone. In his factory, he posted a tin sign with the inscription: "THE RULE THAT GOVERNS THIS FACTORY: 'Therefore Whatsoever Ye Would That Men Should Do Unto You, Do Ye So Unto Them.'"[16] Jones's commitment went beyond platitudes. Workers at the Acme Sucker Rod Company received wages 50 percent higher than those paid by his competitors. Jones did away with time clocks, created a profit-sharing plan, and provided paid vacations, a company cafeteria, and day-care facilities. In his oil fields, men worked only eight-hour shifts. While many thought his actions radical, Jones insisted that he was just practicing "applied Christianity."

Jones devoted himself to improving the lives of Toledo's citizens as well as his employees. In 1896 and 1897, he brought Jane Addams, Washington Gladden, Henry Demarest Lloyd, and other advocates of humanitarian reform to the city to give lectures. He supported a settlement house, created a free kindergarten for the children of his employees, and pioneered a cooperative insurance plan. Also notable were his efforts to develop a system of public parks in Toledo. He bought the lot next to his factory and transformed it into a grassy area complete with benches, swings, and a maypole. There were free lectures and concerts and a place for working-class people to spend Sunday afternoons.

Jones was unconventional by anyone's standards. While he defied the business practices of his day, he lived well in a comfortable home characterized by patriarchal domesticity. Later in his life, Jones became a vegetarian. He took up running long before it was popular and tried standing on his head on occasion to improve his health. Above all, he was fascinated by the idea of brotherhood, by the need to sacrifice in the greater cause of social justice and humanity. Whatever the source of his commitment to living by the Golden Rule, he put his money where his mouth was. Maintaining the park next to his factory cost him $500 a year. And he gave away so much money that his personal fortune fell from around $1 million in 1894 to around $333,000 when he died in 1904.

Jones was chosen as the Republican candidate for mayor of Toledo in 1897 because the party was divided. He won a narrow victory, then was reelected three times as an independent. In 1899 he launched an unsuccessful campaign for the governorship of Ohio. Even though he finished third, he won Cuyahoga and Lucas Counties and did well in Hamilton County. Far from discouraged, Jones saw his loss as another step in the moral progress of Ohio. His repudiation of Republicans was part of his general rejection of institutions that he believed had grown stale and corrupt because they were more interested in greed and power than in doing good. Although a devout Christian, Jones believed that churches as well as political parties were responsible.

Jones's goal as a political leader was to build community by defeating selfishness. He was an indifferent administrator, and his record as mayor was mixed. While Jones made Toledo the first American city with an eight-hour workday for municipal employees, he was unable to win municipal ownership of utilities or rein in highhanded police courts. But all these things mattered less to him than a revival of humanity. Like most respectable citizens, Jones was a teetotaler and a foe of prostitution, saloons, and gambling. Where he diverged was in his tolerance of vice. After all, prostitutes and saloon keepers had to make a living. Jones did not blame individuals for social problems. He blamed corrupt institutions that neglected to work for the common good.

Jones was not representative of Ohio's middle-class reformers. Most of his support came from working-class neighborhoods whose interests he championed. Like Gladden, his interest in reform was largely personal. His philosophy was summarized in a quotation from his favorite poet, Walt Whitman, that he posted on a wall at the Acme Sucker Rod factory: "Produce Great Persons, the Rest Follows." If people would improve themselves and learn to treat each other with respect and dignity, the city of Toledo, the state of Ohio, and the United States would surely prosper. "There is," Jones wrote, "a heroic and spiritual core to our national life. . . . We are developing a free-spirited, tolerant robustness of character which will set us free from small and petty conceptions of life. We shall yet have *men to match our mountains, rivers and prairies*—large-natured men, too generous to be tyrannical and too strong to be selfish."[17]

Jones's famous counterpart in Cleveland, Tom Johnson, was neither as idealistic nor as religious as the mayor of Toledo. Born in Georgetown, Kentucky, in 1854, Johnson accumulated a considerable fortune as inventor of an automatic streetcar fare box. In 1879, he outfoxed Cleveland's preeminent businessman, Mark Hanna, to establish himself in the streetcar business in the city. Later he made more money as a manufacturer of streetcar rails. While he was converted to the single-tax notion of the New York reformer Henry George, Johnson was a relatively conventional businessman who lived in a fine home on Euclid Avenue and served as a Democratic congressman from Cleveland from 1891 to 1895. Elected mayor in 1901, he was finally defeated in 1909, and died two years later. The overweight Johnson was a great conversationalist who was able to charm many people. Far less empathetic and more worldly than Jones, he also was less tortured by a need for personal perfection.

Johnson's record as mayor was controversial. Although he revised the city's tax system, his great crusade for municipal ownership of streetcars failed. After years of struggle, he was unable to sustain a three-cent fare for streetcar rides, the issue that had been the cornerstone of his campaigns. Meanwhile, his repeated attempts to win home rule for cities were unsuccessful. Johnson was also seen as something of a hypocrite. A vociferous critic of political corruption, he built a personal political machine in Cleveland. To many, he seemed just a gadfly businessman.

But over the long term, Johnson had a significant impact on Cleveland. He attracted professional experts and placed them in important positions in city government. As important, he received considerable support from Cleveland's immigrant population. Johnson, like Jones, frightened many middle-class people who saw him as too radical. Like Jones (and any good Democrat), Johnson avoided cultural issues. He did not campaign for temperance or public education. Instead, he focused his energy on reclaiming government for the people. His most visible legacies were parks, public works, and revised public health policies.

Following Jones's lead, Johnson's administration operated a liberal parole system for criminals, encouraged police officers to use more discretion in dealing with juvenile delinquents and petty criminals, and emphasized rehabilitation in workhouses and reformatories. Johnson blamed "crime and vice and misery" on "involuntary poverty," which was itself "the result of law-made privilege, whereby some men get more than they earn while the vast mass of mankind earns more than it gets."[18] The Johnson administration opened parks to everyone, let people walk on the grass, and built tennis courts and playgrounds. Characteristic of Johnson's more democratic style were tent meetings in which the mayor discussed civic life.

Johnson shared with Jones (and with Gladden) a commitment to the idea that the history of Ohio, like the history of the world, was a ceaseless struggle between the people and privilege. Progress occurred only through the victories of the former over the latter. Such triumphs were not easy because, wrote a disappointed Johnson a few months before his death, the people were "slow to wake up, slow to recognize their own interests, slow to realize their power, slow to invoke it," while privilege was "always awake and quick to act." Still, there was hope. Government embodied the popular will, and Cleveland demonstrated the possibilities of collective action. "The chief value of any social movement," Johnson explained, "lies perhaps in the influence it exerts upon the minds and hearts of the men and women who engage in it."[19]

Newton Baker, who became mayor of Cleveland for two terms starting in 1911, was less charismatic than Johnson. Broadening his sense of reform into a spirit of what he called "civitism," or civic patriotism, Baker relied even more heavily on experts to manage the city and plan its development. He built alliances with the businessmen-dominated Cleveland Foundation, later reorganized as the Municipal Association. Baker advocated municipal ownership of utilities for its efficiency and low cost. Among other things, his administration created city dance halls to woo people away from decadent private ones; improved the safety of streetcars; enhanced public education; built a municipal lighting plant in 1911, which helped force down the cost of lighting; and spent ten thousand dollars in support of a city orchestra. According to his biographer, "Baker believed that the greatness of a city did not depend on its buildings, either public or private, but rather on the intensity with which its citizens loved the city as their home."[20]

Revising the State

Reform mayors such as Jones and Johnson were continually frustrated by the enormous power of the state government. Cities were subject to rules made by the General Assembly, which is why the mayors were such strong supporters of municipal home rule. The constitution of Ohio hindered Johnson's struggle against the streetcar companies because it forbade municipal ownership of transportation companies. No wonder he thought he could achieve little as long as a legislature dominated by men from rural areas and small towns made laws in Ohio. The popular explanation of politicians' alleged aversion to reform was corruption. To Christian reformers, no one seemed less Christ-like than the men who ran the state government and represented Ohio in Washington, D.C.

In 1895, Allen Myers of Pickaway County published an indictment of political corruption, arguing that bribery was so widespread in the General Assembly that U.S. Senate seats were bought and sold. Myers marveled at the changes in Ohio in a century. Forests had become fields, cities had become great, and "the savage so dreaded has disappeared forever." But the struggle was not over. In the place of the Indian now arose "other foes, more dangerous to our civilization, our homes and our institutions than the untutored red man." "In our modern politics we have savages that exceed in brutality the most atrocious deeds of the relentless Indians." Myers contended that the writers of Ohio's 1802 constitution had made the executive too weak and the legislature too powerful. The latter's control of patronage inevitably led to abuse. Ohio's admirable founders "did not seem to realize that they were laying the foundations of a state that would soon rise and stand as a master-miracle in an age of miracles."[21] Now, the combination of bossism (direction of a political machine) and boodle (bribery on the grand scale) was destroying their fragile creation.

Was Ohio politics as corrupt as Myers and others claimed? To some extent, yes. Money from Standard Oil and other companies did lubricate the legislative process. Public officials accepted retainers from industrialists; lobbyists were omnipresent in ways that would horrify people a century later. A notorious example was Republican Joseph Foraker. An attorney from Cincinnati, Foraker worked for railroads, public utilities, and corporations throughout his career. Elected governor in 1885, the thirty-nine-year-old Foraker was an able administrator who supported the interests of big business and greased the palms of key supporters. He was elected to the U.S. Senate in 1896 and wielded immense influence until he lost his seat after the publication of letters from a vice president of Standard Oil showed that Foraker had received at least $29,500 for supporting the corporation's agenda.

In many ways, Foraker's career embodied the history of the Republican Party. As a young man, he had marched to the sea with William Tecumseh Sherman. Later, he earned the nickname "Fire Alarm Joe" because of his passionate oratory, much of it directed against Southerners. Over the decades, however, Foraker had aligned himself with businessmen, accepted bribes, and become an unscrupulous opponent of Senator John Sherman, the distinguished brother of William. Somewhere along the way, Foraker, it seemed, had made himself his primary cause.

The poster boy of political corruption was George B. Cox of Cincinnati. A native of the city, born in 1853 to British immigrants, Cox worked a variety of jobs as a youth. He was a bootblack, a newsboy, a lookout for gamblers, a delivery boy, a bartender, and a tobacco salesman. Eventually he bought a saloon at the corner of Longworth and John. From his headquarters, he won election to city council in 1879 and regularly delivered the votes of his ward to Republican candidates. By the late 1880s, Cox was a recognized force in Cincinnati politics. Although he held some minor offices, the source of his power was his control of patronage. Insisting on absolute loyalty, he distributed political favors widely and built a solid core of voters that was decisive in close contests.

Cox was everything middle-class reformers despised. Indifferently educated, a saloon keeper, a man who forthrightly declared that he was looking out for his own interests, he was anything but the enlightened citizen of brotherly love imagined by Washington Gladden and Golden Rule Jones. Yet Cox won support on more than one occasion from leading Republicans in Cincinnati and from middle-class, reform-minded voters who lived on the hills north of the down-town area. Many people thought that Cox made Cincinnati work. They tolerated his excesses because he brought order to a rapidly changing city. He got things done and did so relatively inexpensively. The Cox machine provided citizens with a professional police force and fire department; expanded the city (and its tax base) with a series of annexations; engaged water, electricity, and transportation issues; and modernized the public schools.

In the early 1900s, the onslaughts of reformers and journalists de-stroyed Cox's political power. His machine had become associated too closely with corruption, special privilege, slum life, and immorality. In the late nineteenth century, however, Cox's way of doing things had seemed to many to be a viable response to the chaos of urban life, an alternative method in which efficiency mattered more than character, in which getting things done mattered more than one's personal be-havior. Cox maintained power for a long time not simply through bribery but by being reasonably responsive to the needs and interests of his constituents. The existence of corruption does not necessarily mean an absence of democracy. Or as Cox put it, "a boss" was "not necessarily a public enemy."[22]

Perhaps more important than corruption in inhibiting reform at the state level was the essential conservatism of many Ohio politi-cians. Rarely the kinds of citizens idealized by Gladden and Jones, they were not men of broad vision. Many went into politics for self-ish or parochial reasons—to satisfy ambition, to become famous, powerful, or wealthy, or to advance their interests and those of peo-ple like them. The successful ones quickly learned that winning of-fice, while occasionally a reward for genuine merit, was a combination of talent, hard work, and luck. Indeed, being the right person at the right time was more than half the game. Smart men learned that political ascent usually depended on the ability to get along, keep people happy, be popular without being controversial, and have the right friends. Even the honest and talented William Howard Taft of Cincinnati rose to the U.S. presidency in 1909 on the basis of a string of appointments that began with a federal judge-ship arranged by Senator Joseph Foraker.

No one better exemplified the rules of the game than Warren G. Harding, a man of modest talents who became president of the United States in 1921. Harding believed in the conventional pieties of small-town Ohio life. Born in the village of Blooming Grove in November 1865, Harding accepted the editorship of the struggling *Marion Star* in 1884. Through hard work and some innovation, he made the newspaper into a success. By the time he married the strong-willed music teacher Florence M. King in 1891, Harding was a force in Marion, a growing presence in Republican circles. In 1899 he won election to the Ohio Senate, and in 1903 he became lieutenant governor. Defeated for the governorship in 1910, Harding won election to the U.S. Senate in 1914. Six years later, as a good-looking, popular senator from an important state, he became the Republican nominee for president and defeated another Ohioan, James M. Cox, the Dayton newspaper editor, in the election.

In his inaugural address, the man from Marion proclaimed that "our supreme task is the resumption of our normal way."[23] Harding was talking about recovery from the crisis of World War I and its immediate aftermath. In many ways, however, the sentence summarized his character and career. Harding was always committed to normalcy as he understood it, that is, to the respectable world of middle-class men and women in small towns. He stood for progress, for prosperity, and for men of good character. Never mind that Harding had a series of lovers, including a young Marion girl, Nan Britton, whom he impregnated in 1920 and with whom he happily cavorted in hotel rooms and the White House. Never mind that Harding's circle of friends—the Ohio Gang—turned his administration into one of the most corrupt in American history. What mattered was the way he handled himself in public.

Harding's great gift was his friendliness. He liked to hang out with men as well as women, playing cards and talking. When he got to Columbus as a novice legislator, he made his name as a boon companion rather than as a serious thinker. According to a reporter, he was "the most popular man in the legislature. He was soon regarded as a coming man in Ohio politics. He was an excellent 'mixer,' he had the inestimable gift of never forgetting a man's face or his name, and there was always a genuine warmth in his handshake, a real geniality in his smile. He was a regular he-man according to the sign manual of the old days—a great poker player, and not at all averse to putting a foot on the brass rail."[24] Twenty years later, Harding held twice-a-week poker parties with his friends. Although he ate well and put on weight, the president continued to play golf.

People genuinely liked Harding, and he genuinely liked them. "I *love* to meet people," he told his secretary when he worried that the president was overwhelmed with visitors. "It is the most pleasant thing I do; it is really the only fun I have. It does not tax me, and it seems to be a very great pleasure to them."[25] The problem was that Harding was so eager to please that he sometimes seemed to have no real convictions. He navigated the complicated shoals of Ohio's politics well, keeping party leaders happy. When he was talked into running against the aging Senator Foraker in the 1914 Republican primary, he did so reluctantly. Foraker had done him more than one favor. Harding won and promptly sent the senator a gushing letter in which he virtually apologized for running against him.

Harding wanted to have it both ways. He was a politician who wanted to win elections without offending anyone—an ambition he often fulfilled. Harding's biographer attributed his obsession with "mindless conformity" to widespread rumors, which dogged him from childhood, that he had an African American ancestor. Harding would do anything to win acceptance.[26] No doubt the rumors were part of it. But in another sense Harding simply embodied the affable (and occasionally hypocritical) gentility of small-town Ohio men at the turn of the century.

Harding's rival in the 1920 presidential election, the Democrat James M. Cox, was the most successful statewide representative of the reform impulse. Less moralistic and less radical than Jones or Johnson, Cox had ridden the success of the *Dayton Daily News* to the governorship in 1912. He won in part because reform was at high tide in the state. For years, some reformers had lobbied for a convention to revise the state's constitution. They had won some limited successes in the General Assembly, including the passage of constitutional amendments, ratified in popular elections, that created veto power for the governor and placed state elections in even-numbered years. In 1906, the legislature required that all members of the General Assembly as well as local officials (including school boards and most judges) be nominated in open primaries. Welcoming these changes, reformers nonetheless saw them as piecemeal. Only a convention could engage in a systematic overhaul of state government.

They finally got their wish in 1911 when Ohioans elected 120 delegates (including bankers, farmers, lawyers, teachers, laborers, and editors) to a Constitutional Convention. Meeting in January 1912, the delegates divided themselves into committees to consider specific issues and eventually proposed forty-one amendments to the constitution. When the citizenry considered the amendments in September, they passed thirty-three of them. Taken together, they amounted to a serious revision of Ohio's political structure. The process of initiative and referendum, whereby voters could participate more directly in their government, was adopted, as were the direct primary, civil service protections, and a line item veto for the governor. The General Assembly gained the power to establish work hours, a minimum wage, and provide for "the general welfare" of workers. The eight-hour day for public work and workman's compensation became mandatory. The state government assumed more responsibility for public education. The state was empowered to finance better roads and to regulate the use of timber, water, and natural resources. And, although Tom Johnson did not live to see it, Ohio created home rule for cities with a population of five thousand or more. They could now govern themselves as long as they did not violate the state constitution. Defeated were provisions for women's suffrage, the abolition of the death penalty, and the removal of the word "white" from the requirements for the right to vote. Even though African American males had voted in Ohio since 1870, it was not until 1923 that color was no longer specified as a legal requirement for participation in elections.

Elected in the fall of 1912, Governor Cox pressed for more reform. The General Assembly strengthened some of the amendments and passed a stronger workman's compensation bill and child labor act. Under pressure from Cox, the legislature created a rural school code that consolidated school districts and established standards for teachers and students. There also was support for road improvements. The reform wave subsided during Cox's term. Defeated for reelection in 1914, he returned to office in 1916 and 1918 with a more moderate agenda.

Why, if Ohio politics was dominated by men such as Harding, did the state experience such a brief, intense period of serious reform? Why did Cox succeed to some extent where others had failed? In part, the answer lies in the fact that Ohio politicians, while not immune to bribery and boodle, were never as unresponsive to the wishes of voters as reformers charged. As we saw in the previous chapter, Ohio's major parties tended to co-opt the agendas of popular third parties. And in the early 1910s, voters on both the left and right were pressing for reform.

On one side, Democrats and Republicans had to reckon with the success of the Socialist Party. Ohio Socialists were relatively respectable. Attracting native-born and immigrant voters, Socialists sponsored public lectures and concerts, published newspapers, and distributed leaflets. The Columbus party had a dramatic club and a glee club. Meanwhile, its agenda was a little more radical than those of Jones and Johnson. Socialists called for government ownership of industries and utilities as the best means of restoring democracy and justice to Ohio.

A prominent Socialist was Charles Emil Ruthenberg, a noncomformist intellectual and an assistant manager in the Selmer Hess Publishing Company of Cleveland. Ruthenberg had been born in Cleveland in 1882 to German immigrants and led a bookish, domestic life. Inspired by Tom Johnson, he gradually moved to a more radical position, accepting state control as the best way to end poverty and inequality. "Capitalism stands for individualism gone to seed," he wrote in 1911, whereas socialism "would make its appeal to all those qualities which capitalist ethics glorify theoretically but ignore in practice." Sounding like Johnson, he argued that socialism would make service rather than profit the guiding principle of life. "It would give an opportunity of living happy, healthy lives, which would be an incentive to each individual to give the best that is in him to the service of society."[27]

A disillusioned Ruthenberg became more radical in the 1910s, eventually joining the Communist Party. But his brand of respectable socialism did well in Ohio in the early decades of the twentieth century. In the election of 1910, Ohio led the nation in the number of Socialist voters. A year later, Ohioans elected Socialists to the city council in Columbus and as mayors of St. Marys, Salem, Cuyahoga Falls, Barberton, Lorain, Martins Ferry, Canton, Mount Vernon, Fostoria, Toronto, and Lima. The party peaked in 1912 when it garnered nearly 10 percent of the statewide vote.

Reform benefited from activism on the right as well as the left. In 1912, the national Republican Party divided between supporters of President Taft and insurgents committed to both reform and the return of former president Theodore Roosevelt to the White House. The latter supported some of the limited political reforms that Ohio voters accepted in the fall of 1912. It was hardly coincidental that major constitutional revisions took place in the same year when the Republicans were seriously divided and Socialist candidates were doing well. The eagerness of some politicians to tap into the popular reform impulse fueled the passage of the constitutional amendments and the election of Cox and Democrats to the legislature.

As Republicans healed their breach and Socialists waned, reform faded. The sudden reform insurgence seemed to have satisfied many critics. Few Ohioans had ever wanted to do more than tinker with their government. As usual, politicians chose a middle path, offering revisions but not revolution. As usual, Ohioans endorsed limited political and economic reform but refused to accept social reform, especially that which would recognize the rights of women and African Americans.

The Great War and Normalcy

The outbreak of World War I in April 1917 brought efforts to revitalize public culture in Ohio through municipal and state governments to a temporary end. But before the impulse expended itself completely, it took a turn into cultural repression. While Protestant values had informed reform movements from the beginning, leaders such as Jones, Johnson, and James Cox had tried to one degree or another to avoid ethnic and religious divisions. Their whole point, in many ways, had been to get people to emphasize what they had in common with each other.

Such attitudes informed even the temperance crusade. The Anti-Saloon League, which had been founded at Oberlin College in 1893 and operated under the leadership of Wayne B. Wheeler, was much more pragmatic than the Woman's Christian Temperance Union. Wheeler insisted only that a man vote for temperance, not that he practice it. He wanted enforcement of existing laws and local option laws so that parts of the state could go dry if they chose to do so. In 1908, the Rose Law made local option in a county possible if 35 percent of voters approved. By April 1909, fifty-eight Ohio counties had voted to go dry. All told, sixty-three of Ohio's eighty-eight counties had prohibition. The holdouts were metropolitan areas and counties with large German populations. So strong was the Anti-Saloon League that the United States Brewers' Association decided to meet the organization halfway. The brewers admitted that there were too many saloons and committed themselves to the promotion of temperance. They then had enormous influence on the development of a liquor license law in 1912 and 1913. The "Ohio Plan" of self-regulation was a success. Voters refused to add a prohibition amendment to the state constitution in 1912.

World War I reinvigorated support for prohibition and other reforms designed to enforce a particular set of cultural values. The conflict lasted a year and a half, from April 1917 until November 1918. While Ohioans such as air ace Captain Edward V. Rickenbacker of Columbus distinguished themselves in combat, few became heroes. The 225,000 citizens who fought in distant Europe might have told themselves, in the words of President Woodrow Wilson, that they were making the world safe for democracy, but the sense of a moral crusade that had characterized the Civil War was largely absent. The roughly 6,500 men who died from wounds and disease died for a cause to which few people in Ohio were deeply committed.

The Great War's impact on Ohio, however, was profound. Fighting the war increased the size of the federal and state bureaucracies. The notion that government was the best embodiment of the people's will, especially when it operated like a business corporation, received a stern test. The Ohio branch of the federal Council of National Defense supervised the conduct of the war. It directed the work of the Ohio Industrial Commission, which, in an effort to ensure the efficient use of labor, dealt with emergency needs and found jobs for more than five hundred thousand people. Government officials also coordinated use of the state's transportation network.

By far the greatest immediate impact of the war came in the widespread insistence on cultural homogeneity and absolute patriotism. The Great War marked a major turning point in ethnic identification in Ohio. Anti-German feelings were intense in the Cincinnati area and the state as a whole. Anything or anyone perceived to be German was at risk. The president of Baldwin-Wallace College was dismissed for not being vociferous in his anti-German beliefs. Meanwhile, schools and universities began to teach "Americanization." A state Americanization committee drew up lists of approved readings and urged libraries to remove suspicious books from their shelves. Both public and private school teachers had to swear their loyalty to the constitutions of the United States and Ohio. The attack on things German continued after the war with the Ake Law (1919), which forbade the teaching of the German language below the eighth grade in any school in Ohio.

As the war continued, the Americanization crusade generalized to include anything that seemed foreign. Authorities arrested Socialist Charles Emil Ruthenberg, who got more than a quarter of the hundred thousand votes cast in the 1917 Cleveland mayoral election, for criticizing the draft. He served a year in prison. For an antiwar speech in Canton, Socialist Eugene V. Debs was sentenced to ten years in jail, while Socialists were dismissed from the Canton city council and the school board. The Cleveland branch of the American Protective League reported cases of un-American activity to the U.S. Department of Justice. Ohioans, like other Americans, became more conspicuous in their public displays of patriotism, whether they were saluting the flag, pledging allegiance to the United States, or talking about the necessity of law and order. Understandable as some of this hysteria was in the midst of war, it represented a coercive period in the evolution of a public culture. At no point in the history of Ohio had a citizen's political identity been so critical. Loyalty to the United States and to Ohio had to trump any and all personal loyalties.

As a result, not just Germans but all peoples of central and southern European origins confined displays of ethnic and religious loyalties to their homes. It was not that they mattered less, but that they were not welcome in the public world of Ohio. For decades, ethnicity had been an important dimension of public conversation in the state. A major theme of the efforts to reform Ohio in the early twentieth century had been to get people to transcend their differences and come together as a great community of broad-minded citizens. For the most part, reformers had assumed that cultural homogeneity would follow from a renewal of public culture. Christian brotherhood or Republican prosperity, the idea was the same: let us dwell on what we have in common.

The Americanization crusade changed all that. Now it became the public interest and the business of the state to demand and enforce homogeneity defined by middle-class Protestant values. No wonder, then, that the prohibition campaign, with its suspicion of the drinking habits of European immigrants, finally achieved success in 1918.

Events in Cleveland revealed that some Ohioans were ready to resist coercive governments. On May Day in 1919, more than thirty thousand people gathered in Public Square to hear a speech by Charles Ruthenberg, who had become even more radicalized with the success of the Bolshevik revolution in Russia. Nervous officials and police arrested hundreds of the participants, most of whom were foreign-born, and physically assaulted countless others. Two people died from their wounds. The Socialist and Communist Parties were all but destroyed by the repression.

To some degree, this incident marked a break with a pattern of trying to find ways to subsume ethnic diversity within a larger conception of a public interest. Politicians such as Tom Johnson had cultivated working-class voters. Public occasions had also served as moments of public reconciliation. On July 4, 1894, Cleveland celebrated the dedication of the Soldiers and Sailors Monument, a tribute to the sacrifices of the Civil War. Military units and representatives of civic and ethnic groups paraded. Irish, Poles, and Czechs participated, and the Catholic bishop rode in a carriage. Symbolically, the march demonstrated both the inclusiveness and the diversity of the city. If this event and others like it did not compensate for prejudice and discrimination, they nonetheless indicated a public endorsement of diversity that evaporated during World War I. Although in 1919 seventy-five thousand Germans, Hungarians, and others paraded through downtown Cleveland in a public display of their patriotism, they were unable to overcome a pervasive fear of foreign radicalism that would climax in immigration restriction in the 1920s.

Officially, at least, Ohio had a public culture in 1918. Its residents were first and foremost citizens of Ohio who could treasure their various religions and ethnic communities in private but not in public. We can safely assume that neither Golden Rule Jones nor Tom Johnson had imagined the role of government in enforcing such an outcome. They and many others had hoped that revising the landscape, eliminating corruption, and promoting spiritual renewal would eventually achieve the same end. This path reflected their values; it also was voluntary. People had to choose to see themselves as part of a larger community, something neither prohibition nor police action permitted.

While some Ohioans devoted themselves to reform in the late nineteenth and early twentieth centuries, most were busy with other things, not the least of which was survival. Meanwhile, a handful of writers and artists filled notebooks and canvases with stories, essays, poems, and paintings about a variety of subjects. A large number of them chose at one time or another to reflect on life in Ohio. They did not always like what they saw. Ohio had progressed at an almost incomprehensible rate in the nineteenth century. But the price of progress had been high. Writers repeatedly turned to what many believed was the quintessential Ohio landscape, its small towns, and reluctantly concluded that the greatest transformation in the state involved the disappearance of its citizens' belief in the possibilities of life, both public and private, within its borders. Somewhere along the way, Ohio had lost its soul.

Three men and a boy standing at the corner of Railroad and Main Streets in Clyde, Ohio, ca. 1880s. Clyde was where Sherwood Anderson grew up and became the model for the fictional town of Winesburg, Ohio. *(Courtesy of the Clyde Public Library, Clyde, Ohio)*

8

The End of the Beginning

——

Until he reached his early twenties, William Dean Howells was the model of a respectable Ohioan. Born in Martinsville (now Martins Ferry) in 1837, Howells lived in Hamilton from 1840 until the mid-1850s. His family then moved to Jefferson in the Western Reserve. Staunchly abolitionist and Republican (previously Whig) in their politics, Swedenborgian in their religious predilections, and ambitious for their children, Howells's parents embodied the emerging middle-class culture. The young Howells was much like Rutherford B. Hayes, whose campaign biography he would write in 1876. Curious about the world, he taught himself languages and devoured books. Howells was an expert typesetter from an early age and grew up in the world of print. For him as for Hayes, Ohio was a place of endless possibilities whose real history lay in the future.

When he was nineteen, Howells got a job as a reporter with the *Ohio State Journal* in Columbus. Covering the legislature by day, he enjoyed the lively society, especially the young women, of the capital in his free time. He also wrote, publishing a volume of poetry and a campaign biography of Abraham Lincoln. The industrious Howells seemed destined for a career as an important Ohio journalist and writer.

However, Howells's life diverged from that of Hayes. As a reward for his Lincoln biography, he was appointed American consul in Venice, Italy. There he spent the entire duration of the Civil War. While in Venice, he married Elinor Mead, the daughter of a New England family he had met in Cincinnati. After returning to the United States, the Howellses lived briefly in New York City and then in Boston. As assistant editor and editor of the *Atlantic Monthly* from

239

1866 to 1881 and then as a regular contributor to *Harper's Monthly* from 1886 until his death in 1920, Howells was at the center of American literary culture for half a century. He became an influential man, but not in Ohio. Living comfortably in Boston and then again in New York City, to which he and Elinor moved in 1891, Howells nurtured the careers of dozens of young men and women. He was an indefatigable writer with an enormous literary output. More often than not, Howells explored what he considered real life using characters whose problems reflected the values and tensions of the middle-class world in which he was raised. Most of his novels were set in the northeastern United States. Not until he reached his fifties did Howells publish anything about Ohio. He had "nothing to do with day before yesterday. I deal with the present and fear to trespass on the morrow," he told a reporter in 1886. Although he "came from Ohio," he had "not written anything about the people and their characteristics."[1]

A struggle between conventional and unconventional behavior permeated Howells's work. A good son of Ohio, he was forever torn between a need to conform and a need to rebel. In his own life, he was thoroughly respectable. His life with Elinor was the stuff of affectionate Victorian domesticity. Rarely did his writings address the concerns of workers or immigrants. From his perch in an easy chair in Boston and New York, Howells enjoyed a life of refinement that even the most starry-eyed of ambitious, improvement-crazy Ohioans could scarcely have imagined in the 1850s.

Howells was a pioneer of a new social type, the Ohio expatriate. As early as the 1850s, more people were moving out of the state than were moving in. Most of them went west, to Iowa, Kansas, Oregon, and especially California. Howells traveled in the opposite direction and for reasons that were as much cultural as economic. Turning the conventional story of Ohio on its head, he did not describe it as a harbinger of a new world whose history was an inexorable march of progress. Rather, it was a place whose glory lay in the past. What it had to offer the United States was its origins, not its prospects. Fond as he was of Ohio, he had to escape it. To have stayed would have been to circumscribe his possibilities as a person as well as a writer.

Ohio writers and artists in the late 1800s and early 1900s were remarkably united in seeing their state as a place whose time had come and gone, as a world where the white heat of promise had cooled into comfortable conformity. Unlike reformers and politicians, writers and artists tended toward pessimism. For most of them, the source of Ohio's decline into banality, the transformation of hope into sterility, had little to do with immigrants, cities, or the growth of big business. No, the root cause of the problem lay in the prototypical landscape of Ohio, the small towns whose futures had been trumpeted with such glee in the 1840s and 1850s. Within the minds and hearts of their residents, the attitudes and expectations that had nurtured faith in the possibilities of Ohio were atrophying. Writers and artists wanted to understand how that had happened, how in pursuing unprecedented material and moral progress the citizens of the state had lost their vision of a happier world.

Ambivalence and Alienation

Despite his protestations to the contrary, William Dean Howells wrote in abundance about Ohio. Indeed, people came to think of him as something of an expert on the subject. On the occasion of his seventy-fifth birthday in 1912, Colonel George Harvey gave a dinner for more than four hundred people in New York City. The host asked that the guest of honor remember that he had begun his "splendid career as a native of Ohio." Another Ohioan, President William Howard Taft, traveled to New York to honor the writer. Years later a critic saluted Howells as someone who "knows the Ohio state of mind; at least—since there may be no Ohio state of mind—he knows that one Ohio family."[2] For the most part, that family was his own. Taken together, Howells's memoirs and stories, while written at different times and for different purposes, constitute a coherent narrative of the evolution of his ambiguous relationship with the place of his birth. They trace his alienation from a world that he loved but that he ultimately found limited and limiting.

In 1897, Howells published *Stories of Ohio*. Intended for young men (shaping the character of boys was a preoccupation of his), the tales focused primarily on the struggles between whites and Indians in the late eighteenth century. Indeed, two-thirds of the book dealt with events before Ohio became a state. According to Howells, "Nearly all the Ohio stories since 1812 have been stories of business enterprise and industrial adventure." Much as he insisted that they could be "as exciting, as romantic and pathetic as any I have set down concerning the Indian wars," he devoted very little space to them.[3] Howells was much more interested in stories that tested manhood. He wrote about settlers' triumphs over doomed Indians distinguished by their noble resistance to their inevitable fate of extinction.

Pioneer adventures were in part an antidote to the increasingly sedentary nature of middle-class life. They reinforced a growing emphasis on the importance of physical activity in the development of masculine character. Howells's stories taught the importance of perseverance in the face of a powerful enemy. Overcoming strong Indians made the conquerors better people, preparing them for important battles against other enemies who would threaten their world, including slaveholders and corporations. Ohioans had improved the landscape they took from the Indians primarily because they "are that sort of idealists who have the courage of their dreams. By this courage they have made the best of them come true." Aside from occasional flirtations with "fanaticisms," such as the temperance crusade, they had maintained a "matter-of-fact and practical character." Their mistakes had "helped to keep them modest in the midst of their prosperity and their eminence in saving and governing the union of these states." They were "historically, the first of the Americans" who "have perpetuated and imparted their character to the whole country on the westward."[4]

Howells was presenting the story of Ohio as the epitome of American progress. He implicitly agreed with a state history textbook published in 1906 that the events of state and local history "illustrate the principles of national history." Certainly Ohio had prepared great men. In his hyperbolic campaign biography, Howells claimed that the source of Rutherford B. Hayes's greatness was his abiding interest in the world around him. Hayes embodied the educated man concerned with the behavior of all human beings. Most striking, however, was his determination. Affable in private, he was a bulldog in public. He had an "iron *fight* which instantly replaces what seems the normal repose, almost indifference, of his nature, when once he is called into action of any sort."[5] Like all good Ohioans, Hayes was willing to stand up for what he believed.

As Howells aged, he romanticized life in early-nineteenth-century Ohio. Small towns were a lost world. In *A Boy's Town,* his fictional account of growing up in Hamilton, Howells remembered a happy place. Along the Miami River, boys found "places to swim, to fish, to hunt, to skate." Although there were few events of any importance, "every day was full of wonderful occurrence and thrilling excitement" in a "very simple little town." He enjoyed the uncivilized customs of boys interested in immediate gratification. He testified to the power of mothers in the lives of boys. He enjoyed the rhythms of life in a village constructed around a courthouse, school, churches, stores, and mills, learned about temperance and defiance of it, went to circuses and minstrel shows, admired the local militia, worried about becoming a "girl-boy," and dreamed of faraway places such as Granada that he encountered in books.[6]

Howells imagined that his introspective bent differentiated him from other boys. He had "an inward being that was not the least like [his] outward being." He came to feel that "he was dwelling in a wholly different world within him, . . . a world of dreams, of hopes, of purposes" that he discovered in enchanting books. The shy Howells came to live much of his life as a boy in this inner world. He learned to "conceal his gift" for writing because his reputation with his young friends suffered when he revealed it. People thought him "*soft.*" Living vicariously, he attended theater performances and started a multitude of projects that he never finished. There was the torment of his "double life . . . the Boy's Town life and the Cloud Dweller's life" and the fact that the latter was a source of public shame.[7] Only the guidance of his practical older brother saved him from his angst. Far more than a nostalgic memoir, *A Boy's Town* describes the origins of Howells's alienation from life in Ohio.

While Howells's memoir is an older man's idealization of his youth, *A Boy's Town* is also a prototype of a common Midwestern story written by sensitive young men and women in which the limits of the happy world of their youth become clearer as they mature. Howells's fictional memoir emphasizes a gradual shrinking of possibilities. Pleasant places for children, Ohio towns were crippled by ignorance and prejudice and above all by the apparent inability of many of their citizens to develop a larger vision of life. They could not deal with diversity. They could not handle alienation. Youths who imagined great things for themselves, who coveted adventure and nonconformity, sought solace in books and dreams, in exotic tales of faraway places. A good place to grow up, Ohio was no place to live a rich and full life as an adult.

Howells elaborated on this theme in another memoir, *Years of My Youth*. While he had begun to squirm during his comfortable life in Hamilton, he lost his patience altogether in Jefferson. He "felt the life very dull and narrow which I had once found so vivid and ample." No matter the charms of social life and holidays, of young girls and dances, Howells developed "the sense of spent witchery and a spell outworn" and "chose to revolt from it all and to pine for a wider world and prouder pleasures." He and his sister confided in each about their "discontent with the village limit of our lives. Within our home we had the great world, as least as we knew it in books, with us, but outside of it, our social experience dwindled to the measure of the place."[8]

Accordingly, brother and sister set out for Columbus in 1856. Meeting a diverse group of people, including Germans, living with young journalists and lawyers, Howells attended many "brilliant [social] affairs." He and his friends "read the new books, and talked them over with the young ladies" they were courting. As they broadened their experiences, Howells admired a lack of conformity—most of the time. In an 1860 review of Walt Whitman's *Leaves of Grass,* Howells praised some of the poetry but not the author. Whitman was "not a man whom you would like to know. . . . He has told too much. The secrets of the soul may be whispered to the world, but the secrets of the body should be decently hid. . . .Whitman exults to blab them."[9] Howells would never lose his instinct for respectability.

By the time he got to Venice, Howells was talking about "the meanness and hollowness of that wretched little village-life." The mere thought of returning to Ohio filled him with "morbid horror." Several short stories he wrote in the late 1850s explain why. Unpublished in his lifetime, they were about the residents of a small town named (what else?) Dulldale. The longest, "Geoffrey: A Study of American Life," tells of a sensitive and weak young man who has returned to the village of his youth after an absence of several years in order to win the hand of his widowed cousin, Clara. Largely unrecognized by his former neighbors, Geoffrey finds himself alienated from life in Dulldale. Gloomy, unfinished, unpolished, and unbearably quiet, it is a place where people while away the hours with gossip and go to bed at sunset. Through their "hard antipathetic eyes," they see Geoffrey only as a "rather quiet unsociable man." When Clara's mother dies, Geoffrey and Clara marry. Geoffrey edits the local newspaper and befriends "odd people" more easily than respectable folks whose "friendship would have been of greater use to him." Intensely antislavery, he is an indifferent politician. His marriage is a mistake because he does not really love Clara. After she dies, Geoffrey becomes a bitter recluse. Despite his sensitivity and intellect, or perhaps because of them, Geoffrey never knows happiness. He lacks the capacity to change. Querulous and unreasonable, he is a lonely man whose future "is blurred with doubt."[10] Part of his problem lies with Dulldale. Who could find happiness in such an isolated environment, surrounded by people unable to connect with each other or the world?

No wonder Howells wanted to escape Ohio. No wonder Columbus could not contain his ambition. No wonder he sought validation outside the state, sending poems to editors in the East, some of which were published in the *Atlantic Monthly* and other magazines. Years later, Howells could give no reason for abandoning his friends and prospects in Columbus "except my belief that my work would be less acceptable if I remained in the West; that I should get on faster if I wrote in New York than if I wrote in Columbus. Somehow I fancied there would be more intellectual atmosphere for me in the great city."[11] When Lincoln was elected, Howells actively sought a consulate, hoping for Munich in order to study German literature but ending up in Venice on the way to Boston and New York City.

Lamenting Conformity

Other writers shared Howells's profound ambivalence about life in Ohio. Struggling to balance nostalgia and criticism, they told stories of squandered opportunities and repressed emotions. Much of what they were feeling was personal alienation. Collectively, however, they offered an indictment of what the state had become. Once full of enthusiasm and promise, Ohio now seemed increasingly petty, provincial, and stagnant. What had gone wrong?

The extent to which even popular writers addressed this question is striking. Born in Morgan County in 1860, James Ball Naylor practiced medicine in Malta until his retirement in 1934. The novels Naylor wrote in his spare time constitute a fictional history of the Muskingum Valley. In *Under Mad Anthony's Banner, The Kentuckian,* and *Ralph Marlowe,* Naylor described how difficult it was for even good citizens to realize the possibilities of Ohio. Lamenting the loss of freedom and independence he associated with the frontier period, Naylor had no patience with deception and the mindless conformity of the late nineteenth century. The only way to survive is to know who you are and stand up to those who would tell you otherwise. Religion and morality are well and good to the extent that they do not distort the ability of people to connect with each other, to choose each other freely, to put personal happiness above social conformity.

Women were writing about similar themes. Mary Hartwell Catherwood was born in Licking County in 1847. When she was nine, her family moved to Illinois. Shortly thereafter both parents died, and Mary and her two younger siblings went to live with their grandparents in Hebron, Ohio. The energetic Mary was a schoolteacher at the age of fourteen and a published poet soon thereafter. She attended the Granville Female College, worked for a year at a magazine in Newburgh, New York, and ended up in Cincinnati, where she supported herself as a writer. Eventually, financial constraints forced her to live with relatives in Illinois until she married James Steel Catherwood in 1877.

Marriage did not compromise Catherwood's independence. During her long career, she presented female characters as shrewd social observers who were quite capable of making their own decisions. "[W]oman is no helpless, weakling species of the genus man," she wrote at the end of her first novel, *A Woman in Armor,* "but an independent, a cherishing, a strong, a daring nature, who in the armor of her own uprightness can fight the battles of the world and win them."[12] Set in a fictionalized version of Granville, a village shorn of its indigenous flora and fauna as well as Native Americans and indifferent to social reform, the novel highlighted the need of women and children for legal protection from difficult men. *A Woman in Armor,* which was published in 1875, paralleled the actions of the Woman's Crusade. Catherwood advocated independence from social conventions as redemption from provincialism. Like Naylor, she mixed stories of an idealized past with tales of the problematic present.

Catherwood's novel *Craque-O'Doom* was set in Licking County. In the small village of Barnet live the Chenoworths, a family of unrefined, lazy, and apathetic individuals descended from Tennesseans. Their daughter Tamsin, who despises her parents and brothers, possesses "the spirit which her people had lacked for generations." Reserving her love for her younger sister, Tillie, she has developed a tough exterior that masks an inner rage. Aunt Sally Teagarden, a kindly gentlewoman who lives in the local mansion, remarks that Tamsin cannot make a "woman of herself" because "it isn't in the stock to take an education; they are all ignorant." A local writer, Rhoda Jones, pities Tamsin: "It is like living under some crushing weight, or in swamps where the live-oak moss would make one want to commit suicide,—worse than being a homeless and kinless orphan."[13]

Life in Barnet is respectable and rigid. "[I]ts solid people" get richer with the years, send their sons and daughters to colleges and seminaries, and love "to prove to all strangers that they were not a whit behind the age." They indulge "a jealous conformity" to what they consider city life. "But while the citizen is a free agent, with his own set, perhaps his own club or several clubs, and his amusements, . . . the villager is hampered by a heavy etiquette and a servile imitation of what he considers standard models." Local folk frown on dancing and playing cards. In Barnet, progress means that when respectable people gather, they "stood up straight and conversed with miserable effort, or promenaded, or listened with hypocritical enjoyment to piano-playing."[14]

Tasmin overhears the spirited Rhoda warning her friends not to rush into marriage. "The woman of to-day, when she gets ready to marry, marries, and it doesn't make any difference to her whether she's twenty-five or a hundred. . . . We learn how to take care of [our bodies] and how to bring ourselves in happy relations to society, . . . I just learned how to live, and I'm *going to live* . . . as many days as are granted." In Rhoda, Tamsin sees "a vast example," someone who offers her escape from poverty and provincialism through independence and education. Tired of sentiment, Rhoda wants a rich husband who "won't thwart me." To be in love with him would simply "give him an advantage over me." Men can be "very tyrannical and abusive toward the women of their families. . . . Therefore I want to protect myself as much as possible from the miseries of matrimony."[15]

Salvation arrives for Tamsin in the form of a dwarf named Isaac Sutton, better known as Craque-O'Doom. Sutton is a smart, wealthy man with a love of music. His only problem is his size. Respectable girls recoil from him, even though unconventional Rhoda calls him "a rare gentleman" with a nature "like a woman's." Tamsin, working as a maid, serves Sutton coffee and treats him kindly. Sutton responds warmly to this young woman who does not "shudder at sight of me."[16]

The rest of the novel narrates their courtship and marriage. Tamsin's family may be ignorant and lazy but she has a gentility of soul that her wealthier, educated neighbors lack. Sutton, used to ostracism, finds in her a kindred spirit. He wins her hand from her parents, who are more interested in his money than his appearance. Rhoda alone thinks Tamsin lucky to have such a suitor.

Their marriage is a curious one. Sutton and Tamsin do not live as man and wife. Treating her as a ward, he sends her away to New York to a boarding school. Pygmalion-like, Tamsin becomes refined. She improves her language, writing, and social skills. She endures the death of her sister, Tillie. Eventually, Sutton offers to give her up to a handsome young man. But the good-hearted Tamsin will have none of it. She loves Sutton because he cared about her. His kindness overcame her anger as her kindness trumped his bitterness. Tamsin thought Sutton "real tall." He was beautiful to her.[17] She moves in with him, continues her education, and bears Craque-O'Doom a child whom they name Tillie.

Catherwood's novel is a tale of two social outcasts finding love amid provincial prejudice. It is also an indictment of what had happened in Ohio towns. The problem with Ohio in both Catherwood's and Naylor's novels is that the vision of a better tomorrow has faded into a shallow conformity. There is no discussion, no serious exchange, no diversity of opinion. Rud and Lucy Hayes's eager embrace

of the possibilities of reading and conversing had by the 1880s con-
gealed into empty rituals. People sought refinement thoughtlessly.
They lived less to improve themselves and the world around them
than to fulfill the expectations of their neighbors.

Like Howells and Naylor, Catherwood longed for the old days before rigor mortis set in. Critical of the late-nineteenth-century village,
she idealized its origins. Once upon a time, the people of the Ohio Valley were creating new standards of human behavior, not conforming to
old ones. Catherwood detailed her idealization of lost vitality in a series of romantic novels about the French conquest of North America.
Covering four centuries and ranging from Quebec to the Mississippi
Valley, the tales celebrated the exotic qualities of the earliest European
pioneers. In writing about a lost world of possibilities, Catherwood
found her largest audience. The tough-minded realist Hamlin Garland
criticized fellow writers such as Catherwood for catering to "the great
intelligent middle class of America, curiously enough, who are apparently most provincial." "American literature can not be built up out of
romantic tales of medieval France," warned Garland, "and stories of
country life will be false if they deal only with June sunshine, roses,
and strawberries."[18] True enough, perhaps, of Catherwood's novels of
early settlers, but not of her tales of nineteenth-century Ohio. If her
plots were sentimental, her themes were harsh.

Constance Fenimore Woolson also wrote about the limits of life in
Ohio. Woolson had an adventurous if troubled life. She was a grand-
niece of James Fenimore Cooper who moved to the Western Reserve
shortly after her birth in Vermont in 1840. As the daughter of a well-
educated industrialist, she enjoyed the benefits of an excellent education in both Cleveland and New York City as well as long summer
vacations in Michigan. After her father's death in 1869, Constance
and her mother moved to New York City, North Carolina, and
Florida, and then in 1879 to Europe, where she lived until her death
in 1894. Restless emotionally as well as physically, Woolson never
married, although she had intense emotional relationships with several men, including Henry James.

Woolson suffered from recurrent periods of severe depression. In
1876, she described them as something "that comes unexpectedly, and
makes everything black." "[A]t times," she told a friend, "in spite of

all I can do, this deadly enemy of mine creeps in, and once in, he is master." Bereft of self-confidence, Woolson considered herself an ugly outcast. Her personal pessimism permeated her fiction. "Why do literary women break down so?" she famously asked. "It almost seems as though only the unhappy women took to writing."[19] To combat her insecurities, she traveled incessantly, rowed, and worked long hours. In the end, however, nothing helped. Her death in 1894 was undoubtedly a suicide, the result of a fall from the second story of her rented villa in Venice.

Only a few of Woolson's stories were set in Ohio. Originally published in *Harper's* and *Atlantic Monthly*, they became part of a collection entitled *Castle Nowhere: Lake-Country Sketches*. German Moravian communities in Tuscarawas County particularly fascinated Woolson. In a couple of tales, she described visits by young, affluent Cleveland women who saw the region as a "hiding-place" "almost as isolated as a solitary island."[20] While they played at being simple rural folk, they also learned the enormous cost of life in an isolated village where the emphasis was on conformity.

"Solomon" is the story of a coal miner in Zoar. Two female cousins from Cleveland visiting the neighborhood encounter Solomon's wife in her isolated home. According to the once beautiful woman, Solomon cannot keep a job outside of the Moravian community because of his love of painting. Solomon is a primitive artist whose work lacks perspective and refinement. But he has talent and feeling—both of which have gone to waste in the isolation of rural village life and in his devotion to his wife. One of young women remarks: "[H]e had his dream, his ideal; and this country girl with her great eyes and wealth of her hair represented the beautiful to his hungry soul. He gave his whole life and hope into her hands, and woke to find his goddess a common wooden image." He had been "hopelessly ship-wrecked."[21] The other cousin blames Solomon as much as his wife. After all, the wife had her dreams, too, even if they were about finery.

Caught in a storm, the two cousins end up spending a night at the couple's "lonely house in its lonely valley." In the evening, they finally meet Solomon. His dreary attic studio is full of "crude" paintings of scenes from the Bible and "flat and unshaded" representations of his wife's face. Community and marriage have stifled both expression and opportunity. One of the cousins gives the eager man a poignant lesson in perspective. The next day the women learn that Solomon is dying and return to the house. With his eyes, he directs them to a charcoal sketch he has just begun. It is "wonderful to behold—the same face, the face of the faded wife, but so noble in its idealized beauty that it might have been a portrait of her glorified face in Paradise. It was a profile, with the eyes upturned—a mere outline, but grand in conception and expression." Before he dies, Solomon tells his wife that the sketch is "how you looked to me, but I never could get it right before." For all its melodrama, "Solomon" is a powerful story of blighted dreams. Solomon might have been a great man, if only he had lived in a place that connected him with the outside world and not devoted his life to an unworthy subject. Self-sacrifice by both husband and wife had achieved nothing but pain and gloom.[22]

Even writers who were personally happier than Woolson and who were frequently humorous portrayed small-town life negatively. Jessie Brown Pounds, a Disciple of Christ from the Western Reserve, supplied the lyrics to hymns such as "The Touch of His Hand on Mine" and "The Way of the Cross Leads Home." Born in Hiram in 1861, she grew up in what appears to have been a happy family. Her mother was a schoolteacher and her father a minister. Her 1896 marriage to another minister was happy, and she and her husband lived with two adopted daughters in Hiram until 1921. Although she had no interest in leaving Ohio and published most of her work in Christian periodicals, Pounds was an unsentimental critic of life in provincial towns. Like others, she romanticized the pioneers of Ohio as brave people who had conquered heathenism as well as a wilderness. But while Pounds lamented the impact of urbanization and industrialization in corroding village life, she also believed that small towns had more than their share of "self-satisfied bigotry and complacency."[23]

Among the best of Pounds's creations is a series of five character sketches called "Hillsbury Folks." The "dull little village" of Hillsbury, like thousands of others in the Midwest, has been "swallowed" by the world of the "Great City" (Cleveland). But its residents do not seem to care that they are provincial. Hillsbury folks prefer a cottage in their town to "a castle in Spain"; they would rather be the village postmaster than a U.S. senator. Public conversation generally pits "Republicanism, and Righteousness" against "Democracy and Depravity."[24]

Pounds's gentle sketches expose the complexities of life underneath the veneer of respectability. The guardians of Hillsbury's "great pride . . . the 'graded school'" are the kind Miss Emily and the principled principal, Mrs. Carolina More, who is "the Old Testament in female form." After Miss Emily fails to persuade a habitual truant named Conrad Wetzel to reform his ways, Mrs. More beats him with a ruler for two hours. He repents. She forgives him, as does a weeping Miss Emily. Humor just barely balances the bleakness of the tale. In the end, the narrator tells us, Mrs. More's corporal punishment had no more effect than Miss Emily's moral suasion. As an adult, Conrad Wetzel "made half a million in the manufacture of glue," becoming "the only Hillsbury man" to achieve wealth. A "liberal education" only got in the way of his "pursuit of wealth."[25] Success, Pounds suggests, does not necessarily follow from the moral lessons of the schoolroom.

"Trouble at Craydock's Corners" expertly reveals Pounds's ambivalence about small towns. Lucy Reid, the nineteen-year-old bride of the local preacher, makes the fatal mistake of wearing the wrong kind of hat to Sunday services. Instead of the bonnet expected by the married women of the congregation, Lucy appears in "a cheap little white chip, trimmed with a wreath of corn flowers and daisies, and with a knot of ribbon under the brim." Mrs. Seakin, "a large and solemn woman, with a tremendous sense of her responsibilities," visits Lucy to tell her to forsake her vain hat for a proper bonnet. Meek Lucy does not think a bonnet will look good on her. She surrenders nonetheless, and Mrs. Seakin buys her a black bonnet. For weeks Lucy wears the new bonnet, the symbol of her sacrifice of her independence, while her spirit evaporates and her indignant husband smolders. Then one Sunday, when he insists that she wear her original hat, her action precipitates a major crisis. The shocked congregation, led by Mrs. Seakin and her friends, adopts "a studied coldness . . . toward the preacher and his wife."[26] Soon the members vote, in Lucy's presence, to replace their preacher.

The meanness of this trivial episode represents the small-minded intolerance of village life at its worst. Pounds keeps the tone light. But the experience is as bad as anything in Catherwood or Woolson. It takes tragedy to rectify matters and give the story something of a happy ending. Before the couple can leave Craydock's Corners, Lucy loses a baby. The event brings the community to its senses. Mrs. Seakin rushes to the Reids's home and takes charge. At the funeral, Lucy wears her black bonnet with a black crepe in it. The next day, the congregation votes to rehire Lucy's husband. All is forgiven. "The trouble at Craydock's Corners had been buried in the grave of a little child."[27] Still, this resolution does not expunge the nastiness that had preceded it. Whatever their capacity for compassion, Mrs. Seakin and her friends have also demonstrated their capacity for cruelty.

No Ohio writer did more to popularize the image of life in the state as a mindless mix of conformity and hypocrisy than the ultimate expatriate, James Thurber. In 1933, Thurber published a hilarious satirical memoir of growing up in the overgrown small town of Columbus. Written when Thurber was close to forty, *My Life and Hard Times* comprised the reminiscences of a man who, like Howells, had left Ohio for the big city and achieved fame and some fortune, mostly as a regular contributor of essays, stories, and cartoons to the *New Yorker,* a weekly magazine that took pride in looking askance at the country west of the Hudson River. *My Life and Hard Times* has droll wit, offbeat anecdotes, and self-deprecating humor in abundance; it also is a bitter diatribe.

According to Thurber, Columbus is "a town in which almost anything is likely to happen and in which almost everything has." But what happens is mostly small stuff: beds fall, people have nightmares, dams break, cars won't work, families squabble. Dogs are more perceptive about human beings than human beings are about each other. Thurber's account of the 1913 flood turns the citizens of Columbus into lemmings, unable or unwilling to think for themselves. A rumor spreads that a dam has burst, and people, without thinking, flee their businesses and homes. The whole affair lasts two hours, during which time a few people reach Reynoldsburg, twelve miles east. While Thurber tells us that "[o]rder was restored," he notes that a "visitor in an airplane, looking down on the straggling, agitated masses of people below, would have been hard put to it to divine a reason for the phenomenon."[28]

Some of Thurber's humor comes at the expense of the family's female servants, whose "loose" behavior offends their employers and gets them fired. While Thurber sympathizes with the women, he deprecates them as ignorant and deceptive. His descriptions, moreover, reveal serious class and racial tensions. Dora Gedd is "a quiet, mousy girl of thirty-two who one night shot at a man in her room," while Gertie Straub is "big, genial, and ruddy" and drinks too much. The African American woman Vashti is forever finding jewelry Thurber's mother has supposedly lost. Meanwhile, Vashti's boyfriend is angry because her stepfather is trying to sleep with her. Mrs. Robertson, a freedwoman from Georgia who professes not to know what the Civil War was about, takes "a prominent part in the Negro parade" in celebration of Jack Johnson's boxing victory on July 4, 1910, claiming that it proved "de 'speriority ob de race.'"[29]

Who would want to live in Columbus after reading *My Life and Hard Times*? Just as the slew of servants reveals the complexity of social relationships that middle-class families will not acknowledge, the false dam rupture reveals that skepticism is in short supply in Columbus. "The Day the Dam Broke" is as pointed an exposé of mindless conformity as any number of drearier tales. So too is Thurber's characterization of The Ohio State University as an institution more concerned with "mechanics" than with "beauty," a place where dumb oafs are led by the nose through classes so that they can qualify to play football and sensitive souls have to suffer through gym and military drill.[30] There was nothing to be done about life in Ohio, it would seem, except mock it.

Celebrating Diversity

Ohio-born artists had similar criticisms of their home state, but they tended to express them more indirectly. Many of those with any talent as painters fled Ohio as soon as they could, seeking inspiration in Europe or New York City. Like Howells and Thurber, they were expatriates as long as they could afford to be. For the most part, they had little interest in Ohio as a place. Ohio-born painters were interested in scenes of ordinary people or landscapes rendered with broad, quick brush strokes and vibrant colors. In the late nineteenth century, their

concern with exotic characters and settings startled viewers used to
the formal canvases of early-nineteenth-century artists. Unlike Ohio
writers, Ohio artists, many of whom grew up in cities, directly engaged the themes of immigration, urbanization, and industrialization.
Rather than critique the limitations of life in small towns, they celebrated diversity and change. Admiring personal independence in defiance of conventional expectations, their work was often noted for its
"virility" rather than its subtlety. They put a premium (at least rhetor-
ically) on pleasing themselves rather than pleasing others.

And yet for all their rebellion, many Ohio-born artists managed to
find audiences, patrons, and jobs in the state. The fact that the
Cincinnati and Columbus gentry hired "Bohemians" such as Frank
Duveneck and George Bellows to paint their portraits, that they
sought to appropriate artists in order to boost their cities as centers of
refinement, suggests that the artists' reputations as rebels may have
been largely superficial. In fact, while Ohio-born artists were free in
style and diverse in content, while their paintings were bold and
bright, their proclivity for romanticizing their subjects meant that
their work disoriented rather than threatened wealthy and middle-
class citizens. Generally more intuitive than intellectual, they made
the exotic familiar.

The grand old man of Ohio painters was Frank Duveneck. Born
Frank Decker in Covington, Kentucky, in 1848, he was the son of
immigrants from northern Germany. After the death of his father in
1849, his mother married Joseph Duveneck, a grocer who would
eventually open a bottling plant and a beer garden. While Frank Duveneck grew up in Kentucky, he was part of the extended German
community of Cincinnati, just across the Ohio River. Because he was
German and Catholic, Duveneck was not welcome in artistic circles
in Cincinnati. Instead, he learned about art in the altar-making shop
of the Institute of Catholic Art in the Diocese of Covington. The decisive moment in Duveneck's life came in November 1869, when he
left to study in Munich. In many ways, the son of German immigrants was simply going home, or rather to what he might have
imagined was home. After enrolling in the Royal Academy of the
Fine Arts, Duveneck soon completed some of his most famous
paintings.

Whistling Boy revealed Duveneck's emerging style and content: a young street urchin, cigarette in hand, hardly the stuff of drawing room art, painted in quick, bold brush strokes, probably in one session, wet paint upon wet paint. The boy, however, is idealized. Quiet and dignified, he might titillate middle-class audiences without making them nervous.[31] The painting was exotic without being dangerous. The same was true of most of Duveneck's work, which consists mostly of single figures. He mixed portraits of friends and patrons with more unusual subjects such as a Turkish page and a cobbler's apprentice. The latter is slightly insolent in both his expression and the way he holds his cigar. But the Turkish boy seems wan and wasted, a figure to be pitied, not feared.

Duveneck spent most of the 1870s and 1880s in Europe. Although he experimented with landscapes in a mildly impressionist style, he returned again and again to the solitary human figure. Moving out of doors in the sunlight of southern Europe, his Italian paintings are overly bright, romantic stereotypes of peasant life. After the sudden death in 1888 of Elizabeth Boott Duveneck, whom he had married two years earlier, Duveneck's productivity dropped off sharply. He returned to the United States, living until his death in 1919 mostly in Covington (with long summer sojourns in Gloucester, Massachusetts) and teaching at the Art Academy of Cincinnati.

Duveneck was a legendary teacher. For most of his life, he was surrounded by pupils and acolytes—"my boys"—on whom he doted. Elizabeth described the "professor," as she and others called Duveneck, as "genial, simple, and friendly." She saw him as "a child of Nature" and "a natural gentleman." Recognizing his laziness, she made a virtue of it. "He is the frankest, kindest-hearted of mortals and the least likely to make his way in the world." Because he "never looks at all to the main chance," he would always be poor. While he had plenty of suggestions, Duveneck believed in giving his students "endless freedom" to find their own way.[32] "He did not try to make little Duvenecks. But he expected all students to really work hard."[33]

In the early twentieth century, Duveneck produced little art, and while he became a local icon in Cincinnati, his larger reputation declined. He was considered a talented painter who never achieved greatness. The Cincinnati middle class lionized him, nonetheless, and displayed his paintings in their homes and in the Cincinnati Art Museum. The city's elite transformed the Bohemian painter of working-class boys into the stuff of local boosterism.

Cincinnati tried to do the same with Duveneck's pupils, including Elizabeth Nourse, who worked with "the old man" briefly in 1874 and 1875. The daughter of a genteel but poor Massachusetts family who made a dramatic conversion to Roman Catholicism after their migration to Cincinnati, Nourse devoted herself to her career as an artist. In 1887, she left Cincinnati, and except for a brief visit in 1893, she remained in Europe until her death in 1939. While she traveled all over the continent and in North Africa, her favorite subjects were French peasant women performing the basic rituals of life: tending children, working in homes or fields, or resting. Like Duveneck, Nourse was revolutionary in her focus on people rather than on landscapes. Like him, she was accused of painting "ugly" people. "To me, these people are not ugly," she replied; "their faces, their toil-stained hands tell the story of their lives. I cannot paint 'pretty' people; they do not appeal to me."[34]

The appeal of Nourse's work lies in her ability to convey a sense of empathy with the women she portrayed. The content of her paintings was not as challenging to middle-class mores as it may have first appeared. Nourse tended to idealize French peasant women, as she had the African Americans she had painted before she left for Europe. She did not represent real poverty or alienation. Rather, writes a critic, "the peasants in her pictures are . . . the virtuous poor, devout and hard working and endowed with the essentials of their physical and spiritual needs."[35] As with Duveneck's paintings, Nourse's work exudes respect for the vitality and dignity of all human beings who share much in common even if their clothes and customs diverge.

John Henry Twachtman presented a more difficult case for Cincinnati boosters. The son of Hanoverian immigrants, he studied art as a youth and then worked extensively with Duveneck in the 1870s, accompanying him to Munich, Venice, and Florence. The ambitious Twachtman was more original and less congenial than Duveneck. He did not try to hide his dislike of Cincinnati. The city was "an old fogied place" without "good art influence" that he was "glad to leave." "[O]ne naturally falls into a state of doing nothing out here," he complained.[36] Twachtman was much taken with impressionism and began to paint in the style during extended stays in France and Holland. In the 1890s, he moved his family to Connecticut, where he lived until his death in 1902.

Twachtman became one of the primary exponents of American impressionism, which was quieter, darker, and more contemplative than the French variety. Unlike his Ohio contemporaries, he did not paint many people, in part because he did not do it well. Twachtman's forte was the austere, silent landscape. Refusing to mellow as he aged, Twachtman directly confronted the tastes of Midwesterners. He once famously wondered to an audience in Chicago "why you should invite me, an American artist, to deliver an address on 'American art,' a subject in which you are not interested."[37] Of all the Ohio-born artists, Twachtman was perhaps the most daring and confrontational—and therefore the most unusual.

Like Duveneck, Robert Henri achieved as much fame as a teacher as a painter. Born in Cincinnati in 1865 to an entrepreneurial father of French Huguenot and Dutch ancestry and a Virginia-born mother, Henri spent only the first fourteen years of his life in Ohio. The family moved to Nebraska in 1879. Seven years later, Henri enrolled in the Pennsylvania Academy of Arts. After the necessary sojourn in Paris and Italy, where he became fascinated with the work of impressionists, Henri worked in Philadelphia and then New York City. He became immensely popular as one of the teachers at the New York School of Art. While he was more obviously influenced by impressionist experiments with light and form than Duveneck, many of Henri's mature paintings are similar to his in style and content. Henri's portraits, especially those of Spanish and Native Americans, are bright and romantic. Doing their subjects the honor of taking them seriously, they also familiarize them and make the exotic reassuring. No wonder the modernists who put together the Armory Show in 1913 thought Henri and his "Ash Can" students old-fashioned. Although they played with conventional subjects, they had never really broken with them.

As a teacher, Henri, like Duveneck, dedicated himself to encouraging self-expression. He urged his students to "cultivate your individual vision. Don't think as I think, but think as you think." He encouraged them to have prejudices. As recorded by one of his students, his lessons seem like greeting-card encomiums. "Be a master, not like anyone else, but like yourself." "There are no rules. I give you no rules, I only want to help you." Refinement was a matter of gaining control, of finding out who one was. Painting was like reading a book or writing in a diary; it was a means of engaging the world. The difference was that the goal was as much personal fulfillment as personal improvement, and it was achieved by in part by avoiding mindless conformity of the kind Ohio writers lamented. "All I can hope to do is to incite you to do something for yourself—to create something," said Henri. "What it is, I can't guess. I'm eager to see."[38]

This emphasis on personal realization through defiance of social conventions was profoundly liberating for many of Henri's students. None felt his impact more than George Bellows, perhaps the most successful of all Ohio-born artists. Born in Columbus in 1882, he was the son of Anna Smith Bellows of Long Island and George Bellows, a fifty-three-year-old building contractor who had dedicated his life to sound principles and sound craftsmanship. The Bellows were Republicans and Methodists and provided their son with a thoroughly middle-class upbringing. In an autobiographical fragment, Bellows remembered feeling alienated from his peers as a child. Interested in art from an early age, he felt awkward and out of place growing up in Columbus. Bellows compensated by making himself into an athlete. Hard work trumped a lack of natural talent. He became a baseball and basketball player of some local renown. After graduating from Central High School in 1901, he enrolled at The Ohio State University, where he also overcame a feeling of exclusion through athletics.

Bellows was a complex figure. He simultaneously complained about feeling alienated and celebrated his ability to work his way into social acceptance. The mere act of becoming a painter was tantamount to rebellion against his father's middle-class world. Yet Bellows also craved approval, and he became good at winning it. He had the usual complaints about life in Ohio: it was too materialistic, too conformist, too insensitive to the needs of artists. Typical was the comment of the Reverend David Gregg, the speaker at Ohio State's 1903 commencement, that "brains are money," a thesis Gregg illustrated with a story of how the painter Millet bought some supplies for sixty cents and sold the painting he made with them for $105,000. In 1904, Bellows left Ohio State, and after a summer of playing semi professional baseball and drawing cartoons, he moved to New York City. He did so with his parents' reluctant blessing and the promise of financial support for a year. It was not a bitter parting.

In New York, Bellows quickly proved adept at both painting and winning friends. He enrolled in the New York School of Art, where he found a mentor in Robert Henri. "My life begins at this point," he later said.[39] Bellows loved Henri for the freedom he gave his students. Consciously modeling himself on the manly Henri, he rejected the personality of the aloof artist. Bellows relished playing baseball and basketball with his fellow artists. He wanted to experience the world. He admired Henri's democratic informality and his celebration of manliness. In the gender-segregated studios of the art school, the gregarious Bellows was right at home.

Under Henri's influence, Bellows came into his own. He developed a vigorous style with exceptionally clear colors and striking composition and concentrated on representations of technological progress in both rural and urban settings. *Stag at Sharkey's* established Bellows's reputation. Like *River Rats* and *Club Night,* it evokes a world unfamiliar to the Columbus middle class: violent, intense, competitive, male. He also painted landscapes built around trains and steamboats and scenes of urban development and working-class life. In addition, Bellows did a great many seascapes and scenes of rural life, often set in the snow and suffused with a sense of romantic loss.

As more than one critic has noted, Bellows's paintings were ambiguous. They could be read as both tributes to and critiques of urban development and urban life. Bellows had a genius for offering unusual compositions in ways that stimulated but did not disturb his largely middle-class viewers. He made alienation popular. Bellows, as Marianne Doezema has observed, found a way to reconcile his sensitivity with his masculinity, a means to balance his critique of progress and conformity with his love of innocence and energy. Bellows's claim that his life began when he met Henri was wrong. His strong sense of justice, his desire for acceptance, his ability to make the uncouth attractive were part and parcel of his Midwestern heritage.

We should not be surprised that virtually no Ohio painter in this period was attracted to abstract forms of expression. Archibald Willard of Wellington, whose most famous painting was *The Spirit of '76,* and Howard Chandler Christy, whose large canvas romanticizing the signing of the Treaty of Greenville hangs in the rotunda of the state capitol, were at the other extreme. But whether they were among the avant-garde or not, most Ohio painters produced solid representations of the world as they saw it, finding beauty in everything and emphasizing the dignity of everyone. As they celebrated their bohemian individuality, they affirmed the cultural traditions in which they had been born and raised.

The World of Winesburg

Sherwood Anderson's *Winesburg, Ohio,* which appeared in 1919, was the climax of a long period of artistic consideration of life in the state. Like others, Anderson was concerned with the ways people found to connect with each other. *Winesburg* is more than another indictment of small-town conformity or a celebration of defiance, however. The book was part of a larger movement away from self-discipline and toward self-realization as the key to living a good life. Anderson's characters were thwarted in their efforts to connect with each other, to find personal happiness and public participation, less by the repression and isolation of small towns than by their own confusion about what should matter in their lives. Defiance and exile were not satisfactory solutions to the problem of conformity, for everyone who grew up in Ohio—from Howells to Bellows—carried something of it with them wherever they went. Rather, Anderson's book suggested that the goal was to imagine not a civic community that transcended personal and local interests but one that fulfilled them. Influenced by a growing interest in psychology manifested in the popularity of Sigmund Freud, Anderson represented an effort to find the meaning of life within oneself. Good citizens were happy, not dutiful.

Born in Camden in Preble County in 1876, Anderson was the son of peripatetic Methodist parents. His father was an indolent harness maker and blowhard who wanted to be a musician. Like a character in *The Music Man,* Irwin Anderson loved his cornet and played in parades and summer concerts. When Sherwood was a year old, the family moved to Clyde. Located some eighteen miles south of Sandusky, it became the model for Winesburg. Anderson worked at several jobs, including journalism, before he became a successful businessman in Cleveland. In 1912, he suffered an emotional breakdown. He divorced his wife and moved to Chicago, where he made a living as a writer until his death in 1941.

Winesburg, Ohio is a collection of short stories about the inhabitants of the town. Anderson called the characters "grotesques." The term was not meant to be pejorative; rather, Anderson used it to describe people distorted by the failure of reality to match their expectations. Home to about two thousand people, Winesburg is a relatively prosperous place in the late nineteenth century, when most of the stories take place. The affluent live in solid houses on paved streets lined with trees. There are two banks, several businesses, a weekly newspaper called the *Winesburg Eagle,* a post office, a railroad station, a telegraph office, a town hall, an opera house, and, of course, a high school. On the outskirts of town is a fairgrounds for baseball games and horse races. All in all, Winesburg is like any other turn-of-the-century Ohio town.

Beneath the veneer of respectability and material comfort, human beings struggle to make connections with each other. Elizabeth Willard is a sensitive, exhausted, middle-aged woman who helps her son, George, resist his father's advice that he "get ahead" as a local businessman. Elizabeth does not want George to repeat the lives of his parents. She wants him to develop his artistic, feminine qualities. Alas, Elizabeth has trouble expressing herself directly, even to her son. Nonetheless, it is clear that she has influenced George. George Willard is the central character in *Winesburg* because people feel comfortable talking to him. What he does well is listen to people tell stories about their lives. They trust George because he takes them seriously and does not judge them.

Most of the stories tell of loneliness. Alice Hindman pines for a reporter named Ned Currie with whom she was intimate when she was sixteen and in search of "something beautiful" in her life. Currie left for Chicago, promising to send for Alice. He never did. Alice grows old, saving money and realizing that time is passing her by without fulfilling her need for love. One rainy night she runs naked into the street, trying vainly to make human contact. Crawling back into her empty house, she turns "her face to the wall" and begins "trying to force herself to face bravely the fact that many people must live and die alone, even in Winesburg."[40]

More often than not, people are lonely because they do not trust themselves. Repressing desire and exercising self-control, they are confused and frustrated. Presbyterian minister Curtis Hartman is insecure about his work and unhappy with his wife. One night, he accidentally sees thirty-year-old schoolteacher Kate Swift smoking and lying on her bed. Disgusted with himself, he finds solace in the strength of God. And yet Hartman returns night after night to watch her, even breaking a stained-glass window to do so. One night he sees her fall naked on her bed; she cries, beats her pillow, and then starts to pray. There is another side of the story. Kate, who controls her emotions behind a cold facade, lusts after one of her students, George Willard. The reason she is thrashing about and praying is that she had briefly lost control of herself while visiting George at the newspaper where he works. Kate is as ashamed of her desire as Curtis Hartman is of his. In Winesburg, even the guardians of institutions such as the church and the school are lonely human beings.

Anderson is not suggesting that people give in to every urge, but he is showing what happens when people neglect themselves in order to meet others' expectations. Winesburg's filthy telegraph operator, Wash Williams, who paradoxically keeps his hands very clean, is a drunken misanthrope who fascinates George. Why is he the way he is? Once he was married to a respectable woman he loved in a respectable house in Columbus, Williams tells George. Then he discovered that his wife had had three lovers. Hurt and disappointed, he sent her home to her parents in Dayton. When he went to see her, his mother-in-law shoved his wife naked into the parlor. Appalled by the crassness of both women, as if his marriage was only about sex, Wash hit the mother and left. Now he wallows in rage and alienation.

Warning George to overcome his need to be like other people, one character urges him to "begin to dream" and "shut [his] ears to the roaring of the voices." George finally achieves something important in his friendship with Helen White, who has returned home from college for a visit. They walk about town and sit together at the fairgrounds. They kiss. They hold each other. They connect. They "had for a moment taken hold of the thing that makes the mature life of men and women in the modern world possible."[41] Here at last is expression; here at last is love, however fleeting.

In the end, George leaves Helen and Winesburg for Chicago. The town has become "but a background on which to paint the dreams of his manhood." What will become of him, we do not know. We do know that while Winesburg is the home of unhappy people, it is not the cause of their unhappiness. No one should think that life will be any better in Chicago or New York or Europe. James Thurber was glad to be away from Ohio, but he knew he would never really be able to leave it. If he lived in the South Seas, his "horn-rimmed glasses and [his] Ohio accent [would] betray" him. Cursed by the mark of the Buckeye, unable "to be inscrutable," he "might just as well be back at Broad and High Streets in Columbus sitting in the Baltimore Dairy Lunch." When he says that "nobody from Columbus has ever made a first rate wanderer in the Conradean tradition," he does not intend it as a compliment. The only people who disappear in Columbus are husbands who wander from their wives but suffer for it. No matter where you go, you are who you are.[42]

Unlike Thurber, Anderson insists that there is a way out, at least emotionally. *Poor White,* a novel published in 1920, is a story of the transformation of the Midwest of possibility into the Midwest of limitations. Hugh McVey was born in a Missouri town. His southern-born family is poor because slavery has made them indolent. Adopted by an ambitious New England–born schoolteacher and her husband, Hugh acquires an education and ambition. He embodies nineteenth-century regional stereotypes. Growing up right after the Civil War, he lives in a place where "in every mind the future was bright with promise. Throughout the whole Mid-American country . . . a hopeful spirit prevailed. In every breast hope fought a successful war with poverty and discouragement." Later, as a young man, Hugh wanders through the small towns of Indiana and Ohio. There, "a quaint interesting civilization was being developed. Men worked hard but were much in the open air and had time to think. Their minds reached out toward the solution of the mystery of existence." Reading widely from Tom Paine to Edward Bellamy, they conversed with each other with "a feeling, ill expressed, that America had something real and spiritual to offer to the rest of the world." Bidwell, Ohio, where Hugh finally settles, is like a booster's dream come true. Its residents "were to each other like members of a great family. . . . A kind of invisible roof beneath which every one lived spread itself over each town. . . . For the moment mankind seemed about to take time to try to understand itself."[43]

The construction of a factory in this near paradise leads to a loss of respect for labor as well as poverty, inequality, filth, and unrest—all the ills decried by working people and reformers at the turn of the century. Anderson, however, does not see the transformation as the work of unseen or malevolent forces. The leaders of the Industrial Revolution are the ambitious, educated young sons of the small towns of the Midwest. Like Rockefeller and Kettering, they have been taught to seek improvement, to embrace progress, to make things better, which is what they think they are doing with their factories. They have learned to equate money with success and greatness with prosperity. Hugh becomes an inventor and creates practical machines.

Everywhere, everyone feels "the new impulse toward progress" without taking stock of its costs. It is a kind of "madness." As industry thrives, architecture, art, music, and poetry languish. People lose their "native energy and strength." Once upon a time, Ohio towns were full of people who had "read books and believed in a God born in the brains of men who came out of a civilization much like their own. On the farms and in the houses in the towns the men and women worked together toward the same ends in life." Before they cared about money, they cared about nurturing "art and beauty."[44] Hugh becomes rich but he does not become happy, with only his educated and independent wife, Clara, to comfort him, to remind him of the possibilities of children and art.

Poor White makes a point about Ohio that Willa Cather made about Nebraska. If the day of the pioneer was over, so too was the day of the respectable, middle-class improvers such as Rud and Lucy Hayes. With them, wrote Cather, "the attainment of material prosperity was a moral victory, because it was wrung from hard conditions, was the result of a struggle that tested character." Now their children and grandchildren were consumed "with material comforts."[45] This sense of loss gave much of Midwestern literature and art an elegiac quality. The dream of development had crashed, at least temporarily. But where others blamed Yankees, bureaucrats, and such for their woes, Anderson argued that the source of the problems lay within Ohioans themselves. Industrialization was not the work of demons. It was the logical outgrowth of a state focused uncritically on unlimited progress and possibilities, on building a public culture that subsumed desire and diversity.

Winesburg, Ohio was the end of that story and the beginning of another. Hayes and Howells, for better or worse, had sought meaning in the development of individual character as the foundation of the improvement of the world as a whole; Samuel Jones and Tom Johnson had reformed but not rejected this idea. In their world, self-analysis was a duty. People lived with the expectation that a good citizen put aside his or her personal loyalties and interests in order to serve the public good. Thus, they had given themselves over to the grand causes of reform, from temperance to antislavery, from municipal ownership to home rule. But in the twentieth century, Ohioans increasingly devoted themselves to realizing public possibilities by fulfilling personal possibilities. A good citizen was no longer a dutiful proponent of material and moral progress. A good citizen was now a complete person, healthy in mind and body, someone who found meaning less in self-denial than in self-fulfillment. For George Willard and thousands of others who left small Ohio towns in the twentieth century, the only sure path out of Winesburg, with its well-intentioned citizens whose lives had withered, led not to Chicago but to an understanding of themselves as members of a public community that recognized the importance of personal happiness.

The Live Wire Club was one of several social organizations formed by African Americans in Cleveland in the 1920s. (Courtesy of The Western Reserve Historical Society, Cleveland, Ohio)

9

Ohio in Black and White

———

SOUTHERNERS flooded into Ohio in the middle of the twentieth century. Hearing stories of a better life north of the Ohio River—and feeling overwhelmed by the economic and social changes that were transforming life in the South—they migrated north with their own ideas about the possibilities of life in Ohio. They formed enclaves in the Miami Valley, in the Columbus and Toledo areas, and from Akron to Cleveland that were similar to earlier immigrant communities. Craving familiarity, Southerners sought to perpetuate the cultures in which they had been born and raised. They established churches and organizations and maintained distinctive languages and forms of expression. Like other immigrants, Southerners encountered hostility and discrimination. Many people denounced them as ignorant and undisciplined, the opposite of what good citizens should be. Southerners nonetheless remade Ohio in the twentieth century as much as Germans had revised it in the nineteenth century.

Despite their similarities to earlier migrants, the Southerners were different in at least two major ways. First, they were not as far from home as Germans and Hungarians had been. Trains and cars made it possible to return to Kentucky or Alabama for extended stays, and telephones kept them in regular contact with family members. Because they were Americans who spoke English and tended to be Protestant, Southerners, while occasionally disoriented, did not face the same kind of challenges as Italian Catholics. Ohio was unfamiliar but not alien.

The second difference was race. The label Southern, like the label European, obscures enormous complexity. Southern immigrants included African Americans from Mississippi, Alabama, Georgia, South Carolina, and Louisiana as well as whites from the Appalachian regions of Kentucky, West Virginia, and Tennessee. White Appalachians and blacks from Alabama found themselves competing for the same jobs and the same housing in their new state. Rather than direct their frustrations at the not-so-promised land of Ohio, they frequently lashed out at each other.

The near simultaneous decline in European immigration with the rapid increase in Southern immigration after World War I made Ohio far more racially diverse than it had been in the nineteenth century. The color line became both more visible and more controversial. The presence of significant numbers of African Americans tended to reduce ethnic conflict as the grandchildren of Europeans began to think of themselves less as German or Irish than as white. So strong was the power of racial identity that many Ohioans found it increasingly difficult to believe in the idea of a public interest that transcended diverse private interests. Many African Americans suspected that talk of a larger public good was a means of ignoring them, while many whites believed that blacks wanted to force public institutions to serve their needs at the expense of others.

Race and Class

Bishop Benjamin William Arnett of the African Methodist Episcopal Church caused a bit of a stir when he rose to address the audience gathered in Chillicothe in May 1903 to mark the centennial of Ohio statehood. Sponsored by the Ohio State Archaeological and Historical Society, the celebration included speeches on the state's history that were later published by the society. Bishop Arnett's talk was printed as well, even though it was "extemporaneous" and had to be recorded by a stenographer. The bishop was not one of "the regular speakers." Still, Arnett's "witty and eloquent remarks greatly pleased the audience." As the official history of the event noted, "[t]he distinguished colored divine was never in better form or feeling."[1]

Arnett was well known to his audience. A sixty-five-year-old native of Pennsylvania, he was a graduate of Wilberforce University and had spent most of his career as a minister in Ohio. Arnett had made similar addresses on similar occasions, including the centennial of Marietta's settlement in 1888. He had been the chaplain of the 1896 National Republican Convention. Well educated and respectable, he was a life member and trustee of the Archaeological and Historical Society. No wonder cries of "Hear him" greeted his attempt to speak. What better person to answer the shouted question, "What shall we do with the Colored Race?"[2]

Bishop Arnett's answer was music to his white audience's ears: education would make blacks into good citizens and unite the races in the special place that was Ohio. Arnett's speech was a passionate paean to the state. He had risen, he said, "to represent in part ninety-six thousand Buckeyes of the buckeye color." Over laughter and applause, Arnett asserted that "no class of people in this land" had been more interested in the fulfillment of the promises of the Northwest Ordinance, "the Ten Commandments" for "the land of Canaan" that was the Northwest Territory. It had not happened at first. Law and custom restricted the rights of African Americans. But at the dawn of the twentieth century, no law in Ohio "discriminates against any man or woman on account of race. . . . [W]e stand to-day equal before the law." Instead of lingering on the failures of the past, people of color should seize "the opportunity to make of themselves men" and become responsible citizens. After all, some black men were veterans of the Civil War. They owned houses, supported schools, and used courthouses, although in the case of the last, Arnett remarked, "You furnish the judge and we furnish the prisoner."[3]

As the audience's laughter died away, Arnett grew earnest and gingerly pushed at the underside of life in Ohio. The black man was not going to go away. Arnett "would not move out of Ohio if I could." He appreciated the assistance whites had given blacks. He appreciated the importance of education and civic duty. All people of color wanted was sympathy and fairness. Let newspapers "record our virtues as well as our vices." For all the praise the bishop heaped on Ohio, he knew that race relations had deteriorated in recent years.[4]

Segregation by custom, if not law, was becoming more pronounced throughout the state. Nor was the explosion in the number of black men hanged without trial for alleged crimes against whites limited to the American South. At least six black men had been lynched in Ohio in the 1890s, and others had come close to suffering a similar fate. In 1896, the General Assembly passed the Smith Law (after its prime sponsor, Harry Smith, a Cleveland man of color), which allowed survivors or relatives of victims of mob violence to sue the county for five hundred to a thousand dollars for victims and up to five thousand dollars for their kin. It was called the most progressive antilynching law in the United States. Yet the very next year a crowd in Urbana pulled a young black man from his jail cell and hanged him for raping a wealthy white widow, who watched the proceedings from her porch. No wonder, then, that Bishop Arnett pleaded for Ohioans to observe their own laws. "If a negro is lynched," said the bishop, "tell why he is lynched, but if the negro does a good deed put it in your paper." As important: "If you find a negro man going to jail, let him go on like any other man, and hang him like any other man but don't hang the wrong man and try him after he is hung." Arnett sounded this note briefly before concluding with assurances that blacks would do their duty as educated citizens. "Loud and long continued applause" followed.[5]

Arnett's speech outlined the dilemma African Americans would face in twentieth-century Ohio. On the one hand, segregation was illegal; most restrictions on African Americans had been repealed. The Ohio Civil Rights Law of 1884 made it a misdemeanor to refuse to grant "to all citizens . . . regardless of race the full enjoyment of accommodations, advantages, facilities, and privileges." On the other hand, Arnett knew that the civil rights law and other legislation were weak, vague, and indifferently enforced. His joke about white judges and black prisoners said so indirectly, and his comments about lynching did so directly. Yet his white audience seemed mostly reassured by his speech. He threatened no revolution. Like most middle-class African Americans, Arnett had faith that with education and demonstrations of character, class might yet matter more than race. Arnett was not unusual in his response to the necessity of negotiating a color line in a place that claimed not to have one. While whites fretted about conformity and stagnation, many black citizens in the early 1900s tended to reinforce traditional middle-class ideals. No group of people, at least until the middle of the twentieth century, was more anxious to embody respectability than African Americans.[6]

At the dawn of the twentieth century, less than 5 percent of Ohio's population was African American. Most people of color were poor and lived in rural enclaves or urban neighborhoods created by a combination of white discrimination and their desire for community. Their living standards were lower, they found it more difficult to find work beyond manual labor, their children received inferior educations, and they often were denied entry to public facilities and accommodations. De jure freedom in the promised land of Ohio was not de facto freedom. Because civil rights legislation was only sporadically enforced, local custom dictated race relations. Although whites tolerated occasional black patronage of hotels and restaurants, blacks had to fight in courts to win even slight advances. African Americans gained the right to public education and to vote as long as they kept their distance and remained deferential.

Not all was bleak, however. Throughout the Midwest in the late 1800s and early 1900s, a self-conscious black elite was emerging. The families of professionals, merchants, and skilled artisans defined themselves as much by their light-colored skin and their behavior as by their occupations or wealth. Constituting upwards of 15 to 20 percent of the black population in Milwaukee, Chicago, Cleveland, and Indianapolis, middle- and upper-class African Americans exuded respectability. They dressed well, maintained neat homes, mastered grammar and diction, listened to the proper music, and read the proper books. They supported economic development and boosted their cities. In essence, they sought citizenship through assimilation, arguing that class was more significant than race. They proclaimed their willingness to subsume their identity as black people within their public identity as decent citizens. By 1900, there were few more obvious examples of bourgeois respectability in the Midwest than the members of black service clubs and self-improvement associations.

In the early twentieth century, Charles W. Chesnutt, who made a small fortune as the owner of a firm of black legal stenographers, lived with his family in one of Cleveland's wealthiest suburbs. The first black member of the city's chamber of commerce, Chesnutt was also the first person of color invited to join the weekly meetings of the Rowfant Club, a literary society. His wife, Susan Chesnutt, was an important member of the nearly all-white Emmanuel Episcopal

Church and belonged to several social clubs. The Chesnutts gave their children highly polished upbringings and sent their two daughters to Smith College and their son to Harvard College and the Northwestern School of Dentistry.

No one was more conscious of the intractable problem of race than Charles Chesnutt. Born in Cleveland in 1858, he was the son of free mulattoes from Fayetteville, North Carolina, to which the family returned after the Civil War. Charles attended the Howard School, a free public school for blacks, learned several languages, and developed an interest in writing. He embarked upon a career as a teacher and became principal of the Howard School (later called the State Colored Normal School) in 1880. Charles grew dissatisfied with life in North Carolina and in 1883 moved his family to Cleveland, where he lived until his death in 1932.

Chesnutt was thoroughly bourgeois in his aspirations, as were many self-identified members of what W. E. B. Dubois called the "talented tenth," educated black men who intended to lead their race out of degradation. Like Rutherford Hayes, he filled his journals as a young man with discussions of the ways he could become a better person. He sought to improve his personal appearance. He read history, rhetoric, and fiction. He listened to music. Chesnutt hoped to experience a religious conversion because he had "made up [his] mind to try and do right." He was delighted that he was acquiring "some degree of *self-reliance.*" Chesnutt was fair-skinned enough to be "taken for 'white'" on more than one occasion. Ambivalent about his color, he thought class should be more important. Character and money should be the measures of success. After returning to Cleveland, he hoped to "exalt [his] race" and depend on the "good" to "honor true merit wherever discovered." He intended to find out "if it's possible for talent, wealth, genius to acquire social standing and distinction."[7]

Chesnutt became a writer in order to contribute to "a moral revolution." His goal was "not so much the elevation of the colored people as the elevation of the whites." Impossible to achieve by force, it had to happen by internal conversion. Slavery was gone; legal rights had been won in Ohio. "But the subtle almost indefinable feeling of repulsion toward the negro, which is common to most Americans . . . cannot be stormed and taken by assault." In this crusade, "the negro's

part is to prepare himself for social recognition and equality." Literature would "open the way for him to get to it, to accustom the public
mind to the idea; and while amusing them to lead them on impercep-
tibly, unconsciously step by step to the desired state of feeling."[8]

How did Chesnutt imagine this transformation taking place?
There are clues in stories he wrote about life in Groveland, a fictional
stand-in for Cleveland, which were published in 1899 in *The Wife of
His Youth and Other Stories of the Color Line*. Chesnutt confronted the
world of Midwestern black elites, light-skinned people who prided
themselves on their refinement. In Groveland, these men and women
belonged to the Blue Vein Society, so named because the members'
skin was white enough to reveal their veins. Much as he approved of
the Blue Veins' efforts to improve themselves, Chesnutt was troubled
by their attitudes toward race.

He himself was ambiguous on the subject. On the one hand, he
suggested in "Her Virginia Mammy" that in the end race should not
matter—much. In this contrived story, a young woman named Clara
resists the marriage proposal of a man she loves because she was
adopted by a German couple and is therefore uncertain of her family's history. Her lover, John, meanwhile, is descended from a passenger on the *Mayflower* and a governor of Connecticut. Unconcerned
about Clara's past, John advises her to concentrate on the future and
to remember that "we are all made after God's own image, and
formed by his hand, for his ends; and therefore not to be lightly despised, even the humblest of us, least of all by ourselves." When
Clara begins to teach dance to a group of black people, she tells the
story of her early life to a woman named Mrs. Harper, who gleans
enough to inform Clara that she knows her, that she was her "colored
nurse." Clara's parents were from an aristocratic Virginia family and
were good people. Why, they were even opposed to slavery! A delighted Clara is free to marry John and, "impulsively," to accept Mrs.
Harper as a member of her family.[9] Throughout the conversation between Clara and Mrs. Harper, Chesnutt more than implies that the
latter is the young woman's real mother. But John and Clara are
happy, and Clara and Mrs. Harper have formed what is clearly a permanent attachment. Why spoil things by making Clara aware of her
mixed ancestry?

Would the news matter to Clara? Earlier, she was reassured to learn from people in her dance class that while people of color may not be able "to make the fine distinctions that are possible among white people," they do "draw certain lines of character and manners and occupations." They may not have a "prejudice against color." But they "must have standards that will give our people something to aspire to." Clara admires her students and comes to feel "perfectly at home" with them because they are no "different from other people."[10] But how would she react if she discovered that she too was a woman of color? We never find out.

Chesnutt parodies the racial pretension of Groveland's black elite humorously in "A Matter of Principle." Here one of the most prominent exponents of the idea of a brotherhood of man, Cicero Clayton, also accepts the idea that people of color who are more than half white should be allowed to belong "to the most virile and progressive race of modern times." A good man in many ways, Clayton is a hypocrite in his efforts to deny his color. When Alice, his beautiful, "nearly white" daughter, travels to Washington, D.C., she attracts the attention of an African American congressman who writes of his intention to call on the young woman and her family during an impending visit to Groveland. Alice and her relatives are excited at the prospect; the trouble is, neither she nor anyone else can remember what the congressman looks like. Deciding that he must be light-skinned, the Claytons invite him to stay in their home and arrange a grand ball to celebrate his visit. But when Mr. Clayton and a young man who loves Alice go to the train station to greet their visitor, they confuse him with "a stout and very black man." Horrified at the prospect of entertaining, let alone having as a son-in-law, a man who is "palpably, aggressively black, with pronounced African features and woolly hair, without apparently a single drop of redeeming white blood," Clayton sends the congressman a note saying that his daughter has diphtheria and his family is quarantined. The father assures himself and everyone else that his decision is not a question of "prejudice," but "principle."[11]

While sympathetic to Clayton, Chesnutt mocks his liberal attitude. And he makes him pay for his prejudice when he discovers that the man he thought was the congressman was really his traveling companion. Welcomed into the home of another Groveland family, the light-skinned congressman becomes engaged to their daughter. The farcical story ends happily: Alice marries the man who really loves her. Clayton learns nothing, however, and goes on mouthing platitudes about how whites need to accept "a higher conception of the brotherhood of man. For of one blood God made all the nations of the earth."[12]

More poignant is "The Wife of His Youth." Mr. Ryder, "the dean of the Blue Veins," has risen to prosperity and prominence. He owns a nice home where he can enjoy music and indulge his "passion for poetry." Like Clayton, he denies that he is prejudiced, yet he laments the situation of "people of mixed blood" such as himself. Like Clayton, he clearly thinks that white is superior. "Our fate lies between absorption by the white race and extinction in the black. The one doesn't want us yet, but may take us in time. The other would welcome us, but it would be for us a backward step."[13]

As the story opens, Ryder has decided to hold a party in his home in which he intends to propose marriage to an equally refined, light-skinned widow. Their children will obviously advance the cause of "the upward process of absorption." But on the afternoon of the ball, a small, aged, tastelessly dressed, "very black" woman "with toothless gums" arrives on his porch and announces that she is looking for the husband from whom she was separated while they were slaves in Missouri. The woman has been searching for her spouse for a quarter of a century, certain that he has remained loyal to her, even if he has risen in the world. That night at the party, Ryder tells the woman's story and asks his guests what her husband should do, especially if he has improved his condition, knows that his marriage to a slave woman was not legally binding, and has created a new and better life for himself. They all agree that he should acknowledge her. Gratified by their response, Ryder introduces the old woman as "the wife of my youth."[14]

There is more than a little shame in Ryder's story and a strong sense that his noble act will drastically affect the life he has built for himself. He and his former wife have little in common except the past and feelings of obligation to each other. Would that every story could end like "Her Virginia Mammy." But they cannot. If Groveland's Blue

Veins would improve themselves, they cannot do it at the cost of obliterating black people. Color may be invisible on occasion, but in the end, it will out.

Chesnutt liked to say that "[i]n the North, race prejudice is rather a personal than a community matter, and a man is not regarded as striking at the foundations of society if he sees fit to extend a social courtesy to a person of color." Neither "wealth or blood or birth," he insisted, had much to do with his success.[15] Yet they did, especially race. Mixed marriages held out the possibility of love triumphant, of a better world in which people treated each other without regard to anything other than the content of their characters. But even for a bourgeois proponent of progress such as Chesnutt, interracial love was a dubious proposition. The ending was unlikely to be happy, or so Chesnutt suggests in "Uncle Wellington's Wives."

Wellington Braboy, a middle-aged, mixed-race man living in North Carolina, sees "in the North a land flowing with milk and honey,—a land peopled by noble men and beautiful women, among whom colored men and women moved with the ease and grace of acknowledged right."[16] Braboy decides to migrate. The problem is his wife does not want to go. Learning that their marriage is not legal because they were married while slaves, Braboy steals money from her and takes off for Groveland. He arrives in the city in the 1870s and stays with relatives. Impressed that he can sit anywhere on a streetcar, he gets a job as a coachman for a wealthy white family.

Braboy marries one of the other servants, who happens to be an Irishwoman named Flannigan. "According to all his preconceived notions," writes Chesnutt, "this marriage ought to have been the acme of uncle Wellington's felicity." Wrong. Braboy and his wife try to live in an Irish neighborhood but are forced out by people who will not live "'wid naygurs.'"[17] Life in the black community proves to be no better, largely because Mrs. Braboy condescends to her neighbors. She begins to drink heavily, as does Braboy. An accident leads to the loss of his job, and Mrs. Braboy has to take in washing to support them.

At this point, Wellington reflects on life in Groveland. With "his rose-colored conception of life at the North" in tatters, he has "discovered more degrees of inequality than he had ever perceived at the South." Class matters. Even if race is overcome, no one "was of any special consequence without money, or talent, or position." Welling-ton lacked the education and the self-discipline to "take advantage" of what the North had to offer him. While Chesnutt thinks that Braboy's plight is to a large extent his own fault, he is not unsympa-thetic. A black lawyer tells Braboy that he "might have expected" such a result when he "turned [his] back on [his] own people and married a white woman. You weren't content with being a slave to the white folks once, but you must try it again. Some people never know when they've got enough."[18] Fortunately for Braboy, his wife deserts him for her previous husband, and he returns to North Carolina, where he finds his first wife missing him and resumes his previous life.

Despite the dismal portrait of Braboy's mixed marriage, Chesnutt saw miscegenation as the most likely means of overcoming racism. Miscegenation would resolve the issue of the color line by eliminating it. "The mixture of races will in time become an accomplished fact," and "it will be a good thing for all concerned. It is already well for-ward and events seem to be paving the way to embrace the Negro in the general process by which all the races of mankind are being fused together here into one people." In Chesnutt's view, race was a social construction. No wonder persons of mixed race tried to pass as white in order to gain the rights of citizenship. Who would not choose to emphasize that part of their identity that promised them the most sta-tus? While he continued to talk in terms of black and white and clearly favored the latter, implicit in Chesnutt's writings was the as-sumption that people of mixed race were unique. The challenge was less to confront double consciousness than to assert a single con-sciousness fused out of European and African ancestries. The model for this kind of a world was Latin America, especially Brazil. Chesnutt summarized his position in the title of an essay: "The Future Ameri-can: A Complete Race-Amalgamation Likely to Occur."[19]

Other black writers from Ohio were less sanguine about the fu-ture. Miscegenation seemed far from inevitable—and not necessarily a good thing at that. Chesnutt's contemporary, Paul Lawrence Dunbar, who was born in Dayton in 1872, took greater pride in being black, although much of his poetry and prose followed white models and dealt with conventional themes. Unable to find a job other than that of elevator operator, Dunbar nonetheless became a published poet and novelist in the 1890s. In his writings, he transformed the tales and traditions he learned from his family into powerful statements of racial pride. Unlike Chesnutt, Dunbar did not try to mix with whites. In fact, he insisted on identifying himself on his own terms.

Dunbar was a realist. His home state was better for blacks than the South, but it was no paradise. Prejudice was as strong north of the Ohio River as it was south of it. Still, Dunbar knew the importance of industry and perseverance. Nothing would do more for his race than the success of individuals in winning "the confidence and respect of [their] neighbors." Their examples would redound to the credit of all. The reasons for their achievement would be "the same that account for the advancement of men of any other race: preparation, perseverance, bravery, patience, honesty, and the power to seize the opportunity."[20]

Dunbar's fiction, however, suggests that character is not enough. In "One Man's Fortunes," the young black man Bartram Halliday graduates from the state university with optimism about his future. He listens to a friendly debate between a white and a black acquaintance about the challenges of finding a job. Halliday accepts the former's argument that he is the master of his own fate. Reality strikes when he returns to his hometown of Broughton and cannot get a job in a law firm, notwithstanding his willingness "to work and to work hard." "I am an American citizen," Halliday tells a white lawyer and prospective employer; "there should be no thought of color about it." "Oh, my boy," replies the white man, "that theory is very nice, but State University democracy doesn't obtain in real life."[21]

Unable to find respectable work, Halliday becomes an under janitor in a factory. A year later, a white lawyer offers him a job but only to win black votes in an election. When he wins, he dismisses Halliday. Chastened, Halliday writes to his black friend from college that he is going south in search of a teaching job. Middle-class pieties are not enough. Race matters more than class. He no longer "judge[d] so harshly the shiftless and unambitious among my people. I hardly see how a people, who have so much to contend with and so little to hope for, can go on striving and aspiring. But the very fact that they do, breeds in me a respect for them. . . . We have been taught that merit wins. But I have learned that the adages, as well as the books and the formulas were made by and for others than us of the black race." Of course, the friend thinks as he reads the letter, "A colored man has no business with ideals—not in *this* nineteenth century!"[22]

Dunbar's story effectively undermined middle-class assumptions about life in Ohio. Halliday does everything right: he gets an education; he dresses well; he speaks properly; he is ambitious, industrious, and generous. But none of it makes any difference. As obvious as this conclusion may seem to us, it was a novelty in its time. Dunbar did not give up. Hoping that things would turn out for the best, he talked about forgiveness, if only because it demonstrated the great spirit of black people. Indeed, Dunbar's answer to the problem of the color line was not miscegenation. He would not obliterate the black race but uplift it. "Be proud, my Race, in mind and soul," he wrote in "Ode to Ethiopia." "Thou hast the right to noble pride, / Whose spotless robes were purified / By blood's severe baptism. . . . / No other race, when free again, / Forgot the past and proved them men / So noble in forgiving." Now was the time for black men to "proudly tune their lyres to sing of Ethiopia's glory."[23]

Dunbar and others began to talk of race pride in no small part because they had no choice. The history of nineteenth-century Ohio had demonstrated that it was whites, not blacks, who insisted on the inevitability of race, maintained the color line, and continued to restrict admission to hotels and amusement parks by custom, if not law. When James Hathaway Robinson, a Kentucky-born Yale Ph.D., and other faculty at Cincinnati's Frederick Douglass School greeted eight hundred black students every morning with placards proclaiming "Self-Control," "Self-Reliance," "Self-Respect," and "Race Pride," they were sustaining a parallel universe.[24]

The Great Migration and Ohio

Whether pushed by economic change and institutionalized racism in the South or pulled by the prospect of jobs and freedom in Ohio and the Midwest, a stream of black migrants, what Langston Hughes called "a great dark tide," rose in the late 1800s and accelerated dramatically in the 1900s, particularly in the decades following World War I and World War II. This growth was almost exclusively urban.

The number of African Americans in Cleveland rose from 1.5 percent of the population in 1910 to 16.2 percent in 1950 to 43.8 percent in 1980; in Cincinnati, from 5.4 percent in 1910 to 15.5 percent in 1950 to 33.8 percent in 1980; in Dayton, from 4.2 percent in 1910 to 14 percent in 1950 to 36.9 percent in 1980; in Columbus, from 7.0 percent in 1910 to 12.4 percent in 1950 to 22.1 percent in 1980; in Toledo, from 1.1 percent in 1910 to 8.2 percent in 1950 to 17.4 percent in 1980; and in Akron, from 1.0 percent in 1910 to 8.7 percent in 1950 and 22.2 percent in 1980. "This is when the South all came up here," remembered Clevelander Bertha Cowan, "and it turned into a new world."[25]

African Americans who came to Ohio in the twentieth century entered a hostile world. Whites who tolerated the presence of a handful of blacks were unwilling to do so when they felt overwhelmed by blacks. While employers welcomed black workers in tight labor markets, they dispensed with them as soon as possible and almost always paid them less. As competitors for jobs and houses, blacks were on their own. Many white Ohioans, anxious about the decline of their state, became more rigid about racial borders. Even whites in the northeastern section of the state, long sympathetic to the plight of blacks, became more hostile. African Americans in Ohio found the practice of segregation nearly everywhere. The color line became more visible in Cincinnati, Columbus, Akron, and even Cleveland. In the early 1900s, students at Oberlin College, once the bastion of abolitionism, segregated their extracurricular activities.

Most spectacular were the lynchings and attempted lynchings in southern Ohio. The first was in Oxford in Butler County in 1892. A group of white citizens broke into the town jail and hanged a black man for the murder of a white woman and an assault on her daughter. None of the participants was punished, and the *Cincinnati Enquirer* all but applauded their action. In 1894, a crowd lynched a young African American for the murder of an elderly white couple in Adams County. Over the next couple of years, two more men were executed without trial in Bellefontaine and New Richmond. Others barely escaped the same fate, including an alleged rapist in Washington Court House. After the 1897 lynching in Urbana, attacks on black prisoners stopped. But violence against African Americans did not.

In 1904, a black Kentuckian with a reputation for drunkenness shot his female companion, a black woman, in Springfield. When a policeman attempted to arrest him, he killed the officer. The next day, a group of citizens took him from the local jail and lynched him. The following night, a white mob launched a full-scale assault on the Levee, a row of saloons, brothels, and gambling houses in a run-down black neighborhood along the railroad tracks. Springfield was notorious in the early twentieth century for providing just about anything a man could pay for. Despite lax police enforcement of laws and widespread corruption, whites blamed blacks for the immorality of the place. Some whites were upset about the integration of local schools. Even more were disturbed by the fact that blacks had served as strikebreakers in the late 1800s. And growing numbers of whites associated African Americans with sexual promiscuity. In 1913, there was a strong effort, ultimately unsuccessful, to sentence married interracial couples to five years in prison.

From the Civil War to the 1880s, African Americans had made significant progress toward achieving legal integration. But from the 1890s on, they faced rising anger among frustrated whites who were afraid of the expanding numbers of blacks in their midst. African Americans were no longer a tiny minority, most of whom lived in rural areas. They had become a visible presence, and whites were unhappy about it. The sight of unfamiliar young black men from the countryside or the South arriving regularly in search of work unsettled white people. The attack on the Levee in Springfield, which resulted in the destruction of black homes as well as white- and black-owned businesses, was seen as a moral defense of community values. Never mind that the gamblers and prostitutes moved to a white working-class area when the smoke had cleared. More unrest followed the 1906 arrest of blacks accused of attacking whites.[26]

Black immigrants, a majority of whom were young, male, unattached, and eager to test the boundaries of northern freedom they had heard so much about, struck many whites as vulgar and uncouth. Their rural pasts had not instilled the proper values. Their music was unrefined, their gestures uncontrolled. White middle-class disgust at Southern blacks echoed traditional complaints about rural people and European immigrants. Racial prejudice reinforced class prejudice. But it was more than that. In many ways, whites gave up easily on blacks, concluding it was impossible to raise them to the proper levels of civilization. Even in "liberal" Cleveland, according to the writer Langston Hughes, "the color line began to be drawn tighter and tighter."[27]

Middle-class blacks were just as horrified by their new neighbors. Uncouth hordes of people swarming across the Ohio River threatened to undo the efforts of black elites to cultivate respectability, to argue for the power of class to overcome race. In Cleveland, the city's black elite worried that "the loud-mouthed individual of color on the streets, in the streetcars and other public places" threatened their social positions. The editor of a black newspaper insisted that "whites had been old friends of the race" in the city. The behavior of migrants, he worried, would transform the Midwest into the South. The large numbers of noisy and undisciplined blacks would lead whites to institutionalize segregation. As important, black middle-class residents just did not like their new neighbors. One minister lamented the rise of shouting in church. "The more education the people had, the less noise you heard out of them."[28]

In February 1921, George Myers, a black man who had turned his hotel barbershop into a gathering place for leading politicians and become a Republican stalwart, complained to a white friend about the new Negroes in Cleveland. Many were "of the lowest and shiftless class" and needed to be assimilated into life in Ohio. The challenge was "to get them to see themselves from a northern, inste[a]d of a southern standpoint and leave their old condition and customs back in the South. Speaking in the vernacular—to quit being a southern darkey." Like his peers, Myers worried that Southern black immigrants would cause a revival of racial prejudice. In the meantime, he put his faith in religion, organizations, and the creed of the Midwestern black man: "Give the negro an equal opportunity to work, equality before the law, and he will work out his own salvation."[29]

Southern blacks *were* different, of course. They had grown up in a rural world where there was far less concern about self-discipline, moral improvement, and social and sexual respectability. Southern blacks' ecstatic forms of worship, their preference for gospel music, their choices about how to spend free time, as well as their clothes, language, and customs offended bourgeois sensibilities. While most Southern immigrants were Protestants, their behavior in church was far more emotional and demonstrative. Worshipers were more likely to punctuate sermons and readings with shouts, more likely to clap and sway. To some extent, Southern blacks were more interested in finding their own mode of expression than in adhering to middle-class notions of respectability.

Nothing reveals this better than blues music. Born in the Mississippi Delta, the blues is a simple, direct form of music with lyrics arranged in an AAB rhyme scheme and the first line often repeated. Typically the songs address personal and collective problems. They dealt with pain and frustration by sharing it. They also are fun. People have a good time with the blues, even if the songs were melancholy. The blues is the music of the street and of speakeasies— smoky, dark places that were anything but respectable. As important, the songs are fatalistic about human failings and difficult relationships. They talk about the pleasures of sex, drugs, and alcohol, the antithesis of middle-class respectability. The blues is an emotional, personal response to the constant harshness of life. The songs could be bleak, as in Sweet Papa Tadpole's "Sing Sing Blues": "And you're motherless and you're fatherless, friendless in this old world, too, / A deck of cards and a deck of dice and underworld woman ain't no friend to you." Or more upbeat, as in Walter Coleman's "I'm goin to Cincinnati, the times is good, / I'm goin to Cincinnati where they eat fried food, / And I'm goin to Cincinnati, boys, where the bottle is good. . . . Now when you come to Cincinnati stop on Sixth and Main, / That's where the good hustlin women get the good cocaine."[30]

Consciously or not, the blues defied white culture and a middle-class emphasis on self-discipline. In song, black men asserted themselves and their ways of doing things. In the words of Johnny Shines, a Cincinnati bluesman, "[Everyone thinks of] the bluesman as bein' stupid, illiterate, not able to think for himself, that's why he's singin' these dirty, lowdown songs. They don't realize that THEY'RE the one that's STUPID because they've been taught that these songs was dirty. . . . I AM the privileged character. I'm the one wearin' the crown, even though it don't show."[31]

Equally defiant was the writer Chester Himes, who was born in Missouri and spent much of his early life in Cleveland and Columbus. Himes was the son of "a short black man with bowed legs, a perfect ellipsoidal skull, and an Arabic face with a big hooked nose" and a woman who was "a octoroon, or perhaps whiter" and quite proud of her English ancestry. The family moved to Cleveland in the 1920s because Himes's father, a professor of mechanical arts at several colleges, had relatives in the city.[32]

An instinctive rebel, Himes repeatedly defied his mother's insistence on respectability. When he entered The Ohio State University in 1926, he spent most of his time and money on looking good and enjoying himself. He joined one of the two black fraternities, bought a coonskin coat and a Model T roadster, went to black musical shows, and visited Columbus prostitutes, whom he found generally more attractive than their counterparts in Cleveland. He experienced the strange sensation of living in a place where racial discrimination was forbidden by law but enforced by custom. The same black students who attended classes at the university could not live in dormitories or eat in restaurants.

As much as Himes despised the color line, he had no faith in the saving grace of class. He ignored white people who stared at him because he "didn't need them, didn't want to know them, and always felt that they couldn't reject me any more than I could reject them." Although he did not understand his behavior at the time, he later came "to understand [that he] hadn't accepted [his] status as a 'nigger.'" Despite his light skin, his respectable family, and his relative affluence, he did not feel comfortable putting class above race. He "liked dark black people" and was "at ease with them. Among them, I felt as black as the next person and as good as anyone."[33]

Himes flunked out of Ohio State and returned to Cleveland, where he became involved in illegal gambling operations. While his brother Joe graduated from high school with honors and went to Oberlin College, Himes hustled for money. With his friend Benny, also "light-brown-skinned," he participated in a series of burglaries.[34] He also passed bad checks in Columbus. In 1928 he was arrested for breaking into the home of a wealthy white couple, whom he held at gunpoint. Already on probation for previous infractions, Himes was sentenced to twenty to twenty-five years' hard labor in the Ohio State Penitentiary. He served only seven and a half years, but in that time he developed more self-discipline and began to write.

Himes's life was the nightmare of white (and middle-class black) Clevelanders come true. He seemed to have wasted incredible opportunities. Yet, without holding Himes up as a paragon, it is possible to accept his reading of his early behavior as the product of an unhappy home and a larger society that promised him one thing and gave him another. People of color in Ohio could dress up like respectable whites, they could live in decent houses, attend public universities, and accept white values. But they were still black. Salvation for Himes lay not in rejecting or ignoring his color, but in rejecting the identity that he thought white Ohioans were trying to force on him. If his behavior was criminal, it was also a stumbling assertion of autonomy, his refusal to allow others to tell him who he was and to define his significance. Before or after prison, Himes had no intention of surrendering himself to become a citizen.

This theme reached its fruition in the novels of Toni Morrison, who was born and grew up in Lorain, an industrial city east of Cleveland on Lake Erie. Morrison left Lorain in 1949 when she was eighteen to attend Howard University in Washington, D.C. Except for occasional visits, she has never returned to Ohio. And yet most of her novels are set in the state or in an imagined world that strongly resembles it. Morrison herself frequently notes the importance of her origins. Although she "never felt like an American or an Ohioan or even a Lorainite . . . [if she] never felt like a citizen," she retained from her life in Lorain "a very strong sense of place, not in terms of the country or the state, but in terms of the details, the feeling, the mood of the community, of the town." "I am from the Midwest," Morrison said more generally in a 1983 interview, "so I have a special affection for it. . . . No matter what I write, I begin there." Morrison adds, however, that a sense of place is more of a curiosity than a critical factor in the lives of African Americans. "Black people take their culture wherever they go," she has said. "If I wrote about Maine, the black people in Maine would be very much like black people in Ohio. You can change the plate, but the menu would still be the same. . . . They cook a little bit differently, but I know what the language will be like."[35]

Morrison's first novel, *The Bluest Eye,* is set in her hometown. On the eve of World War II, Pecola Breedlove, an eleven-year-old girl of color, believes she will find love and happiness if only she had the blue eyes and blond hair of the Shirley Temple dolls idolized by white girls. A devastating critique of the damage racial prejudice and mass consumer culture can wreak on innocent children, *The Bluest Eye* may also be read as a guide to black life in twentieth-century Ohio. Although racism is pervasive, there is little legal segregation by color in Lorain. Rather, the borders between whites and the small number of blacks are negotiated through the stuff of daily lives, in schools, homes, stores, and on the streets. Lorain's blacks tend to be recent immigrants from the South struggling in a new environment without a clear sense of its cultural rules. Opportunity and discrimination are contrapuntal themes in its history. "Ohio," Morrison has written, "is a curious juxtaposition of what was ideal in this country and what was base." Ohio "offers an escape from stereotyped black settings. It is neither plantation nor ghetto."[36]

In general, blacks in *The Bluest Eye* fall into two categories: those with middle-class aspirations and those without. Pecola's family is in the latter group. Living in a shabby apartment, they have few connections with others. They believe in their own ugliness, accepting the larger society's description of them. Pecola thinks she is ugly not only because movies and advertisements portray beauty as white but because family and friends are complicit in her ruin. Unable to define themselves either for or against white, middle-class norms, often lost in a perverse pain, they can provide neither encouragement nor alternative models of life in Ohio.

Morrison is especially tough on light-skinned women who accept their alleged inferiority and devote themselves to winning the respect of white people. To do so, they have to "get rid of the funkiness. The dreadful funkiness of passion, the funkiness of nature, the funkiness of the wide range of human emotions." They paint their lives from a narrow palette. They go to school "to instruct black children in obedience" and to learn, above all else, "how to behave. The careful development of thrift, patience, high morals, and good manners."[37] Geraldine is one of these women, a person who distinguishes between colored people and niggers on the basis of their behavior. "Colored people were neat and quiet; niggers were dirty and loud." She values her well-ordered, elaborately decorated home as a refuge from the volatility and irregularities of the world. When Geraldine finds her son has brought Pecola, resplendent in her dirty clothes and dirty hair, into her clean and neat home, she banishes her: "'Get out,' she said, her voice quiet. 'You nasty little black bitch. Get out of my house.'"[38]

Pecola's family only makes things worse. Her mother, Pauline, has destroyed herself and her children with her obsession with "respectability." Morrison suggests that the stomping out of funkiness makes people afraid—afraid of breaking the rules, afraid of other people, afraid of life.[39] Pecola's father, Cholly, has abandoned all connections with other people, finding independence in utter isolation. Lost in alcohol, he rapes Pecola out of a mixture of hatred and despair.

The only happy characters in the novel are the three prostitutes—China, Poland, and Miss Marie—who live in the apartment above the Breedloves. Hardly innocents, they have nonetheless accepted who they are. They have found a way to laugh, to sing, and to value their own opinions. Pecola visits them because unlike virtually everyone she knows, the prostitutes do not "despise her."[40] With them, she is, briefly, who she is, not someone forced into the emotional straitjacket of respectability.

Morrison's most powerful meditation on the necessity of imagining our place, of escaping the prison we create for ourselves by accepting the judgments of our larger society, is her 1987 novel, *Beloved.* Set along the Ohio River, the novel elaborates on the true story of Margaret Garner, a young woman living near Cincinnati in the 1850s who slit her children's throats rather than see them returned to slavery. Beloved is a young woman who suddenly appears in the lives of Sethe (a fictional version of Garner) and her family during the 1870s and who may be the ghost of a murdered child. In telling the story of Beloved and Sethe, Morrison echoes and transcends the ways in which white and Ohioans have imagined themselves for almost two centuries.

The pragmatic black man Stamp Paid knows that in Ohio even educated blacks—"the long-school people, the doctors, the teachers, the paper-writers and businessmen[—]had a hard row to hoe. In addition to having to use their heads to get ahead, they had the weight of the whole race sitting there." Class could never override race. The color line was inescapable. For "[w]hitepeople believed that whatever the manners, under every dark skin was a jungle." Stamp Paid accepts the existence of that jungle even as he sees it largely as the creation of "whitefolks." "The more coloredpeople spent their strength trying to convince them [whites] how gentle they were, how clever and loving, how human, the more they used themselves up to persuade whites of something Negroes believed could not be questioned, the deeper and more tangled the jungle grew inside."[41] There is no solace, in other words, in trying to act like whites, indeed, in trying to act like anyone but yourself.

Most of all, the people of *Beloved* are unable to embrace the future because they cannot escape the past. Sethe's experience is a common one. She "was not interested in the future. Loaded with the past and hungry for more, it left her no room to imagine, let alone plan for, the next day." Her life is a daily struggle "of beating back the past." "[T]he future was a matter of keeping the past at bay." The horrors and grief of history cannot be erased, nor should they be. The idea, as Sethe's lover Paul D urges her, is to accept that they have "more yesterday than anybody" and that they "need some kind of tomorrow."[42]

The key to making that future is taking hold of the past and making it your own. It is your own story, not the one others may tell you. That, in fact, was what Sethe was doing when she cut her daughter's throat. Because she loved her, she would take her future to allow her to avoid her mother's past. She would not let "anybody white . . . take your whole self for anything that came to mind. Not just work, kill, or maim you, but dirty you. Dirty you so bad you couldn't like yourself anymore. Dirty you so bad you forgot who you were and couldn't think it up." Sethe's children were her future, and they had to be kept clean. It was her responsibility to see that "nobody on this earth, would list her daughter's characteristic on the animal side of the paper. No. Oh no."[43]

Running away from slavery, giving birth to her daughter on the banks of the Ohio, helped across the river later by the resourceful Stamp Paid, Sethe enjoys twenty-eight days of freedom—of family and community, of dancing and eating, of talking about public issues, of living without fear—followed by a life of misery defined by white men coming to take her children away. Sethe lives on the memory of the promise of that month, something Ohio with all its racism gave her, something that slaveholding Kentucky could never offer her. It gave her hope, and she would not surrender it even at the cost of her children's lives. Ohio was not a perfect place. But it was a place that seemed to offer the opportunity, the space, to make your own story, to decide who you were and what mattered in the past, and what the future could be. It is a place where Baby Suggs, Sethe's mother-in-law, can at last experience life through her own eyes and on her own terms. This Sethe forgot in years of shame and shunning. This Beloved teaches her again with the help of Paul D. Within Sethe's house, "the women . . . were free at last to be what they liked, see whatever they saw and say whatever was on their minds."[44]

Beloved can be read in many ways. It is about the horrors of slavery and the need for black Americans to embrace the future by claiming their history. *Beloved* is history written in a circular fashion, a dialogue between the present and the past. But it also is a reimagining of a place called Ohio. African Americans may have been disappointed by life in the state, but they were not silenced by it. While for some white writers and artists Ohio became an ossified promised land, a place from which sensitive and ambitious souls escaped as soon as they could do so, for many blacks it remained a world of possibilities. Even as some people of color defied the conventions of middle-class respectability, even as they felt the frustration of unfulfilled promises, they more than anyone continued to insist that the Midwest was a world defined by a commitment to material progress and moral improvement. What was different about that insistence by the second half of the twentieth century was the idea that progress depended on assertion of the particular interests and identities of black citizens as they themselves defined them. Ironically, pervasive racism inspired black Ohioans to think, sing, and write self-consciously about what it meant to be a citizen of Ohio.

Appalachian Ohio

White Southern migrants also experienced serious discrimination. Since most of them were from Appalachia, they were frequently and derisively called "hillbillies" or "briarhoppers" (especially in southern Ohio) and linked with undesirable social traits. The Kentuckians and Tennesseans who moved by the tens of thousands into southeastern Ohio and the West Virginians who arrived in Columbus, Akron, Canton, Youngstown, Cleveland, and Cincinnati were ridiculed by other whites. "What's the best thing to come out of Kentucky?" asked one joke, to which the answer was, "An empty Greyhound bus." Another asked: "Did you know that Kentuckians could walk on water to cross the Ohio River?" "Yes, they walk across the scum left by the other hillbillies."[45] Appalachian whites, like black Southerners, found it difficult to obtain jobs beyond the level of unskilled workers. Clustered in urban communities that paralleled and occasionally overlapped with black communities, they were also called poor, dirty, lazy, and ignorant. They were not, in a word, "decent."

Many native Ohioans saw white Appalachians, like Southern blacks, as competitors for jobs. They also feared them as threats to their self-image. Appalachians streaming into Ohio were reversing the outcome of the Civil War. If the Midwest had conquered the South militarily in the nineteenth century, Southerners were conquering Ohio demographically in the twentieth century. According to one joke, there were only forty-eight states left in the U.S. by the 1960s because "all of Kentucky moved to Ohio, and Ohio went to hell."[46] There was some outrage in the 1960s when many counties in southern and southeastern Ohio were included in the federal government's designation of Appalachia.

Middle-class Ohioans wanted as little to do with Appalachians as possible beyond deriding their lack of manners, education, and self-discipline. Perhaps the most insidious thing about the regular demeaning of Appalachians was its effect on children. Even in schools they were the victims of insults. Their large families, their supposed inability to control their sexual behavior or to figure out how women got pregnant, were evidence of their general lack of character and their unsuitability as citizens. After all, joked Ohioans, a "virgin in Kentucky" was either "the ugliest girl in the fifth grade" or "the sister who can outrun her brothers." Woody Hayes, the legendary Ohio State football coach, told his teams that a Tennessee woman had assured a census taker that she and her husband would not be having any more than the thirteen children they already had "because we found out what was causing them."[47]

Was there any truth to these stereotypes? Appalachian families in Ohio cities in the 1970s tended to live in poorer areas where a high percentage of people had not finished high school. Household incomes were lower in Columbus (median family income in Appalachian-dominated areas was $7,712, compared to $9,731 in other parts of the city). But Appalachians in Dayton were closer to the city's median income, although they also tended to have larger families and more children living at home than other residents. Appalachians in Cleveland also had roughly the same median income as other families, and those in Toledo not only had similar incomes but similar educational levels. An extensive study of Cincinnati Appalachians found that they had done well but not as well as other groups. Appalachians in the 1970s had the lowest unemployment rate in the city, 44 percent had experienced upward social mobility from one generation to the next, and almost two-thirds lived in suburbs rather than the inner city. On the other hand, their suburban homes were in working-class areas, they remained largely in semi-skilled or unskilled jobs, and their overall household income was low. High school dropout rates in Cincinnati's Appalachian neighborhoods in the 1980s hovered around 50 percent. And Appalachians made up around one-third of the residents of Ohio's penitentiary system in the mid-1990s.[48] In sum, Appalachians were more likely to be less educated, poorer, and in trouble with the law than the average Ohioan.

Still, the impact of Appalachians on twentieth-century Ohio was enormous, rivaling if not exceeding the impact of Germans in the nineteenth century. The Appalachian conquest of Ohio originated in a need for labor precipitated by the decline of European migration during and after World War I, coupled with the modernization of agriculture in the American South. By 1930, Ohio's population included 54,043 native-born Tennesseans, 206,353 Kentuckians, and 130,363 West Virginians; by 1960, the numbers were 119,388 Tennesseans, 409,059 Kentuckians, and 311,134 West Virginians, for a total of 839,581. Ohio's industrial cities were transformed by their presence. Akron became known as "the Capital of West Virginia." By the late 1960s, one-third of Cincinnati's population was Appalachian, clustered in such distinct communities as Price Hill, Over-the-Rhine, and the separate city of Norwood.

Appalachians also began to populate smaller cities and towns such as Hamilton, Middletown, Chillicothe, Portsmouth, Ironton, and Lorain. By 1970, one of every two residents of Hamilton and Middletown was Appalachian. Since around one-third of white Appalachian migrants before the 1960s were illiterate, low-skill jobs in factories such as the Inland Container Corporation and Armco Steel Corporation in Middletown were attractive. These companies, moreover, encouraged Appalachian migration by actively recruiting them and, in the case of Armco, by developing a policy of hiring the children and relatives of workers. As a result, nearly everyone who worked at these plants was Appalachian. One Kentuckian noted that there was little discrimination because "there weren't no buckeyes to get along with." The same process was at work in northeastern Ohio, especially in Ashtabula County. When former miner Frank Myers got a job as a guard at the Union Carbide Plant, he was able to arrange for jobs for all five of his sons and five of his sons-in-law.[49] With such connections, one of every three industrial workers in Ohio in 1973 was Appalachian.

Behind the stereotypes lay a commitment to a way of life unfamiliar to many middle-class Ohioans. Family was among the most important aspects of Appalachian life. Ohioans joked that Appalachian migrants went home every weekend. Reportedly, "half the people" in "the Ohio room" in heaven were "tied up and not permitted to move" on the weekends; otherwise, "they would leave heaven and go back to Kentucky." It is true that many Appalachians returned home frequently. Yet we should see this behavior as a positive commitment to strong extended families; "home" for white Appalachians was physically closer than it had been for any other migrant group in the history of Ohio. The ubiquity of cars and improved roads, especially after World War II, made the trip relatively easy and inexpensive. No doubt Yankee or European immigrants would have done the same thing in the nineteenth century, if they could have. The Adlers of Toledo frequently returned to West Virginia in the 1950s and 1960s. The family had migrated in the early 1950s in order to find better work and to "improve them-selves." They had no intention of going home permanently. They just wanted to visit family, hike, and pick apples.[50]

Close connection with home and relatives allowed Appalachians to maintain a way of life that mattered a great deal to them. In many ways, Appalachians were as critical of the world they encountered north of the Ohio River as Ohioans were critical of theirs—and with good reason. They generally worked at low-skill, tedious jobs in hot, polluted, stinking plants. One man described a dirty factory in northeastern Ohio as "not a safe place to work." Urban neighbor-hoods were no better. Appalachians clustered in Peck's Addition in Hamilton in the mid-1900s lived in shacks, about half of which were without electricity or running water. No wonder the mountains looked good in contrast. Members of the Brown family of Toledo, despite severe stress in the relationship between father and mother, prided themselves on their family ties. The wife blamed her hus-band's drinking and that of his friends on the "fast pace society" of Toledo. Life "in the hills" was slower. In the city, men felt pressure to succeed. When they did not, they turned to drink. Janis Lewis said that while she would never return to Kentucky permanently because there was "no work to be found there," she hated city life with its "corruption and pollution" and preferred to live on a rural road with lots of space between houses.[51]

Much as Appalachians missed home, most were realistic about the possibility of ever living there again. One Cleveland couple with two children had mixed feelings; the wife was proud of her heritage and wanted to return to West Virginia permanently, while her husband did not like the teasing about his accent that he got at work. Another couple in their fifties, with little education and ten children, had come to Cleveland around 1960 in search of work. Currently unem-ployed, they wanted to return to West Virginia. In fact, they had tried to do so the previous summer but had come back to Cleveland after three weeks.[52]

Unlike black migrants, who sought freedom as well as economic opportunity, most white Southerners came to Ohio almost exclusively to find jobs. Few left Appalachia because they felt uncomfortable there. So, as the historian Jacqueline Jones has observed, their "relocation" often had "an elegiac quality." A migrant in Columbus in the early 1970s was proud of his origins. "The least offensive name people can call me is 'hillbilly.' The most offensive is 'city slicker' or 'Buckeye.'" Were he able to get a good job in West Virginia, he would live there. In the mountains, he could have a garden and chickens. He disliked not having a yard. When he went outside, he had to sit on a porch. "Back there you can get your breath a lot better—smell that good hillbilly air."[53]

A twenty-seven-year-old native Kentuckian, Mrs. White, had lived in Columbus for ten years and had four sons and a disabled husband. She thought hostility to Appalachians would never go away. She "wasn't accepted very easily in the city of Columbus. . . . There's just an atmosphere that when people have worked to build up a town they don't want intruders. . . . It takes a while for them to get to know you and to realize that you're not a bad person just because you come from another state." Miss Walker, a West Virginian in her early fifties, had been in Columbus since 1962. Still, she described herself as "just a plain old hillbilly. You can't get it out of me." She loved to go back to West Virginia whenever she could. But Columbus had become her home. Walker lived with her mother, even though she had five illegitimate children; a sister lived next door and a brother across the street. Now she just "live[d] one day at a time."[54]

A middle-aged West Virginian who accepted his "hillbilly" origins and had many friends who were not from Appalachia reflected that work dominated life in the city. He missed the free time of country life when he could go fishing and hunting. "It's a different lifestyle, really . . . different culture, different kind of people. Here, people are too busy going to and from work to stop and talk to you. . . . [U]p here they don't socialize as much as they do down south."[55]

Not all Appalachian migrants preferred home to Ohio. For one woman, life in her new state was "a real shock." She had grown up in closed Appalachia without the "different ethnic groups" she found in Columbus. In Ohio, she had to learn how to drive on an interstate highway, shop at a department store, eat at a "nice" restaurant, and deal with a big university campus. The city was intimidating. Urban life was different, especially in the details. She could not throw her garbage out in the backyard, as she did at home. Shocked that girls wore blue jeans and did not use makeup, she was intrigued by the idea that women participated in what she considered male activities. While the young woman was hardly rejecting her eastern Kentucky origins, it was clear that she found life in Ohio as liberating as it was confusing. She was not alone. Other Appalachian women were able to band together informally and formally against what they called "snobbery" to protect their interests and those of their children from both unfeeling institutions and abusive husbands.[56]

Appalachians were not culturally inferior; they were just culturally different. Many had difficulty seeing the value of education. Jobs, one woman remarked, came "from people you know. So it doesn't matter whether they have a diploma or not."[57] Appalachian parents encouraged their children to take jobs rather than delay employment in order to finish high school or college. They tended to put loyalty to family in the present above the development of the individual for the future. When relatives got sick, young women stayed home to care for them. When money was short, students left school to go to work. An overriding sense of family loyalty overrode larger civic responsibilities. Where middle-class families devoted an enormous amount of their time and income to preparing their children for college and a professional life, working-class Appalachians expected their children to contribute to the household as soon as they could. Viewed from the perspective of their local worlds, these were admirable traits. Their problem in Ohio went beyond their accents or their customs. Their lack of sustained interest in education and their unwillingness to delay gratification were the opposite of what middle-class citizens expected.

Whether or not Appalachians appeared to be model citizens, they had a major impact on the cultural landscape of the state. The proliferation of evangelical Protestant congregations is one example. Frank Adler of Toledo told an interviewer in the 1970s that the Baptist Church was "the closest thing to the 'folks back home.'"[58] Baptist and Pentecostal churches in particular were the center of life for many Appalachians. Not only did they worship in familiar ways among familiar people, they also attended church picnics and programs and built support networks that helped them deal with the difficulties of relocation.

Southern-based religious movements were especially prominent in Akron. In 1934, Kentucky-born Dallas Franklin Billington formed the Akron Baptist Temple with six families. Within months, the temple had two hundred members, and by 1949, fifteen thousand. Other ministers in the Akron area such as Rex Humbard and Ernest Angley not only brought religion to large numbers of people, they reassured people in strange surroundings and helped them build a sense of community. Starting with little money and few supporters, these evangelists exploited the expanding media markets to build huge religious empires throughout Ohio and beyond.

Meanwhile, "hillbilly" and "country" music grew in popularity in the second half of the twentieth century, winning acceptance on radio and television stations by the 1960s. WLW in Cincinnati offered the radio show *Boone County Jamboree* and the television program *Midwestern Hayride*. After World War II, Sidney Nathan, the president of King Records in Cincinnati, developed a particular sound by blending bluegrass and mountain performers with a background of steel guitars and wind instruments. The result was a mixture of Cajun and black-influenced country music. Meanwhile, country performers such as Hank Williams and Patsy Cline were popular in southern and central Ohio and paved the way for Elvis Presley. Country music star Dwight Yoakam, a native of Kentucky, grew up in Columbus in the 1960s and 1970s. Among his songs was "Readin', Rightin', Rt. 23," which talked about migration along a main road from central Kentucky to central Ohio. Like blues songs, country lyrics frequently dealt with the problems of male-female relationships and focused on divorce and adultery. Also like blues songs, they were generally fatalistic about the hand life deals people, advocating acceptance rather than reform.

Just as important were local musicians who perpetuated the traditions of the mountains. Herschel Blevins was born to a sharecropping family in Floyd County, Kentucky, in 1931. When he was ten or eleven years old, his aunt gave him a banjo and he began to mimic the musicians he heard on the *Grand Ole Opry* and other radio shows. When Blevins moved to Ashtabula County in 1952 to get a decent job, he continued to play country and bluegrass music. His sons learned how to play the bass, drums, and banjo. In the 1960s and 1970s, father and sons toured the state as the Blevins Band.

Beyond religion and music, Appalachians were slow to develop formal institutions and cultural expressions. Rarely joining organizations, they had no distinctive rituals or holidays to bind them together as a community. The O'Tucks, an organization of Kentucky-born Ohioans, was the exception rather than the rule. Only in the 1960s did there appear such organizations as the Urban Appalachian Council in Cincinnati, Our Common Heritage in Dayton, Appalachian People's Service Organization in Hamilton, and Central Ohio Appalachian Council in Columbus. Under the leadership of people such as Michael Maloney, a former seminarian and one of the founders of the Urban Appalachian Council, these groups conducted research and promoted community awareness of Appalachian history and culture in order to debunk stereotypes and improve the image and self-image of Appalachians. In the 1970s and 1980s, meetings of scholars and activists produced books and articles attacking myths and encouraging a more positive approach to Appalachians. They worried that Appalachians were accepting the pejorative labels of the larger world, that they had come to believe that they had "a unique culture . . . incompatible with the mainstream of society" and were losing hope about competing for better jobs and improving their lives.[59]

Maloney and other students of the community were convinced that they had to establish a positive identity for Appalachians before they could make any progress. They worked to develop a notion of ethnic identity so that Appalachians could not only think better of themselves but create institutions and lobbies.[60] The depth of support for their activities, however, is difficult to measure. Because white Appalachians tended to ignore politics as well as social organizations, their indifference made the formation of a political interest group difficult, if not impossible.[61]

Nothing was more important in initially impeding and then encouraging the development of Appalachian consciousness than race. For all the jokes about their accents and behavior, for all the discrimination they suffered, white Appalachians identified with a large community of whites more than people from their place of origin. Tellingly, black

Appalachians were absorbed quickly into a generic black community, both in perception and in reality. Black Appalachians experienced discrimination because they were black, not because they were Appalachian.[62]

In contrast, white Appalachians who acquired middle-class characteristics, who managed to get a college degree, buy property, adopt a more generic way of speaking and dressing, were quickly assimilated into the general population. They enjoyed a degree of residential mobility unknown to African Americans. Many second-generation Appalachian immigrants abandoned the identity altogether in public as they acquired the characteristics of middle-class Ohioans. Those Appalachians and their descendants who were unable to climb the ladder of class continued to suffer serious discrimination from white employers and neighbors. But for the most part, race mattered more than class.

Similarly, while white Ohioans may have found Appalachians unpleasant, most preferred them to African Americans. And white Appalachians seemed much more comfortable blaming blacks than whites for their predicament. They were jealous of what they perceived as a stronger sense of community among African Americans and resented what they thought was greater political and journalistic attention to the world of blacks. The public schools by the 1970s emphasized African American history but rarely mentioned Appalachian history. White families, struggling with large families and low incomes built around tedious and unreliable jobs, flared at a supposedly disproportionate public concern with African American poverty and discrimination. Much racial tension centered on the ways in which government (or "welfare") dealt with whites and blacks. Because black and white Southerners increasingly made up a huge percentage of the populations of Ohio's cities, they lived side by side with each other in an uneasy truce that fell apart completely in the 1960s and 1970s. Indeed, Appalachians became more conscious and assertive about their identity in no small part as a reaction against the increased visibility of African Americans as well as governmental response to their needs.

A West Virginia migrant in his twenties spoke openly of his dislike of African Americans. His welfare caseworker was "a sassy . . . colored" woman. He guessed she did not like "the white." The same was true of his neighbors, who "were pretty bad" when he first came to Columbus. "We lived amongst the colored people. There weren't any blacks where we grew up. We didn't even know what a black looked like. We'd probably been scared stiff if we'd seen one." Matters soon deteriorated. The man and his family said that their black neighbors had thrown rocks at them and broken windows; others were noisy; some were thieves. Indeed, whites often complained about "uppity" blacks. In nearby Detroit in the early 1940s, white Appalachians had proclaimed that "down home we know how to keep niggers in their place" and "Southern niggers aren't like these bold brassy Northern niggers."[63] The ubiquity of these attitudes and the growing assertiveness of all people in the face of unending discrimination and declining employment opportunities did not bode well for the civility of public discussion in Ohio in the second half of the twentieth century.

The Great Migration of Southerners highlighted many of the most important themes in the history of Ohio, especially the linkage of middle-class respectability with citizenship. It also exposed the contradictions in that story and the limitations of progress. One way or another, the color line would be at the center of nearly all twentieth-century conversations about what Ohio was and what it could become. And more than anything else, it would focus discussion once again on the question of whether citizens needed to subordinate personal interests and loyalties to some larger public interest. Increasingly, Ohioans suggested that public culture was important as long as it facilitated rather than restrained private lives.

Part of the famous eleven-mile line drawn by members of the United Rubber Workers during the Goodyear strike in Akron in February and March 1939. The strikers said that neither police nor strikebreakers would cross the line. They didn't. (Courtesy of The Walter P. Reuther Library, Wayne State University, Detroit, Michigan)

10
Labor and Liberty

—

Louis Bromfield looked at Ohio in the second quarter of the twentieth century and fretted about its future. People who spent much of their lives working in increasingly mechanized and bureaucratic jobs crowded its cities and their suburbs. Machines did what skilled workmen had once done. The smoke and filth of industrialization suffused the atmosphere. Corporations and governments had grown ever more powerful. Above all, the family farm, that mainstay of nineteenth-century life in the Midwest, was disappearing. Bromfield, a Mansfield native who had accumulated a small fortune as a popular novelist in the 1920s, feared that this brave new world was deadening the spirit of Ohio's citizens, turning them into automatons dependent on the whims of big business and big government. Bromfield believed that the possibilities of Ohio had been lost in a mad pursuit of money, in a generalized commitment to progress at any cost. He had seen it happen himself when his parents sold his grandparents' farm near Mansfield, a place he had idealized since his birth in 1896. For Bromfield, there was "in all the world no finer figure than a sturdy farmer standing, his feet well planted in the earth, looking over his rich field and his beautiful shiny cattle." His "security and independence" were obvious. Who would want to live "wholly in an industrial civilization where time clocks and machines rule man instead of man ruling them[?]" Good farmers could teach others the secret of getting machinery to serve them instead of serving machinery.[1]

After service in France during World War I, Bromfield lived in New York City. His first novel, *The Green Bay Tree,* was based on his life in Mansfield and became a best-seller; his third, *Early Autumn,*

won a Pulitzer Prize. Success allowed him to move his family to Sen-
lis, France, in 1925 and to write, travel, and lobby against the rise of
fascism in Europe. In 1939, with war imminent, the Bromfields returned to the United States. Forty-two years old and full of nostalgia
for the lost life of his youth, Bromfield bought several farms in Richland County. There he and his wife had a house built large enough to
accommodate hordes of visitors. His thousand acres he called Malabar
Farm after a hill overlooking the harbor of Bombay, India. Bromfield's
goal was simple: "To be on my own land, on an island of security
which could be my refuge not only for myself and my family but my
friends as well."[2]

In the 1940s and 1950s, Malabar Farm became famous. Celebrities visited the Bromfields. Movie stars Humphrey Bogart and Lauren
Bacall were married there. Journalists followed Bromfield's effort to
reconcile large-scale production and respect for individual producers.
Modeling Malabar on his understanding of collective farming in the
Soviet Union but disdaining both government subsidies and regulations, Bromfield supplied the capital and received 5 percent of the
profits from the farm. Laborers lived on the property with their families in rent-free houses equipped with running water and electricity
and were paid a decent salary (plus part of the profits) and most of
their expenses.

Bromfield devoted himself to lush descriptions of the beauties of
Ohio and the pleasures of plowing, fencing, and gardening. "It was a
brilliant day," Bromfield wrote in his journal on March 1, 1945, "and
that corner of the farm is one of the loveliest spots—a kind of bowl
with the big trees of the virgin forest on one side raising their top
branches a hundred feet and more above the sugar camp. A spring
stream wanders through the pasture with oxbow ponds filled with
young fish and bordered by water cress, marsh marigold, and skunk
cabbage. The steep cemetery field is planted to wheat which has
grown prodigiously in a few warm days and looks like a carpet of
emerald green velvet." Finding beauty in the stillness of an Ohio landscape, Bromfield loved rural people as well. Farmers were "humble
and simple people" who knew that "the tragedies and the suffering of
their own lives [were] only a part of a general vast pattern."[3] Idealistic
to the point of naïveté, Louis Bromfield was not unlike his hero,

Thomas Jefferson. He was a gentleman-farmer who loved farm life because he was wealthy enough to not have to do any of the work and an intellectual who relished taking his turn at the plow so that he could fill his journals with elegant prose.

Bromfield's world was unfamiliar to most Ohioans. Struggling through the crises of global depression and war, few people had time to consider long-term developments. The notion of creating a farm as an oasis from change, as an experiment in making progress more humane, was ludicrous to all but a handful of wealthy citizens. Nonetheless, many people shared aspects of Bromfield's idealism. As they worried about better wages and working conditions, about their ability to buy houses, cars, radios, washing machines, televisions, and the other trappings of the middle-class life to which most aspired, they continued to believe in the importance of personal dignity and collective tradition. However, sharing a vision of a world in which most people enjoyed both material comfort and individual respect did not mean that they agreed on how to achieve it. From the 1920s through the 1940s, as Ohioans struggled with a series of catastrophes, they argued about the roles of labor unions and government, and about the emergence of a society of consumers in which many people, whatever their ethnicity, race, religion, or class, seemed to value self-fulfillment more than self-discipline and personal satisfaction more than civic participation.

Labor and the Rights of Citizens

Few people would have predicted in the middle of the 1920s that in the 1950s labor unions would be among the most influential institutions in the state of Ohio. The decade that followed World War I was a disappointment to union organizers because their prospects had seemed much brighter in the 1910s. Ever since their initial appearance in the nineteenth century, labor organizations had been far more interested in improving wages and working conditions than in mounting a serious challenge to capitalism. The various craft unions allied in the American Federation of Labor were essentially conservative in their goals and methods. Restrictive in their membership and tentative in their protests, the AFL members wanted respect. They wanted to be treated fairly. More radical were the United Mine Workers and the Industrial Workers of the World. The latter in particular welcomed all workers into an organization dedicated to using direct action (such as sit-down strikes) to achieve its goal of an industrial order controlled by workers rather than owners. Only a few thousand Ohioans joined the IWW during the height of its popularity in the 1910s, and many of them did so because, in the words of an Ohio Senate committee, "they hoped through collective action to increase their wages and improve their conditions of employment."[4]

World War I put labor in a strong position. Demand for manufactured goods increased while the supply of workers stabilized or decreased. Employers had little choice but to accommodate the demands of their employees. Between 1914 and 1919, the annual real earnings of workers increased by 36 percent. More numerous and more powerful than ever before, labor unions asserted the presence of working people in the larger public conversation about life in Ohio. Workers had every reason to expect even greater progress toward a more equitable and just society in the wake of the triumph over Germany in 1918.

Postwar economic dislocations, however, dashed such hopes. As demand for goods fell and the supply of workers grew, employers no longer had to court employees. Moreover, the antiforeign hysteria of the war years inspired a reaction against ethnic laborers in the steel mills and coal mines of Ohio, which climaxed in the Red Scare of 1919. Recoiling from the Bolshevik Revolution of 1917 in Russia, rural and middle-class citizens distorted all working-class rhetoric into calls for class warfare and the overthrow of legitimate government. In late 1919, the federal Justice Department raided homes and union halls in Cleveland, Youngstown, and Toledo as well as dozens of other American cities and arrested mostly innocent people tarred with the brush of communism. Real earnings fell, and the gains of the 1910s evaporated in a multitude of corporate decisions to cut wages, reduce hours, and lay off employees. Meanwhile, the right of workers to engage in collective action in order to protest these changes was widely denounced as anti-American. Angry laborers, however, did not step aside quietly. In 1919, one of the most violent years in the history of Ohio labor, there were 237 strikes.

In Toledo, returning soldiers and recently laid-off workers directed their ire at the Willys-Overland Company. While Willys-Overland had developed a training school, reasonably priced housing, and a profit-sharing plan, the company announced plans to expand the workweek from forty-five to forty-eight hours and to limit wage increases. After months of negotiation, seventy-five hundred frustrated workers (two-thirds of the company's employees) went on strike on May 5, 1919. Within a few days, picketers clashed with those who continued to work. Rocks were thrown, scabs were assaulted, and respectable residents worried about impending revolution. When Willys-Overland defied the strikers by bringing in five hundred deputies hired by the mayor of Toledo, the situation deteriorated even further.

Kenneth Rexroth, at the time a teenager radicalized by the strike, later described its climax as "the most spectacular battle" he ever saw "in my years in the labor movement." A phalanx of mounted police advanced toward the picketers and moved them slowly away from the main gates of the plant. When an officer ordered the strikers to disperse, the men pushed forward with long poles and the police responded with canisters of tear gas. The wind blew the gas back into the ranks of the police, and pandemonium followed. "The horses were enveloped in clouds of tear gas, which made them scream with the bloodcurdling scream of horses in a fire and they took off up the steep banks, spilling their riders, as the boys with the poles, with wet handkerchiefs wrapped round their faces, charged." Company guards ran out of the gates with fixed bayonets, and "the strikers vanished like snowflakes."[5] Although the police fired their guns, no one was seriously hurt. Rexroth was so taken with the riot that he immediately joined the IWW. Rexroth's enthusiasm aside, the outcome of the Willys-Overland strike did not bode well for organized labor. Governor James Cox refused to intervene. But a U.S. District Court issued a temporary restraining order that limited the number of strikers to a handful of American citizens. With both government and community opinion against them, most of the strikers gave up.

The Great Steel Strike of 1919 was similarly unsuccessful. Steelworkers who had received wage increases had seen little improvement in working conditions and had no say in factory operations. In September,

100,000 Ohioans in Steubenville, Cleveland, Youngstown, Canton, and other northeastern industrial cities were among 250,000 American steelworkers who went on strike in order to gain some control over their workplace and win some measure of dignity. A man whose son had died in Europe fighting to make the world safe for democracy promised "to help my fellow workmen show [the chairman of the United States Steel Corporation] that he can't act as if he was a king or kaiser and tell them how long they have got to work."[6]

If most workers saw themselves as acting within a great American tradition of respect for labor, most middle-class, affluent, and rural Ohioans did not. Laborers were struggling against public opinion as well as corporations. In Youngstown, respectable citizens formed vigilante committees to protect their city against largely immigrant workers, and local officials openly sided with the steel companies. By late 1919, strikers were beginning to go back to work. The Great Steel Strike officially ended in January 1920, having accomplished nothing.

The year 1919 marked the high tide of labor activity in Ohio until the 1930s. As the nation cultivated normalcy, unions declined in both numbers and influence. The defeats in the Willys-Overland, steel, and other strikes inaugurated a long period of apathy and disillusionment. The American Federation of Labor was relatively quiescent in the 1920s. William Green, who became the national president of the AFL in 1924, epitomized the movement's enthusiasm for accommodation. Green, a former president of the Ohio district of the United Mine Workers, was not interested in confrontation. Nor were most of his members. Willing to work with employers, unions avoided trouble. In 1927, there were only twenty-one strikes in Ohio. Two years later, only six thousand Ohioans risked their jobs and security in job actions.

Because the 1920s was a period of relative prosperity for Ohioans who were not miners and farmers, they were reluctant to risk what they had for something more. Like all Americans, they were increasingly caught up in a world of consumption. As long as they had enough money to buy a car, get the latest household appliance, see an occasional movie, and buy cheap versions of the latest fashions, they seemed relatively contented. Whatever indignities they suffered at work were compensated for by the benefits they enjoyed at home. Americans in general were more likely to define themselves as consumers than as producers by the 1920s. More and more were involved in service rather than manufacturing jobs.

Ohio employers encouraged their employees' concern with material comfort. As they established the principle of the open shop (the right of anyone to take a job, whether or not they belonged to the union) as the true American alternative to collective action, they also practiced what became known as welfare capitalism. Many, including Procter and Gamble, Willys-Overland, Goodyear Tire and Rubber, and National Cash Register, formed company unions, which concentrated on minor improvements and the development of sports teams and group activities. These actions gave employees a sense of community but not serious power.

Workers also impeded collective actions themselves because of their frequent movement from one job to another. Skill was less important than it had been in the nineteenth century. In the rubber industry, technological advances made work "faster, simpler, and less labor intensive."[7] The number of turnovers dramatically increased at Goodyear, Firestone, Goodrich, and U.S. Rubber. Between 1921 and late 1929, Goodyear hired 87,525 people but employed only an average of 12,995. The number of layoffs far exceeded the number of voluntary departures.

At the same time, immigration restrictions and public pressure to privatize ethnicity made Ohio workers, who were never particularly radical, seem less alien to middle-class citizens. As the number of new European arrivals declined, workers appeared to become more conventional. Increasingly, workers themselves were less aware of ethnicity than of race. Working-class Ohioans were no happier about the arrival of African Americans than middle-class Ohioans. Worried about losing jobs to blacks who would work for less, many laborers became more conscious of being white than of being Italian or Polish.

Blacks were no more welcome in union halls than they were in small towns. More frequently arrested and harassed by local authorities, they were confined to certain sections of most cities. After World War I, the Cincinnati Real Estate Board declared that "no agent shall rent or sell property to colored people in an established white section or neighborhood and this inhibition shall be particularly applicable to the hill tops and suburban property."[8] When the number of blacks in

Cincinnati's West End doubled in the 1920s, the number of white residents fell by more than half. Rent structures and zoning restrictions encouraged segregation.

Whites made no effort to hide discrimination against blacks when it came to hiring. A 1930 survey of Cincinnati employers found that some refused to hire blacks because they were "unable or unwilling to mix white and Negro workers" or wanted skills that blacks allegedly lacked. Only slightly less important were a lack of "separate facilities" and a fear of negative reaction from unions, the public, and white workers. The color line mattered as much to workers as to employers. Kimberley L. Phillips has argued that in Cleveland in the 1920s, "white workers gradually constructed a new vision of themselves that linked racist attitudes and a working-class consciousness, even when they organized black workers." African Americans were not allowed to join craft unions. As a result, according to Phillips, "black workers remained as unorganized [in 1929] as they had been" in 1920.[9] African Americans were most likely to belong to unions in industries whites found unpalatable, such as the Sanitary Drivers and Helpers' Union.

Indeed, the vast majority of black workers were unskilled, which meant that they tended to do the lowest and meanest work. Men were hired in the building and metal trades and in the clothing, soap, and leather-tanning industries, while African American women were most likely to earn money as domestics. In Cleveland, more than three-quarters of black women worked as household laborers. They went from constituting less than a tenth to almost one-third of the household laborers in the city as a whole. Occupations requiring more skill and offering more autonomy, such as beautician or waitress, were almost exclusively reserved for white women.

Nothing better reflected the obsession of whites with drawing racial (and religious) lines than the flourishing of the Ku Klux Klan. Influential in industrial cities such as Youngstown and Akron, the Klan was especially powerful in rapidly changing areas. While racial prejudice was central to the organization, much of its popularity reflected a desire among native-born Protestants to save their world from an onslaught of diverse immigrants. The Klan was both nativist and nationalist. It called upon people "whose reputations and vocations are respectable" and "whose habits are 'exemplary' to conserve, protect and maintain the distinctive institutions, rights, privileges, principles, traditions and ideals of pure Americanism."[10]

The Klan won the support of Protestants, including ministers, interested in enforcing morality (such as prohibition) and a range of people from many backgrounds, including women. Working-class Ohioans also joined. In Akron, many Southern-born workers were members of the Klan. There, as elsewhere, the Klan empowered men and women who wanted to assert their interests and demand that attention be paid to them. The Klan served many constituencies: middle-class people in search of greater law and order and working-class people looking for some way to ensure the representation of their interests in the larger public sphere. Membership in Ohio peaked at four hundred thousand.

The Klan thrived in cities such as Youngstown, where the steel industry attracted immigrants from all over the world and whose population in 1920 was 59.8 percent foreign-born and 5 percent African American. Since 1880, Youngstown's population had increased by more than eight times and the black population had more than doubled. Tensions between native-born Protestant and Catholic and Jewish immigrants ran high, especially over the issue of alcohol. In the 1920s, Klan and Klan-backed candidates won several elections in the Mahoning Valley, appealing not just to prejudice but to citizens concerned with a perceived decline in personal morality. The Klan promised to restore law and order and Protestant values over an unwieldy and assertive population of immigrants and blacks. When in 1924 the mayor of Niles appointed some 150 members of the Klan to a quasi-police force, Italian and Irish Ohioans refused to take any more. Trying to keep Klansmen from marching into the downtown area, they defied efforts to enforce values on immigrant communities. Almost no one was punished, but the incident was one of several that tarred the Klan as narrow and intolerant. People who considered themselves respectable increasingly deserted it.

If white male laborers had little interest in opening their unions to blacks, they were equally unhappy about the participation of women, whatever their color. In the 1920s, about 20 percent of people who worked outside the home were women, about half of whom were married. Typically, they earned about half the wages of men in the same jobs. During the decade, the number of women in manufacturing jobs fell from 25 to 18 percent while the number in clerical or menial service jobs increased. Even those in manufactures were concentrated in garment and candy industries, making goods associated with women. A female's earning power peaked in her late twenties; the typical sixty-year-old woman earned less than a twenty-year-old woman. A 1925 report suggested that women who supported themselves in Cleveland received monthly wages that averaged ten dollars below the poverty level. Notwithstanding the desire of many women to work full time, about half of those employed in industries were part-time employees.

Organized labor did virtually nothing for women. Except in the garment industry, few women belonged to unions. Men tended to see women, like blacks, as competitors who would work cheaply and drive down wages. They fretted that working women threatened family and community life. If women were busy in plants and stores, who would take care of children, manage households, and maintain family networks? Many men could not take the idea of working women seriously. Unions were brotherhoods, groups of men, almost exclusively white. The dignity they fought for was as gender specific as it was race specific.

Government and the Crisis of the 1930s

The prosperity of the 1920s obscured deep problems in the nation's economy. Particularly alarming was the inability of demand to keep up with supply. Manufacturers were producing consumer goods much faster than workers could afford to buy them. By the end of the decade, many companies had surpluses that could be reduced only to the extent that Americans were willing to buy on credit. When runaway speculation in stock and real estate led to the crash of the stock market in October 1929, the nation's weak financial system collapsed. Rural Ohioans had been living with hard times for years. As prices for farm products fell during the 1920s, farmers could not keep up with everyday expenses, let alone buy new products. Because many families were overextended, bankruptcy and repossession became common. The price of land declined, as did the percentage of Ohioans who lived on farms.

In the early 1930s, most people experienced similar problems. With demand for goods in a free fall, industries laid off thousands of workers. The unemployment rate in Ohio climbed to 13.3 percent in 1930 and 37.3 percent in 1932. Two-thirds of construction workers and close to half of factory workers were without jobs. Only half of industrial workers in Cleveland had jobs. In Akron the percentage was less than half, and in Toledo it was around 20 percent. Meanwhile, employers cut the hours and wages of those who were still employed, often by a third. In one Cleveland neighborhood, 44 of 234 families had no obvious source of income, while dozens of others lived off money earned by women and children or borrowed from relatives.

African Americans felt the effects of the Depression acutely because they often worked in marginal jobs and were the first hired and the last rehired. By 1934, four of five blacks in Cleveland were on relief, either directly or indirectly. In 1933, unemployment among African Americans in Cincinnati stood at 54 percent. Even though blacks comprised only 10 percent of the population, they constituted 25 percent of the unemployed. With jobs scarce, racism became more pronounced. Ninety percent of Cincinnati employers in 1930 either said they did not want to hire African Americans or refused to answer the question. Want ads for domestic workers suddenly specified white women.

Even people with jobs had to deal with reduced incomes and buying power. The Depression stunned Ohioans emotionally as well as economically. Nothing like it was supposed to happen in the Midwest, where a belief in progress was fundamental. From the beginning, Ohioans had built their lives on the assumption that things were going to get better. Economic expansion was so much a part of Ohio that people took it for granted. In the 1890s and early 1900s, some had worried about the progress of the state. Yet they tended to argue that whatever was wrong could be fixed with minor tinkering over a relatively long period of time.

The crisis of the 1930s demanded more immediate solutions. Ohioans in distress turned to government for answers. Constitutional revisions enacted in the early twentieth century had led to an expansion in the size of government at all levels, including the hiring of trained professionals eager to collect information and guide progress.

In response to exposés about the exploitation of children, the General Assembly passed the Bing Act of 1921, which required students to attend high school until they earned their diploma or reached the age of eighteen, and restricted children under the age of sixteen from working in most industries. In 1923, the General Assembly passed a civil rights act for women. (Ohio had been the fifth state to ratify the Nineteenth Amendment to the Constitution, which gave the right to vote to women.) In 1925, the state created a gasoline tax to fund the paving and improving of roads now traversed by automobiles. And then there was prohibition, which lasted until the Twenty-first Amendment to the U.S. Constitution repealed it in 1933. Under the Crabbe Act of 1920, the General Assembly created an agency to enforce prohibition in tandem with agents operating under the national prohibition act of 1919. The Depression not only intensified similar developments, it made the expansion of government more visible. Bucking the odds, the population of Columbus increased by 15.5 percent in the 1930s because of the growing numbers of people working for the state government.

Even more obvious was the emergence of the U.S. government as a powerful force in the lives of Ohioans. State and local governments could not handle the Depression alone. Indeed, much of their expansion reflected their roles in administering programs created by the U.S. Congress as part of the New Deal of President Franklin Delano Roosevelt. Under the Federal Housing Act of 1933, the General Assembly authorized city officials to obtain federal grants to improve urban neighborhoods. A 3 percent sales tax raised nearly $48 million in 1935 for schools, local governments, pensions, and poor relief. The federal Agricultural Adjustment Act of 1933 and the Soil Conservation and Domestic Allotment Act of 1936 brought millions of dollars to Ohio. The most dramatic program was the Rural Electrification Act, which brought electricity to farm families throughout the state.

At the same time, the Civilian Conservation Corps kept up to fourteen thousand men busy each year, while the Civil Works Administration, the Public Works Administration, and the Works Progress Administration (WPA) came to the aid of people in dire straits. Within months of its inception in July 1935, the WPA had 187,000 Ohioans employed in rearranging the landscape of their state. In

Summit County, the WPA improved nearly four hundred public buildings; built seventeen new ones; laid forty miles of sewers and water mains; paved or improved six hundred miles of streets; constructed forty-six playgrounds and parks, a reservoir, and the thirty-five-thousand-seat Akron Rubber Bowl; and presented free plays and concerts.

Among the most significant actions of the Roosevelt administration was recognition of the rights of labor unions. Section 7-a of the National Industrial Recovery Act of 1933 guaranteed workers the right to "organize unions of their own choosing" and to engage in collective bargaining. The appearance of government support for unions inspired job actions across the country. In 1933, twenty-five thousand Ohioans went on strike. One member of the United Mine Workers noted that "they had heard organizers before, but this was a new message. The Government of the United States guaranteed the right for them to have a union! They began to believe; then they did believe; then they started to move. . . . Local unions reappeared as if by magic, at mines where almost everyone thought they had been destroyed."[11] Although there was no provision for enforcement of Section 7-a, unions gained new life after a long period of quiescence.

According to Ruth McKenney, a prolabor reporter, the growing assertiveness of workers in the rubber industry was directly tied to their perception of a sympathetic Roosevelt administration. McKenney claimed that the number of union members in Akron rose from fewer than three hundred in June to twelve thousand by the end of August 1933. Coleman Claherty, an American Federation of Labor field representative, had a ready answer when a man asked him how he was going to fulfill his promise of getting the rubber industry to recognize the unions. "Everybody in this room knows that President Roosevelt is for the unions," Claherty replied.[12] In the midst of the Depression, Roosevelt helped restore some faith in the possibility of collective action because government appeared to be on the unions' side. Never mind that the prolabor measures of the New Deal were often half-hearted gestures. Workers had begun to believe.

Their elation dissipated somewhat as it became clear that a labor millennium was not at hand and that government was not as sympathetic as workers had hoped. When thousands of workers walked off the job at the Toledo Auto-Lite Plant in 1934, Governor George White dispatched more than a thousand National Guardsmen to re-store order. At least two people were killed and many others wounded before the union won modest concessions. Meanwhile, militancy ar-rived in the onion fields of Hardin County when families, many of them Southerners, tired of wage cuts and horrid conditions, quit working. Adamant growers refused to accede to their demands. In Au-gust, vigilantes took union president Okey Odell from the sheriff's of-fice, beat him, and told him to leave the county. When he refused, hundreds of people gathered in front of his home. Not only were none of the people who attacked him prosecuted, Odell was indicted for threatening his assailants with a gun. When a court injunction stopped workers from meeting as a group, the strike quickly disinte-grated. As the Depression continued, these and other strikes through-out the nation led Congress to rise to the defense of employees with the Wagner Act of June 1935. Guaranteeing the right to form unions, to engage in collective bargaining, and to protest against unfair treat-ment, the act created the National Labor Relations Board to enforce its provisions.

Whatever government did, some workers had long since con-cluded that only defiance would win them the dignity to which they were entitled as citizens. In 1935, the United Mine Workers, led by John L. Lewis, and other unions broke away from the AFL, com-plaining that it was too accommodationist. In Akron, hostility to-ward the pragmatic AFL was intense. The election of West Virginia–born Sherman H. Dalrymple as president of the United Rubber Workers and the rejection of Coleman Claherty's less con-frontational style were symbolic of a change. Appalachian whites and other rubber workers believed that by creating their own union, they were fulfilling the promise of a democratic society. "Your destiny is in your own hands," Lewis told two thousand supporters in Akron in January 1936. "I hope you'll do something for yourselves."[13] The break with the AFL became official in 1938 with the formation of the Congress of Industrial Organizations, which included automo-bile and rubber workers.

Meanwhile, sit-down strikes became common. Workers and their supporters saw these events as collective democracy in action. They represented the refusal of men to suffer in silence. On June 19, 1934, eleven hundred General Tire workers in Akron held a brief sit-down in response to yet another wage cut. On the signal of Rex D. Murray, a native West Virginian and an activist in the United Rubber Workers of America, the employees turned off their machines. Although the work action was brief, the workers celebrated something of a victory in their negotiations a month later. Stopping the machines was an act of empowerment. The ensuing quiet reminded people of their humanity, that they, not the machines, were in control. The Appalachian-born residents of East Akron "expected to win. . . . These were mountain people" who had suffered poverty and humiliation. "Now at long last they were striking back." Thousands of rubber workers marched in a parade in Akron that same month. Many in their ranks or on the sidelines were white Southern immigrants. "'How do you like us?' big tall mountaineers whooped to the sidelines, and men from the curbs yelled back, 'That's shown' 'em, boy; that's showin' 'em.'" They were "confident and happy and proud."[14]

In late January 1936, a manager in the truck-tire department of the Firestone Tire Company in Akron suspended Clay Dick, a union committeeman who had had a fight with a nonunion laborer. Coming in the wake of another wage cut, the incident precipitated a fifty-five-hour work stoppage. Ruth McKenney gave an embroidered but powerful account of the sit-down. At close to two in the morning on January 29, "the tirebuilders stepped back from their machines. Instantly, the noise stopped. The whole room lay in perfect silence. The tirebuilders stood in long lines, touching each other, perfectly motionless, deafened by the silence. . . . [T]here was absolute stillness, no motion anywhere, no sound." Suddenly, one man said: "Jesus Christ, it's like the end of the world." With "the magic moment of stillness" broken, men began to shout: "'We done it! We stopped the belt! We done it!' Slowly, their cries gave way to the singing of the 'Battle Hymn of the Republic.'"[15] The song was appropriate. Ohioans had found meaning in it as they tramped through the South in the 1860s. Laborers now did so again as they sat down in the middle of factories. What the workers got in an immediate sense was small; they returned to work when management agreed to give them and Clay Dick half-pay. But they won something more, including self-respect and faith in their ability to act collectively.

Wildcat strikes were everywhere in 1936 and 1937. They happened at Firestone, Goodyear, and Goodrich plants. In December 1936, workers at the General Motors Fisher Body plant in Cleveland spontaneously began a sit-down strike that precipitated the huge strike at the General Motors plant in Flint, Michigan, a milestone in the unionization of the automobile industry. Most of the sit-downs were not so successful. The Little Steel Strike against the smaller companies centered in northeastern Ohio, which was suffused with violence and dependent on workers' physical control of the mills, ended in a defeat for labor. Governor Martin L. Davey, a New Deal Democrat who had been friendly to unions, called out the National Guard against the strikers.

Even in the face of opposition, workers persisted. African Americans did, too, although they rarely had much support from white unions. Initially ignored by the Roosevelt administration, blacks found much of the New Deal legislation, including that dealing with labor, to be discriminatory. Some called the NRA (the National Recovery Administration) the "Negro Run Around" and "Negroes Ruined Again." But in the second half of the 1930s the situation changed. With greater relief as well as access to federal programs and public housing, African Americans became more sympathetic to the New Deal. In Ohio as elsewhere, they began to move from the Republican Party to the Democratic Party in one of the most significant political shifts in the history of the United States.

Like white union members, black workers became more assertive about their rights as citizens. In early 1935, under the leadership of John O. Holly, a handful of African American men and women in Cleveland formed the Future Outlook League (FOL). Its purpose was to boycott white-owned stores in black neighborhoods that welcomed their business but refused to hire them. A native of Tuscaloosa, Alabama, Holly had worked as a coal miner in Virginia, as a laborer for the Packard Car Company in Detroit, and as a porter and shipping clerk in Cleveland. Aware of the power of boycotts, he believed in the importance of collective action. Predictably, middle-class African

Americans disliked the FOL and its aggressive tactics. But working-class blacks, many of them recent Southern migrants, warmed to it. Despite a fondness for confrontations, Holly was thoroughly conventional in his hope that African Americans would become respectable capitalists. He wanted blacks to gain the experience working "under the white man's instructions," which would permit them to become "the merchants of tomorrow."[16] Nonetheless, the FOL became a genuinely radical organization in its demands for jobs and an end to racial discrimination.

Overcoming legal injunctions, middle-class opposition, and internal disagreement, the FOL mobilized thousands of African Americans. In 1939, its eighteen thousand members, many of them women, refused to buy where they could not work. The boycotts, which won the approval of the U.S. Supreme Court in 1938, forced businesses such as F. W. Woolworth and the Woodland Market to hire the same people to whom they sold their goods. As with other labor actions, the FOL was fighting for human dignity as well as jobs. "Of course we didn't call it civil rights," remembered Isabelle Shaw. "[W]e didn't use those terms then, but it was really about civil rights." One offshoot of the FOL, the Employees' Union, pledged itself to establishing "the fact that the Negro can and will organize themselves into a strong labor movement, thereby putting the Negro on equal footing with other labor movements."[17]

In 1938, continued economic recession soured some people on the New Deal and frustrated their hopes. Still, from a longer perspective, unions had emerged as formidable organizations. While they did not always achieve their goals, they had mobilized thousands of workers. In many ways, the sheer act of collective defiance was the most important thing. In asserting themselves, moreover, workers won the support of other citizens. Most local officials and newspaper editors strove to be fair in labor disputes, largely because they recognized the growing clout of unions. In Canton, Warren, and Youngstown, unions could not be ignored. Some strikes failed, but working people in general in the 1930s had forced themselves into a larger public conversation. They had found their voice in their demands that they were entitled to full participation in the possibilities of life in Ohio.

Liberty and the Rights of Citizens

Labor organizations were strong from Toledo eastward into the industrial cities of Lorain, Cleveland, Akron, and Youngstown. There, many families welcomed the increased presence of the government in their lives; they celebrated the tentative movement of the Democratic Party under Franklin Delano Roosevelt toward championing the rights of labor and a conception of American society as a pluralistic conglomeration of diverse constituencies. The commitment to collective action, the belief that material and moral improvement would come only through defiance of established institutions and union organization across occupational and ethnic lines, was a liberating notion for many Ohioans.

Outside of industrial and mining centers, however, enthusiasm for labor militancy and cultural pluralism scarcely existed. To the contrary, Ohioans in rural areas and small towns saw the demands of labor unions and the expansion of governments as new ways of organizing Ohio's society and explaining Ohio's history. Silly as it would have sounded to the steelworker interested only in respect and a decent standard of living for his family, or to the automobile worker or secretary whose dream was to raise children who would enjoy the benefits of middle-class life, many respectable Ohioans feared their actions as rejections of everything nineteenth-century middle-class citizens had striven to create. Resenting the intrusion of officials in their communities, many Ohioans believed that relief, government jobs, and unions threatened the process by which people became good citizens. The solution to the Depression, which they saw as a moral as well as an economic crisis, lay in what they now called traditional values of hard work and self-control. What had been in the 1850s a radical commitment to the potential of self-discipline and production was becoming a conservative defense against the attractions of self-fulfillment and consumption. The political champions of this perspective were Robert A. Taft and John W. Bricker.

The bald and bespectacled Taft was the scion of a distinguished Cincinnati family who would become one of the most influential politicians in the country from the late 1930s until his death from cancer in 1953. As minority and then majority leader in the U.S. Senate and as the candidate of the conservative wing of the Republican Party for the presidency in 1952, Taft earned the title of "Mr. Republican." Smart and honorable, more comfortable with family and close friends than the hurly-burly of politics, Taft harked back to the days of Rutherford B. Hayes. A lawyer from an affluent family, he had no burning need to become a politician. That he did so anyway was a tribute to a family commitment to public service that began with his grandfather, Alphonso Taft.

Alphonso arrived in Cincinnati in 1839. He was a native of Vermont, a lawyer with a degree from Yale who disapproved of making money for the sake of making money. A good Whig and then a Republican, Alphonso Taft was ambitious and stern. From his children he expected great things. "Mediocrity" would not do.[18] Alphonso's second wife, Louise, also from New England, reinforced her husband's attitude.

Among their children was William Howard Taft. Born in 1857, William was temperamentally the opposite of his father. Genial, fat, indulgent, he enjoyed laughter, often at his own expense. But his affability only superficially obscured his deep ambition and self-discipline. Like Alphonso, he graduated from Yale and became a lawyer; he then accepted an appointment to the federal bench. In 1900, Taft was put in charge of the American commission to the Philippines. Four years later, President Theodore Roosevelt made him secretary of war, and four years after that Roosevelt engineered his election as president of the United States. Defeated for reelection in no small part by the revived ambition of Roosevelt, who split the Republican Party in 1912, Taft served as chief justice of the U.S. Supreme Court in the 1920s until his death in 1930. This was the job he most coveted and the one for which he was best suited.

Taft's wife was Nellie Herron of Cincinnati, the daughter of a Republican lawyer and a good friend of Rutherford and Lucy Hayes. Never shy, Nellie wanted to get ahead. Some people found her cold; others thought her principled. In any case, she shared William Howard Taft's commitment to the idea that public service must come before private interest. If the latter served the former, so be it, but the former must be paramount. "Character," wrote Taft, "is formed by the practice of self-restraint and self-sacrifice, by overcoming obstacles. . . . Of

the sons of those who have luxurious homes and cherishing surroundings only the few who have force of character successfully to resist
these enervating influences will be among the leaders of the next generation."[19] No one summarized the values of middle-class Ohioans
more succinctly.

Into this world in 1889 was born Robert Alphonso Taft. Like his
father and grandfather, he went to Yale and became a lawyer. Like
them, he sought public office. But Robert Taft lived in a world transformed. His grandfather and father had been able to have it both ways
politically. They disdained the dirty business of politics even as they
courted and served Republican leaders in Cincinnati. Successful as
William Howard Taft was, he rarely faced the voters because he was
appointed to most of his positions.

Practicing law in Cincinnati, Bob Taft ran for office in 1920 because he thought he ought to do so. After election to the state senate,
he devoted himself to tax reform. Ohio cities suffered from an absurdly
low cap on the amount of money they could raise through taxes. The
Smith Law of 1910 limited local property tax to 1 percent. After
county commissioners allocated money to schools and county government, they gave the remainder to cities. Moreover, Ohio's constitution
required a uniform rate of taxation, which meant that all forms of
property from buildings to stocks were taxed at the same rate.

In the senate, Taft led an effort in 1921 to give cities a three-year
break from these requirements. His "chief aim" was "to relieve the
cities from restrictions which have made most of them bankrupt."[20]
Cincinnati, which faced a deficit of $2.4 million in 1923, and other
cities were in dire need of income to support schools and social services. Passed over the veto of Governor A. Victor Donahey, the so-
called Taft Law of 1923 raised the cap on property taxes and restricted
cities' ability to issue bonds. Assessment procedures and county control over cities were also reformed. Taft's success with such a delicate
issue revealed his great strengths as a legislator: his talent for principled compromise and his skill at working out acceptable solutions to
potentially explosive challenges. While out of office briefly, Taft supported a successful effort to eliminate the uniform rule of taxation.
Back in the senate, he engineered passage of the Property Classifica-
tion Act of 1931, which provided for the assessment of personal prop-

erty and established a tax rate of 5 percent of income for intangible property such as stocks and bonds, as well as a motor vehicle fee and a tobacco tax.

Few men could have ridden such an arcane, if important, issue to political triumph, especially a man with as limited a public personality as Robert A. Taft. But his name was golden. And Republican politicians in Cincinnati were happy to have someone so respectable on their ticket. Taft won by large margins because he was a decent, smart man from a famous family with a sure instinct for compromise and getting things done. Realistic about political chicanery, he was personally above reproach. Living in a mansion on Sky Farm in Indian Hill, Taft was a public man, dedicated to supporting the arts and education. No wonder he seemed the ideal candidate for the U.S. Senate in 1938. Middle-class and rural Ohioans could hardly have created someone more likely to meet the requirements for leadership in the state. Taft won his races for the Senate in 1938, 1944 (barely), and 1950. Yet he did so not as the kind of forward-looking candidate of a new energy and optimism personified by Hayes and Garfield in the 1800s. Rather, he represented people interested in preserving a world that seemed to be disintegrating.

Taft spoke for the old values, for character and public service. But Ohio was changing. Surrounded by advertising in print and on the radio, caught up in worlds conjured by their radios and magazines, by movie stars and sports heroes, its citizens were spending more time and more time thinking about conspicuous consumption. As important, many looked to government to regulate economic behavior, to provide relief when things went bad, and to ensure equity for everyone. Above all, many were disillusioned by the economic collapse of the 1930s. Given the challenges of the era, self-reliance seemed quaint at best. Only through collective action, through government, through defiance of entrenched institutions could ordinary people claim their dignity and create a sense of autonomy in their lives. For those who saw the world in this way, Robert A. Taft was an anachronism, a man who seemed to be saying that people could will improvement.

Taft was smarter than that. Suspicious of government, he was committed to a nineteenth-century notion of liberty as freedom from coercion. The New Deal was more than a problem. It was a revolution, an overthrow of everything that Ohio and the United States stood for. Emergency measures were taking on a life of their own, threatening socialism and "complete government control of all business, agriculture, manufacture, and distribution." The real solution to the nation's ills lay in "a balanced budget and an international stabilization of currency." "[I]f democracy is to be preserved," Taft wrote, "we must have more local self-government instead of less. The more government is removed from the people, the less interest they take in it, . . . and the more likely it is to become unresponsive and tyrannical." "The progress of America had been due to the retention of the spirit of liberty and individual initiative," he said in a 1938 radio address, "kept alive by the freedom of the different localities and by the freedom of the individual."[21]

Much more charismatic than Taft and far less thoughtful and sophisticated was John W. Bricker, governor of Ohio from 1939 to 1945, vice presidential candidate with Thomas Dewey in 1944, and U.S. senator from 1947 to 1959. Bricker also was a lawyer. He, too, stood for a revival of nineteenth-century homilies. But Bricker was more typical of Ohioans who worried about big labor and big government. He was born in 1893, the son of small Republican farmers who lived near Mount Sterling in Madison County, about twenty-five miles southwest of Columbus. His bloodlines were Scots-Irish and German, not Yankee. Bricker attended a one-room schoolhouse and several churches. He went not to Yale but to The Ohio State University. Unable to realize his dream of playing football, he became such a campus leader that his fraternity brothers nicknamed him "Governor." An extrovert, Bricker made friends easily. He was a conservative supporter of prohibition and states' rights. After graduation, Bricker entered the law school at Ohio State and passed the bar in 1917. A slow heartbeat kept him out of World War I. Married in 1920 to Harriet Day, a Columbus native who had grown up in Urbana, Bricker took a job with a law firm in Columbus and spent the 1920s building his practice as well as serving in the state attorney general's office.

The popular Bricker was an Ohio Babbitt. He had done very well, all within a thirty-mile radius of the statehouse at Broad and High Streets. Unlike Taft, he had not traveled the world. Having turned down a job in Washington, D.C., Bricker was a Buckeye by inclination as well as circumstance. He loved the state and he loved the values—free enterprise, individualism, character—that he believed had made it a great place. Most of his friends were white, middle-class Republican businessmen and professionals. He enjoyed the regular meetings of his clubs, including the Rotary, the Eagles, the Moose, and the Odd Fellows. Bricker was a farm boy who had thrived in Columbus, the least diverse of Ohio's major cities with an economy that revolved around government and education more than industry. Bricker was sincere; he was also familiar. Ohioans in small towns and rural areas trusted him because he was one of them, a good Protestant, Republican, family man.

Bricker lost a race for attorney general in 1930. Two years later, however, he bucked a Democratic tide by winning the office. While he lost the governorship in the Roosevelt landslide of 1936, he did well enough to get the nomination again two years later. This time he rolled to victory. Nineteen thirty-eight was a banner year for Republicans, with Bricker taking the governor's mansion and Taft the U.S. Senate seat. Their victory was a repudiation of years of Democratic rule at both the state and federal levels, a populist uprising by Ohioans in small towns, rural areas, and cities such as Columbus against the growing assertiveness of labor and the celebration of government as the solution to Ohio's woes.

Union members despised Bricker—and with good reason. In the wake of sit-down strikes in 1937, Bricker attacked the tactics and influence of unions. In 1938, he attempted to portray his Democratic opponent as beholden to the CIO and John L. Lewis of the United Mine Workers. He suggested that communists were influential in unions. He attacked the Wagner Act, saying that he did not "believe that any labor union has the right to compel any worker to join against his will, any more than an employer has a right to prevent his joining if he so desires." Sit-down strikes were "illegal" and would "not be tolerated when I am Governor." Bricker would not allow "Ohio's government to come under the domination of labor," which was "selfish" and did not have "the interest of Ohio and all its citizens at heart."[22]

These sentiments hardly endeared Bricker to the people of northeastern Ohio. In the election of 1938, the Republican lost Cuyahoga

County by sixty-four thousand votes, as well as the cities of Akron, Youngstown, and Toledo. But he garnered an overall state majority of 53 percent by carrying seventy-seven of eighty-eight counties. Like Taft in his bid for the Senate, Bricker won by playing on the fears of people outside the heavily industrial cities of the northeast that unions and government were, with the possible help of outside radical agitators, threatening their way of life. Suspicion of big government, big labor, and radicalism would remain at the center of both men's careers. While Taft was less strident in his criticism, it is no coincidence that the one major piece of legislation associated with the Ohio Republican was the Taft-Hartley Act of 1947. Amending the National Labor Relations Act of 1935, its supporters sought to redress what they thought had become an unfair balance between labor and management. Unions were too strong and needed their wings clipped. Among other things, Taft-Hartley outlawed the closed shop, told states they could supercede federal labor legislation, provided for cooling-down periods, and made unions responsible if their members violated no-strike provisions in their contracts. Among its supporters in the U.S. Senate was John W. Bricker.

As governor from 1939 to 1945, Bricker preached the value of local government and individual character in order to promote traditional notions of public culture. "The individual citizen must again be conscious of his responsibility to his government, and alert to the preservation of his rights as a citizen under it. This cannot be done by taking government further away but by keeping it at home." Bricker eliminated jobs and cut budgets. "The paternalism of the New Deal has weakened the old homely virtues of initiative and self-reliance," he said. "We have been led to believe that we can do very little to help ourselves."[23] His most dramatic act was his refusal to call a special session of the legislature to come to the aid of Cleveland when the city ran out of relief funds. Earning himself the national nickname of the "Starvation Governor," Bricker worried more about people taking advantage of relief than about their needing it.

Taft, characteristically, was more measured. He believed that Republicans had to woo ethnic voters and laborers in order to revitalize large cities. Above all, Taft counseled tolerance and reconciliation, dreaming that public conversation could take place without recrimination. People "can adhere to sound principle, without stirring up class hatred," he said on the radio, "if they will admit the good faith of their opponents, avoid personalities, and try to present in clear and calm language the reasons for their own faith. . . . Peace on earth depends not on surrender, but on meeting opposition in a spirit of tolerance, sympathy, and good humor."[24]

Solidarity Forever

From the 1930s through the 1960s, Ohioans remained rather evenly polarized between those who embraced a more activist government and endorsed collective action and those who saw the solution to the Depression as a modified revival of what had become traditional values of self-discipline and civic responsibility. During and after World War II, this division manifested itself in continued controversy over unions, government, and charges of radicalism and anti-Americanism aimed at people who called for significant reform in the political and economic structures of the country. At the same time, the long-term impact of World War II—which began for the U.S. with the Japanese attack on Pearl Harbor on December 7, 1941—and its aftermath was to stimulate the American economy into an extended period of prosperity. Increasingly comfortable with their lives as consumers, Ohioans were not interested in prolonged controversies.

During World War II, which lasted until August 1945, unemployment in Ohio fell to almost zero, industrial wages rose by 65 percent, farm income grew by close to 200 percent, and defense contracts brought $18 billion to the state. Ohioans built thousands of airplanes, ships, and ordnance. The Willys-Overland Company produced the most distinctive vehicle of the era, the Jeep. Synthetic rubber was developed in Ohio and quickly adopted by rubber companies in Akron. The average weekly wage of laborers in manufacturing rose from $29.55 in 1940 to $52.52 in 1944, and the average number of work hours increased from thirty-eight to forty-seven.

Once the United States entered the war, unions overwhelmingly pledged not to strike in war-related industries. Long hours, poor conditions, as well as food and consumer goods shortages strained that promise, however. Many protested by changing jobs, filing grievances, or simply staying home. Collective action soon followed. In 1943, close to 300,000 workers held some 467 work stoppages; another 549 strikes took place in 1944. A high percentage of angry workers were new immigrants from the South unused to factory labor. Whether white or black, male or female, they also had grievances based on their treatment by both employers and fellow workers who often discriminated against them on the basis of their accent, their color, and their gender.

The fact that African Americans constituted just over 8 percent of Ohio's skilled and industrial work force by 1945 did not translate into equality. Employment opportunities and higher wages for blacks did not survive the war. "We became black blue-collar workers," remembered one Cleveland woman, "but there was no mobility for blacks in private American industry." Racism persisted. In Cincinnati, where the demand for labor attracted black migrants from the South, a group of between fifty and a hundred white men stoned the houses of the first black families to move into the Mount Adams neighborhood. Intimidated, the blacks left, and a white woman who criticized the incident was hanged in effigy outside her home by an angry crowd. In another incident, a prospective employer began to discuss a job in detail with a light-skinned African American woman until he noticed on her application that she was black.[25]

With men overseas fighting Germany and Japan, many workers were women. In most cities females comprised roughly one-third of the total work force, while the number of female workers in plants rose from 16 percent to 32 percent. Women experienced blatant discrimination. Even though they were paid more in manufacturing than in service and domestic jobs, they averaged a third less than men doing the same jobs. Males often were unhappy working with white Southerners, blacks, and women. Their unions were no better, although members of the CIO tended to be more sympathetic than members of the AFL. White workers in Cincinnati, where the African American population rose from 55,593 (12.2 percent) in 1940 to 78,196 (15.5 percent) in 1950, protested the hiring of blacks at several factories by striking. The gains won by Appalachian whites, blacks, and women during World War II were usually the results of labor shortages rather than union activity. And the end of the war meant that women and blacks were often either forced out of industries or relegated to lower paying jobs.

The challenges of the postwar era were no less severe. In addition to dealing with the problems of readjustment, workers found themselves in an economy that was increasingly automated. The war solidified the transition to mass production. While wages rose and employment was relatively regular, both agricultural and industrial work declined. More and more, Ohioans found jobs in transportation, public utilities, wholesale and retail trades, finance, insurance, real estate, government, and professional occupations. The dominant occupations in the state by the 1970s were service rather than production related.

Despite these changes, unions were never stronger than they were in the decades that followed World War II. In 1945, some 36 percent of nonagricultural workers in Ohio belonged to a union. That fell to 21 percent by the end of the 1980s, the sharpest drop experienced by any American state. Still, unions were powerful institutions. As strikes became a normal dimension of negotiations for higher wages and better benefits, major automobile, steel, and rubber companies moved to long-term contracts. Unions benefited from a close alliance with the Democratic Party, whose leaders had supported government programs from the Social Security Act of 1935 through Medicare and Medicaid in the 1960s, which alleviated the fear of workers that they would grow old or become disabled without adequate income. Building on the traditional loyalty of ethnic and urban voters, Democrats in the 1950s remained strongest in northeastern Ohio.

Critics of unions did not surrender, however, and in 1958, they provoked what amounted to a referendum on their existence. The Ohio Chamber of Commerce and other probusiness organizations supported a "right-to-work" amendment to the state constitution. Voters had to decide whether they wanted to make it illegal to deny anyone in Ohio a job because they were, or were not, a member of a union. Advocates argued that the act would restore freedom to the workplace and control "big labor." People should be allowed to associate with whomever they wished without paying a penalty in the workplace. Requiring employees to join a union, creating what was called a closed shop, was a violation of individual liberty. Unions, on the other hand, characterized right-to-work legislation and open shops as an effort to destroy them. If workers could choose whether or not to join a union, their collective power would be fatally diluted.

Running for reelection in 1958, Senator John W. Bricker initially ignored the right-to-work amendment. By October he was speaking out in favor of it. Bricker had built his popularity in Ohio's rural areas and small towns in no small part on his denunciation of unions. Events in the 1950s gave him considerable ammunition. Unions suffered from nasty internal squabbles and rivalries. The 1955 reunification of the AFL, an older, more conservative group of skilled crafts unions, and the CIO, a militant group founded in the 1930s primarily among unskilled laborers, was fraught with distrust. Charges of corruption, including the misappropriation of dues and racketeering, dogged several major unions. Unions also suffered more than their share of accusations of communist influence during the McCarthy era.

Senator Bricker, however, was positive as well as negative in his support for open shops. It was, he said, a matter of liberty. Ohio citizens should not have to suffer the tyranny of corrupt bosses. They should have a choice. Contributing money to union leaders who used it for their own ends was wrong. Bricker held to "the ideal of voluntary membership." "I oppose the power of big business over inalienable individual rights," he said. "I oppose the power of big unions over the inalienable rights of men; and I oppose the rights of big government to suppress the rights of individuals."[26]

In November, Bricker lost his Senate seat in a startling upset. Labor had organized at all levels to defeat the proposed amendment. Unions paid for advertising campaigns and volunteered to register voters. More Ohioans voted in this election than in any other contest in state history with the exception of the presidential election of 1956. The result was a complete triumph for organized labor. The right-to-work amendment carried only sixteen of the state's eighty-eight counties and was defeated statewide by a two to one margin. No less amazing was the victory of Democrats who supported the unions' position. Michael DiSalle ousted C. William O'Neill to become governor of Ohio, and long-time Democratic gadfly Stephen Young ended the career of the sixty-five-year-old Bricker by a surprising margin of

155,000 votes. Bricker, as usual, did well in southern and rural Ohio, where he carried 57 counties and the city of Cincinnati. But he lost decisively in the industrial cities of the northeast.

A mild recession and six years of Republican rule aided organized labor's victory. It was also testimony to the degree to which unions had become part of the landscape of Ohio. Workers had to be taken seriously in public conversations about the meaning and future of the state. Indeed, the legitimization of unions was one of the great themes of twentieth-century Ohio. With the decline of ethnic immigration, the growth of suburbs, and the general affluence of postwar America, working-class families began to find more in common with each other. The vast majority of union members were interested in improving wages, working conditions, and the material lives of their families; few harbored dreams of revolution. Overwhelmingly, they saw themselves as middle-class people whose dreams centered on a home in which they and their families could enjoy the good life in the promised land of Ohio.

Coda: On Change

One of the most interesting commentators on the changes sweeping Ohio was the painter Charles Burchfield. Born in Ashtabula Harbor, Burchfield grew up in Salem. After high school, he enrolled in the Cleveland School of Art. In 1921, Burchfield moved with his new wife to Buffalo, New York. There he worked as a designer for a wallpaper manufacturer. Concentrating on watercolors, Burchfield achieved almost immediate success. His paintings were frequently shown in New York City, and his reputation was secure long before his death in 1967.

Throughout his career, Burchfield focused on landscapes of manmade or natural settings highlighted by wind, rain, snow, or sun. He located everything within a larger world that is beyond human control, emphasizing the extent to which people are particles of nature swept along by larger forces. Burchfield liked to paint buildings from behind, from a private angle of vision. He said that it was "good to be isolated from the world."[27]

Strong and colorful, Burchfield's work suggests the wear of weather and the world on both objects and human beings. The ironically titled *Civic Improvement* shows a trio of windswept houses looking somewhat off-kilter and worn. While paintings such as *Rising Smoke, Abandoned Coke Ovens,* and *Factories* comment on the presence of industrialization, they do so with a vibrancy that undercuts the horror of its impact. *Black Iron* seems almost celebratory in its depiction of the power of machines.

One of Burchfield's most famous paintings, *End of the Day,* depicts men straggling home from work to dilapidated shanties. It evokes the Depression or, more generally, the routine of industrial labor. Burchfield was not striving for a judgment as much he was for a sense of the moment. In a peculiar way, the transitoriness of these scenes is reassuring because we realize than the transformations wrought by industrialization are part of a larger process that is natural and inevitable.

Burchfield was less interested in the general than in the way the particular reveals the general. "The Capital-Labor quarrel makes such a noise," he wrote in Salem in March 1920, "that we are apt to lose sight of real human tragedy. We are asked to join a revolution to transfer the automobiles from one class to another. We cannot despise" people who fall victim to advertising charms or are consumed with "silly love affairs" or "who strain their ears for gossip—we can only despise those who have no sympathy for other people—There is real tragedy that is independent of time or circumstances—Sometimes a face seen in a crowd brings to mind great gulfs of horrors."[28]

More than anything else, Burchfield strove to convey the complexity of existence. When he visited the upper Ohio Valley in 1932, he found the countryside unchanged from the early 1920s. The fact filled him "with a great intoxicating joy." "The grim primitive country" was "untouched virgin material." He remembered his earlier visits to the region, the taste of coffee in a lunchroom and the sound of a phonograph. One song had "since come to mean 'Ohio River' to me. It is all mine yet—nothing has changed."[29]

Louis Bromfield thought the opposite. In 1954, remembering the snowy night in 1939 when he brought his family to Richland County, he considered himself something of a fool. He had learned in a decade and a half that he could not recreate the imagined world of his boyhood. "A return to the past can never be accomplished and the sense of fortified isolation and security is no longer possible in the world, of automobiles, of radios, or telephones, and airplanes," Bromfield lamented. "One must live with one's times, and those who understand this and make the proper adjustments and concessions and compromises are the happy ones." In the end, he believed, he had lived "a useful life."[30] Alas, Bromfield the realist was not nearly as interesting as Bromfield the visionary. Better to put aside the "concessions and compromises" and remember him in full tilt against the brave new world of the twentieth century.

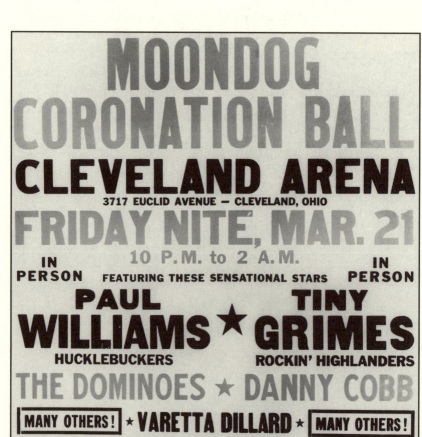

Announcement of the Moondog Coronation Ball at the Cleveland Arena, March 1952. (Courtesy of The Western Reserve Historical Society, Cleveland, Ohio)

11

The Good Life

—

JACK NICKLAUS was the son of a middle-class family who achieved international fame and fortune as one of the greatest golfers in the history of the game. Nicklaus was not the most naturally talented player. What distinguished him was self-control, what a competitor called his "ability to organize himself and maintain his discipline, concentration and composure." It seemed that Nicklaus could do anything he decided to do, simply by willing himself to succeed. His secret, according to rival Gary Player, "is his ability always to remain calm or on an even keel."[1] Nicklaus, who ascribed his intense concentration to a German heritage he otherwise ignored, embodied Rutherford B. Hayes's belief that a disciplined person could achieve whatever he thought important.

While Nicklaus represented traditional middle-class values, he played a sport that represented a new middle-class world. Golf required self-discipline but not self-sacrifice. To the contrary, golf was about self-interestedness. Nicklaus worked hard to win fame and money for himself and his family. Offering personal comfort in a manicured world designed for the diversion and convenience of affluent men and women, golf was the perfect sport for a suburban world. It celebrated character as the surest path to personal happiness.

It was no coincidence that Nicklaus grew up in the Columbus area. Most of the hundreds of thousands of people who lived in and around Columbus in the late 1900s considered themselves middle class. Being middle class entailed financial independence. It also continued to mean sharing certain attitudes with like-minded people. But while from the early 1800s to the mid-1900s those attitudes revolved

around a celebration of hard work, self-discipline, and personal refinement, they now focused on a celebration of personal happiness,
self-satisfaction, and leisure. Citizens were consumers more than they
were producers. They lived in suburbs rather than cities or towns and
worked in government jobs, education, high-tech companies, banks,
insurance firms, department stores, fast-food restaurants, hotels, air-
ports, and movie theaters.

Suburbs were more than a century old in the 1950s. It was their size
and influence that was new, a development made possible by the ubiquitous automobile. Providing convenience and independence, privately
owned cars allowed people to think that they had control over their
lives. As governments constructed intricate networks of highways, cars
transformed the landscape of Ohio. Work and home were now often
miles apart. Businesses moved away from urban centers, and retailers
developed shopping malls, first as strips along highways and then as en-
closed commercial villages with acres of parking spaces.

Suburbs, with their green spaces, their rigid separation of work
and home, their promise of quiet and beauty, reflected the possibilities
of a good life won through victory in a good war. Work had its occasional rewards, but the center of life lay in and around well-appointed
family homes. Ohioans wanted a car (or two), air-conditioning,
stereos, color televisions, vacations, and new clothes, among other
things, all of which had to be replaced with newer, improved versions
as soon as possible. Buying goods and services with loans and credit
cards, suburban Ohioans lived amid relentless advertising. Suburban
Ohioans lived better than their parents had, and had even higher expectations for their children, who were multiplying rapidly as part of
a national baby boom.

The expansion of suburban life after World War II was a major re-
organization of the Ohio landscape. In 1900, children in an Ohio city
would have expected to live, work, and die within a few miles of their
parents' home among neighbors with a common ancestry, religion,
and customs. By 2000, teenagers were mobile, culturally sophisticated
creatures who thanks to popular culture belonged to a world that
went far beyond a self-contained local area. Their major concern was
less with finding a job that would feed and house them than with
achieving that most nebulous and elusive of human goals—happiness.

Goodbye to the Cities

Between the world wars, Ohio's great cities experimented with political reforms. In order to increase efficiency and reduce corruption, several cities tried the city manager form of government pioneered by Dayton in the 1910s. In Cleveland, where manager W. R. Hopkins quarreled constantly with the city council, the system lasted barely a decade, from 1921 to 1931. Cincinnati's experience was more positive. In 1924, voters adopted a new charter that centralized power in the hands of a small council elected at large and an appointed city manager. Some worried that proportional voting would encourage voters to choose on the basis of ethnic, religious, or racial identity and, in the words of Robert A. Taft, put "selfish and particular interest ahead of the general welfare, and ahead of every principle of American government." Proponents countered that proportional representation would increase participation and diversity in city government, arguing that "the various minority groups would . . . forget their differences and vote as citizens instead of groups."[2] By the 1930s, Cincinnati's government, while less democratic, was winning acclaim nationally for its business acumen rather than its partisanship.

Despite political reform, cities were no longer as dynamic as they once had been. Massive migration to suburbs, especially after World War II, bled aging industrial cities of people and resources. By the 2000, the populations of Cincinnati and Cleveland had fallen to 331,285 and 478,403 respectively. Akron, Dayton, and Toledo remained relatively stable, while Youngstown's population plummeted from more than 160,000 in the 1940s to 82,026 in 2000. Only Columbus escaped the trend. In 2000, it was the largest city in Ohio, with 711,470 residents.

Ohioans increasingly associated urban areas with rampant crime and vice. Kenneth Rexroth described Toledo around 1920 as a sanctuary from which "[e]xtradition was extremely difficult. You could commit a crime somewhere else and run to Toledo and as long as you behaved yourself, it took all hell to get you out." Toledo was "wide open," replete with "brothels, cardrooms, and burlesque shows." In 1971 Columbus native Wil Haygood's brother hid from police on Dayton's West Side. The area was "Dayton's mecca of vice. . . . It wasn't difficult to disappear there."³

Once strong immigrant neighborhoods disintegrated as children and grandchildren learned English, moved to suburbs, became preoccupied with popular culture and material convenience, and married people from different backgrounds. In Cleveland, second- and third-generation immigrants were much more mobile, depending on family size and education. Romanians, Italians, and Slovaks moved into skilled and white-collar jobs. Marriages tended to mix ethnic but not religious identities. Many residents who refused to leave apartments they had inhabited for decades felt overwhelmed by growing numbers of African Americans and white Appalachians with whom they thought they had nothing in common.

Born in Cleveland in 1915 to an Italian father and a mother who was the daughter of Italian immigrants, Michael DeCapite graduated from Ohio University and worked as a laborer and a reporter. His novel *Maria* tells of a young girl forced to marry Dominic, an abusive man she does not love. She lavishes "[a]ll the affection and love absent in her marriage" on her son, Paul. When the ambitious Dominic moves his family out of Cleveland's Italian community to a house near the Flats and its factories, he ignores his ethnicity. "He did not seem to be bothered by his being Italian, he was not afraid of his new country. He seldom talked of the old world."⁴

Maria, meanwhile, adjusts to an ethnic diversity she scarcely imagined while growing up in Little Italy. Her Jewish neighbor, the wife of a tailor, complains about leaving her "own people. It is not good to leave your own people." Surrounded by Poles, Russians, Greeks, and now Italians, the Jewish family has no synagogue; they cannot teach their sons their religion because they cannot read or write. Losing contact with his parents' world, Paul speaks English more than Italian. Dominic crudely encourages his son to assimilate because of the material possibilities of life in Ohio. In spite of his own difficulties, he still believes that "in this country . . . you can do anything and you can go anywhere—if you got the brains and education." Even Maria is not immune to temptation. She flirts with a man who is "an American of Italian parents, but . . . now [is] more American than anything else." Deserted by Dominic, Maria goes to work in a garment factory where she witnesses the depth of ethnic rivalries and racial prejudice. With Little Italy a distant memory, Maria finds Cleveland "gloomy and cold, a stranger with a pitiless sneer on its face." Mother and son, coming from "two worlds," are left to find ways "to touch each other."[5]

In *No Bright Banner,* DeCapite continues the story from Paul's perspective. Rejecting his family, Paul moves to New York City and reads philosophy and literature in order to understand the "puzzling elegiac sadness of America, the profound uprooting of individuals." Eventually, he makes peace with his past. Ironically, the memory of his father helps him do so. While Dominic was not a good man, he "believed in himself; he had a kind of integrity in everything he said and did; more, he left me with the impression it was possible to have integrity."[6] To DeCapite, who died in an automobile accident in Mexico in 1957, the greatest lesson of the immigrant experience in Cleveland was that determination in the face of repeated disappointments is the surest foundation of self-respect. Whether people are Italian or American matters less than their respect for themselves as human beings.

Michael's younger brother, Raymond, enjoyed greater popular success, exploring similar themes with a much lighter touch. After attending Ohio University in the 1940s, Raymond worked as a clerk, a writer, and a journalist before he published his delightful novel *The Coming of Fabrizze.* Young Cennino Fabrizze becomes obsessed with the promise of the United States when his Uncle Augustine returns to Italy for a visit. Augustine warns his nephew about unrealistic expectations before he agrees to take him back to Cleveland. "Look outside," he says. "The sun must climb the mountains to bring light into this village. Always the same hard climb to win the day. It was the same for me in America. . . . America is a good place. For the young it's even better. But it means work."[7]

In Cleveland, hard-working Fabrizze marries Grace and they have a son. Defying prohibition, Fabrizze uses the money he makes selling wine to open a store and sell cheese and olives. Meanwhile, a character named Vivolo teaches the Italians that "there is one blessing" and that "blessing is life"—which is DeCapite's point. People should not take life too seriously. To be happy, we have to take chances and avoid getting mired in angst about disappointments. Fabrizze is admirable mostly because he does not let life defeat him. When he becomes involved in the stock market, Fabrizze characteristically invests everything he has. If we did not take chances, he says, "[w]e would never leave our beds." "Tomorrow may be the best day of all."[8]

When Fabrizze loses everything, including his friends' money, in the stock market crash of 1929, he disappears, leaving his store to his neighbors. Some grumble, but most retain their faith. "Fabrizze says that each one of us is born with an empty barrel," remarks one man. "We have to fill this barrel with trouble and then it's time for happiness." The point is not to give up hope, to survive with dignity. When Fabrizze returns, they will have a party. "Open your heart," says one character. "The music is there. I tell you I heard it."[9]

The whimsy of *The Coming of Fabrizze* contrasts strongly with the grimness of *Maria*. Still, both DeCapites stress the importance of persistence. They both admire the faith of their father in the American dream. As Raymond's second novel, *A Lost King*, makes clear, however, the generations diverge in defining that dream. Paul Christopher is a young man living with his widowed father in a working-class neighborhood "overlooking the industrial valley of Cleveland. Below was a sprawl of steel mills and oil refineries and chemical plants" along the "old brown Cuyahoga River." In the spirit of Fabrizze, Paul wants to see beyond the grime, to "[l]ook at that sun and sky" and to believe that "something good is happening." He is as optimistic as his father is tired. "For you everything is good," says the latter. "For me everything is bad. It's a little difference of opinion we have." While the father wants his son to work hard in a good job, Paul prefers to indulge his fondness for playing the harmonica. His father says that with Paul, "It's words and music." He "belong[s] to the wind." Paul is content to ride in a wagon and sell watermelons. His lack of industry, his ambition to be happy rather than to have a job, costs him the woman he loves. She marries a man with a position in a bank who wants to move to the suburbs away from "this smoke and dirt."[10]

Paul and his father both dream of the good life. But for one it means a steady job, while for the other it means happiness. When the father dies, the son refuses to accept the drudgery of his father's life.

He insists that he "must make a song for [his father]. And for [his] mother and [his] brother. And for everyone else, too."[11] Which, of course, is exactly what Raymond DeCapite had done with *The Coming of Fabrizze.* The younger DeCapite has made peace with his parents' generation. He celebrates their spirit even as he chooses a life that places self-fulfillment above self-discipline.

A focus on personal happiness also permeates the work of Ruth Seid, a Jewish woman born in Brooklyn in 1913 who moved to Cleveland when she was three. In *The Changelings,* Seid (using the pseudonym Jo Sinclair) describes growing racial tensions in the aftermath of World War II. Thirteen-year-old Judith Vincent, the daughter of a first-generation Jewish family, lives next door to Italian immigrants in a Cleveland neighborhood. Families hoping to rent floors of their houses are dismayed that no one is coming to see them except blacks, the "Schwartze," as the Jews call them. Judith's family thinks they will soon have to leave their neighborhood. Her father's friend, Mr. Levine, complains that African Americans even bought the synagogue for their church. He decries the "American habit" of blacks following you "no matter where you move." Like the Depression, "the coming of the Black Ones," says Levine, rolls "like a flood over you until you are naked and penniless as the day you came to America. A nothing again." The longer Judith's grandmother lives in the United States, "the less I feel trust. Jews are surrounded by disasters here, too."[12] She decides to move to Palestine.

Seid understands the degree to which ethnic and racial tensions originate in a fear that is partly physical and partly about self-worth. Everyone seems to understand life in Cleveland as a zero-sum game. Everything that makes someone "something" makes someone else "a nothing again." Judith nonetheless refuses to give in to fear. "I'm not going to run around crying and hating people," she bravely announces. She calls herself a changeling. Like "lots of kids," she does not belong with her parents or grandparents "because they want different things out of life. They don't talk—well, the same language. I mean, in their hearts!"[13] Befriending a black girl named Clara, Judith dreams of a day when Jews, African Americans, and Catholics can find common ground in a place where no one is an outsider. To the older generation, however, to tolerate is to move away from one's faith, to begin to blend into a homogenized America rooted in material comfort.

Part of the tragedy of racial tensions was that both white and black urban citizens faced the same challenge in the middle of the twentieth century: making their way in cities in decline. Beneath the general affluence of life in postwar America, long-term developments were working against all residents of Midwestern industrial cities. Companies were beginning to move plants to suburbs and rural areas. Automation was eliminating jobs, especially for unskilled or semiskilled laborers. Government spending on defense was declining in industrial areas, and overtime pay cut the need for new employees.

Pervasive racism made a bad situation worse for African Americans. With the desegregation of Cincinnati's Coney Island amusement park in 1961 under pressure from local civil rights organizations, virtually no restaurant, hotel, or business in Ohio publicly refused service to African Americans. A de facto segregation nonetheless flourished in everyday life. While black men could get jobs in certain industries, opportunities for advancement were rare. And labor unions had little interest in taking up their cause. Black women tended to weather the decline of the cities better than men. As domestic jobs evaporated, they found jobs as health-care workers or secretaries. The fact that employers in service industries put a greater emphasis on education and appearance than plant managers meant that prejudice, conscious or unconscious, affected the hiring of black men. By the 1950s, the unemployment rate for African Americans in Midwestern cities was more than double that of whites. The situation deteriorated even further in the 1960s and 1970s. Increasingly, black men had to accept low-skill, low-paying jobs.

The problems of the cities were related to an influx of unskilled labor at precisely the time that the demand for such workers was evaporating. Whether black or white, people saw cities decaying before their eyes. White urban residents struggling with children who were looking for something different from their parents, who were dealing with the impact of deindustrialization and suburbanization, saw blacks and white Appalachians as more than competitors for jobs and housing. They were harbingers of an urban apocalypse. Blacks and white Appalachians, on the other hand, resented the exclusivity and hostility of long-time residents. By the late 1960s, cities seemed at times to be armed camps divided between whites and blacks from which people were fleeing in droves.

Over time, escalating racial tensions weakened the Democratic Party in Ohio. As blacks moved away from their traditional support for Republican candidates and into the Democratic Party of Franklin Delano Roosevelt and Harry S Truman, white ethnic voters became increasingly uncomfortable with Democratic candidates. By the late 1960s and 1970s, sizeable numbers of Catholic and working-class voters were supporting Republicans and insurgent candidates such as George Wallace. Democratic leaders, envisioning their party as a coalition of interest groups united by their support for government protection of the rights of all, were flummoxed. Since everyone saw politics as a zero-sum gam, they resented any and all attention paid to "others." Visible signs of difference attracted hostility. To some extent, white Appalachians who lost the "hillbilly accent," acquired an education, and worked in professional jobs could disappear into the burgeoning middle-class suburbs. African Americans, on the other hand, could change their accent, get a college degree, and display all the signs of respectability, but they could not change their skin color. Middle-class blacks still had to contend with daily discrimination, no matter where they lived.

Residential segregation and the creation of so-called ghettoes resulted from a combination of black migration patterns, white prejudice, and the choices of businessmen and politicians. In 1940, 64 percent of African Americans in Cincinnati lived in a neighborhood north and west of downtown called the West End. After World War II, middle-class black families began to move out of the deteriorating West End into Walnut Hills and South Avondale, largely white communities north and east of the University of Cincinnati. As blacks moved in, whites moved out. In the 1950s, Avondale went from being a largely white neighborhood to a largely black neighborhood. Real estate agents abetted the process with a practice called "blockbusting." Agents would arrange the sale of a home to a black family and then use a variety of techniques to play on the fears of whites and encourage them to sell their homes, often at bargain prices. Local government did nothing to fight this behavior. Indeed, city plans and officials supported urban renewal projects, including limited access expressways, that isolated black neighborhoods. Interstate 75 ran through the West End, essentially destroying the neighborhood, while Interstate 71 separated Avondale and Walnut Hills from more affluent neighborhoods on Cincinnati's east side.

Opposition to residential segregation became widespread in the 1960s. Some Cincinnatians argued that poverty was not an individual failing but a structural problem that could be remedied to some degree by integration. While the city council did little to change things, the Ohio General Assembly in 1965 passed the Fair Housing Law, which was intended to allow people to choose where they wanted to live, to create basic minimum standards, and to outlaw blockbusting and other shady real estate techniques. The Ohio law was weak (it exempted one- and two-family buildings with resident owners), and enforcement was lax at best. Racial discrimination kept black communities together while ethnic communities were breaking up.

If whites felt threatened by blacks in Ohio's deteriorating cities, African Americans reciprocated the feeling. Mel Watkins grew up black in Youngstown in the 1940s. His father, Tennessee, an itinerant bluesman from Mississippi, had stopped off in Youngstown on his way to Detroit in 1939. His wife, Katie Bell, followed. Tennessee got a job at Republic Steel Company and supplemented his income with street hustling, while Katie took care of their children, dealt with occasional abuse, and found community in the Baptist Church. In retrospect, Watkins saw his maternal grandmother, Miss Aggie, as a decisive influence in his life. Although Miss Aggie lived with the family for only a few months, she taught her young grandson the importance of being a "Dancer," that is, of learning how to fool white people while maintaining his own integrity. She told him of a young enslaved African who knew who he was and did not let anybody tell him otherwise. "Dancer was thinkin' somethin' else even whilst he smilin' and puttin' them white folks on. Didn't matter what *they* said or thought, child knowed he weren't nobody's property."[14]

In many ways, Mel Watkins's life was similar to that of thousands of other young Ohioans. He listened to radio shows, developed a passionate interest in baseball and basketball, admired charming, confident men, and lived through sundry personal crises and joys. Getting into trouble from time to time, he won a basketball scholarship to Colgate University and became a successful journalist, writer and editor of the *New York Times Book Review*. Race, however, forever complicated Watkins's story. "[T]o grow up in Ohio," he learned, "was to confront a congenial Midwestern atmosphere and surface tranquility that insistently suggested all was right with the world. Everyone was promised a bright future. Well, nearly everyone."[15]

Race began to define Watkins's world slowly. He became conscious of it when his family fell out with the white family from West Virginia who lived next door. "Goddamn white trash," Tennessee called them, "they ain't never goin' to be nothin' but trouble." A series of squabbles over music, chickens, and dogs ensued. A year later, the white family left the neighborhood, following a larger pattern of white flight from black residents.[16]

One day a four-year-old girl broke Mel's happy mood by pointing to him as he walked by and yelling, "Nigger! Nigger! Nigger!" When her taunts did not break his confidence, she grew frightened and began to cry. Mel was baffled by the incident. He learned its full meaning soon enough. Mixing with other children in the public schools taught him that people thought he was different. Textbooks and teachers strove to make American history as positive as possible, ignoring blacks altogether. "Through avoidance and silence, and seemingly with the best of intentions, my grade school teachers perpetuated a myth of equality that many white Midwesterners publicly embraced and, perhaps, even imagined was real." But Watkins knew it to be false. When a friend who was the only black member of a championship baseball team was forbidden to enter a public pool for a party to celebrate their team's triumph, Watkins was outraged. Life in Youngstown, he concluded, meant experiencing "a subtle, seemingly inexplicable sense of outwardly imposed restraint and negation of self-worth." "[S]urface politeness and amicability" was the tip of an ugly iceberg. No wonder Watkins was anxious to leave Youngstown; no wonder he returned less and less after he went to Colgate. He wanted to explore the "diversity and richness" of African American life in Harlem and other places far removed from the restricted congeniality of Ohio.[17]

Wil Haygood was born in 1954, the son of a mother from Alabama and a father from Georgia. He grew up in Columbus and went on to become a successful journalist for the *Boston Globe*. In 1994, Haygood returned to Columbus for a year as the James Thurber Fellow at The Ohio State University. He and his family lived in a renovated home on Jefferson Avenue in which Thurber had lived as a child. Haygood concluded during his time in Columbus that "much had changed." The once vital African American business community located on Mt. Vernon Avenue had become moribund. People talked of bankruptcies and departures. The Mt. Vernon Avenue District Improvement Association continued to meet but to little effect. When Carl Brown, a worn-out, seventy-seven-year-old proprietor of a grocery store, died of a heart attack, a packed church celebrated more than his life and mourned more than his passing. Like ethnic neighborhoods, black neighborhoods were disintegrating. The friends and relatives of Haygood's youth had moved away or settled down. As he visited old haunts along the Olentangy River, Haygood called Columbus "[o]ur town; my family. The family I've loved, the family that has times frightened me. It has come to this: we've survived, held on." Or, more precisely, the women had. "The men in my family fled. The women stayed put, giving us a place to come home to. I now see there's plenty of bravery in staying put, claiming ground." The irony was that Wil Haygood, like many men and women, had spent much of his youth dreaming of other places. "More than anything in the world," he recalled, "I wanted to travel, to visit any place beyond Ohio. There were times when I felt the rest of the world was calling my name." When Haygood moved to New York City in 1979 to become an actor, he celebrated by walking all over Manhattan and feeling "a million miles from Columbus, Ohio."[18]

Haygood, like Watkins, enjoyed a happy youth. Until he was a teenager, he lived in an integrated neighborhood in a home on North Fifth Street owned by his grandparents. He loved going to movies, fishing, hanging out with his friends, and playing basketball. On Sunday afternoons in the summer, "the voice of Joe Nuxhall, the Cincinnati Reds baseball announcer . . . was like background music" as generations of male Haygoods gathered on the front porch, "holding hats, holding cigars and tapping away the ash."[19]

Race was present for Haygood, but not as viscerally as it was for Watkins. Haygood's mother moved her children into an apartment in a three-acre housing project, the Bolivar Arms. Four years old, the project had taken the place of "a huge eyesore" of "shacks" and "lean-tos" devoid of indoor plumbing and located in muddy fields. Haygood attended high schools that were mainly or all black. He felt the presence of racial antipathy in some sections of the city's west side, which was the home of "transplanted West Virginians; it was Appalachia all over." The west side was a place where "white boys . . . didn't back down from fights with black boys, as the suburban boys mostly did." When he graduated from high school, Haygood went to Miami University in Oxford, one of the least diverse campuses in the state, and survived. Ambitious and earnest, he dreamed of becoming a basketball player, a journalist, or an actor. His mother, who had her own struggles with alcohol and a string of boyfriends, did not always understand. "You're the only one of my children who eats Jim Crow," she told Wil when he announced his intention to play basketball at a white suburban high school. The remark stung her son but did not stop him from pursuing that which he thought would make him happy. "I only wanted to play basketball."[20]

Unlike Watkins, Haygood seems to have experienced being black more as a source of pride than alienation. Race was inevitable but not necessarily an obstacle. Loving his family and his home, Haygood found Mt. Vernon Avenue, with its nightclubs and bars, theaters and shops, exciting and seductive. It had "blood and rhythm." It had a "special way" of drawing "a long-necked woman out of her waitress uniform and into her girdle, her sequins and lame."[21] By day, blacks went to Mt. Vernon Avenue to hear evangelists or to buy clothes and food. By the 1990s, the community that enlivened the neighborhood had dispersed. The decline of Mt. Vernon Avenue and the rise of the Bolivar Arms reflected the fate of Ohio cities in the second half of the twentieth century. Postindustrialization, suburbanization, generational conflict, and race ate away at African American neighborhoods as well as white ethnic ones and, in the process, encouraged people to imagine themselves as divided by race rather than united as citizens.

Goodbye to the Towns

Perhaps the only places that suffered more than cities in the second half of the twentieth century were small towns. Villages within an hour's drive around Cincinnati, Columbus, and Cleveland, especially those located on expressways, were absorbed within the cultural borders of the metropolitan areas. Meanwhile, rural counties in west-central and southeastern Ohio suffered significant population losses or stagnation. By 1990, three-quarters of Ohioans lived along a diagonal axis that runs from Cincinnati through Dayton and Columbus to Cleveland, Akron, and Youngstown. As residents left in droves, small communities withered.

The birthplace of Sherwood Anderson, Camden in Preble County, enjoyed a certain vitality in the 1920s. Improved living standards along with automobiles, radios, and motion pictures had reduced its residents' sense of isolation. Camden was not an unusual village. Centered on the intersection of Main and Central Streets, it had a red-brick town hall, a drugstore, a hardware store, a bank, a phone company, a clothing store, and a theater—all within a couple of blocks of each other. The car dealership was relatively new, as was a two-story, yellow-brick school.

Most people in Camden worked in farming or related businesses. Women had jobs as maids and clerks. Virtually everyone thought of themselves as middle class, although there was a clear-cut local hierarchy. The gentry lived in better houses and dominated influential organizations such as the Presbyterian church, the Masons, and the Progressive Club. People who were respectable but not affluent constituted about half of the town. They, too, belonged to local organizations, although most were Methodists and Brethren. Perhaps one-quarter of the population consisted of unskilled laborers with little interest in the community; their children tended to quit school early to find work. Those who were religious were Baptists. Whatever their class differences, the people of Camden were not divided by race or ethnicity because blacks and immigrants were few and far between. The majority were Republicans whose primary interest was in maintaining prosperity and social order. Nothing mattered more than keeping taxes as low as possible. "Camden doesn't have a chamber of commerce, a commercial club or a civic boosting organization," observed a visiting journalist in 1927, because "it doesn't need one. Everyone who lives here see to the matter of broadcasting the advantages of the town as a place to live and do business."[22]

Real or imagined, this congenial atmosphere dissipated during the Depression and World War II. Local efforts to deal with the economic crisis foundered and fostered a long controversy over whether the town should accept federal public works money. Despite a brief economic boom after World War II, Camden disintegrated in the 1950s and 1960s. As the attractions of jobs and businesses in the expanding Cincinnati and Dayton metropolitan areas proved irresistible, people moved to those cities' suburbs or became commuters. Like other small towns, Camden raised children who left for greener pastures when they finished high school. Popular culture as well as jobs lured people away. Increasingly, people went to the outskirts of Dayton or Cincinnati for diversions and goods they saw advertised on television in between the programs they watched rather than attend local sporting or civic events. The closing of theaters in 1952 marked the shift from local sources of entertainment to metropolitan ones.

By the late 1950s, Camden's economy was suffering, school enrollments were falling, and interest in local civic affairs was evaporating. Downtown stores went out of business as people drove miles to shop at malls and supermarkets. As improvements to Route 127 took traffic around the town rather than through it, Camden lost its newspaper, its school, and its bank. One older person described it as "a ghost town," while a former resident said it was "dead compared to when I lived there."[23] Some people looked for someone or something to blame. But the sad fact is that the town's fate was part of a larger transformation of Ohio in the twentieth century. Nothing could have saved Camden.

By the 1970s, public conversation about small towns increasingly centered on nostalgic memories of the way people imagined things used to be. The writer John Baskin compiled brief oral histories of the village of New Burlington near Wilmington into a tough-minded elegy for a lost world. Baskin came to live in New Burlington as it was literally disappearing; the U.S. Army Corps of Engineers was planning a reservoir that would obliterate the town and its environs.

Ohioans would now water ski where they had farmed. "[O]nce people had something to do," Baskin concluded, "and now they do not."[24] Melodramatic overstatement, perhaps, but indicative nonetheless of a profound sense of loss.

Older people remembered New Burlington ambivalently. People "were so close," said one person, revealing both the advantages and disadvantages of community. "Everyone watched everyone else. How could you possibly get out of line?" The hard and isolated life had an undeniable appeal when viewed from the perspective of "modern brick ranch houses" clustered in suburbs. According to a woman in her seventies, the transient population of New Burlington had been held together by the church and the school in a "dull" and "safer" world. A former teacher warned of the danger of "glorifying the past. We are very sentimental about the countryside these days, forgetting that the farm once gave us overworked hearts, little profit, and an early grave." Ruby Higgins did not lament the passing of the staid, provincial world of the village she loved. She had defied the notion that "we are on the earth to make a living and live for God. But I was what I was and if I wanted a drink, why, I had one." Yet despite "the hypocrisy we were all very close. . . . We seek community today and we do not find it."[25]

The residents of New Burlington did not blame others for its fate. They knew that the town declined because its residents chose to leave one world for another. Like the citizens of Camden, they sought jobs and the promise of a good life in metropolitan areas. "Life in the cities was enticing to the rural children," recalled a farmer, "no matter how firm their foundations. City life was said to be a better life." And so by the early 1970s, almost "all of New Burlington [was] gone," with only a few scattered buildings and a few stubborn residents marking time before the literal flood.[26]

While the decline of cities created crisis, the decline of small towns created nostalgia. Where many white Ohioans associated cities with African Americans, poverty, and crime, they tended to see the small towns as relics of a bygone era when life was simpler and people imagined themselves as one community. Suburban Ohioans, living in the midst of rapid change, enjoyed romanticized versions of village life.

By the 1980s, some towns were actively promoting themselves as lost worlds. Marietta offered the imagined life of a river town where steamboats had once plied the waters while residents enjoyed ice cream socials and band concerts. In east-central Ohio, communities and entrepreneurs appropriated the Amish, often with their cooperation, to market the good old days and sell "traditional" foods and decorations. Towns closer to cities, such as Worthington and Montgomery, redesigned their central business districts to highlight their nineteenth-century origins. Virtually every Ohio village proudly announced at its borders that it was the home of a unique event, celebrity, or historic first. Tourist bureaus and chambers of commerce built festivals and fairs around the connection in order to boost business. Greenville had the sharpshooter Annie Oakley, Cadiz was the birthplace of the actor Clark Gable, and Steubenville celebrated itself as the hometown of singer Dean Martin and gambler Jimmy "the Greek" Snyder.

Ironically, small towns liked to associate themselves with people who had left them and become celebrities. It was as if they were saying, talented people can get out of here. Focusing on pioneers and inventors, Civil War generals and ministers, villages were marketing the past to eager consumers. Like all good entrepreneurial boosters, they avoided controversy. Small towns emphasized ethnicity, race, or religion only to the extent that they reassured everyone they were a united community of decent people.

Consumers All

Some suburbs had a largely working-class population. Norwood developed early in the twentieth century when a factory owner moved his plant several miles out of Cincinnati and his laborers followed. Chagrin Falls was a largely African American suburb of Cleveland. In the 1920s and 1930s, black families moved there because of cheaper housing, greater space, less crowding, and more control over daily life. Unlike many white suburbs, Chagrin Falls was the home of extended families, working women, sizeable gardens, and efforts to replicate aspects of life in the rural South. Clara Adams, who arrived with her husband in 1940 from an apartment in Cleveland, "didn't like *in* the city—too congested. I liked *out.* I like the fresh air, and it's nice and quiet."[27]

The significance of post–World War II suburbanization lay in its scale and character. By the 1950s, white Ohioans, whatever their origins, wanted to live in safe, quiet, homogeneous places distinguished by their lack of diversity and controversy. Owning their own homes, they prized nuclear family life. Domesticity dominated the new suburbs. There was a premium on women's staying at home, maintaining beautiful houses, and raising children. Fathers entered a different world when they arrived home from distant jobs. Indeed, a division between work and home defined suburban life. Adults were primarily parents, and work was something fathers did in order to support leisure activities and education.

North of Cincinnati, the suburb of Forest Park started as North Greenhills, a New Deal experiment in the creation of greenbelt communities around large cities. After the war, metropolitan planners, local government officials, and private developers scrambled to control the growth of North Greenhills. Huge demand for suburban housing, however, overrode their conflicts. Renamed Forest Park in 1954, the suburb soon mushroomed. By 1960, its population exceeded eight thousand. Social organizations flourished, including a women's club, a civic association, a baseball association, and a volunteer fire department. By 1970, the population had nearly doubled to 15,174. In order to deal with crime, road construction and repairs, water, and sanitation, the village had incorporated itself. Local elections revolved around issues of development, including the location of malls and industries, social services, schools, and taxes. Zoning laws were critical to the growth of Forest Park as they were to other suburbs because they segregated commercial and residential areas.

In the 1960s, Forest Park was a community of young people who were remarkably mobile and whose attachment to the place was fleeting at best. The median age was 20.7, with 43.1 percent of residents under fifteen and only 2.9 percent over sixty-five, the reverse image of the aging populations of cities and small towns. Some three-quarters of residents lived in households consisting of a married couple with children. In well over half of the households, only one person worked. Civic identity did not come easily to people who rarely contemplated living the rest of their lives in the area. While Forest Park gained a municipal building, a post office, and a branch library in the 1960s, its police force was small and it lacked a hospital and a health department. Meanwhile, many of its residents seemed more interested in private development than the preservation of public space. The village suffered from constant traffic congestion on roads that could not keep up with growth and that were increasingly cluttered with dozens of small businesses and retail outlets in strip malls.

More than the infrastructure of community was lacking. Forest Park residents tended to identify themselves almost exclusively in terms of their families. Their interests were less parochial than personal. When voters overwhelmingly approved a local income tax in 1974 in order to provide better services, the event marked the transformation of a community defined by shared values into a community defined by autonomous individuals whose mantra was personal happiness. The new government's "primary goal," writes historian Zane Miller, "was not to foster civic, ethnic, religious, neighborhood, or some other form of social cohesion, but rather to provide a convenient, comfortable place for those liberated individuals to move through, or linger within, as their self-defined commitments and lifestyle choices might determine."[28]

Like most postwar suburbs, Forest Park was a white enclave until the late 1960s. Blacks arrived in large numbers in the following decade, buying homes and working in service industries. By 1972, just under 10 percent of the people of Forest Park were African American. Race tested the image of the suburb as a free enterprise zone with regard to culture as well as commerce. The same whites who believed that individuals should be able to live where they wanted were frightened by black neighbors whom they often saw as the advance guard of urban problems such as poverty, crime, low property values, and deteriorating services and institutions such as schools. As blacks became a significant presence, whites either learned to accept the change or moved further away into suburbs beyond the Interstate 275 beltway.

Although ethnic identities faded in the world of suburbs, many Ohioans remained faithful to the religions of their ancestors. Young, native-born Jewish professionals and their families moved to Cleveland

Heights and Shaker Heights and established new synagogues and community centers. Ethnic and class tensions dissipated as immigration dwindled and the horrors of the Holocaust united Jews. Simultaneously, Jewish families in Cincinnati migrated north into Roselawn, Golf Manor, Amberley Village, and Wyoming. A new synagogue in Amberley Village superseded the original Plum Street building as the home of the Isaac M. Wise Temple. Neither migration nor the loss of national power with the transfer of the headquarters of the Union of American Hebrew Congregations to New York City destroyed a sense of a Jewish community in greater Cincinnati.

The homogeneity of suburban life worked to stir interest in religion. Cleveland novelist Herbert Gold recalled that he had learned growing up as a Jew in Lakewood, Ohio, before World War II that being "American is enough." And if it was not, "pleasure will be enough." And if it was not, "art and the life of art will be enough." Or "health, love, money, luck and words will surely suffice." Gold's story is the tale of a man who returned to "tribal myths." He rejected a bar mitzvah because as an American he did not need one. But eventually he decided that it was "wise to cultivate strangeness" because there were privileges in being "exotic when what was normal was dead-white, bland, and suburban." Gold, like more than a few suburban Ohio youths, escaped "the emptiness of history in Lakewood" as soon as he could. He headed for Columbia University in New York City, "the belly of America, where I could do anything, the freedom of art, the freedom of self-creation, in the image and pattern of nobody else," or so he imagined. In the 1950s, a brief return to Cleveland convinced Gold that he had had enough of "midwestern flatness." And yet he continued to consider himself "bound to both Cleveland and Jerusalem, the American idea and the history of Israel," Gold sought "a salvation on earth, right now; not in heaven, but today. Or at least tomorrow. Or, please God, next year in Lakewood, Ohio."[29]

Powerful as religion was, consumerism was more important in defining suburban life. Women and teenagers worked in stores in increasingly elaborate malls that catered to an insatiable demand for new clothes, shoes, records, appliances, books, and equipment. Suburban homes required care; lawns had to be manicured, cars had to be maintained, living rooms had to be decorated, kitchens had to be equipped with the latest devices. Advertising saturated the suburban world with a seemingly infinite number of choices. Newspapers, magazines, and billboards touted the latest in everything. But it was radio and then television that brought the art of advertising to near perfection. Countless ads urged people to rush to sales, heralded new and improved versions of products, and encouraged people to devote leisure time to buying commodities. A weekly trip to a movie and a restaurant became a regular expectation for many people.

For many teenagers, life focused on dating. Guys cruised the streets in souped-up cars designed to impress young women. In couples or groups, teenagers went to movies, amusement parks, and sporting events. According to journalist Bob Greene, who grew up in Bexley, outside Columbus, the Eskimo Queen and the Pancake House became as important as the public library on his town's Main Street. When he was seventeen, he spent the night in bed with a twenty-seven-year-old married woman. Greene thought "about the moral questions." But it did not "seem wrong" to him. It was "wonderful." And rather than worry about "why it was happening," he concentrated on "the fact that *it was happening.*"[30]

Television and radio fed this emphasis on finding personal happiness. Especially in the daytime, stations catered to women isolated in suburban homes with multitudes of small children. In Cincinnati, WLWT produced much of its own programming. In the morning, viewers could watch the antics of Paul Dixon, who shamelessly clowned his way through an hour and a half, praising products, telling slightly risqué jokes, and leering at the world in a cheerful way. At noon, Ruth Lyons, the energetic and opinionated doyenne of local television in southeastern Ohio, presided over the 50-50 Club. With a live band and wholesome young singers, her program reached a vast regional audience made up primarily of young white women. Never shy, Lyons hawked products with such sincerity that her endorsement of a particular brand was as good as gold in the Cincinnati market. She also wrote her own songs, boosted the city's sports teams, entertained celebrities and politicians as if they were visiting her home, and made the Christmas season a gargantuan festival of sentiment and spending. Lyons's appeal went beyond entertainment, however. While she presented herself as a domestic figure, she was anything but bland. Speaking her mind on everything from fashion to politics, Lyons provided a forum for women who otherwise felt disconnected from public conversation.

The logical successor to Ruth Lyons was Phil Donahue, a young man from Dayton who launched his own talk show, as the genre was now called, in the late 1960s. Unlike Lyons, Donahue did not sell products or sentiment. Instead, he offered his audience of young to middle-aged white women a more intellectual and interactive version of what Lyons had given them. Donahue would interview a single guest for an hour and encourage members of the audience to participate in the discussion, either in person or via phone. Although Donahue featured celebrities, he also tackled controversial subjects such as divorce, drugs, and sexuality. Wildly successful, his program moved to Chicago in the 1970s and spawned a slew of imitators. Suburban women had their own spokespersons. Dayton-area housewife Erma Bombeck became a popular newspaper columnist and guest on the Donahue program by satirizing suburban life. In collections of columns such as *The Grass Is Always Greener over the Septic Tank,* Bombeck offered short takes on the dilemmas of suburban women—what to make for supper, how to shop, how to deal with mystifying children and the strange behavior of husbands. In her way, Bombeck was a social critic. As much as her humor reinforced social expectations about women's roles, her sharp wit also pointed out their costs.

Suburbanites generally organized their lives around their many children. Frequently alienated from their own parents, they had more money and time to lavish on the development of the next generation. Parents measured their worth by the success of their offspring in Little League games and academic competitions. Where a child went to college or the kind of job he or she found became markers of respectability and success.

As they grew into teenagers, children did not always conform to their parents' expectations. Generational tensions had little to do with ethnic and religious questions and everything to do with sexuality and style. As baby boomers matured, some reveled in defying authority. While the sheer act of rebellion was often the end in itself, teenagers superficially rejected the supposedly conformist, white, consumer world of their parents by consciously adopting the styles of people their parents feared or despised. To dress like a laborer, to go into the dangerous city for fun, to value the eccentric, to smoke, drink, take drugs, or swear were acts of defiance. If the essence of middle-class life was still respectability, whether defined by character or affluence or a combination of the two, then the thing to do was to be as disreputable as possible.

Music was often a source of serious controversy. In the early 1950s, what had been labeled "race music" or rhythm and blues began to attract the attention of large numbers of young whites. This music was direct in its depiction of sexuality, both in lyrics and the driving rhythms of the music. Rejecting sentimental romantic ballads, young whites began to buy records put out by black artists and record companies.

In the early 1950s, Alan Freed, a deejay in Cleveland, began to pitch black music to a wide audience. Freed claimed to have coined the term "rock and roll," which dealt with the problem of the association of rhythm and blues with blacks by renaming it. Born in Pennsylvania in 1921, Freed grew up in Salem. After briefly attending Ohio State, he embarked on a career in radio. His big break came in 1951 when he landed a job introducing rhythm and blues records on WJW, whose owner, Leo Mintz, was ready to experiment with music and audiences, in particular the expanding black market in Cleveland.

Debuting in July 1951, Freed let loose with an unabashed style that appealed to young Americans. He called himself Moondog and developed a patter of jive talk shouted into the microphone. Playing music by black artists for black audiences, Freed was unique in only one major way—he was white. Freed became a phenomenon (his dances attracted tens of thousands of mostly black youths). Other Cleveland stations started to imitate Freed's high-energy style. By 1953 and 1954, growing numbers of whites were buying rhythm and blues records. Roughly 20 percent of Freed's audience was now white. Freed became so popular that he was wooed away by a New York City radio station in 1954. Freed did not create rock and roll, nor was his tenure in Cleveland responsible for the growing national interest of young, suburban whites in "race music." But it was no coincidence that Cleveland, with its burgeoning black and young suburban white populations, was at the forefront of this cultural development.

Rock and roll appealed to both black and white youths because it seemed countercultural. The driving beat, the ragged rhythms, and the suggestive lyrics directly challenged a white, middle-class world that defined the good life as the accumulation of possessions and the development of character. The music was anything but respectable. Rock and roll was often denounced for its "smutty" lyrics and "animal" rhythms that contrasted strongly with the romantic ballads favored by white, middle-class audiences. Listening to this music offered kids in the new tract houses of Ohio's suburbs a window into a different world—a place they imagined was more diverse, freer, less restrictive and bland than the one in which they lived. The immense popularity of Elvis Presley crystallized this appeal. Presley was not only one of the first white artists to embrace rhythm and blues, he was overtly sexual. For thousands of young Ohioans more interested in self-gratification than self-restraint, he became a minor deity.

By the late 1950s, rock and roll was not nearly as raw as it had been earlier in the decade. As record companies and radio stations marketed the music to suburban white audiences, they tamed it to a significant extent. Increasingly, songs were about romantic love rather than sexuality and emphasized the importance of finding an elusive personal happiness rather than challenging the fundamental structures of American society. To be sure, rock and roll celebrated the world of the suburb, of cars and dances, of sex and defiance. But ultimately, most of the music pointed its listeners toward the middle-class ideal of domesticity. The good life, it would seem, involved a necessary period of rebellion in the teenage years before young Ohioans would settle down into the world of their parents. Like nearly everything else in suburban life, teenage defiance was part of a process of self-fulfillment made possible by consumerism.

The Sporting Life

Sports defined public culture in Ohio in the second half of the twentieth century. White or black, suburban or urban, many Ohioans, mainly but not exclusively male, were loyal to the Ohio State Buckeyes, the Cleveland Browns, or the Cincinnati Reds. Sports was consumerism perfected. Fans bought tickets, pennants, programs, and hot dogs. Seeking a public identity, they wore clothes emblazoned with their teams' insignia. Sports was popular on radio and television, attracting advertisers eager to associate themselves with a successful team. As significant was the fact that sports combined old and new attitudes about the possibilities of life in Ohio. Sports was leisure, not work. It was a source of pleasure and pain for thousands of people who lived vicariously through the exploits of athletes with whom they identified. Yet Ohioans understood sports as about something much greater than diversion or consumerism. Sports was about self-discipline and self-sacrifice for a cause greater than oneself. Sports integrated nineteenth-century notions about the value of work and character with twentieth-century ideals of gratification. As much as coaches and journalists emphasized that sports was fun, they justified the enormous amount of time and money devoted to it as investments in future citizens. Sports, they argued, makes men (and later women) fit in mind as well as body. Sports built character. It demonstrated the value of delaying gratification, of working hard, of dealing with other human beings directly and fairly.

Prominent Ohioans offered these clichés throughout the 1900s. Byron Bancroft "Ban" Johnson, son of a Marietta College professor, led a successful movement at the turn of the twentieth century to create the American League as an alternative to the entrenched National League. "Clean ball," insisted Johnson, a notorious drinker, "is the main plan in the American League platform. There must be no profanity on the ball field." He offered fans "purified baseball." No one agreed more than Judge Kenesaw Mountain Landis, a native of Millville whose father named him (with the spelling modified) after the Georgia battlefield where he had lost a leg. Landis was appointed commissioner of baseball in the wake of the 1919 scandal in which some members of the Chicago White Sox were accused of throwing the World Series to the Cincinnati Reds. A tough, no-nonsense judge with no sense of self-irony, Landis restored the integrity of baseball even as he kept it all white. "Baseball is something more than a game to an American boy," said the judge. "It is the training field for life work. Destroy his faith in its squareness and honesty and you have destroyed something more; you have planted suspicion of all things in his heart."[31]

Jesse Owens was born in Oakville, Alabama, in 1913 and grew up in Cleveland. Owens developed into a champion sprinter and long jumper, and became an international celebrity when he won four gold medals at the Berlin Olympic Games in 1936. White Ohioans rushed to claim him as one of their own. "We are proud of Jesse because he is a clean gentleman wherever he goes," said the mayor of Cleveland during a public celebration. "By his high character, his clean living and attention to duty, he has brought this credit and honor to his Race, to this the greatest city of the world, to his alma mater, Ohio State, to our great commonwealth, to this country at large." While whites exploited Owens, he proved quite adept at promoting himself. He made a career as a celebrity who celebrated core public values. He wanted to be a "worthy citizen," and until his death in 1980 he continued to believe that "in America, anyone can become somebody." Owens urged black men and women to think of themselves as humans first and to move up in the world not through defiance but through traditional middle-class values of self-control and education. Without illusions about the difficulties of being black in a white society ("it can be pure hell at times"), he saw no future in "making his hand into a fist."[32] Jesse Owens was a black man white Ohioans were happy to know—at least in public.

The most fervent exponents of the idea of sports as the last outpost of nineteenth-century values were several midcentury football coaches. Paul Brown, who launched his career with a successful stint at a high school in Massillon, won a national championship at Ohio State in 1942, led the Cleveland Browns during their glory years of the 1950s, and founded the Cincinnati Bengals in 1968. Born in Norwalk, Brown never really left Ohio. He attributed his achievements to his emphasis on football fundamentals and his gift for organization. Brown believed that his success flowed from his commitment to character. He took seriously the words of Elizabeth Hamilton, a dean at Miami University when he was an undergraduate: "The eternal verities will always prevail. Such things as truth, honesty, and good character will never change no matter how people and times change." As a coach, Brown wanted men who were both "solid citizens and solid football players." That meant respectable players who understood the "team concept," the importance of sacrificing for "the overall good of the team." "The only people who couldn't play for us were the selfish or the disloyal."[33]

Brown's players found him distant. A brilliant control freak, according to running back Jim Brown, the coach was an anachronism who insisted that his players become "extensions of his personality. . . . They dressed as he would have them dress, and if they were prone to habits that he considered to be vices (smoking, drinking, cursing, women, etc., etc., etc.) they pursued them with the furtiveness of CIA agents." To Jim Brown, the coach seemed ill-equipped to deal with a new world in which players wanted to express their individuality or objected to the hypocrisy of sneaking around behind the coach's back. Jim Brown was right. Paul Brown represented the hardening of middle-class mores into inflexible "tradition." Idealizing "the healthy and wholesome life-style of a small community," Paul Brown had led "a very ordered existence" as a child under the supervision of firm but fair parents.[34] He had learned, above all, that verities governed the world and that success depended on obedience to those rules.

Woody Hayes, who became the Ohio State football coach in 1951 despite serious pressure for the university to rehire Paul Brown, also believed in those verities. He was born in Clifton in 1913, the youngest child of a schoolteacher and his wife. Like Paul Brown, he grew up valuing education, work, and discipline. As the football coach at Denison College, Miami University, and then at Ohio State, Hayes advocated organization and hard work as the keys to success. "The only smarts I have are that I'm smart enough to know that I can outwork 'em," he remarked. Like Brown, he required discipline both on and off the field. Hayes prided himself on the fact that his players acquired "all of the games' values he held so dear—hard work, discipline, teamwork, respect for rules, sacrificing for a goal, and overcoming adversity, among others." In 1986, when he received an honorary doctorate from Ohio State, the former coach exhorted graduating students to "make sure they don't beat themselves." Success was a personal choice. "Hard work, tough decisions, teamwork, family values, and paying ahead will help to change this world and make it a better place."[35]

Hayes's teams were immensely successful. Close to ninety thousand people crowded into Ohio Stadium five or six Saturday afternoons every year to watch the Buckeyes play Big Ten rivals. Hayes was the most famous citizen of Ohio. On his weekly television show, he presented his athletes to a statewide audience as models of human character as well as physical skill. Football games, Hayes suggested, were won by men who were disciplined, industrious, obedient, responsible, and willing to sacrifice themselves for the greater cause of their team. The annual clash with the University of Michigan became a rivalry that tested culture as well as ability. Many people imagined that the victors triumphed as much because of their characters as their talent. When Michigan won, they noted that many of the Wolverines were from Ohio.

Unlike Brown, Hayes had a difficult time controlling his emotions. He did not always possess the self-discipline he demanded of others. He lost his temper frequently and often abused players. When a frustrated Hayes struck a Clemson player during the 1978 Gator Bowl on live television, he lost his job after twenty-eight years of dedicated service to his university. Rallying to their coach, player after player testified about how Hayes went out of his way to help them when they needed help and how much they had learned from him. Speaking to a group of elementary students in the 1970s, two-time Heisman Trophy winner Archie Griffin, a running back from Columbus, summarized the close relationship that existed for Brown and Hayes between character and sport. "Football," Griffin said, "is a game plan, and so is life. . . . Coach Hayes always told us at Ohio State that you could never get anywhere if you can't take direction, learn, and discipline yourself."[36]

Bob Knight, a product of a small Ohio town who lost his job as head basketball coach at Indiana University after years of success because he could not control his temper, told his team in 1987: "Follow our rules, do exactly what we tell you and you will not lose."[37] This credo was, as Griffin suggested, about life as well as sports. Like Brown and Hayes, Knight believed that success resulted from following the rules of respectable and respectful behavior. Nothing was more likely to trigger his players' deviation from their accepted code of conduct than their perception that selfishness was being rewarded. Alas, for these men, even in sports, more and more people defined the good life as freedom from the rules they championed.

The scene on the Kent State University campus at around noon on May 4, 1970. National Guardsmen advancing toward people protesting American intervention in Cambodia on Blanket Hill below Taylor Hall. (Courtesy of The Kent State University, Kent, Ohio)

12

The Future Is Past

⟡

ON MAY 4, 1970, most people in the Portage County town of Kent were going about the ordinary business of their lives. Many were working or attending classes at Kent State University. On the Commons, an area at the center of the campus, approximately two thousand people were publicly protesting President Richard M. Nixon's decision to send U.S. soldiers into Cambodia. Nixon's action was an expansion of American participation in a long conflict for control of the southeast Asian country of Vietnam. The demonstration at Kent State was not unusual. Growing numbers of Americans were frustrated by the actions of their government. They saw the war as pointless or, worse, as an act of imperial aggression that was destroying Vietnam and killing tens of thousands of innocent people. They also objected to the military draft, which they saw as coercion.

Nixon had announced the incursion into Cambodia on Thursday, April 30. Over the next few days, angry protests occurred throughout the country, especially on university campuses. In Kent on May 1, a crowd started a bonfire and broke windows in local businesses. On May 2, the ROTC building, a symbol of the military, burned from unknown causes while some students tried to keep firemen from putting out the blaze. Many citizens began to worry about the security of their businesses, homes, and lives. Governor James Rhodes, who was running for the U.S. Senate, called out the National Guard and traveled to Kent to denounce the demonstrators. Those who rallied again on the Commons on Sunday night were dispersed with tear gas.

Ohioans, like all Americans, were polarized by the Vietnam War. Ken Hammond, a member of the Kent chapter of Students for a

Democratic Society, recalled "a true revolutionary moment. People were living very much in the present, and were acting out their feelings of outrage with the war, and with their more or less total alienation from American society." Twenty-three Kent State faculty members formally called for the withdrawal of the National Guard. Much as they "deplore[d] this violence," they wanted it viewed "in the larger context of the daily burning of buildings and people by our government in Viet Nam, Laos, and Cambodia."[1]

On the other hand, many townspeople in Kent blamed everything on "'the students,' mixed up with communism," according to Quaker activist Mary Vincent. Another Kent resident, fifty-nine-year-old Lucius Lyman Jr., who was a car dealer active with the campus ministry center, later recalled the palpable sense of fear among the townspeople. On the evening of May 2, when they saw the flames rising from the ROTC building, "many people in this town thought their houses and their property was going to be next." Lyman thought that "the destruction of property [in particular] had a great impact" on "those of us who are in the system." Robert Gabriel, a Vietnam veteran and lieutenant in the National Guard, flew a helicopter patrol over Kent on the night of May 2. He remembered "looking down and seeing groups of people, just running around; there were fires. It was anarchy. I'd never seen anything like that."[2]

Gabriel spoke for many when he saw the events in Kent as a disintegration of an older world. He believed his hometown of Logan had been "an interlocking society." Before Vietnam, "things were different; things were simple. Everybody had the same values that I had; work hard, pay your taxes, obey the law, respect other people's property— and opinions." In other words, people had played by the rules, by "very strong notions of right and wrong." Wanting the law enforced equally, Gabriel was upset that students were being treated like "a privileged class." "Everybody ought to be treated the same," Gabriel reasoned. "That's part . . . of our American heritage." Years later, he still did not understand "how somebody feels that a group, for whatever reason, can violate the law and do what they want."[3]

Ruth Gibson, a student from Wheeling, West Virginia, who was indicted along with others for her role in the May demonstrations (the charges were dropped in 1971), also saw a world coming apart.

But Gibson looked to the future rather than the past. She dreamed of a coming revolution in which working people, African Americans, and Mexican Americans, among others, would unite and overthrow a political system that no longer "express[ed] the will of the people." Like Gabriel, Gibson believed in rules. But she insisted that the U.S. government was violating its "own rules and regulations." The people were primarily "concerned about the lack of democracy." A decade later, Gibson knew that "we weren't successful in bringing about the great revolutionary change; but we had it in our hearts that day, and I think that there are many of us still who have that in our hearts." She had hoped that the events would be the beginning of a more egalitarian and more just social order. "[T]he students weren't the enemies of democracy; the government was and probably still is."[4]

As the university held its normal schedule of classes on Monday, May 4, hundreds of people formed a volatile crowd on the Commons. Some were cursing, jeering, and throwing rocks at the 113 young, inexperienced National Guardsmen clustered off to one side on an elevated area called Blanket Hill. Launching tear gas canisters and pointing their rifles in the direction of the protestors, the citizen-soldiers started retreating. At 12:25 P.M., the guardsmen reached the crest of Blanket Hill, where they suddenly turned and fired into the crowd. Sixty-one rounds of ammunition exploded in thirteen seconds. When the firing ceased, four students—Allison Krause, Jeffrey Miller, Sandra Scheuer, and William Schroeder—were dead or dying and another nine were wounded. Ironically, Scheuer had been on her way to a class and Schroeder was a ROTC student. Neither had been involved in the demonstration on the Commons.

The events that Americans simply called "Kent State" were a horror that precipitated years of legal wrangling and personal recriminations as the participants struggled to understand what had happened. Each side blamed the other for overreacting, for breaking the law, for failing to respect the rules of a democratic society. Rhodes and some townspeople were as sure of the students' radicalism and disrespect for authority as the protesters were of the officials' repression of free speech and support for a bloody war. In time, it became clear that the meaning of Kent State went well beyond the tragedy of May 4 and even the war itself. In Ohio, as in the United States as a whole, the dead and wounded became a symbol of a profound crisis in American society. Something seemed to have broken, and no one knew how to fix it. "What's the use?" asked one Kent State student shortly after the shootings. "What can we do? What kind of democracy is this?"[5]

Richard T. Cooper, a reporter for the *Los Angeles Times,* argued later in 1970 that the problem was partly generational. Kent State students were anything but intellectual radicals. Mostly they were first-generation college students, the sons and daughters of hard-working Americans. Cooper believed that the students were "no longer quite comfortable with themselves or their society." Surely that was true of many adults in Ohio. The special state grand jury that indicted twenty-five people but refused to criticize the guardsmen saw the tragedy in a much larger context. The jurors, a cross-section of Portage County residents, lamented a breakdown in moral authority. The university administration had "fostered an attitude of laxity, over-indulgence, and permissiveness with its students and faculty to the extent" that it had lost control of both. "What disturbs us," concluded the jurors, "is that any such group of intellectuals and social misfits should be afforded the opportunity to disrupt the affairs of a major university to the detriment of the vast majority of the students enrolled there."[6]

No matter whom they blamed, almost everyone agreed that they were living in the midst of a major social crisis. The very word "Ohio" became a national symbol of disillusionment. A popular song written by Neil Young in reaction to the news of Kent State and recorded by Crosby, Stills, Nash, and Young contained the lyric "Four dead in Ohio" repeated over and over. Ohio, once the land of endless beginnings, had become a place of deadly endings.

Stagnation

Frustration defined Ohio from the late 1960s through the early 1990s. It went deeper than opposition to the Vietnam War or calls for civil rights or fears that traditional values were disintegrating. The good life that had flourished in the aftermath of World War II seemed lost. The nation as a whole was unable to deliver on promises of inclusion. Mired in an increasingly unpopular war, buffeted by rampant inflation and political corruption, Americans seemed to delight in exposing the underbelly of their society. They wanted to know the story behind the story, dismissing public rhetoric as propaganda. Popular culture and history—whether in the media or the academy—reveled in exposés of hypocrisies and corruption.

Ohioans had good reason to be disgruntled. The state had experienced difficult times before, particularly in the late 1800s and the 1930s. This time, however, the problem was a question of stagnation rather than economic collapse. By the 1970s, neither agriculture nor industry was thriving. Rural residents, threatened with competition from larger, more efficient farms, found it impossible to sustain life on a family farm even with federal subsidies. Agribusiness, with its plethora of machines, chemicals, and hired labor, harvested the corn, soybeans, and dairy products that still made Ohio one of the leading agricultural states in America. By 1985, the number of Ohio farms had fallen from 221,000 in 1945 to 89,000, while their average size had risen from 100 to 178 acres. Ohio farm families survived only when women found work in urban areas and all members held part-time jobs. Increasingly, farm children could not continue their parents' way of life. While 27 percent of Ohioans lived in a rural areas in 1980, only 3 percent of Ohioans were full-time farmers.

Meanwhile, industry also was in decline. The obsolescence of factories combined with relatively high labor and property costs led larger corporations to close plants and move either to the southern or western U.S. or out of the country altogether. Automobile companies preferred to pay seventeen dollars a week to Mexican workers rather than twenty dollars an hour to Ohio workers. In addition, oil was replacing coal in importance, which put Americans in general at the mercy of oil producers in other parts of the world. Labor unions, which had played such a key role in the improvement of working conditions and wages in the middle of the twentieth century, lost their influence. By 1980, fewer than 30 percent of Ohio's nonagricultural workers belonged to a union (down from around 36 percent in the late 1960s).

Between 1972 and 1982, Ohio suffered a loss of 246,553 jobs, an 18.3 percent decline. In Toledo, corporate mergers and relocations led to the disappearance of 12,000 jobs. From 1969 to 1977, in the eight most industrialized counties the number of manufacturing jobs fell by an average of 15.6 percent. In 1980, U.S. Steel shut down two huge mills in Youngstown, and unemployment in the region rose to almost 15 percent, a figure not seen since the Great Depression. More than 10,000 steel factory jobs evaporated in Youngstown in a five-year period and 8,000 jobs in Akron rubber plants.

For the first time in its history, Ohio was not growing demographically. A 22 percent increase in population in the 1950s fell to under 10 percent in the 1960s and barely struggled to 1.5 percent in the 1970s. There were approximately 10.6 million Ohioans in 1970 and roughly 10.7 million a decade later. Faced with dismal job prospects, young and middle-aged Ohioans went south and west. Older people, attracted by air-conditioned retirement communities in Florida, Georgia, and South Carolina, did the same. Those who stayed in Ohio more often than not found work in low-paying jobs at fast-food restaurants or retail stores with few or no benefits. Residents of "the rust belt," Ohioans were living in a stagnant world.

In the popular imagination, Ohio was the place where the Fernald Feed Materials Production Center, northwest of Cincinnati, released hundreds of thousands of pounds of uranium byproducts and other unhealthy materials into the air, and the Olentangy River in Columbus was desecrated with plastic bags, soft-drink bottles, tires, car parts, and canisters of household products full of chemicals. Cleveland was "the mistake on the lake," a city where the Cuyahoga River caught fire in the early 1970s, a city that lost its professional football team in 1996. Cleveland's population plummeted from 914,800 in 1950 to 573,800 in 1980. The drop was especially precipitous in the 1970s, falling by close to 25 percent. In 1983 Cleveland-area native Chrissie Hynde of the rock group The Pretenders sang of the transformation in "My City Was Gone." She "went back to Ohio," but "[t]here was no downtown." "My pretty countryside / Had been paved down the middle / By a government that had no pride. / The farms of Ohio / Had been replaced by shopping malls / And Muzak filled the air / From Seneca to Cuyahoga Falls."[7]

Like other cities, Cleveland staged a comeback in the 1990s. The Rock and Roll Hall of Fame and new stadiums for the Cleveland Indians and the Cleveland Browns anchored a multimillion dollar downtown redevelopment called the Central Market Gateway Project. On television, native son Drew Carey starred in a popular sitcom that poked good-natured fun at Cleveland's working-class population and contended that "Cleveland rocks." Visitors and suburbanites did trek to bars and restaurants in the Flats area to spend lots of money. But little of it benefited the people of Cleveland. In 1970, 17 percent of them lived in poverty; in the mid-1990s, the number was 40 percent, and only 38 percent of high school students graduated.[8]

Economic decline fueled a sense of crisis. Why follow middle-class nostrums about decorum and self-discipline when it led to so few tangible rewards? In their dress, in their manners, in their predilection for the abuse of drugs and alcohol, and in their taste for music and movies, many Ohioans—especially young people—expressed frustration and hostility. Cynical about politics, few people looked to government for answers. Instead, they sought solace in diversions and vented their bitterness at each other. As early as March 1968, a union member in Youngstown argued that many people did not participate in the public culture because they had given up. They believed that "there is no sense in voting because all politicians are crooks, and look out for their own, and special interests." They were tired of "so called liberals" who wanted to spend their money. They were "tired of Viet-Nam, foreign aid, civil rights 'give away programs,' political corruption, and high taxes."[9] Novels written by Ohioans often told of alienation. Even popular mystery writers such as Jonathan Valin and Les Roberts, who set their stories of hard-bitten individuals in the dark worlds of Cincinnati and Cleveland, suggested that life in Ohio was a matter of survival. There was no sense in putting one's faith in institutions or middle-class shibboleths. In a corrupt world, decency was a matter of maintaining one's own integrity on one's own terms.

An important early spokesman for this point of view was the poet and underground publisher d. a. levy. Born in Cleveland in 1942, levy was at the center of the city's countercultural community until his death in 1968 following his prosecution for contributing to the delinquency of minors by reading his poetry to teenagers. Levy was eager to expose middle-class hypocrisy and celebrate a Cleveland without pretense. One friend said that levy showed him "the actual Cleveland." Levy "imagined frescoes were painted under the bridges." In his mind, "Cleveland fell out of the gloomy steel mill smog of daily bread and suffering into some other stream of jewels, something lovely and familiarly strange." He thought about "what could be and probably is, beyond the struggle of problems to keep bodies fed and children growing in a culture of receding wisdom."[10]

Yet levy's vision was bleak. His history of Cleveland was one of exploitation and repression, starting with Indians and "Mose Ass Cleaveland" and moving to the triumph of "money myth and warped tradition." A city inhabited by African Americans, "hillbillies," Puerto Ricans, and prostitutes, Cleveland in the 1960s was a lonely place lost in a kind of "indian summer." It was a city "where the mayor and councilmen suck money from the federal govt and cosa nostra and syndicates," believe that they should "never let the little people know whats happening," and blame problems "on the communists . . . or the black militants or the illiterate hippies." In such a world, people can only live in the here and now, finding solace in sex and drugs and defiance.[11]

Many Ohioans lamented this attitude and the moral decline they attributed to it. Pilot Paul Tibbets, who dropped the atomic bomb on Hiroshima in August 1945, lived a conventional middle-class life in Columbus after World War II. In the late 1990s, Tibbets worried that his generation had lost a more important war. Americans were no longer patriotic. They no longer had "Discipline." They opposed the military draft because "they don't want to be told what to do." Tibbets wondered why he had fought to produce a world in which people were purposefully "undignified . . . in their conduct and mannerisms," in which there were so "many loudmouths . . . walking around, not caring who they are offending."[12] Tibbets simply did not understand the frustrations experienced by people for whom the possibilities of life in Ohio seemed to be narrowing. Like d. a. levy, they saw no reason to abide by rules that they thought worked only for a few.

In Mike Henson's 1980 novel, *Ransack,* a young Appalachian man is lost in a world that seems to be falling down around him. Finding solace in using drugs, abusing women he cannot understand, fending off policemen who seem intent on harassing him, working at a job that involves tearing down buildings, Seth just wants "to be let alone." He lives in the Over-the-Rhine section of Cincinnati, not because he likes it but because it is what he knows and because things are less likely to go wrong there than elsewhere. Cincinnati is "the only city he could remember where anything ever went halfway right." Even there, however, much is wrong. While Seth is taking apart a mantle in a condemned building, he finds an old silver dollar with a "Liberty's head" on it that he hopes will be worth some money. "But when he tried to pick it up, it broke into foil and black dust and the foil dropped to the floor and the dust capped his finger-tips and he felt them burn as if they had made their own acid until he rubbed them on his shirt." It is literally as if every time he reaches out for something better, it disintegrates. No wonder Seth despairs. Although his friend Ray tells him they can survive by working together, the police kill Ray. Seth is left to survive by himself. Redemption, if it comes, will come only if he concentrates on the task at hand and doesn't dream of future possibilities. "[H]e never thought so much about the chances he had lost, or on his failed nerves or on the rubble that had nearly buried him, but on what he had to do."[13]

James Wright expressed similar disillusionment about life in southeastern Ohio. Born in Martins Ferry in 1927, Wright grew up in a working-class family. He graduated from Kenyon College in 1952 and after a year on a Fulbright scholarship in Austria attended the University of Washington in Seattle. W. H. Auden chose Wright's *The Green Wall* to win the Yale Series of Younger Poets award; it was published in 1957. Wright taught at the University of Minnesota and Hunter College in New York City and published several books of poems. He loved traveling in Europe, especially in Italy. Wright won the 1972 Pulitzer Prize for his book *Collected Poems*. He died in 1980 from throat cancer at the age of 52.

Wright wrote frequently about Ohio, although he did not live in the state after he left Kenyon. His second wife, Annie, thought that "he carried the Ohio Valley and its people with him where ever he went." Wright said that his "feelings about [Ohio] are complicated." It was his "place, after all," and for better or worse, he was "stuck with it." Martins Ferry was ethnically diverse, with many "distinct communities in one small town." Life for most people was tough. Work of any kind was rarely rewarding. For many, high school football gave them purpose and community. No wonder Kenyon College was exciting. Suddenly, possibilities existed.[14]

Despite the travails of life, Wright believed in the story of Ohio as a dream betrayed. "My rotted Ohio"—with his family, friends, and history—was by the early 1970s a place Wright had to confront. He did so in *Two Citizens,* comparing Ohio to Italy and finding it wanting. The book, according to Wright, contains "some severe poems about Ohio." His anger was palpable. He had "loved [his] country, / When [he] was a little boy." Now, he had "nothing. / Ah, you bastards, / How I hate you." Wright wrote of the "ugliness" of Ohio, where people were prejudiced and mean, where they had desecrated the earth with their mines and farms, where men raped women and got away with it. People worked hard and accumulated little, least of all happiness. "[T]he Ohio / River was dying." Ohio was in decay. "Steubenville, / Ohio is a hell of a place to be buried," wrote Wright. "But there are some lovely places to be buried. / Like Rome."[15]

And yet, even if Italy was the home of artists and poets, tradition and history, and Ohio was dirty and ugly, Ohio was also home. It was inescapable. "The one tongue I can write in / Is my Ohioan. / There, most people are poor. / I thought I could not stand it / To go home any more. / Yet I go home, every year, / To calm down my wild mother, / And talk long with my brother." Steubenville was "a black crust" and America a "shallow hell where evil / Is an easy joke, forgotten / In a week." But it was Wright's hell. Knowing that no one is without sin, he looked somewhat unconvincingly for redemption. Alienated from Ohio, he was in love with it as well. Indeed, he grasped at anything to make it beautiful. In "Beautiful Ohio," Wright wrote of a sewer main emptying its "shining waterfall out of a pipe / Somebody had gouged through the slanted earth." The people in Martins Ferry, "my home, my native country," were caught in the light that revealed the waterfall, that revealed the "solid speed of their lives." "I know what we call it / Most of the time," wrote Wright. "But I have my own song for it, / And sometimes, even today, / I call it beauty."[16] While much of Wright's angst is personal, his mixture of rage and love reflected a gray period in the state's history when those who would love life in the state sought connection and beauty in waste and decay.

Feeling isolated, powerless, ignored by traditional institutions, Ohioans were less and less likely to value public civility. Indeed, the whole idea of a public culture that transcended local and individual interests was increasingly ridiculed. It was not that people were abandoning middle-class values as much as they believed that those values had abandoned them. Conservative critics lamented the disintegration of "traditional" values, not understanding that most of those values were historically constructed and that people upheld them only to the extent that they seemed to work for them and their friends and neighbors.

Perhaps the most important cultural development in Ohio in the last third of the twentieth century was a pronounced tendency to focus on private or group interests rather than some amorphous public interest. This was not simply a product of economic decline and personal frustration. It was also an assertion of particular interests within a larger society that promised much to everyone. The growth of identity politics based on race, gender, and ethnicity was a logical extension of the great expectations of the good life and the basic story of Ohio. Feminists, African Americans, and others in the 1960s and 1970s were simply demanding what they understood to be their rights as citizens. Yet many people were uncomfortable with their assertions of themselves from the margins to the center of public life in Ohio. What some saw as rights, others saw as privileges. What some saw as a necessary broadening of public life, others saw as a fragmenting of public life. Racism and sexism were important parts of the reaction as well. But much of the frustration in late-twentieth-century Ohio was born of fear, fear that the world was changing too much and that the demand for resources was far outrunning the ability of Ohio to provide enough for everyone.

Race and the Politics of Frustration

Nothing polarized Ohioans in the second half of the twentieth century more than race. By the 1960s, the African American migration from the South was nearly over. Blacks who had come north expecting both economic security and greater freedom were largely clustered in urban areas and a few suburbs. By 1980, African Americans constituted roughly 43 percent of the population of Cleveland (up from 16.2 percent in 1950), roughly one-third in Cincinnati, Dayton, and Youngstown, and about 22 percent in Akron and Columbus. Increasingly, whether people were white or black, there were fewer jobs in the cities, except in low-paying, low-benefit service employment. Living in segregated neighborhoods, partly by choice and partly because of discrimination in housing, blacks experienced the worst of the decline of Ohio's once vibrant urban areas. As cities lost industry and population, they also lost the resources to support and replace infrastructure. Roads, bridges, and basic services such as fire and police protection disintegrated. Public school systems were unable to provide the same quality of education as mostly white suburban districts. Even when city governments engaged in urban renewal projects in the 1970s and 1980s, they tended to improve certain sections, particularly those areas that featured the stadiums, theaters, and restaurants that attracted large numbers of visitors and suburbanites. Like many American cities, Cleveland, Cincinnati, and Columbus by the 1990s featured lavish downtown areas with huge hotels, elaborate restaurants and shopping areas, and state-of-the-art sports arenas and concert halls, all easily accessed from expressways. Meanwhile, neighborhoods suffered from neglect and disrepair.

By and large, cities in Ohio by the end of the twentieth century were home only to those people who could not afford to live in the suburbs. Urban residents had every reason to distrust local governments and real estate developers. They had no incentive to support a larger civic culture. When city leaders started to talk about the greater good of the city, they seemed more often than not to be talking about their private interests and those of white suburbanites. Meanwhile, many people blamed blacks for the condition of their neighborhoods. If only they would work harder, save more money, and practice self-discipline, they would achieve what others had achieved before them—the good life. Knowing full well that racism blocked many possibilities, many black Ohioans were no longer willing to believe that class would triumph over race.

In the late 1960s, declining economic opportunities and urban institutions combined with national promises of an end to racial discrimination (ranging from the 1954 Supreme Court ruling in *Brown v. Board of Education* to federal civil rights legislation of the mid-1960s) to create tension. In Cincinnati, angry black residents took to the streets of Avondale in June 1967. A more extensive protest took place on the east side of Cleveland from July 23 to July 28, 1968. Arson and looting of property permeated the Glenville area, a Jewish center in the 1940s that had become a black neighborhood. Sixty-three businesses were damaged or destroyed, with losses totaling more than $2 million. More disturbing was the personal violence, much of it directed at whites. One gunfight, which lasted for more than an hour, left seven people dead and another fifteen wounded. Of the twenty-two casualties, fifteen were policemen. This was unusual because urban unrest usually resulted in far more black than white casualties. The 1968 uprising followed a smaller one in 1966 in Cleveland's Hough neighborhood, a black slum since the 1950s. Twenty-two hundred National Guardsmen brought in to restore order could not prevent the deaths of four blacks.

The violence in Ohio cities followed in the wake of slow progress toward the achievement of civil rights. In the early 1960s, Cleveland had around fifty separate civil rights organizations, some of which briefly united in the United Freedom Movement. Members of the UFM pushed for an end to de facto discrimination in city hiring and the public schools. Calls to desegregate Cleveland's public schools through busing aroused the ire of white ethnic citizens. In Murray Hill, the center of Little Italy, public demonstrations in January 1964 led to violence against blacks and journalists. Other incidents intensified growing awareness of the serious racial divisions in Cleveland. Essentially, blacks who were demanding their full rights as citizens were running into opposition from whites who saw black assertiveness as a threat to their way of life.

The Glenville gunfight resulted from escalating tensions. In July 1968, Fred (Ahmed) Evans lived in an apartment on Auburndale Avenue. Evans was a leader of the Black Nationalists of New Libya. The police believed that Evans and his allies were hoarding guns in his apartment in preparation for assassination attempts on prominent public figures, but they could not arrest him because they had no direct evidence of his possession of automatic weapons. Meanwhile, Evans was upset because a white landlord was evicting him from a long-deserted storefront on Hough Avenue where he was trying to start an African American culture shop. Black leaders visited Evans on the evening of July 23 in an attempt to prevent violence. Later that night, an anxious Evans responded to the sound of shots by firing, precipitating the gun battle that produced twenty-two casualties. News of the encounter brought thousands of people into the streets. Mayor Carl B. Stokes attempted to control the situation by sending only black policemen into the area on July 24. He hoped that blacks would settle the problem among themselves. The next day, the mayor, bowing to pressure from worried whites, reversed himself and called for the National Guard. The presence of armed white soldiers and police officers restored order to Glenville.

While many whites saw the loss of property and life as symbolic of the general lawlessness of blacks, some blacks believed that the only way African Americans could overcome the effects of racism was to take the law into their own hands. Why should they obey institutions that served the interests of those who would keep them in subjugation, who blamed their problems on them? After his conviction on seven counts of first-degree murder in May 1969, Evans refused to express regret for the loss of life. He did not think his punishment would end the trouble. Nothing would stop "the black man who are willing, who are able, who are strong enough to stand up. . . . I feel justified in that I did the best I could." The white judge who sentenced him to the electric chair rejected Evans's argument. He thought it "perfectly obvious that we cannot have a system where every man is his own law."[17]

Ironically, the Glenville uprising occurred shortly after Cleveland had elected a black mayor. In 1967, 95 percent of African American voters and 19.4 percent of white voters united to make Carl B. Stokes the first popularly elected mayor of a major American city with a majority white population. Stokes had grown up in Cleveland. A lawyer and former liquor enforcement agent, he had served three terms in the Ohio General Assembly and had lost a race for mayor in 1965. Stokes lived the life of a politician, trying to steer between expediency and commitment.

The ambitious Stokes had not sought a seat on the Cleveland city council. He wanted to become a state legislator, which meant that he had to win one of the top spots in a countywide Democratic primary. Running in 1960, Stokes courted white voters. He went to the suburbs and spoke before groups of working-class ethnic whites. Stokes prided himself on his respectable appearance and his command of language. Needing white support to win, he formed a slate with white candidates. Stokes narrowly finished eighteenth in a race for seventeen slots on the Democratic ballot. When he ran again in 1962, he won in no small part because he had proved to both blacks and whites in 1960 that an African American could compete. Once in Columbus, he focused on civil rights, housing, and welfare but not on regular attendance. Like his brother, Louis, who was elected to the U.S. Congress in 1968, Carl Stokes was important less for what he did than who he was. When he became mayor of Cleveland in 1967, his narrow victory suggested that a black man could make it to the highest levels of power in Ohio.

As mayor, Stokes was a mixed success. He collaborated with real estate interests and lobbied the federal government. During his four years in office, 5,496 public housing units were constructed in Cleveland. In the aftermath of the assassination of Martin Luther King Jr. in April 1968, Stokes spearheaded a movement called Cleveland: NOW! to rebuild the city. In the late 1960s, the program raised and spent more than $5 million on public housing, day care centers, recreation centers, drug-treatment centers, and jobs while fostering a sense of community action. Stokes appointed blacks to key political offices, saw to it that black businesses won government contracts, and tried to change the attitudes as well as the demographics of the police department, with little success.

Stokes was proud of his record, and when he left office he believed that he had been driven out by people who were afraid of him. "When you start dealing with real change," he wrote in his self-serving autobiography, "you are talking about interfering with those who are in possession of something. . . . [W]hen you start dealing with the basic fundamentals of housing and schools and jobs, then you are dealing with a resistance that is not going to yield peacefully." In some ways, business interests and journalists were the least of Stokes's problems. The real challenge was to overcome the hostility of "those who are in possession, the middle-class people who have the jobs, who live in the neighborhoods with the nice decent housing and the recreational areas that are well maintained."[18] By 1978, 132 black men and women held political offices in Ohio. Most sat on city councils and boards of education.[19] Yet they were a tiny minority of officeholders and rarely represented an area that was not predominantly black. The progress made by blacks in public life was uneven at best. For all the attention on the Stokes brothers in Cleveland, their success did not herald a revolution in black participation in politics.

Race nonetheless dominated local politics because of the chasm between whites and blacks. No issue was more critical in this regard than the busing of public school students to achieve racial balance. Mandated by federal judges in cities such as Cleveland, the integration of public schools began and ended with race. To be sure, the crucial issue for most parents was the quality of education. But urban school systems had neither the tax base nor the morale of largely white suburban districts. More than an effort to make schools diverse, busing was also an effort to give black students in inner cities the same opportunities enjoyed by white students in suburbs.

White parents generally resisted busing, whether it involved taking their children to urban schools or bringing black students to suburban schools. Parents worried that busing would lessen the quality of all schools while making them more dangerous for everyone. Beyond race, busing challenged an age-old truism: that control of public education was largely a local concern, and that the kind of education and the amount of support it received in each school district was a matter for local people to decide.

In Dayton, the local board of education (by law, after 1920, the regulator of public schools) maintained separate elementary school buildings for black students. White students attended a high school in their neighborhood, while Dunbar High School took black students from all over the city. Everyone at Dunbar, from the principal through the students, was African American. Despite the fact that some blacks attended other schools, in 1951 and 1952, thirty-eight of forty-seven schools in Dayton were more than 90 percent white or black. The board of education contended that the de facto segregation was strictly voluntary.

The 1950s saw a rapid increase in African American residents and a national movement for civil rights, spawned in part by the 1954 U.S. Supreme Court's decision in *Brown v. Board of Education* declaring separate but equal facilities unconstitutional. Dayton voters elected a black man, the Reverend J. Wellby Broadus, as one of the seven at-large members of the board of education. There also was concerted pressure from the African American community for integration. School officials contended that they were doing all they could. Still, in the early 1970s, strict segregation remained the rule, even as the number of black students in the district as a whole rose above 40 percent. Like other Ohio cities, Dayton experienced heightened racial tensions in the late 1960s and 1970s. The problem went beyond the social injustice of segregation. Black parents believed that the city school district was suffering in terms of financial support and overall quality in comparison with largely white suburban districts.

Under federal order, the Dayton school board worked unsuccessfully to reduce segregation in the early 1970s through a policy of voluntary compliance. Meanwhile, the issue of integration polarized voters and school board members. Tension increased exponentially in 1972 with discussion of a plan to bus students from suburban districts into the city. The idea was to address the problem as a metropolitan one that required the integration of suburban and urban students. Opposition to the proposal was fierce among supporters of local control.

Opponents of busing dominated the Dayton school board throughout the 1970s. Nonetheless, busing occurred, beginning in 1975 as a result of a federal court order. Some white parents chose to send their children to private schools, usually religious in nature. Others moved to the suburbs as part of "white flight." In 1968, roughly 62 percent of Dayton school students were white; by 1980, the percentage had fallen to 43.4 percent. While white parents supported racial integration in theory, they were generally critical of busing. Meanwhile, a more multicultural curriculum could not compensate for the decline in the city's tax base that followed suburban growth. Dayton's public schools, like those in other urban areas, did not have the resources to compete with the suburban districts that surrounded them. Of the six hundred school districts in Ohio, the Dayton suburb of Oakwood ranked sixth in 1995 in standardized test scores; Dayton was 596. Predominantly white Oakwood was worlds away from Dayton in the possibilities available to its children.[20]

The same was true in the Columbus metropolitan area. In March 1977, a federal court decision in *Penick v. Columbus Board of Education* mandated the desegregation of the deliberately segregated school system. When East High School opened as a desegregated school in September 1979, its population went from 55 percent black to 55 percent white. Columbus had avoided the public racial tensions that had occurred in other Ohio cities. Indeed, civic and business leaders, taking pride in the fact that Columbus was peaceful, tried to turn the business of desegregating schools into a way of boosting the city as a great place to live and invest. Focusing only on the successful implementation of busing, they ignored long-term problems in race relations and school funding. In the words of historian Gregory S. Jacobs, they tended to put "civic order over civil rights."[21]

Columbus got by with so little public trouble because of the ways in which it grew. In the 1950s and 1960s, the city had expanded rapidly through annexation. City officials used their near monopoly on water and sewage services to entice suburbs to become part of Columbus. Beginning in 1965, they also encouraged the development of "common areas" within the city that would be served by suburban schools. That is, people could live in the city of Columbus and send their children to schools run by suburban school boards. The growth of the city and the growth of the schools were severed. Meanwhile, the financial resources available to the city schools declined precipitously. In the late 1970s, the district cut its budget by $28 million. Columbus had greater poverty, a stagnating tax base, and fewer voters with children.

Many critics of busing blamed desegregation for the decline of city school districts. Some saw busing as a pipe dream that alienated white middle-class families and did nothing for the quality of education. Yet over the years, the real culprit appeared to be the loss of revenue. Columbus simply could not keep up with its affluent suburbs of Dublin and Worthington. In the 1980s, the city district faced a 16.2 percent decline in the taxable value of personal property, while taxable value of personal property in the common areas doubled.

The generally dismal state of urban school districts reflected the state of Ohio's cities beyond areas benefiting from commercial development that lured suburbanites downtown for diversion. The population of the Over-the-Rhine section of Cincinnati in 1990 was 9,752,

71 percent of which (6,875) was African American. With a median household income of $5,000 (compared to $21,006 for Cincinnati as a whole), the area was rife with drugs, crime, and disrepair.

In the middle of the twentieth century, Cincinnati leaders and planners proposed to demolish neighborhoods such as Over-the-Rhine that they deemed slums. The idea was to create new industry and housing and make way for expressways. The cost, of course, was the dislocation of residents. By the 1960s and 1970s, the city focused on the rehabilitation and renewal of neighborhoods. Leaders hoped to make Over-the-Rhine into an attractive area for young professionals interested in reviving neighborhood life in an integrated neighborhood. This plan foundered on the growing assertiveness of black and Appalachian residents in Over-the-Rhine who wished to protect their neighborhood from takeover by commercial developers and affluent white professionals aided and abetted by city government.

Stanley "Buddy" Gray was perhaps the most prominent of the many community organizers in Over-the-Rhine. Born on a farm east of Cincinnati, Gray was white and middle class. Radicalized by participation in the antiwar movement while a student at Purdue University, he returned to Cincinnati in the 1970s to work with the poor. Gray saw himself as "a hard-nosed radical, a street fighter for street people," who would contest every effort to renovate Over-the-Rhine into a haven for "urban gentry." His major opponent in the 1980s was James Tarbell, who had grown up in Hyde Park and had owned nightclubs in Clifton and near Over-the-Rhine. Initially distrustful of politicians and businessmen, Tarbell grew as disdainful of "sloppy people" who seemed disinterested in improving themselves as he was of some activists.[22] Tarbell wanted middle-class and commercial development to transform Over-the-Rhine, while Gray and company stood for local control. The city council eventually sided with Gray and his vision of a neighborhood controlled by the people who lived there, their poverty notwithstanding. Residents of poor, multicultural areas of the city wanted no part of urban renewal that would drive them away and enrich developers and middle-class professionals. Buddy Gray's personal campaign ended ironically. On November 15, 1996, Wilbur Worthen, a man whom Gray had befriended and helped, shot and killed the activist in his office in the Drop-Inn Shelter in Over-the-Rhine. Despite Worthen's long history of mental illness, the tragedy heightened the tension between distrustful local residents on the one side and developers and politicians on the other.

Racial hostility compounded the challenges facing Ohio's cities. Both African Americans and working-class whites confronted the same problems, including fewer industrial jobs, deteriorating public schools, and a declining urban tax base. Nevertheless, they tended to lash out at each other, seeing the world as a zero-sum game in which one's group's gain was another's loss. On radio talk-shows, coarse and angry words increasingly characterized discussions of everything from sports to politics. A Youngstown union member exclaimed in 1968 that "so called white racists are getting tired of being blamed for some thing that has been aided and condoned by the politicians of this country for years. I refer to the so called ghetto or slum. . . . Even these people [African American homeowners] do not want to live with the low class, shiftless, the majority of whom are unwed mothers, and fathers who do not wish to work and are satisfied to live like pigs and be supported by us suckers. In my opinion these people should be forced to live like human beings, deprived of the right to vote and perhaps shipped off to some reservation."[23]

Black or white, urban Ohioans, confronted with massive unemployment and underemployment and deteriorating surroundings, tended to think it better to take care of their own world than entrust it to someone else. As long as Ohio seemed to many people to a land of possibility, those who governed it and who benefited from its expansion had legitimacy. But when that sense of possibility all but disappeared in the 1970s, people living on the margins of society had no incentive to support a collective civic culture. It made more sense to put their own agendas first, to argue from particular interests and to identify themselves by race, gender, class, or ethnicity rather than some vague political construct such as citizenship.

Higher Education and the Politics of Development

Arguably the most important politician and unquestionably the most colorful figure in Ohio in the second half of the twentieth century was James A. Rhodes. Rhodes was born in Jackson County in 1909 to a middle-class family of Welsh descent. His family moved to Springfield after the death of his father, a mine superintendent. Popular, ambitious, easy to get along with, Rhodes briefly attended Ohio State and then opened Jim's Place on High Street near the university, where he sold doughnuts and hamburgers and presided over a lively atmosphere.

In 1934, Rhodes ran for the local Republican ward committee. He won with a gregarious, overpowering style that would serve him well as he moved up to become school board member, city auditor, mayor of Columbus, state auditor, and four-time governor of Ohio. In the 1940s, Rhodes ran Columbus with ringing endorsements of the value of development. He was a key figure in the annexation of suburbs that fueled the city's growth. On the state level in the 1950s, Rhodes honed a folksy, populist image. As country club Republicans cringed, he made no effort to hide his southern Ohio accent or correct his misstatements. Rhodes pronounced Ohio as "O-hi-ah" and once called Ohio University "a venereal institution."[24]

The work of Ray C. Bliss, who became chairman of the Ohio Republican Party in 1949, was no less important than Rhodes's. Bliss transformed the party of Bricker and Taft into a modern institution with such success that he became chairman of the national Republican Party. Characteristically cautious, Bliss emphasized organization over ideology. He believed that the key to victory in a hard-fought state such as Ohio lay in intensive and extensive preparation. Bliss coordinated candidacies, promoted voting drives, raised money, and ceded some authority to county committees. Most innovative, perhaps, was his attention to polls and his willingness to work with citizen organizations and amateur politicians in Ohio's burgeoning suburbs. He thrived on finding out what he could do to help his party win—and that involved giving voters what they thought they wanted without compromising the beliefs of the party. Pragmatic above all else, committed to victory for the party at all costs, Bliss seemed to many to epitomize the stereotypical organization man of the 1950s and early 1960s.

Rhodes's blustering style and Bliss's thorough preparation paved the way to the governor's victories in 1962, 1966, 1974, and 1980.

They also won, however, because Rhodes championed development as the key to all of Ohio's woes, real and imagined, present and future. Putting aside cultural issues, Rhodes argued that jobs would make everything right. Government could help improve employment by improving infrastructure, that is, by building roads and expanding education, and by making Ohio attractive to investors in and out of state with tax breaks and incentives. Rhodes and Bliss were in essence stealing part of their Democratic opponents' thunder by harping on jobs. More than that, they were responding to the growing perception in the 1960s and 1970s that Ohio's economy was in decline.

Rhodes believed in pragmatic solutions: give as many people as possible a straightforward, useful education and the world would be a better place. Underlying his proposal was lingering resentment about his own mediocre academic performance and lack of a college degree. Nonetheless, his support of vocational education was coherent, if naive. "The solution," the governor argued in 1970, "rests in jobs, employment, and the security which these provide." Vocational education was *"education with a purpose."* Not only would it provide jobs, it would permit Ohioans to adjust to a changing economy and avoid becoming "misfits." Ohio would not prosper unless its schools provided "with equal dedication and honor, the study of art and typewriting, history and accounting, philosophy and plumbing.[25]

The politics of development was nothing new; Ohio leaders had been pressing for infrastructure since the state was founded. But Rhodes's ideas were different. He was focused on jobs, not citizenship. His view of education boiled down to basic needs—income and security—and included almost no emphasis on the opening of the mind or the training of broad-minded citizens.

At the same time, Rhodes's emphasis on development was a clever response to the politics of pluralism. Rather than harp on the social issues that divided Ohioans (and made many suspicious of Republicans), he highlighted what they had in common—a desire for material progress. The governor relentlessly promoted Ohio (and himself). He took a personal interest in the annual state fair and saw to it that it showcased top entertainers. He created the Rhodes Raiders, a group of officials and developers whose assignment was to travel around the world to tout Ohio as a good place for industrial investment. He got the presidents of the six state universities to agree to the creation of a state board of regents in return for his support of a $250 million bond issue that would raise some $175 million for higher education. Before the end of Rhodes's second term in 1970, the number of state universities rose from six to twelve and regional campuses and vocational schools mushroomed. Rhodes promised that there would be some sort of higher education within thirty miles of the home of every citizen of Ohio.

Most spectacularly, the governor got voters to approve four bond issues, totaling $1.8 billion, that financed highways, state parks, industrial developments, and a prison. Across from the Greek Revival statehouse rose a forty-story office building that would eventually carry Rhodes's name. Critics contended that Rhodes's notion of development was short-sighted, that it consisted of bricks and mortar without substance. The explosion of university buildings could not disguise the fact that as a percentage of its budget, Ohio was spending less and less on public education. Rhodes did virtually nothing for the poor and underprivileged in Ohio. In fact, state support of education per pupil fell from 40 to 30 percent while he was in charge. On the other hand, those who wanted better roads, better buildings, easily accessible higher education, and improved state parks admired him.

Ironically, the growth of higher education initially seemed to contradict the governor's insistence that development would float all boats and therefore unify Ohioans. Universities were indeed becoming central to a new kind of economy emerging throughout the United States. With demand skyrocketing for people trained in marketing, sales, health care, law, and technology, higher education was at a premium. By the 1970s, a college degree was virtually required for a professional job, something that had not been true in the 1940s.

Fueled by this rising demand for education and by government funding spurred by the Cold War, universities exploded in the third quarter of the twentieth century. The Ohio State University became one of the largest institutions in the country, with more than fifty thousand students, and one of the largest employers in the Columbus area. The number of faculty members, graduate students, administrators, and clerical and maintenance workers grew with the size of the student body. Hospitals and health-care facilities employed thousands. Meanwhile, all these people spent money on food, housing, clothing, and entertainment. Cheap housing units, restaurants, movie theaters, and strip and covered malls dotted the landscape around Ohio State and beyond it into the northern suburbs of the state capital. A similar process was at work around municipal universities in Cincinnati and Toledo, which were absorbed into the state system, as well as state institutions such as Kent State, Ohio University, and Bowling Green. Universities dominated regional economies. By the 1980s, Miami University was the largest employer in Butler County.

The growing importance of higher education inevitably made universities both centers and symbols of cultural conflict. Governor Rhodes's antipathy toward academics reflected a powerful suspicion among many middle-class Ohioans that universities were dangerous places. The antiwar protests focused this unease. Almost overnight, universities had become enormous presences in the lives of Ohioans, exerting economic influence unimaginable before World War II. Despite the fact that most faculty and students were conventional, universities acquired a reputation as hotbeds of radicalism where leftist faculty encouraged students to defy "the system." Ohioans associated long hair, drugs, rock music, and countercultural behavior with college students and their teachers.

The complaints of residents of Kent, Athens, Bowling Green, and Oxford about unruly students echoed those of neighbors of colleges since time immemorial. Students had always had wild parties and engaged in what could be construed as antisocial behavior. What was different in the 1960s and 1970s was size and volume. Once students had numbered in the hundreds; now there were tens of thousands. Unable to find housing on campuses ill-equipped to handle their growing numbers, students began to live in apartments in residential neighborhoods. Their unruliness took on an image out of proportion to their numbers because they were more visible and because universities were more powerful.

The fear that universities were undermining traditional values informed much of the hostility on the part of Governor Rhodes and other Ohioans to the events at Kent State. They genuinely believed that there were radical forces at work on that campus and others. The citizens of Ohio had lost control of higher education. Universities, which were supposed to train young people to be good citizens, now appeared to be training them to challenge the basic values that had supposedly guided the state for more than a century.

While exaggerated, anxiety about higher education was not unreasonable. Especially in the humanities, some faculty members who had come of age in the 1950s and 1960s were highly critical of American society in general and Ohio in particular. Many believed that there were deep flaws in economic and political structures that inhibited true democracy and promoted injustice. Scholarship in some cases became an extension of social reform, a continuation of movements for civil rights for African Americans and women. Universities drew attention to the diversity of society by creating programs in black and women's studies. They campaigned to draw more minority students, whether African Americans, Hispanic Americans, or Asian Americans. To a remarkable extent, Ohio universities by the 1990s seemed to embody the new general emphasis on the primacy of private identity. No longer willing to trust the workings of a generic civic culture, students and faculty proudly asserted their particular interests, seeing the university as Buddy Gray had seen Cincinnati, as a collection of interest groups who had to demand resources or lose everything.

As universities diversified their curriculum and filled their libraries with books and articles highlighting the multicultural nature of American society and pointing out the hypocrisies of life in the U.S., present and past, many politicians and middle-class citizens reacted with hostility. Journalists and critics declared that university faculty increasingly taught less and published more, that they dedicated themselves to undermining civic culture rather than promoting it, that they filled their students' heads with academic jargon while they neglected the basic skills necessary for surviving, let alone prospering, in the new economy. University faculty countered that they were doing nothing more than empowering people who had long been invisible, giving voice to those who had been shunted aside. The "traditional values" advocated by middle-class Ohioans, they argued, were historically constructed. They served the interests of certain kinds of people—white, middle class, and male; they silenced others by declaring the values of the white middle class to be universal.

These arguments continued within and without the academy. Rather than unifying Ohioans, universities appeared to be dividing them. What some people saw as true democracy and freedom of expression, others saw as signs of moral decay and social disintegration.

Incidents away from college campuses played a central role in the larger debate. One of the more famous was the controversy over an exhibit of Robert Mapplethorpe's sadomasochistic and homoerotic photographs in Cincinnati's Contemporary Arts Center in 1989. City officials, who had a long history of zealously prosecuting anyone who violated what they considered to be community standards of decency—including Larry Flynt, the publisher of *Penthouse* magazine—indicted the center's director for obscenity. The national controversy reinforced Cincinnati's reputation as a bastion of conservatism. But while many snickered at Cincinnati's prudery and voiced outrage at the repression of free expression, others applauded the willingness of city officials to defend their community from the influence of people and ideas they saw as objectionable.

Perhaps nowhere was this cultural war more spirited than over the issue of women's role in society. Ohio was not at the forefront of the new wave of feminism that grew out of the civil rights and anti-Vietnam movements of the 1960s. The number of females in Ohio's civilian workforce doubled between 1950 and 1970, especially in nursing, teaching, and government. Women became more conscious of discrimination in issues such as equal pay for equal work, difficulties in winning promotions, requests for maternity leave, and child care. But for the most part, women in Ohio focused on pragmatic matters. The General Assembly responded to some extent with legislation that outlawed discrimination based on gender as well as race and age.

The most famous Ohio feminist was Gloria Steinem. Steinem's parents were Jews whose own parents had migrated to Toledo from Poland and Germany. Although the Steinems lived in Clarklake, Michigan, their daughter Gloria was born in Toledo in March 1934. The family moved to Toledo in 1945, and Gloria remained there until she left for Georgetown University. Years later, Steinem would emphasize the hardships of her life in Toledo, constructing her story as a kind of conversion narrative of how she found salvation in feminism.

In the early 1970s, Steinem told *Newsweek* that "East Toledo is 'Joe' country, the kind of place where they beat up the first available black on Saturday night. They considered us nuts on two counts: we read books and we were poorer than they were. The girls all got married before they graduated because they were pregnant. I had one girl friend like that who had four children too fast. Her teeth fell out. Now she sits at home and her husband beats her from time to time."[26] Exaggerated as it was, Steinem's story of her early life was powerful both in its suggestion of the possibilities of rising from obscurity and in its indictment of everyday life. While Steinem had little direct influence in Ohio, her narrative of a conventional life in which the possibilities were inhibited by rampant sexism and misogyny was a model of its kind.

By the 1970s and 1980s, other Ohio women were telling similar stories. Subtle and not so subtle discrimination, they believed, kept them from realizing their full potential as citizens. The story of Ohio, they suggested, was a male story—one developed by and for white men. Women had played major roles in the development of the state, but they were rarely part of the narrative. Not holding positions of power, they had been deliberately excluded from decision making. In the last third of the twentieth century, women, finding strength in a common cause, began to move into fields previously dominated by men. There was obvious growth in the number of female doctors, professors, lawyers, journalists, and politicians. In 1992, twenty-nine women served in the Ohio General Assembly. Nancy Hollister of Marietta became Ohio's first female lieutenant governor in 1990 and briefly served as the state's chief executive in 1999 when Governor George Voinovich resigned early in order to start his term as a U.S. senator. Meanwhile, women had some success in improving child-care facilities and winning maternity leave, although the gender gap in wages narrowed only slightly.

By the 1980s, there was a divergence in attitude toward women's issues. While many Ohioans supported the right of women to work, equal pay, child care, and other concrete issues, fewer and fewer applauded the term "feminist." Ohio had ratified the Equal Rights Amendment to the U.S. Constitution in 1974. But a decade later its citizens felt uncomfortable with ardent feminism. As with blacks and other minorities, many felt that feminists had gone too far, demanding special attention for women that went beyond equality and became privilege. Feminists were criticized for putting the interests of some women above the interests of the whole, for emphasizing their particular agenda at the cost of civic culture in general.

Meanwhile, feminism survived, even prospered, on university campuses. Bookstores and community organizations proudly proclaimed their feminist perspective. Yet for Ohioans in general the assertiveness of feminists suggested a distortion of the traditional organization of society. Even though committed feminists were often a relatively small group, they became symbols of a popular perception of universities as centers of extremist politics.

In many ways, the extraordinary popularity of Helen Hooven Santmyer's novel *". . . And Ladies of the Club"* rested on its evocation of a different place and a different kind of feminism. Originally published by the Ohio State University Press in 1982, the hefty narrative of the lives of a handful of middle-class women who belong to the Waynesboro Women's Club became a best-seller after a commercial press picked it up two years later. The key figure in the novel is Anne Alexander, the valedictorian of her high school class in 1868. The book expertly intersects the rather ordinary details of her life—her marriage, her children, her death—with larger national political issues. Alexander is something like Santmyer herself, a woman of strong opinions who is a powerful presence in the lives of her relatives and neighbors. She supports the causes of middle-class Republican women such as temperance. She finds strength and sustenance in her association with her friends. Alexander's club empowers her to publicly preach self-discipline and character, but in no way does she challenge the basic justice of the world in which she lives. Shortly before her death, she worries that Franklin Roosevelt's commitment to government's taking care of the poor (who "would rather be poor than work") "sounds like the decline of the Roman empire: bread and circuses. And once the people get the idea that the government has an obligation to support its citizens, there'll be no end to what they will demand."[27]

To many readers in the 1980s, Alexander's words seemed like a prophecy fulfilled. Old nostrums about character and work apparently had little appeal to modern people who placed their own interests above everything else and who talked incessantly about what was owed to them rather than what they owed to others. Liberals and conservatives alike expressed longing for small-town life and the good old days when things seemed to make sense. Books about lost towns such as New Burlington abounded, as did personal memoirs of life in Ohio villages, such as Ian Frazier's eloquent tribute to his hometown of Hudson in which he presented a complex portrait of a way of life undone by suburbanization and postindustrial development.[28] For good or ill, Ohioans on all sides seemed to agree that something had been lost. The world carefully constructed by middle-class people in the nineteenth century was slipping away.

In politics as in literature, Ohioans seemed happiest with the familiar. Voters returned the irrepressible Jim Rhodes to the governorship in 1975, electing him over incumbent Democrat John J. Gilligan of Cincinnati, who had pushed an income tax through the legislature and dramatically increased spending on education, welfare, mental health, and the environment. Despite the two terms served by Democrat Richard Celeste from 1984 to 1992, voters generally rejected the Democratic notion of development through tax-supported government programs in favor of the Republican version of development through tax relief and bonds. At the beginning of the twenty-first century, the Ohio Democratic Party was a shell of its former self. Issues aside, the majority of Ohioans were more comfortable with moderate politicians such as Democrat John Glenn and Republican George Voinovich.

The Significance of Pete Rose

On Monday evening, August 21, 1989, the Cincinnati Reds defeated the Chicago Cubs six to five. The victory was the last in the managerial career of Peter Edward Rose. Two days later, Rose accepted a lifetime suspension from professional baseball. He refused to admit that he had placed a bet on a baseball game, let alone on a contest in which the team he managed was involved. He took consolation in the fact that baseball commissioner A. Bartlett Giamatti agreed to consider reinstatement after one year and in a clause that said he neither admitted nor denied that he had gambled on baseball. More than a decade later, Rose was still banned from baseball. Particularly galling to him and his supporters was the fact that he was not considered for membership in the Hall of Fame in Cooperstown, New York.

Until 1989, Rose had led a charmed life. Signed by the Reds in 1960, he debuted as the team's second baseman in the spring of 1963. Rose spent the next sixteen seasons with the Cincinnati club, then signed as a free agent with the Philadelphia Phillies in late 1978. In 1983, he joined the Montreal Expos before returning to the Reds as player-manager in August 1984. In a career that spanned more than two decades, Rose had more hits (4,526) and played in more major-league games (3,562) than any other player. In 1973, he was named the Most Valuable Player in the National League. The *Sporting News* called him the Player of the Decade for the 1970s.

Individual success contributed to team success. The Reds and Phillies won three world championships and six league pennants with Rose. Most famous was his association with the Big Red Machine of the 1970s, one of the most successful teams in baseball history. Full of enthusiasm, Rose was the guy who raced to first base when he got a walk, who slid headfirst, who knocked over catcher Ray Fosse in order to score a run in the 1970 All Star game, who commented to Boston Red Sox catcher Carlton Fisk during the dramatic sixth game of the 1975 World Series, "Some kind of game, ain't it?"[29] Yankee stars Whitey Ford and Mickey Mantle gave the intense rookie his nickname, "Charlie Hustle," during spring training in 1963. On September 11, 1985, after his triumphant return to Cincinnati as player-manager, a line drive into left field gave Rose 4,192 career hits, the most in the history of the game.

Rose was popular, particularly in Cincinnati, because he was gregarious in public and quick with a quip. But Rose symbolized other things as well. His story, as he and others told it, was that of a kid from a blue-collar family who lived in Anderson Ferry, west of Cincinnati. His father, Peter, was a local sports hero who worked for a bank and devoted much of his life to inculcating discipline, ambition, and the importance of hard work in his children. Neither an academic star (he failed the tenth grade) nor a naturally gifted athlete, Pete Rose achieved fame and fortune through determination and grit. Avoiding alcohol and tobacco, Rose practiced for hours on end. He liked to work on what he did not do well. He studied pitchers and made a fetish out of statistics, especially his own. As a professional, he was versatile. Above all, he was durable. Blessed with a cocky confidence, he accepted defeat with equanimity, sure that victory would come again soon. Rose's reputation rested on his image as an ordinary guy who made it because he earned it.

The story of Pete Rose was not false, but, as is the case with most human beings, it disguised a multitude of sins. From the beginning, Rose was a notorious womanizer who flaunted his promiscuity. His teammates, moreover, rarely warmed to his self-absorption. Rose was always a hot dog, a preening show-off who craved the spotlight. When he joined the Reds, Rose was most comfortable with Frank Robinson and Vada Pinson, black men dealing with ostracism because of their race. Although he developed friendships with a few players, he was rarely popular in the clubhouse. When his obsession with gambling finally caught up with him in the late 1980s, few people who knew him were surprised. Indeed, Rose's associations with known gamblers had worried more than one teammate and journalist. It was not that Rose was a bad person. Rather, he was so fixated on his own success that he was unaware of his impact on other people.

Despite his good relations with many black athletes, Rose played his success as a white athlete for all that it was worth—literally. He told *Playboy* magazine in the late 1970s that he was marketable in no small part because he was white. "Look," Rose said, "if you owned Swanson's Pizza, would you want a black guy to do the commercial on TV for you? Would you like the black guy to pick up the pizza and bite into it? Try to sell it? I mean, would you want [African American] Dave Parker selling your pizza to America for you? Or would you want Pete Rose?" An incensed Parker believed that Rose was an obvious racist, a "neck," as he put it.[30] No doubt Parker was right, but it was entirely in keeping with Rose's personality to promote himself in any way possible without thinking about the consequences.

Rose's personal behavior led to paternity suits but never affected his popularity because he was generally seen as a man who defied conventions and challenged stuffy institutions. Like Muhammad Ali and other (mostly) black athletes in the 1970s and 1980s, Rose was a hero to people who enjoyed watching him mock the pomposity of the rich and powerful. No one could possibly have imagined a more appropriate nemesis than Commissioner Giamatti, the former Ivy League president who exuded erudition and gentility. Always the outsider, Rose was an alienated figure who did not allow anything or anyone to get in the way of his dreams. Rose succeeded, or so the story went, not because he was favored but because he earned it himself.

Rose revealed the fault lines in middle-class notions of life in Ohio. While he honored self-discipline in some parts of his life, he ignored it in others. He concentrated exclusively on private success and made no effort to contribute in any way to some larger public good. Even his teammates, who were hardly known for their lack of ego, considered him a "me-me-me player."[31] Rose epitomized as much as anyone the emergence of a new public culture in the second half of the twentieth century, one that focused almost exclusively on personal goals.

The furor that surrounded Rose's suspension also reflected the maturation of an increasingly raw public culture. The conversation in local newspapers and on radio call-in shows was bitter and vituperative. Some scorned Rose as a hypocrite who had betrayed his people, while others excoriated his critics. Cincinnatians, especially white males who saw themselves as working men, closed ranks and defended their hero. They attacked Rose's critics and tried to poke holes in baseball's indictment. If they failed to do so convincingly, they gave voice to a resentment that echoed throughout Ohio and the United States in general. Frustrated with life in a world of limited possibilities, they lashed out at everyone from overpaid athletes to effete intellectuals. They wondered why Rose was singled out for such harsh treatment when others guilty of heinous crimes received leniency. Some asked directly if only blacks were accorded special treatment in American society. If Rose had been a lawyer or a professor, would he have suffered such a fate? And look at the members of the Hall of Fame. Were they such paragons of virtue? In language full of class and racial prejudice, born of a profound sense of injustice and alienation, they railed against the system. Ironically, in so doing, they intensified the sense that Ohio—like the nation—was drifting ever more resolutely into a collection of separate groups whose goal was less some generic material and moral progress than getting what they wanted.

Rose's defenders correctly noted that his behavior was nothing new. Baseball players had always been a rough group. But in a culture that valued respectability, their foibles had been kept out of sight, just like those of politicians and businessmen. By the 1980s, however, Americans increasingly saw private behavior as a more reliable guide to a person's true character than public conduct. Removing the veil of public respectability laid bare a complex world of sometimes sordid humanity. A court battle with a former employee revealed Marge Schott, the principal owner of the Reds in the 1980s and early 1990s, as a sometimes petty woman with distinct racial and religious prejudices. In a 1992 deposition, Schott said she admired the "work ethics" of "Japs"; contended that "everybody's used the word [nigger] once in their lifetime"; professed that Jews "are not smarter than us, just sharper"; and argued that she had "met a lot of educated asses that can't do anything." When baseball commissioner Bud Selig suspended Schott for a year in early 1993, he did so because of "substantial and convincing evidence that . . . Mrs. Schott commonly used language that is racially and ethnically insensitive, offensive, and intolerable."[32] To say that such language was commonplace in Cincinnati in 1993 is not to defend or excuse her. Schott's troubles revealed the extent to which the line between private and public had disappeared. If piercing the phony superficiality of public images was a blow for honesty, it also cheapened public conversation into an endless series of exposés of hypocrisy.

Even after Rose went to jail for tax evasion, many Cincinnatians continued to admire him because, as writer Kevin Walzer argued, the citizens of the city really "*do* worship hard work, perseverance, and loyalty to family." Although Walzer conceded that Rose was "a less-than-exemplary husband and father," he knew that Rose on the baseball field was "a glorious embodiment of the work ethic." It was not his lack of talent that mattered. It was his character, his discipline, his commitment, and his endurance. "Who could fail to be inspired by such sights, even with knowledge of the conduct that banished him from the game?"[33]

No one in the nineteenth century believed that human beings were inherently perfect. The business of life, however, was to resist the baser instincts and strive to cultivate discipline so as to allow the better aspects of human nature to win out. Making this vision of progress specific engendered opposition and conflict, leading to dwindling interest in moral improvement and a greater emphasis on material progress and self-fulfillment. Revolutionary values and rhetoric had become stale bulwarks of a status quo. Pete Rose was in many ways emblematic of this new world. Resisting the dictates of middle-class morality and authority, he focused on himself. He recognized no laws, no restrictions, no constraints. No wonder that when he was punished, he resented it. He could not comprehend what he had done wrong.

Epilogue
"Champions of Their Lives"

—

OHIO HAS BECOME so synonymous with American normalcy that setting in the state a television show about aliens pretending to be human beings is an entirely predictable development. According to Terry Turner, one of the producers of *3rd Rock from the Sun,* "The aliens . . . looked at Earth and said 'What's the best cross-section of America and people that we can find?'" Turner had decided that Ohio was the obvious answer to that question during an initial visit in the 1970s. "[I]t looked like what I thought America looked like. Los Angeles doesn't and New York doesn't. . . . America, in my head, is Ohio."[1]

Turner's comment is hardly original. In American popular culture, Ohio, like the rest of the Midwest, is bland and predictable. "Aliens aren't going to land in New York City. They'd fit right in," Robert Thompson, professor of television, radio, and film at Syracuse University told *Ohio Magazine* in November 2000. Ohio, Thompson said, "epitomizes our collective image of what the country should be." On the other hand, "all of the hip, cool, in-the-know shows like *Friends* and *Sex and the City,* . . . are set in New York. There are no trends being set in Ohio." Or, as Turner's wife, Bonnie, with whom he produced both *3rd Rock from the Sun* and a short-lived show called *Normal, Ohio,* about a gay man returning to his family, puts it, "[T]here's something plain about Ohio." "But not in a bad way," her husband quickly clarifies.[2]

Bonnie Turner is a native of Toledo who intended her observation as a compliment. In Ohio, she believes, people "are at peace with where they live." They are "champions of their lives." Occasionally, friends or relatives ask her about Hollywood and wonder how they can get out of Ohio. Invariably, however, those people who visit her in Los Angeles are "blown away" by it and want to go home.[3] Turner no doubt exaggerates. But she is on to something when she suggests that many Ohioans at the beginning of the twenty-first century seem comfortable with their world. No longer seeing Ohio as a land of limitless possibilities, they accept it as a nice place to live; a place somewhere in the middle of everything; a place that is, according to the state tourist bureau, "the heart of it all."

Terry Ryan captured the lingering power of faith in individual character in a best-selling memoir of her mother. Evelyn Ryan was a housewife in Defiance in the 1950s and 1960s with ten children; an alcoholic, abusive husband; and an erratic income. Rather than allow herself to be crushed by her problems, the resourceful Mrs. Ryan began to write advertising slogans. Her cleverness enabled her to win a boatload of prizes—including appliances, shopping sprees, vacations, and cash that helped her family survive. Terry Ryan does not minimize the poverty and stress of her mother's life. But *The Prize Winner of Defiance, Ohio* is ultimately a nostalgic tribute to the perseverance of a woman who made the best of a bad situation. Evelyn Ryan did not wallow in self-pity or demand help from others. By saving herself, she became, in Bonnie Turner's phrase, the "champion of her life."[4]

Ohio, of course, is much more complex than these and other inspiring stories indicate. Its popular image as a land of solid people obscures the fact that it is a state with serious problems, few of which can be resolved by tales of individual persistence. Indeed, the widespread insistence on understanding Ohio as the embodiment of respectability, as a major source of what some describe as traditional American values, as a place that is comfortable, reveals the reluctance of many Ohioans to confront difficult problems that will not go away. It is easier to live in what one of the characters in poet Rita Dove's novel *Through the Ivory Gate* describes as a "calm" region inhospitable to any "human crisis," with minimal colors that offend "no sensibility."[5]

To be sure, Ohio, like the rest of the United States, experienced a sustained period of economic growth in the 1990s. The suburbs ringing large cities reaped the benefits of high-tech industries that located there, while sections of downtown Cleveland, Cincinnati, and Columbus gained new restaurants and shops centered on sports stadiums, museums, theaters, and malls. But all was not well. Cities continued to suffer from out-migration, declining tax revenues, and inadequate public services and the glittering lights of revitalized commercial districts deflected attention from dilapidated neighborhoods.

Overall, the economic malaise that has afflicted Ohio since the middle of the twentieth century has proved to be remarkably tenacious. While 11,353,140 people lived in Ohio in 2000, the 4.7 percent rate of population growth in the 1990s was well below the national average of 13.1 percent. Other Midwestern states were increasing faster, including Illinois at 8.6 percent and Michigan at 6.9 percent. Moreover, the fact that people of Hispanic or Latino origins constituted just 1.9 percent of Ohio's population in 2000, compared to 12.5 percent for the nation and 12.3 percent in Illinois, demonstrates the degree to which Ohio no longer reflects the demographic diversity of the United States. In 1999, per capita personal income in Ohio was $27,171, only 95 percent of the national average. Just 83,808 Ohioans owned farms, down from 99,739 in 1980. And while the number of jobs in service industries increased from 21.9 percent in 1989 to 25.3 percent in 1999, those in durable goods manufacturing fell from 20.8 percent to 16.9 percent in the same period. Sadly, Ohio at the beginning of the twentieth-first century is a portrait in stagnation.[6]

Meanwhile, perennial issues continue to divide Ohioans, none of which is more important than race. In April 2001, large numbers of African Americans in Cincinnati, reacting to yet another fatal shooting of a black man by a white police officer, protested years of racism and neglect. Some expressed their frustration in public meetings; others resorted to attacks on property and people and general defiance of authority. They were angry about racial profiling in stopping automobiles and investigating possible criminal activity as well as the extent to which city leaders focused their attention on the downtown business district and entertainment facilities whose primary users were white suburbanites. Although community leaders and city officials restored calm, tensions remained high. The 2001 mayoral election pitted a white candidate, the incumbent Charlie Luken, against a black candidate, Courtis Fuller. Both were thoughtful men who were well known from their work as news anchormen at television station WLW. Fuller made a virtue of his lack of political experience and ties to local business interests while Luken played on his knowledge and connections. In the end, Luken won. But the fact that most of his supporters were white and most of Fuller's black testifies to the challenges facing Cincinnati in the twenty-first century.

As controversial as race was the question of how to fund public education. For two centuries, the leaders of Ohio have asserted that widespread access to schools is necessary to sustain a democratic society as well as a prosperous economy. Yet they have been reluctant to match their rhetoric with a financial commitment. Requiring everyone between the ages of six and eighteen to attend school (unless they have already graduated), the state government has relied on local school boards and property taxes to make the system work.

By the end of the twentieth century, many public school districts in Ohio were in dire straits. Mismanagement, shifting tax bases, the controversy over busing, and a general aversion to taxes had left some in bankruptcy. Between 1984 and 1994, more than a hundred districts had to seek loans from the state to cover their expenses. In 1996, Cleveland alone had a debt of $155 million. Financial problems disproportionately plagued urban and rural areas. Many people saw a direct connection between the better facilities and equipment of suburban districts and the academic success of their students.

In 1991, over five hundred school districts banded together and filed suit in Perry County (*DeRolph v. the State of Ohio*) charging the General Assembly with failing in its constitutional duty to provide a solid and efficient education system. More specifically, they objected to Ohio's reliance on local property taxes (with some additional funding from the state lottery) to support public schools, arguing that the quality of education varied widely from district to district. In 1994, Judge Linton Lewis, Jr. ruled in favor of the plaintiffs and declared that a 1979 Ohio Supreme Court judgment that local control trumped equal distribution of resources was wrong. With the support of Governor Voinovich and leading legislators, the Attorney-General appealed Lewis's decision. The Ohio Supreme Court upheld Lewis's ruling that the property tax system was unconstitutional because it denied children equal opportunity under the law. The court directed the General Assembly to devise a new system of funding for public schools.

The efforts of state officials to delay or reverse the court's decision were unsuccessful. In 2001, Governor Bob Taft and the members of the General Assembly had to find hundreds of millions of dollars to spend on public education in the midst of a national economic downturn that was seriously reducing the state's income. Because they were generally unwilling to raise taxes, the state's leaders had few options other than cutting budgets and drawing on reserves.

In part, the reluctance to raise taxes and spend money on public services revealed the ways in which Ohioans, along with Americans in general, were rethinking the meanings of public culture. In the 1800s and early 1900s, respectable people had defined citizenship as a universal identity that transcended the particular interests of religion and ethnicity. By the early twenty-first century, more and more Ohioans saw citizenship as involving the assertion of the unique experiences of individuals and communities. Public culture was the process of the interaction of a multitude of private cultures. It was more about making people comfortable with who they understood themselves to be than it was about making them into citizens committed to the improvement of others.

Ohioans increasingly thought of themselves in terms of their city or subregion, or their race, gender, religion, family, or ethnicity. They believed that the fragmentation of the world into groups of strangers was a permanent condition and that in such a world people had to fend for themselves against or in spite of public institutions. Fortified by the democracy of the Internet, which made all kinds of information accessible, and made wary by decades of national political scandal, they questioned the expertise of all professionals and officials. They abandoned the obsession with respectable manners and dress for the freedom of individual comfort and expression. Above all, many tended to see diversity as an asset rather than a liability. Public culture was not about developing universal, enlightened notions of citizenship but about facilitating the acceptance and celebration of individual and group identities.

In the last third of the twentieth century, public attention was finally paid to citizens of Ohio whose contributions had been largely ignored or marginalized. Celebrations and books, often published by local organizations or individuals, revealed a fascination with American Indians and, to a lesser extent, African Americans. Ohioans and visitors flocked to outdoor dramas about Indians and white settlers such as Tecumseh in Chillicothe and Blue Jacket in Xenia. Some Ohioans seemed to sympathize more with the conquered than the conquerors. They were sensitive to an injustice that they thought paralleled their own. Untrustworthy politicians had destroyed Native Americans just as they were destroying rural and small-town worlds.

Growing interest in African Americans reflected the determination of many blacks to win inclusion in the past as well as the present and the future. White Ohioans were generally not averse to this as long as it suggested racial harmony rather than conflict. Thus the explosion of claims about the existence of Underground Railroad locations throughout Ohio, culminating in the development of an Underground Railroad Museum in Cincinnati. Yet few people seemed interested in giving as much attention to the virulent racism that has marked Ohio's history.

Indeed, the celebration of diversity became ubiquitous as long as it was positive. In the 1970s, Cleveland State University printed a series of books in the Cleveland Ethnic Heritage Series which highlighted the history of Irish, Poles, Lithuanians, African Americans, Slavs, Italians, and others in Cleveland. Histories of Jews in Cincinnati, Cleveland, and Dayton appeared. One of the largest cottage industries in scholarship on Ohio consisted of numerous conferences and publications dealing with Appalachians. In the late 1970s, the Ohio Urban Appalachian Awareness Project sponsored volumes on the experiences of Appalachians in every major Ohio city. Community activists such as Michael Maloney in Cincinnati made careers out of advocacy for Appalachians. Studies of African Americans in Ohio and in Cleveland and Cincinnati made their way into print. Fairs, festivals, and parades emphasized ethnic and racial pride within the borders of the state.

The consumption of idealized diversity gave Ohioans a sense of history very different from the nineteenth-century emphasis on progress. It combined a desire for a familiar and an interest in the exotic while it satisfied both personal and public agendas. Hamilton native Randy McNutt devoted himself in the 1990s to learning about

Ohio ghost towns. John Baskin, author of *New Burlington,* noted that "Ohio's peculiar places" were not gothic in their eccentricities. Rather, the state was haunted "by such things as lost ambition, thwarted dreams, vanished culture."[7] McNutt had originally intended to write about lost towns all over the United States. Then one day, while driving across Ohio, he asked "a man what the future might offer his town, and he said, 'We might not *have* a future.'"[8]

This sense of loss fueled writing about the state as a place. Some people conjured up the spirit of Henry David Thoreau and wrote at length about the rhythms of climate and the varieties of the landscape. In *Moods of the Ohio Moon,* Merrill C. Gilfillan, a former wildlife biologist for the Ohio Division of Wildlife and conservation journalist, affectionately recorded the sounds of Ohio's flora and fauna. Few people had ever approached the landscape of the state with such reverence. Gilfillan wrote of an Ohio alive with natural vitality. No need to dream nineteenth-century dreams of progress when there was so much to be seen and heard and experienced right now. "The fragrance of plenty is present everywhere," rhapsodized Gilfillan. "It is a pleasant time to stand downwind from a roadside market to inhale the September breeze. . . . [O]ne may arise to the golden glow of sunlit early fog; move through an active day of color, abundance, and cider-sweet air; witness a brilliant autumn sunset against a violet horizon, and go to bed by the light of a bright harvest moon." Gilfillan admired a cultivated landscape with its regularity and security. Familiar noises and smells made him happy. When he sat on the edge of a swamp in December "listening to owl calls and watching the heavens and the broad valley slopes," he "experienced a great sense of contentment."[9]

Not everyone who wrote about Ohio in the 1990s and early 2000s was so much at peace. Essayist Scott Russell Sanders remembered his childhood in Portage County as "the place where I came to consciousness, where I learned to connect feelings with words." When the government dammed the Mahoning River and the land which Sanders had grown up disappeared under water. He blamed the failure of his family and neighbors to save it on the fact that "our attachments to the land were all private. We had no shared lore, no literature, no art to root us there, to give us courage, to help us stand our ground. . . . The Ohio landscape never showed up in postcards or posters, never

unfurled like tapestry in films, rarely filled even a paragraph in books.
. . . It was a country of low hills, cut over woods, scoured fields, villages that had lost their purpose, roads that had lost their way."[10]

Whatever their ultimate purpose, many people understand the significance of Ohio as lying in the extent to which it was part of who
they are. Ohio is less an area to be transformed or improved than explored, both physically and emotionally. Place somehow molds
human beings as much as human beings mold place. The artist Maya
Lin, who was born in Athens in 1959 and achieved fame as the designer of the Vietnam Memorial in Washington, D.C., attributed the
"fluidity"of her sense of herself and her work in part to the landscape
in which she grew up. Even though the region around Athens was
"quiet" and "settled," "the undulating hills in that part of Ohio
seemed to be forever in motion."[11] Poet and professor David Citino
would not argue that "there is something so distinctly *Ohio* that [he]
could tell by his or her writing or speech or dress that an individual
hailed from here[.]" Nevertheless, "at the center of my work lies Ohio.
This state is ever in my mind as a place nearly too real." He has "been
shaped . . . , formed, reformed and informed (and I hope not too terribly deformed) by Ohio."[12]

In 2001, a Maryland college professor named Jeffrey Hammond,
who had grown up in Findlay, sought to "pin down the essence" of
Ohio. Other states had recognizable identities. Why not Ohio?
Hammond fingered the usual suspects of diversity and decline and
offered them up in pithy phrases that bordered on clichés. Ohio was
"the State of Aiming High but Falling Short." It was "less a place of
new dreams than of old daydreams." "[N]o meaning was possible,"
he concluded, "for a state that had been cobbled together from
shards of this and that, a hopeless mix of conflicting dreams." Like
others before him, Hammond finally embraced his lack of distinc-
tiveness as distinctive. "[C] we truly be bland if we're the products
not of nothing but of damned near everything, an entire spectrum
blending into white light? And besides, who says that blandness can't
be redemptive?" Knowing that Ohio serves as a necessary foil to others' more colorful identities is reassuring. For being an American
"Everybody" is "an identity, however shapeless, that the nation can-

not do without—and I am resolved to embrace it with honor and even a measure of relief. It's nice, at long last, to be somebody."[13]

Novelist Constance Pierce is less grandiose about the relationship between place and identity. A professor at Miami University, she came to Oxford in 1980 somewhat apprehensive about a flat, land-locked landscape full of happy images, boosters, and Babbitts. Over time, Pierce discovered the pleasures of her new world and reconciled herself to life in the Midwest. She was, for better or worse, "here." And she knew that she was "going to stay here." Pierce "concluded that we all live in a world that nobody in her right mind could really desire calling 'home.' 'Home' is a place that is supposed to reflect upon us, and a place we're expected to reflect upon."[14]

The book you are reading exemplifies these sentiments. I was born in Cincinnati in 1954. I grew up in Marietta. I reside in Oxford. I have lived one-quarter of the history I have recounted. My story of Ohio is inevitably a personal one. While I have tried to include as many voices as possible and to emphasize diverse perspectives, I have shaped them into an overall narrative that reflects my personal concerns and those of my generation. This book is the work of a middle-aged white male academic who has lived most of his life in small towns in Ohio.

Like many of the people about whom I have written, I spent much of my youth fantasizing about getting out of Ohio. I imagined myself living in New York City or Europe. When I read *Winesburg, Ohio,* I identified intensely with the character of George Willard. Yet even though I went to college in Virginia and graduate school in Rhode Island, I ended up back in the Midwest writing time and again about this state and its neighbors. I almost declined the invitation to write this book because it coincided with my growing sense that it was long past time to follow George Willard to some other place.

On a clear, cold January day in 2001, I rode on an airplane from Boston to Cincinnati. From my window seat, I could see the landscape that we call Ohio below me. I thought about all the people and places I had encountered in writing this history of the state. But mostly I thought about my own experiences in Ohio. Thousands of feet above the ground, I recognized cities, followed the contours of roads, knew the shapes of rivers. There was a place I spent time with high school friends. There were the places where my sisters live. There was the place where my wife and I decided to get married. There was the place where our daughters were born. So much of my life has happened within the arbitrary borders of Ohio. And still, as always, I felt ambivalent about returning. Wasn't I going the wrong way? George Willard had left Ohio. Why was I going back?

Now, as I sit in my office writing these last words, the answer seems obvious. Through the window I see snow swirling around the red-brick buildings of Miami University. Four young female students walk by, laughing about slipping on the ice. It is snowing all over Ohio, I suppose. Snow is covering the landscape from the southern shores of Lake Erie to the hills of the Muskingum Valley. Snow is covering people living in Cleveland, Columbus, and Cincinnati. The bells chime the hour. And snow covers the graves of the countless people who have lived and died in Ohio, people who imagined it as nothing more and nothing less than home.

Notes

Readers interested in a fuller discussion of the assumptions that inform *Ohio: The History of a People* should consult Andrew R. L. Cayton and Susan E. Gray, eds., *The American Midwest: Essays on Regional History* (Bloomington: Indiana University Press, 2001).

I have used the following abbreviations in the notes:

BCHS	*Bulletin of the Cincinnati Historical Society*
BGSUPP	Bowling Green, Ohio: Bowling Green State University Popular Press
CUP	Cambridge: Cambridge University Press
IUP	Bloomington: Indiana University Press
KSUP	Kent, Ohio: Kent State University Press
OH	*Ohio History*
OHS	Ohio Historical Society
OSAHS	Columbus: Ohio State Archaeological and Historical Society
OSUP	Columbus: Ohio State University Press
OUP	Athens: Ohio University Press
QCH	*Queen City Heritage*
UCP	Chicago: University of Chicago Press
UIP	Urbana: University of Illinois Press
UNCP	Chapel Hill: University of North Carolina Press
UPK	University Press of Kentucky
WRHS	Cleveland: Western Reserve Historical Society
YUP	New Haven, Conn.: Yale University Press

PROLOGUE

1. Granger to Huntington, October 20, 1804, "Letters from the Samuel Huntington Correspondence, 1800–1812," in *Tracts* 95 (WRHS, 1915), 92–93.

2. "Marietta Meeting," *Western Spy,* February 11, 1801.

3. St. Clair to James Ross, December 1799, in William Henry Smith, *The St. Clair Papers: The Life and Public Services of Arthur St. Clair* (2 vols. Cincinnati: R. Clarke, 1882), 2: 482.

4. Tiffin to the General Assembly, December 1805, *Journal of the Senate of the State of Ohio, Being the First Session of the Fourth General Assembly* (Chillicothe: T. G. Bradford, 1806), 16; Tiffin, *Anniversary Long Talk, Delivered Before the Tammany Society or Columbian Order* (Chillicothe: J. S. Collins, 1811), 8; "Journal of Samuel Williams," quoted in William T. Utter, *The Frontier State: 1803–1825* (OSAHS, 1942), 57.

5. Tiffin ("A Friend of the People"), "To the Inhabitants," *Scioto Gazette,* September 24, 1801.

6. Ephraim Cutler, Oration, July 4, 1802, Ephraim Cutler Papers, Marietta College, 69; Michael Baldwin to the Electors of Ross County, *Scioto Gazette,* August 28, 1802.

7. "An Act to Regulate Black and Mulatto Persons," 1804, and "An Act to Amend the Last Named Act, 'An Act to Regulate Black and Mulatto Persons,'" 1807, in Stephen Middleton, *The Black Laws in the Old Northwest: A Documentary History* (Westport, Conn.: Greenwood Press, 1993), 15–17.

8. Joseph E. Walker, ed., "Plowshares and Pruning Hooks for the Miami and Potowatomi: The Journal of Gerald T. Hopkins, 1804," *OH* 88 (1979): 401, 402.

CHAPTER 1

1. Joseph E. Walker, ed., "The Travel Notes of Joseph Gibbons, 1804," *OH* 92 (1983): 124, 111, 116.

2. Walker, ed., "Travel Notes," 106, 128, 129.

3. Dwight L. Smith, ed., "Nine Letters of Nathaniel Dike on the Western Country, 1816–1818," *OH* 67 (1958): 192.

4. Joseph E. Walker, ed., "Plowshares and Pruning Hooks for the Miami and Potowatomi: The Journal of Gerald T. Hopkins, 1804," *OH* 88 (1979): 373.

5. Kenneth J. Winkle, *The Politics of Community: Migration and Politics in Antebellum Ohio* (CUP, 1998), 65.

6. Johann Heckewelder, "To the Falls of the Ohio and Vincennes: 1792," in Paul A. W. Wallace, ed., *The Travels of John Heckewelder in Frontier America* (Pittsburgh: University of Pittsburgh Press, 1985 [1958]), 270.

7. John Sale to Edward Dromgoole, February 20, 1807, in "The Edward Dromgoole Letters, 1778–1812," in William Warren Sweet, ed., *Religion on the American Frontier, 1783–1840* (4 vols. UCP, 1946), *IV: The Methodists,* 160.

8. Walker, ed., "Plowshares and Pruning Hooks," 376; James Tawler to Edward Dromgoole, June 20, 1807, in Sweet, ed., *Methodists,* 165.

9. James Hall, *The West: Its Commerce and Navigation* (Cincinnati: H. W. Derby, 1848), 25; Walker to George Bancroft, August 28, 1830, quoted in Daniel Aaron, *Cincinnati: Queen City of the West* (OSUP, 1992), 64.

10. B. Drake and E. D. Mansfield, *Cincinnati in 1826* (Cincinnati: Morgan, Lodge, and Fisher, 1827), 60.

11. Timothy Flint, *Recollections of the Last Ten Years* (Boston: Cummings, Hilliard, 1826), 52.

12. M. H. Dunlop, "Curiosities Too Numerous to Mention: Early Regionalism and Cincinnati's Western Museum," *American Quarterly* 26 (1984): 524–48.

13. Joe William Trotter Jr., *River Jordan: African American Urban Life in the Ohio Valley* (UPK, 1998), 26, 31, 29, 27, 29; Allan Peskin, ed., *The Autobiography of John Malvin, 1795–1880* (KSUP, 1988), 8.

14. Peskin, ed., *Autobiography of John Malvin,* 40, 39; Trotter, *River Jordan,* 35–36.

15. Quoted in Trotter, *River Jordan,* 42, 36; Peskin, ed., *Autobiography of John Malvin,* 41n3, 39.

16. Quoted in Aaron, *Cincinnati,* 125.

17. Quoted in Stephen J. Stein, *The Shaker Experience in America: A History of the United Society of Believers* (YUP, 1992), 62.

18. Brian Harte, "Land in the Old Northwest: A Study of Speculation, Sales, and Settlement on the Connecticut Western Reserve," *OH* 101 (1992): 121.

19. Quoted in Jon C. Teaford, *Cities of the Heartland: The Rise and Fall of the Industrial Midwest* (IUP, 1993), 18.

20. George Knepper, "Early Migration to the Western Reserve," in Harry F. Lupold and Gladys Haddad, eds., *Ohio Western Reserve: A Regional Reader* (KSUP, 1988), 36; Michael J. McTighe, *A Measure of Success: Protestants and Public Culture in Antebellum Cleveland* (Albany: State University of New York Press, 1994), 22–23.

21. Peskin, ed., *Autobiography of John Malvin,* 9, 12, 60.

22. Huntington to Moses Cleaveland, February 10, 1802, in "Letters from the Samuel Huntington Correspondence, 1800–1812," *Tracts* 95 (WRHS, 1915), 74; Henry Leavitt Ellsworth, *A Tour to New Connecticut in 1811,* ed. Phillip R. Shriver (WRHS, 1985), 74.

23. Ellsworth, *Tour to New Connecticut,* 57, 60, 62, 69.

24. Margaret Van Horn Dwight, *A Journey to Ohio,* ed. Jay Gitlin (Lincoln: University of Nebraska Press, 1991), 16, 18, 37, 39, 25, 61, 63.

25. Cleaveland to Huntington, August 16, 1801, "Letters from the Samuel Huntington Correspondence," 65; Huntington to Cleaveland, November 15, 1801, "Letters," 67.

26. Hannah Huntington to Samuel Huntington, October 30, 1798, in Lois Scharf, "'I Would Go Wherever Fortune Would Direct': Hannah Huntington and the Frontier of the Western Reserve," *OH* 97 (1988): 7–8.

27. Hannah to Samuel, August 30, 1803, August 10, 1807, in ibid., 14, 13.

28. Hannah to Samuel, October 30, 1798, April 25, 1804, in ibid., 19, 20.

29. Dwight, *Journey to Ohio,* 37.

30. Lee Soltow, "Inequality Amidst Abundance: Land Ownership in Early Nineteenth-Century Ohio," *OH* 88 (1979): 143.

31. Sarah Ann Worthington King, *A Private Memoir of Thomas Worthington* (Cincinnati: Robert Clarke, 1882), 31, 32.

32. R. Douglas Hurt, *The Ohio Frontier, Crucible of the Old Northwest* (IUP, 1996), 219–24.

33. A. T. to [?], Richmond, May 10, 1819, quoted in William Buckner McGroarty, "Exploration in Mass Emancipation," *William and Mary College Quarterly Historical Magazine* 21 (2d ser., July 1941): 212; Article in Cincinnati *Gazette,* reprinted in Alexandria (Virginia) *Gazette,* December 7, 1835, quoted in McGroarty, "Exploration in Mass Emancipation," 218.

34. *Cincinnati Gazette,* July 1846, quoted in Leonard U. Hill, "John Randolph's Freed Slaves Settle in Western Ohio," *BCHS* 23 (1965): 181; Hill, "John Randolph's Freed Slaves," 186–87.

35. Madison Hemings, "The Memoirs of Madison Hemings," in Annette Gordon-Reed, *Thomas Jefferson and Sally Hemings: An American Controversy* (Charlottesville: University Press of Virginia, 1997), 247.

36. Gatch to Edward Dromgoole, February 11, 1802, in "Letters from Ohio, North Carolina, and Tennessee (1802–1812)," in Sweet, ed., *Methodists,* 152, 154.

37. Gatch to Edward Dromgoole, June 1, 1805, Peter Pelham to Dromgoole, July 27, 1807, in ibid., 155–56, 172.

38. Sale to Edward Dromgoole, February 20, 1807, Pelham to Dromgoole, February 20, 1807, Bonner to Dromgoole, July 19, 1807, in ibid., 160, 165, 171.

39. William Cooper Howells, *Recollections of Life in Ohio from 1813 to 1840,* ed. Edwin H. Cady (Gainesville, Fla.: Scholars' Facsimiles and Reprints, 1963), 55.

40. Smith, ed., "Nine Letters of Nathaniel Dike," 199, 202, 205, 206.

41. Howells, *Recollections,* 115–16, 62, 81, 82–83.

42. Ibid., 42–43.

43. Walker, ed., "Travel Notes of Joseph Gibbons," 102–3, 134.

44. Smith, ed., "Nine Letters of Nathaniel Dike," 219, 218.

CHAPTER 2

1. Aiken quoted in Michael J. McTighe, *A Measure of Success: Protestants and Public Culture in Antebellum Cleveland* (Albany: State University of New York Press, 1994), 66.

2. Quoted in ibid., 119, 106.

3. Hayes, Diary, September 1851, in Charles R. Williams, ed., *Diary and Letters of Rutherford Birchard Hayes* (5 vols. OSAHS, 1922–1926), 1: 397.

4. Harry N. Scheiber, "Alfred Kelley and the Ohio Business Elite, 1822–1859," *OH* 87 (1978): 367, 366.

5. "Thoughts on Education," Cincinnati *Western Spy,* July 17, 1819; "For the Spy," ibid., August 1, 1818; Message of Gov. Ethan Allen Brown, January 8, 1819; Report of the Committee on Public Canals, January 21, 1824, in John Kilbourn, comp., *Public Documents Concerning the Ohio Canals* (Columbus: I. N. Whiting, 1832), 4, 75.

6. Harry N. Scheiber, *Ohio Canal Era: A Case Study of Government and the Economy, 1820–1861* (OUP, 1969), 8. See also John Lauritz Larson, *Internal Improvement* (UNCP, 2001).

7. Scheiber, *Ohio Canal Era,* 28–29.

8. "Report of the Commission on Canals, 1822," in Thomas H. Smith, ed., *An Ohio Reader* (2 vols. Grand Rapids: Eerdmans, [1975]), 1: 154.

9. Michel Chevalier, *Society, Manners, and Politics in the United States, Letters on North America* (orig. ed. 1836; Gloucester, Mass.: Peter Smith, 1967), 234–35.

10. Brian P. Birch, "A British View of the Ohio Backwoods: The Letters of James Martin, 1821–1836," *OH* 94 (1985): 150, 156, 157.

11. Quoted in Scheiber, *Ohio Canal Era,* 223, 224.

12. Birch, "British View," 156.

13. Quoted in Peter Way, *Common Labour: Workers and the Digging of North American Canals, 1780–1860* (CUP, 1993), 120, 121.

14. On politics in this era, see Donald J. Ratcliffe, *The Politics of Long Division: The Birth of the Second Party System in Ohio, 1818–1828* (OSUP, 2000).

15. Quoted in Scheiber, *Ohio Canal Era,* 278.

16. Ephraim Cutler, *An Oration, Delivered Before the Washington Benevolent Society, at Marietta, on the 22nd of February, 1814* (Zanesville: Putnam and Israel, 1814), 4; "Bacon," Cincinnati *Western Spy,* February 21, 1817; *Western Spy,* November 14, 1818; Worthington to the General Assembly, December 7, 1818, quoted in Alfred Byron Sears, *Thomas Worthington, Father of Ohio Statehood* (OSUP, 1958), 206–7.

17. William Cooper Howells, *Recollections of Life in Ohio from 1813 to 1840,* ed. Edwin H. Cady (Gainesville, Fla.: Scholars' Facsimiles and Reprints, 1963), 32.

18. Hayes in Williams, ed., *Diary and Letters,* 9, 7, 3.

19. Howells, *Recollections,* 142–43.

20. John M. Roberts, July 23, 1853, in J. Merton England, ed., *Buckeye Schoolmaster: A Chronicle of Midwestern Rural Life, 1853–1865* (BGSUPP, 1996), 45.

21. Roberts, July 23, September 19, 1853, August 30, 1854, in ibid., 50, 59, 94.

22. Roberts, April 12, April 16, 1857, in ibid., 116, 117.

23. "Sixth Annual Report of the State Commissioner of Common Schools, 1860," in Smith, ed., *Ohio Reader,* 1: 180.

24. "Report of the Debates and Proceedings of the Convention for the Revision of the Constitution of the State of Ohio, 1850–51"; "Sixth Annual Report," in ibid., 177, 181.

25. "Report of the Debates and Proceedings," in ibid., 177, 178.

26. Allan Peskin, ed., *Autobiography of John Malvin, 1795–1880* (KSUP, 1988), 63–64.

27. Joe William Trotter Jr., *River Jordan: African American Urban Life in the Ohio Valley* (UPK, 1998), 33, 47, 33.

28. Samuel Lewis, *First Annual Report of the Superintendent of Common Schools, Made to the Thirty-Sixth General Assembly of Ohio* (3 vols. Columbus: S. Medary, 1838–39), 1: 4, 8.

29. Ibid., 9.

30. Ibid., 10, 11.

31. Ibid., 12, 18, 6, 7.

32. Roberts, May 6, May 21, October 16, 1858, in England, ed., *Buckeye Schoolmaster,* 154, 163, 159.

33. Roberts, August 30, September 10, September 16, 1858, in ibid., 142, 146, 147.

34. Roberts, October 29, September 30, 1858, in ibid., 168, 152.

35. Quoted in David J. Rothman, *The Discovery of the Asylum: Social Order and Disorder in the New Republic* (Boston: Little Brown, 1971), 143.

36. Daniel Aaron, *Cincinnati: Queen City of the West* (OSUP, 1992), 104.

37. Rothman, *Discovery of the Asylum,* 254, 253, 250.

38. James B. Finley, *Memorials of Prison Life* (Cincinnati: L. Swormstedt and J. H. Power, 1851 [1850]), 41–42.

39. *Annual Report of the Ohio Penitentiary for 1852,* quoted in Rothman, *Discovery of the Asylum,* 100.

40. *Annual Report of the Ohio Penitentiary for 1850,* quoted in ibid., 72.

41. Jed Dannenbaum, *Drink and Disorder: Temperance Reform in Cincinnati from the Washingtonian Revival to the WCTU* (UIP, 1984), 24–25.

42. Howells, *Recollections,* 125, 126.

43. Roberts, December 27, 1853, in England, ed., *Buckeye Schoolmaster,* 69, 70.

44. Dannenbaum, *Drink and Disorder,* 46–47, 59, 50–51, 53.

45. McTighe, *Measure of Success,* 104–5.

CHAPTER 3

1. Isaac Appleton Jewett to Willard [?], August 4, 1831, *Cincinnati Mirror and Western Gazette of Literature and Science,* 1836, quoted in Daniel Aaron, *Cincinnati, Queen City of the West, 1819–1838* (OSUP, 1992), 249, 248.

2. Ronald Weber, *The Midwestern Ascendancy in American Writing* (IUP, 1992), 10.

3. Benjamin Drake, "Address by Benjamin Drake, Esq., Delivered on the Sixth Anniversary of the Erodelphian Society," September 27, 1831, in *Oxford Addresses* (Hanover, Ind.: J. C. Monfort, 1835), 80, 82.

4. Hayes, in Charles R. Williams, ed., *Diary and Letters of Rutherford Birchard Hayes,* (5 vols. OSAHS, 1922–1926), 1: 55, 56, 57.

5. Ibid., 72, 82, 82–83.

6. Ibid., 369.

7. Lucy Webb, "Is America Advancing in Mental and Moral Improvement?," quoted in Emily Apt Geer, *First Lady: The Life of Lucy Webb Hayes* (KSUP, 1984), 14–15.

8. Williams, ed., *Diary and Letters,* 366.

9. Quoted in W. H. Venable, *Beginnings of Literary Culture in the Ohio Valley* (Cincinnati: Robert Clarke and Co., 1891), 319.

10. Hayes to S. Birchard, December 9, 1837; Hayes to Mother, July 7, 1838; Hayes to Harriet Moody, February 24, 1838; Hayes to Birchard, April 28, 1838;

Hayes, Diary, May 23, 1851, in Williams, ed., *Diary and Letters,* 1: 16, 24, 19, 21, 361.

11. Roberts, Diary, February 23, August 21, December 27, 1853, [no date] 1854, January 27, 1853, in J. Merton England, ed., *Buckeye Schoolmaster: A Chronicle of Midwestern Rural Life, 1853–1865* (BGSUPP, 1996), 26, 57, 70, 72, 17.

12. Roberts, Diary, May 22, July 31, 1853, in ibid., 39, 49.

13. Roberts, Diary, January 26, 1853, in ibid., 16.

14. Roberts, Diary, April 3, 1853, in ibid., 34–35.

15. Longworth quoted in Jon Teaford, *Cities of the Heartland: The Rise and Fall of the Industrial Midwest* (IUP, 1993), 14; *Transactions of the Western Art Union, for the Year 1847,* quoted in Robert C. Vitz, *The Queen and the Arts: Cultural Life in Nineteenth-Century Cincinnati* (KSUP, 1989), 48.

16. Vitz, *Queen and the Arts,* 54–55.

17. Robert A. Wheeler, "Land and Community in Rural Nineteenth Century America: Claridon Township, 1810–1870," *OH* 97 (1988): 105, 107, 112.

18. Bishop, "Inaugural Address," in *Oxford Addresses,* 18, 19, 20, 24, 27.

19. Ibid., 32, 34–35; Bishop, "Address by the Rev. R. H. Bishop, D.D., President, to the Graduates of Miami University," 1829, in ibid., 36, 37.

20. Ewing, "Address . . . Delivered Before the Union Literary Society of Miami University, at their Anniversary Celebration," September 25, 1832; Bishop, "Address," September 28, 1831; Gray, "Address at the Inauguration of the Rev. R. H. Bishop, D.D., as President of Miami University," March 10, 1834, in ibid., 12, 49–50, 51–52.

21. Brown to Stone, September 22, 1847, in Carol Lasser and Marlene Deahl Merrill, eds., *Friends and Sisters: Letters between Lucy Stone and Antoinette Brown Blackwell, 1846–1893* (UIP, 1987), 31.

22. Brown to Stone, June 1848, in ibid., 40.

23. Walter Havighurst, *The Miami Years, 1809–1984* (New York: Putnam, 1984), 53, 54, 58.

24. Quoted in Linda L. Geary, *Balanced in the Wind: A Biography of Betsey Mix Cowles* (Lewisburg, Pa.: Bucknell University Press, 1989), 27.

25. Quoted in ibid., 34, 39.

26. Quoted in ibid., 65.

27. Quoted in Teaford, *Cities of the Heartland,* 12, 14.

28. "Constitution," in William Davis Gallagher, *Facts and Conditions of Progress in the North-West* (Cincinnati: H. W. Derby, 1850), 71.

29. Gallagher, "Address to the Historical and Philosophical Society of Ohio," 1850, in ibid., 5, 6.

30. Ibid., 9.

31. Ibid., 26, 27, 47, 59.

32. Ibid., 74; Samuel Prescott Hildreth, *Biographical and Historical Memoirs of the Early Pioneer Settlers of Ohio* (Cincinnati: H. W. Derby, 1852), xii.

33. Samuel P. Hildreth, *Pioneer History: Being an Account of the First Examinations of the Ohio Valley, and the Early Settlement of the Northwest Territory* (Cincinnati: H. W. Derby, 1848), vii.

34. Hildreth, *Biographical and Historical Memoirs,* ix; *Pioneer History,* 275; *Biographical and Historical Memoirs,* 169, 482–83.

35. Caleb Atwater, *A History of the State of Ohio, Natural and Civil,* 2d ed. (Cincinnati: Glezen and Shepard, 1838), 6, 87, 88, 106.

36. Ibid., 171, 355, 356.

37. James B. Finley, *Sketches of Western Methodism* (Cincinnati: R. P. Thompson, 1854), 3.

38. Henry Howe, *Historical Collections of Ohio* (Cincinnati: E. Morgan, 1852), 4.

39. William D. Gallagher, "The Mothers of the West" and "Song of the Pioneers," in William T. Coggeshall, *The Poems and Poetry of the West: With Biographical and Critical Notices* (Columbus: Follett, Foster, and Co., 1860), 140–42.

40. Charles A. Jones, "The Old Mound" and "Tecumseh"; Lewis J. Cist, "Ohio's Pilgrim Band"; William Dana Emerson, "To the Ohio River"; Edward A. McLaughlin, "To Cincinnati"; Sullivan D. Harris, "A Song for Ohio," in ibid., 208, 248–49, 285–86, 340, 402.

41. Dumont, "The Second Anniversary Dinner," in *Life Sketches from Common Paths: A Series of American Tales* (New York: D. Appleton, 1856), 21; *Life Sketches,* 9.

42. Dumont, "Ashton Grey," in ibid., 258, 266.

43. Dumont, "The Picture," in Sandra Parker, ed., *Home Material: Ohio's Nineteenth-Century Regional Women's Fiction* (BGSUPP, 1998), 21, 22, 29, 33, 35, 39, 40.

44. Ball, "A Tale of Early Times," in ibid., 59.

45. Dumont, "The Family History," in *Life Sketches,* 199, 202, 203.

46. Dumont, "Aunt Hetty," in ibid., 45, 47, 48.

47. Venable, *Beginnings of Literary Culture,* 482–503.

48. Cary, "My Grandfather," in Judith Fetterley, ed., *Clovernook Sketches and Other Stories* (New Brunswick, N.J.: Rutgers University Press, 1987), 9; Venable, *Beginnings of Literary Culture,* 490.

49. Venable, *Beginnings of Literary Culture,* 139, 140.

50. Cary, "Mrs. Wetherbe's Party," in Parker, ed., *Home Material,* 130, 131.

51. Ibid., 139, 140.

52. Ibid., 150.

CHAPTER 4

1. Alexis de Tocqueville, *Democracy in America,* ed. J. P. Mayer (New York: Anchor Books, 1969), 345–46.

2. "C. D.," "Slavery," in *The Harbinger,* August 14, 1847, in Philip S. Foner and Herbert Shapiro, eds. *Northern Labor and Antislavery: A Documentary History* (Westport, Conn.: Greenwood Press, 1994), 168.

3. Stuart Seely Sprague, ed., *His Promised Land: The Autobiography of John P. Parker* (New York: W. W. Norton, 1996), 71, 73, 127.

4. Larry Gara, *The Liberty Line: The Legend of the Underground Railroad* (UPK, 1961 [repr. 1996]), 93–96.

5. Allan Peskin, ed., *North Into Freedom: The Autobiography of John Malvin, Free Negro, 1795–1880* (KSUP, 1988 [repr. of 1879 edition], 39, 86.

6. *Address to the Constitutional Convention of Ohio, from the State Convention of Colored Men* ([Columbus]: E. Glover, 1851), 3, 5.

7. Philip S. Foner and George E. Walker, eds., *Proceedings of the Black State Conventions, 1840–1865. Volume I: New York, Pennsylvania, Indiana, Michigan, Ohio* (Philadelphia: Temple University Press, 1979), 223, 225.

8. Ibid., 228.

9. Joseph D. Ketner, *The Emergence of the African American Artist: Robert Duncanson, 1821–1872* (Columbia: University of Missouri Press, 1993).

10. John Mercer Langston, *From the Virginia Plantation to the National Capitol* (New York: Arno Press, 1969 [repr. of 1894 edition]), dedication.

11. Ibid., 90–91.

12. Ibid., 92.

13. Ibid., 125.

14. Ibid., 158, 159, 161.

15. Langston, "The World's Anti-Slavery Movement: Its Heroes and Triumphs," in Langston, *Freedom and Citizenship: Selected Lectures and Addresses* (Miami, Fla.: Mnemosyne, 1969), 61, 62, 63.

16. Robert W. Audretsch, ed., *The Salem, Ohio, 1850 Women's Rights Convention Proceedings* (Salem: Salem Area Bicentennial Committee, 1976), 17, 19–20.

17. Quoted in ibid., 23–24.

18. "The Memorial of the Ohio Women's Convention," "Address to the Women of Ohio," in ibid., 25, 27, 28.

19. J. V. Smith, ed., *Report of the Debates and Proceedings of the Convention for the Revision of the Constitution of the State of Ohio, 1850–1851* (2 vols. Columbus: S. Medary, 1851), 2: 13, 555.

20. Ibid., 1: 56, 57.

21. Lawrence Thomas Lesick, *The Lane Rebels: Evangelicalism and Antislavery in Antebellum America* (Metuchen, N.J.: Scarecrow Press, 1980), 71, 73, 89.

22. Quoted in ibid., 92.

23. Gamaliel Bailey quoted in Leonard L. Richards, *"Gentlemen of Property and Standing": Anti-Abolition Mobs in Jacksonian America* (New York: Oxford University Press, 1970), 43, 96.

24. Quoted in Nat Brandt, *The Town That Started the Civil War* (Syracuse, N.Y.: Syracuse University Press, 1990), 31, 33.

25. Quoted in Stephen E. Maizlish, *The Triumph of Sectionalism: The Transformation of Ohio Politics, 1844–1856,* (KSUP, 1983), 16.

26. Charles R. Williams, ed., *Diary and Letters of Rutherford Birchard Hayes,* 5 vols. (OSAHS, 1922–1926), 3: 242–43.

27. Chase quoted in Eric Foner, *Free Soil, Free Labor, Free Men: The Ideology of the Republican Party Before the Civil War* (New York: Oxford University Press, 1970), 77.

28. Thomas Morris, "Speech on Slavery," *Congressional Globe,* VII, 25th Congress, 3d Session. Feb. 9, 1839, 167–75.

29. Quoted in Foner, *Free Soil,* 95, 157; Maizlish, *Triumph of Sectionalism,* 230.

30. Quoted in Maizlish, *Triumph of Sectionalism,* 202–3.

31. Rutherford B. Hayes to Uncle [Sardis Birchard], October 13, 1854, in Williams, ed., *Diary and Letters,* 1: 470.

32. "Majority Report of the Standing Committee on Federal Relations," Ohio General Assembly, Senate, *Journal* (Appendix), (1857), 569–70.

33. Allan Peskin, *Garfield: A Biography* (KSUP, 1978), 85.

34. Quoted in Charles Royster, *The Destructive War: William Tecumseh Sherman, Stonewall Jackson, and the Americans* (New York: Knopf, 1991), 26, 331.

35. Anderson to James M. Williams, May 2, 1859; Anderson to Williams, October 29, 1859; Anderson to "Nephew," February 17, 1861, in John Kent Folmar, ed., "Pre-Civil War Sentiment from Belmont County: Correspondence of Hugh Anderson," *OH* 78 (1969): 204, 205, 209.

36. Quoted in Robert S. Harper, *The Ohio Press in the Civil War* (OSUP, 1962), 18.

37. Quoted in Thomas H. Smith, "Crawford County 'Ez Trooly Dimecratic': A Study of Midwestern Copperheadism," *OH* 76 (1967): 41–42, 43.

38. Quoted in David D. Anderson, "The Odyssey of Petroleum Vesuvius Nasby," *OH* 74 (1965): 234–35.

39. A. Z. to "Friend Lane," May 15, 1863, in Arnold Shankman, ed., "Vallandigham's Arrest and the 1863 Dayton Riot—Two Letters," *OH* 79 (1970): 121; Mary Ladley to Oscar Ladley, May 14, 1863, in Carl M. Becker and Richie Thomas, eds., *Hearth and Knapsack: The Ladley Letters, 1857–1880* (OUP, 1988), 126.

40. Quoted in Arnold Shankman, "Soldier Votes and Clement L. Vallandigham in the 1863 Ohio Gubernatorial Election," *OH* 88 (1973): 96.

41. Hayes, Diary, January 4, 1861; Hayes to S. Birchard, January 12, 1861, in Williams, ed., *Diary and Letters,* 2: 2, 4.

42. Hayes to Guy M. Bryan, May 8, 1861, in ibid., 13, 14, 15, 16.

43. Hayes to S. Birchard, September 3, [4], 1861, September 3, 1862, in ibid., 85, 340.

44. Hayes, Diary, September 14, 1862; Hayes to Sophia Hayes, September 18, 1862, in ibid., 357, 358.

45. Hayes to S. Birchard, October 19, 1863; Hayes to Lucy Hayes, October 21, 1864; Hayes, Diary, October 19, 1864, in ibid., 441, 528, 527.

46. Hayes to Judge William Johnston, April 10, 1865; Hayes to Lucy, April 16, 1865, in ibid., 574, 577.

47. Quoted in Peskin, *Garfield,* 119.

48. Quoted in ibid., 140.

49. Quoted in ibid., 181.

50. Wise to his father, July 11, 1862; Wise to his brother, June 23, 1864, in Wilfred W. Black, "Civil War Letters of George M. Wise," *Ohio Historical Quarterly* 65 (1956): 58, 75.

51. Ladley to his mother and sisters, July 5, 1863, in Becker and Thomas, eds., *Hearth and Knapsack,* 142–43.

52. Quoted in James McPherson, *What They Fought For, 1861–1865* (New York: Doubleday, 1995), 29, 46.

53. Quoted in ibid., 58, 66.

54. Wise to his brother, March 1865, in Wilfred W. Black, ed., "Marching Through South Carolina: Another Civil War Letter of Lieutenant George M. Wise," *Ohio Historical Quarterly* 66 (1957): 193.

55. Holiday Ames to his wife, April 23, April 16, 1865, in Louis Filler, ed., "Waiting for the War's End: The Letter of an Ohio Soldier in Alabama after Learning of Lincoln's Death," *OH* 74 (1965): 56, 59.

56. Quoted in David A. Gerber, *Black Ohio and the Color Line, 1860–1915* (UIP, 1976), 32.

57. Robert W. Hatton, ed., "Just a Little Bit of the Civil War, As Seen by W. J. Smith, Company M, 2nd O. V. Cavalry—Part I," *OH* 84 (1975), 114.

58. Milton M. Holland to the editor of the *Athens Messenger,* January 19, 1864, in Thomas H. Smith, ed., *An Ohio Reader* (2 vols. Grand Rapids: Eerdmans, 1975), 1: 319; Hayes quoted in George W. Knepper, *Ohio and Its People* (KSUP, 1997), 260.

59. Roberts, Diary, July 5, 1859, August 21, 1864, in J. Merton England, ed., *Buckeye Schoolmaster: A Chronicle of Midwestern Rural Life, 1853–1865* (BGSUPP, 1996), 235, 208, 274.

CHAPTER 5

1. Anne Kelley Knowles, *Calvinists Incorporated: Welsh Immigrants on Ohio's Industrial Frontier* (UCP, 1997), 149.

2. Quoted in ibid., 245.

3. *Turn-Zeitung,* 1851, quoted in Bruce Levine, "Community Divided: German Immigrants, Social Class, and Political Conflict in Antebellum Cincinnati," in Henry D. Shapiro and Jonathan D. Sarna, eds., *Ethnic Diversity and Civic Identity: Patterns of Conflict and Cohesion in Cincinnati Since 1820* (UIP, 1992), 59.

4. Quoted in Ivan D. Steen, "Cincinnati in the 1850s: As Described by British Travelers," *BCHS* 26 (1968): 271.

5. "'Dear Julia': Letter from Cincinnati, written in 1870," *BCHS* 18 (1960): 112.

6. Quoted in Joseph S. Stern Jr., "It Was the Best of Times; It Was the Worst of Times," *QCH* 42 (Spring 1984): 8.

7. Quoted in Levine, "Community Divided," 63–64.

8. William C. Smith, *Queen City Yesterdays: Sketches of Cincinnati in the Eighties* (Crawfordsville, Ind.: R. E. Banta, 1959), 43, 44.

9. Ibid., 55, 59.

10. Quoted in Frederick Trautmann, "Cincinnati and Southwestern Ohio Through a German's Eye: 1846–1847," *QCH* 45 (1987): 23.

11. Don Heinrich Tolzmann, ed., *Cincinnati, or The Mysteries of the West: Emil Klauprecht's German-American Novel,* translated by Steven Rowan (New York: Peter Lang, 1996), 151.

12. Ibid., 623, 624.

13. Ibid., 634, 635.

14. Ibid., 7, 8.

15. Quoted in Werner Sollors, "Emil Klauprecht's *Cincinnati, Oder Geheimnisse Des Westens* and the Beginnings of Urban Realism in America," *QCH* 42 (Fall 1984): 44; Tolzmann, ed., *Cincinnati,* 283.

16. Tolzmann, ed., *Cincinnati,* 487, 490.

17. Ibid., 195, 196, 197, 198.

18. Quoted in Blanche Linden-Ward, "The Greening of Cincinnati: Adolph Strauch's Legacy in Park Design," *QCH* 51 (Spring 1993): 21.

19. Quoted in ibid., 23.

20. Comte Alexandre Zanini, quoted in Guido Andre Dobbert, *The Disintegration of an Immigrant Community: The Cincinnati Germans, 1870–1920* (New York: Arno Press, 1980), 9.

21. Quoted in ibid., 79, 53.

22. Quoted in ibid., 54.

23. Quoted in ibid., 86, 88.

24. Steven Rowan, trans., *Cleveland and Its Germans* (Cleveland: WRHS, 1998 [1907]), 32, 34.

25. Quoted in La Vern J. Ripley, "The Chillicothe Germans," *OH* 75 (1966): 222.

26. Quoted in Don Heinrich Tolzmann, *Cincinnati's German Heritage* (Bowie, Md.: Heritage Books, 1994), 120, 127.

27. Quoted in Don Heinrich Tolzmann, *The Cincinnati Germans After the Great War* (New York: Peter Lang, 1987), 125.

28. Isaac M. Wise, *Reminiscences* (Cincinnati: Leo Wise, 1901), 235–36.

29. Quoted in Jonathan D. Sarna and Nancy H. Klein, *The Jews of Cincinnati* (Cincinnati: Center for the Study of the American Jewish Experience, 1989), 55.

30. Quoted in Lloyd P. Gartner, *History of the Jews of Cleveland* (Cleveland: WRHS and the Jewish Theological Seminary of America, 1978), 155, 85.

31. Quoted in ibid., 85.

32. Jonathan Sarna, "'A Sort of Paradise for the Hebrews': The Lofty Vision of Cincinnati Jews," in Shapiro and Sarna, eds., *Ethnic Diversity and Civic Identity,* 134.

33. Quoted in Sarna and Klein, *Jews of Cincinnati,* 62, 63.

34. Marc Lee Raphael, *Jews and Judaism in a Midwestern Community: Columbus, Ohio, 1840–1975* (OHS, 1979), 237.

35. Josef J. Barton, *Peasants and Strangers: Italians, Rumanians, and Slovaks in an American City, 1890–1950* (Cambridge, Mass.: Harvard University Press, 1975), 39–40, 47.

36. Edward M. Miggins and Mary Morgenthaler, "The Ethnic Mosaic: The Settlement of Cleveland by the New Immigrants and Migrants," in Thomas F. Campbell and Edward M. Miggins, eds., *The Birth of Modern Cleveland* (WRHS, 1988), 105.

37. Daniel E. Wienberg, "Ethnic Identity in Industrial Cleveland: The Hungarians, 1900–1920," *OH* 86 (1977): 183, 184.

38. Quoted in Miggins and Morgenthaler, "Ethnic Mosaic," 128, 129.

39. Quoted in Barton, *Peasants and Strangers,* 80.

40. Emily Greene Balch, *Our Fellow Slavic Citizens* (New York: Arno Press, 1969 [1910]), 398–99.

41. Quoted in Miggins and Morgenthaler, "Ethnic Mosaic," 107.

CHAPTER 6

1. Howard E. Good, *Black Swamp Farm* (OSUP, 1967), 35–44; Rosemary O. Joyce, *A Woman's Place: The Life History of a Rural Ohio Grandmother* (OSUP, 1983),

88; Virginia E. McCormick, "Butter and Egg Business: Implications from the Records of a Nineteenth-Century Farm Wife," *OH* 100 (1991): 64.

2. Wheeler McMillen, *Ohio Farm* (OSUP, 1974), 3–4.

3. Joyce, *Woman's Place,* 66, 90, 94, 98; Good, *Black Swamp Farm,* 43.

4. Quoted in Joyce, *Woman's Place,* 214.

5. McMillen, *Ohio Farm,* 33.

6. Joyce, *Woman's Place,* 98, 140; Good, *Black Swamp Farm,* 245.

7. McMillen, *Ohio Farm,* 153, 155.

8. "Wilbur Wright before the Ohio Society of New York," January 10, 1910, in Marvin W. McFarland, ed., *The Papers of Wilbur and Orville Wright* (2 vols. New York: McGraw-Hill, 1953), 2: 978.

9. Quoted in Wyn Wachhorst, *Thomas Alva Edison: An American Myth* (Cambridge: MIT Press, 1981), 35.

10. Thomas A. Boyd, ed., *Prophet of Progress: The Speeches of Charles F. Kettering* (New York: E. P. Dutton, 1961), 125; quoted in Stuart W. Leslie, *Boss Kettering* (New York: Columbia University Press, 1983), 39, 181, 335, 336, 338.

11. Orville Wright to Bishop Milton Wright [Telegram], Kitty Hawk, December 17, 1903, in McFarland, ed., *Papers of Wilbur and Orville Wright,* 397.

12. Quoted in Fred Howard, *Wilbur and Orville: A Biography of the Wright Brothers* (New York: Knopf, 1987), 10, 148, 431.

13. Francis Rolt-Wheeler, *Thomas Alva Edison* (New York: Book League of America, 1990), 7, 8; quoted in Neil Baldwin, *Edison: Inventing the Century* (New York: Hyperion, 1995), 20.

14. Quoted in Ron Chernow, *Titan: The Life of John D. Rockefeller, Sr.* (New York: Vintage, 1998), 44.

15. Quoted in Chernow, *Titan,* 55.

16. Quoted in Steven J. Ross, *Workers on the Edge: Work, Leisure, and Politics in Industrializing Cincinnati, 1788–1890* (New York: Columbia University Press, 1985), 241, 243.

17. Quoted in ibid., 249.

18. Quoted in ibid., 263.

19. Quoted in ibid., 265.

20. Quoted in ibid., 278.

21. Quoted in Leslie S. Hough, *The Turbulent Spirit: Cleveland, Ohio and Its Workers, 1877–1899* (New York: Garland Publishing, 1991), 147.

22. Quoted in ibid., 108, 111; quoted in Henry B. Leonard, "Ethnic Cleavage and Industrial Conflict in Late Nineteenth Century America: The Cleveland Rolling Mill Company Strikes of 1882 and 1885," *Labor History* 20 (1979): 535.

23. Quoted in Brian M. Linn, "Pretty Scaly Times: The Ohio National Guard and the Railroad Strike of 1877," *OH* 94 (1985): 172.

24. Quoted in Herbert G. Gutman, "The Negro and the United Mine Workers of America: The Career and Letters of Richard L. Davis and Something of Their Meaning: 1890–1900," in Gutman, *Work, Culture, and Society in Industrializing America* (New York: Vintage, 1977), 135.

25. Quoted in ibid., 153.

26. Quoted in Stephen D. Guschov, *The Red Stockings of Cincinnati: Baseball's First All-Professional Team and Its Historic 1869 and 1870 Seasons* (Jefferson, N.C.: McFarland, 1998), 59.

27. Quoted in ibid., 68, 58.

28. Quoted in Carl M. Becker and Richard H. Grigsby, "Baseball in the Small Ohio Community, 1865–1900," in Donald Spivey, ed., *Sport in America: New Historical Perspectives* (Westport, Conn.: Greenwood Press, 1985), 84.

29. Quoted in Jack S. Blocker Jr., *"Give to the Winds Thy Fears": The Women's Temperance Crusade, 1873–1874* (Westport: Conn.: Greenwood Press, 1985), 43, 44.

30. Quoted in Frances E. Willard, *Women and Temperance: or, The Work and Workers of The Women's Christian Temperance Union* (Hartford, Conn.: Park Publishing, 1888), 72.

31. Lloyd J. Graybar, ed., "The Whiskey War at Paddy's Run: Excerpts from a Diary of Albert Shaw," *OH* 75 (1966): 51, 52, 53.

32. Blocker, *"Give to the Winds Thy Fears"*, 126–27, 99.

33. Quoted in Jed Dannenbaum, "The Origins of Temperance Activism and Militancy Among American Women," *Journal of Social History* 15, no. 2 (1981): 244, 246.

34. Matilda Gilruth Carpenter, *The Crusade: Its Origin and Development at Washington Court House and Its Results* (Columbus: W. G. Hubbard, 1893), 35–36.

35. Quoted in Willard, *Women and Temperance*, 86; Mother Stewart, Address to the Fourteenth Annual Convention of the Ohio State Union of the Women's Christian Temperance Union, October 4, 1887, in Stewart, *Memories of the Crusade* (Columbus: Wm. G. Hubbard, 1888), 534–35.

36. Stewart, *Memories of the Crusade*, 27.

37. Quoted in Stephen L. Hansen, *The Making of the Third Party System: Voters and Parties in Illinois, 1850–1876* (Ann Arbor: University of Michigan Press, 1980), 204.

38. Quoted in Michael Pierce, "The Populist President of the American Federation of Labor: The Career of John McBride, 1880–1895," *Labor History* 41 (2000): 13; quoted in Pierce, "Farmers and the Failure of Populism in Ohio, 1890–1891," *Agricultural History* 74 (2000): 63.

39. Quoted in Pierce, "Populist President," 14.

40. Quoted in Richard Jensen, *The Winning of the Midwest: Social and Political Conflict, 1888–1896* (UCP, 1971), 291, 305.

CHAPTER 7

1. Quoted in James E. Cebula, "The New City and the New Journalism: The Case of Dayton, Ohio," *OH* 88 (1979): 284, 285.

2. Quoted in ibid., 287, 289.

3. Quoted in Ronald M. Johnson, "Politics and Pedagogy: The 1892 Cleveland School Reform," *OH* 84 (1975): 198.

4. Quoted in ibid., 203, 204.

5. Quoted in Janet A. Miller, "Urban Education and the New City: Cincinnati's Elementary Schools, 1870 to 1914," *OH* 88 (1979): 164, 165.

6. Quoted in John C. Mulder, "The Heavenly City and Human Cities: Washington Gladden and Urban Reform," *OH* 87 (1978): 157.

7. Quoted in ibid., 157, 160.

8. Quoted in ibid., 161.

9. Washington Gladden, *Recollections* (Boston: Houghton Mifflin, 1909), 329.

10. Quoted in Mulder, "Heavenly City and Human Cities," 166, 167.

11. Quoted in ibid., 169.

12. Gladden, *Recollections,* 294; quoted in Jacob Henry Dorn, *Washington Gladden, Prophet of the Social Gospel* (OSUP, 1968), 300.

13. Gladden, *Recollections,* 311; quoted in Dorn, *Washington Gladden,* 82, 227; Gladden, *Recollections,* 429.

14. Quoted in Edward M. Miggins, "A City of 'Uplifting Influences': From 'Sweet Charity' to Modern Social Welfare and Philanthropy," in Thomas F. Campbell and Edward M. Miggins, eds., *The Birth of Modern Cleveland, 1865–1930* (WRHS, 1988), 159.

15. Frederick C. Howe, *Confessions of a Reformer* (New York: Charles Scribner's Sons, 1925), 52.

16. Quoted in Marnie Jones, *Holy Toledo: Religion and Politics in the Life of "GOLDEN RULE" Jones* (UPK, 1998), 68.

17. Quoted in Jones, *Holy Toledo,* 91; Samuel M. Jones, *The New Right: A Plea for Fair Play Through a More Just Social Order* (New York: Eastern Book Concern, 1899), 472.

18. Tom Johnson, *My Story,* ed. Elizabeth J. Hauer (New York: E. W. Huebsch, 1911), 89.

19. Ibid., xxxvi, 167, 168.

20. C. H. Cramer, *Newton D. Baker: A Biography* (Cleveland: World, 1961), 49.

21. Allen O. Myers, *Bosses and Boodle in Ohio Politics: Some Plain Truths for Honest People* (Cincinnati: Lyceum Publishing, 1895), 13, 91–92.

22. Quoted in Zane L. Miller, *Boss Cox's Cincinnati: Urban Politics in the Progressive Era* (UCP, 1968), 94.

23. Quoted in Francis Russell, *The Shadow of Blooming Grove: Warren G. Harding in His Times* (New York: McGraw-Hill, 1968), 13.

24. Quoted in ibid., 134.

25. Quoted in ibid., 438.

26. Ibid., 26, 403–5.

27. Quoted in Stephen M. Millette, "Charles E. Ruthenberg: The Development of an American Communist, 1909–1927," *OH* 81 (1972): 196.

CHAPTER 8

1. London *Mail and Express,* April 10, 1886, in Edwin H. Cady and Norma W. Cady, eds., *Critical Essays on W. D. Howells, 1866–1920* (Boston: G. K. Hall, 1983), 60.

2. "Colonel Harvey's Prefatory Remarks," John A. Macy, "Howells," in ibid., 219, 245.

3. Howells, *Stories of Ohio* (New York: American Book Company, 1897), 282.

4. Ibid., 287.

5. Frank P. Goodwin, *The Growth of Ohio: A Manual of State and Local History for the Schools of Southwestern Ohio* (Cincinnati: University of Cincinnati, 1906), 7; Howells, *Sketch of the Life and Character of Rutherford B. Hayes* (New York: Hurd and Houghton, 1876), 162, 163.

6. Howells, *A Boy's Town,* in *Selected Writings,* ed. Henry Steele Commager (New York: Random House, [1950]), 711, 712, 713, 757, 762–63, 812, 815.

7. Ibid., 828, 834, 837.

8. Howells, *Years of My Youth and Three Essays* (Bloomington: IUP, 1975), 90, 91, 107.

9. "Real Conversations—I. A Dialogue Between William Dean Howells and Hjalmar Hjorth Boyesen," in Cady and Cady, eds., *Critical Essays on W. D. Howells,* 129, 130; Thomas Wortham, ed., *The Early Prose Writings of William Dean Howells, 1853–1861* (OUP, 1990), 181, 182.

10. Howells to Victoria M. Howells, March 24, 1861, August 25, 1864, in George Arms et al., eds., *Selected Letters, W. D. Howells* (Boston: Twayne, 1979–1983), 1: 76, 197; Howells, "Geoffrey: A Study of American Life," in Wortham, ed., *Early Prose Writings,* 272, 284, 308.

11. Howells to Victoria M. Howells, August 25, 1864, in *Selected Letters,* 1, ed. Arms et al., 197.

12. Catherwood, *A Woman in Armor* (New York: Carleton, 1895), 166.

13. Catherwood, *Craque-O'Doom* (New York: Street and Smith, 1902 [1881]), 15, 22–23.

14. Ibid., 38, 39.

15. Ibid., 27–28, 30, 31, 33, 34.

16. Ibid., 65, 72.

17. Ibid., 235, 236.

18. Garland, "Provincialism," in Jane Johnson, ed., *Crumbling Idols: Twelve Essays on Art Dealing Chiefly with Literature, Painting, and the Drama* (Cambridge, Mass.: Harvard University Press, 1960 [1894]), 10; Garland, *Roadside Meetings* (New York: Macmillan, 1930), 256.

19. Quoted in Cheryl B. Torsney, *Constance Fenimore Woolson: The Grief of Artistry* (Athens: University of Georgia Press, 1989), 16, 19.

20. Woolson, "Solomon," in *Castle Nowhere: Lake-Country Sketches* (New York: Harper, 1875), 238.

21. Ibid., 251.

22. Ibid., 261, 262, 263, 265.

23. Quoted in "Jessie Brown Pounds," in Sandra Parker, ed., *Home Material: Ohio's Nineteenth-Century Regional Women's Fiction* (BGSUPP, 1998), 221.

24. Pounds, "Hillsbury Folks," in ibid., 56.

25. Ibid., 57, 58, 61.

26. Pounds, "Trouble at Craydock's Corners," in ibid., 228, 231.

27. Ibid., 239.

28. Thurber, *My Life and Hard Times* (New York: Bantam Books, 1961 [1933]), 21, 25, 29, 38.

29. Ibid., 50.

30. Ibid., 62.

31. Robert Neuhaus, *Unsuspected Genius: The Art and Life of Frank Duveneck* (San Francisco: Bedford Press, 1987), 21.

32. Quoted in Josephine W. Duveneck, *Frank Duveneck, Painter-Teacher* (San Francisco: John Howell Books, 1920), 78, 79, 80.

33. Elizabeth Boott and Bessie Hoover Wessel, quoted in Duveneck, *Frank Duveneck*, 78, 79, 80, 141.

34. Quoted in Lois Marie Fink, "Elizabeth Nourse: Painting the Motif of Humanity," in Mary Alice Heekin Burke, *Elizabeth Nourse, 1859–1938: A Salon Career* (Washington, D.C.: Smithsonian Institution Press, 1983), 111.

35. Ibid., 133.

36. Quoted in Richard J. Boyle, *John Twachtman* (New York: Watson Guptill, 1979), 13–15, 30.

37. Quoted in Robert C. Vitz, *The Queen and the Arts: Cultural Life in Nineteenth-Century Cincinnati* (KSUP, 1989), 174.

38. "The Teachings of Robert Henri: The Alice Klauber Manuscript," in Bennard B. Perlman, *Robert Henri: His Life and Art* (New York: Dover Publications, 1991), 139, 140, 143.

39. Quoted in Charles H. Morgan, *George Bellows: Painter of America* (New York: Reynal, 1965), 37.

40. Sherwood Anderson, *Winesburg, Ohio* (New York: Viking, 1974 [1919]), 112, 120.

41. Ibid., 30, 243.

42. Ibid., 247; Thurber, *My Life and Hard Times*, 84, 85.

43. Sherwood Anderson, *Poor White* (London: Jonathan Cape, 1921 [1920]), 9, 16, 31, 40.

44. Ibid., 103, 110, 111, 113.

45. Quoted in Ronald Weber, *The Midwestern Ascendancy in American Writing* (IUP, 1992), 18.

CHAPTER 9

1. E. O. Randall, ed., *Ohio Centennial Anniversary Celebration at Chillicothe* (Columbus: Fred J. Heer, 1903), xxi.

2. "Address of Bishop B. W. Arnett," in ibid., 677.

3. Ibid., 677, 678, 680.

4. Ibid., 681–82.

5. Ibid., 682.

6. Ibid. See David A. Gerber, *Black Ohio and the Color Line, 1860–1915* (UIP, 1976), 249–54.

7. Richard H. Brodhead, ed., *The Journals of Charles W. Chesnutt* (Durham, N.C.: Duke University Press, 1993), 69, 78, 93, 106.

8. Ibid., 140.

9. "Her Virginia Mammy," in Charles W. Chesnutt, *The Wife of His Youth and Other Stories of the Color Line* (Ann Arbor: University of Michigan Press, 1968), 33, 55, 59.

10. Ibid., 38, 40.

11. "A Matter of Principle," in ibid., 95, 97, 117, 121, 122.

12. Ibid., 131.

13. "The Wife of His Youth," in ibid., 1, 4, 7.

14. Ibid., 8, 10, 24.

15. Kenneth L. Kusmer, *A Black Ghetto Takes Shape: Black Cleveland, 1870–1930* (UIP, 1976), 128–29.

16. "Uncle Wellington's Wives," in Chesnutt, *The Wife of His Youth,* 207.

17. Ibid., 246, 247.

18. Ibid., 250, 251, 253–54.

19. Quoted in William L. Andrews, *The Literary Career of Charles W. Chesnutt* (Baton Rouge: Louisiana State University Press, 1980), 141, 143.

20. See "Recession Never," "The Negro as Individual," "Representative American Negroes," in Jay Martin and Grossie H. Hudson, eds., *The Paul Dunbar Reader* (New York: Dodd, Mead, 1975), 36–39, 48, 59.

21. "One Man's Fortunes," in Martin and Hudson, eds., *Paul Dunbar Reader,* 139.

22. Ibid., 146, 147.

23. Dunbar, "Ode to Ethiopia," in ibid., 83–91, 278–79, 451.

24. Andrea Tuttle Kornbluh, "James Hathaway Robinson and the Origins of Professional Social Work in the Black Community," in Henry Louis Taylor, ed., *Race and the City: Work, Community, and Protest in Cincinnati, 1820–1970* (UIP, 1993), 209–31.

25. Langston Hughes, *The Big Sea: An Autobiography* (New York: Knopf, 1945), 27; quoted in Kimberley L. Phillips, *AlabamaNorth: African American Migrants, Community, and Working-Class Activism in Cleveland, 1915–1945* (UIP, 1999), 127.

26. Gerber, *Black Ohio and the Color Line,* 249–57

27. Hughes, *Big Sea,* 51.

28. Quoted in Phillips, *AlabamaNorth,* 164, 165, 169.

29. George A. Myers to James Ford Rhodes, February 10, 1921, in John A. Garraty, ed., *The Barber and the Historian: The Correspondence of George A. Myers and James Ford Rhodes, 1910–1923* (OHS, 1956), 124.

30. Quoted in Steven C. Tracy, *Going to Cincinnati: A History of the Blues in the Queen City* (UIP, 1993), 46, 60.

31. Quoted in ibid., xxix.

32. Chester Himes, *The Quality of Hurt: The Autobiography of Chester Himes* (New York: Paragon House, 1971), 15.

33. Ibid., 27, 28, 29.

34. Ibid., 38.

35. Claudia Tate, Interview with Toni Morrison, 1983, in Danille Taylor-Guthrie, ed., *Conversations with Toni Morrison* (Jackson: University Press of Mississippi, 1994), 158.

36. Quoted in Taylor-Guthrie, ed., *Conversations with Toni Morrison*, 158.

37. Toni Morrison, *The Bluest Eye* (New York: Holt, Rinehart, and Winston, 1970), 83.

38. Ibid., 87, 92.

39. Ibid., 128.

40. Ibid., 51.

41. Toni Morrison, *Beloved: A Novel* (New York: Knopf, 1987), 70.

42. Ibid., 73, 42, 273.

43. Ibid., 251.

44. Ibid., 199.

45. Clyde B. McCoy and Virginia McCoy Watkins, "Stereotypes of Appalachian Migrants," in William W. Philliber and Clyde B. McCoy, eds., *The Invisible Minority: Urban Appalachians* (UPK, 1981), 20–21.

46. Ibid., 23.

47. Phillip J. Obermiller, *Down Home, Downtown: Urban Appalachians Today* (Dubuque, Iowa: Kendall/Hunt Publishing, 1996), 22, 24–25.

48. *A Report on Appalachians in Columbus; A Report on Appalachians in Dayton; A Report on Appalachians in Cleveland; A Report on Appalachians in Toledo* (Cincinnati: Ohio Urban Awareness Project, 1978), n.p.; William W. Philliber, *Appalachian Migrants in Urban America: Cultural Conflict or Ethnic Group Formation?* (New York: Praeger, 1981), 43; Michael E. Maloney and Kathryn M. Borman, "Effects of Schools and Schooling Upon Appalachian Children in Cincinnati," in Phillip J. Obermiller and William W. Philliber, eds., *Two Few Tomorrows: Urban Appalachians in the 1980s* (Boone, N.C.: Appalachian Consortium Press, 1987), 96–97; Jerry Holloway, Phillip J. Obermiller, and Norman Rose, "Hard Times: Appalachians in the Ohio State Prison System," in Obermiller, ed., *Down Home, Downtown*, 133.

49. Quoted in Jacqueline Jones, *The Dispossessed: America's Underclass from the Civil War to the Present* (New York: Basic Books, 1992), 243; Carl E. Feather, *Mountain People in a Flat Land: A Popular History of Appalachian Migration to Northeast Ohio, 1940–1965* (OUP, 1998), 32.

50. McCoy and Watkins, "Stereotypes of Appalachian Migrants," 21; *Report on Appalachians in Toledo*, n.p.

51. Feather, *Mountain People in a Flat Land*, 39; Jack Temple Kirby, *Rural Worlds Lost: The American South, 1920–1960* (Baton Rouge: Louisiana State University Press, 1987), 329; *Report on Appalachians in Toledo*, n.p.

52. *Report on Appalachians in Cleveland*, n.p.

53. Jones, *Dispossessed*, 229; *Report on Appalachians in Columbus*, 4, 7.

54. *Report on Appalachians in Columbus*, 10, 14, 16.

55. Ibid., 25.

56. Ibid., 26, 27, 29, 28; Obermiller, *Down Home, Downtown*, 39–42.

57. Quoted in Obermiller, *Down Home, Downtown*, 48.

58. *Report on Appalachians in Toledo*, n.p.

59. Philliber, *Appalachian Migrants in Urban America*, 129 and passim.

60. E. Bruce Tucker, "Toward a New Ethnicity: Urban Appalachian Ethnic Consciousness in Cincinnati, 1950–1987," in Henry D. Shapiro and Jonathan D. Sarna,

eds., *Ethnic Identity and Civic Identity: Patterns of Conflict and Cohesion in Cincinnati Since 1820* (UIP, 1992), 235–40.

61. Phillip J. Obermiller and Robert W. Oldendick, "Two Studies of Appalachian Civic Involvement," in Obermiller and Philliber, eds., *Too Few Tomorrows,* 69–80.

62. William W. Philliber and Phillip J. Obermiller, "Black Appalachian Migrants: The Issue of Dual Minority Status," in ibid., 111–16.

63. *Report on Appalachians in Columbus,* 6; quoted in Lewis M. Killian, *White Southerners* (New York: Random House, 1970), 99.

CHAPTER 10

1. Bromfield, "A Philosophical Excursion," in Charles E. Little, ed., *Louis Bromfield at Malabar: Writings on Farming and Country Life* (Baltimore, Md.: Johns Hopkins University Press, 1988), 3, 4.

2. Bromfield, "The Plan," in ibid., 38–39, 32.

3. Louis Bromfield, "A Year at Malabar," "Fifteen Years After," in ibid., 57, 225.

4. Quoted in Raymond Boryczka and Lorin Lee Cary, *No Strength Without Union: An Illustrated History of Ohio Workers, 1803–1980* (OHS, 1982), 135.

5. Quoted in ibid., 162–63.

6. Quoted in ibid., 165.

7. Daniel Nelson, *American Rubber Workers and Organized Labor, 1900–1941* (Princeton, N.J.: Princeton University Press, 1988), 85.

8. Joe William Trotter Jr., *River Jordan: African American Urban Life in the Ohio Valley* (UPK, 1998), 106.

9. Ibid., 102; Kimberley L. Phillips, *AlabamaNorth: African American Migrants, Community, and Working-Class Activism in Cleveland, 1915–1945* (UIP, 1999), 99, 121.

10. Quoted in William D. Jenkins, *Steel Valley Klan: The Ku Klux Klan in Ohio's Mahoning Valley* (KSUP, 1990), 2, 3.

11. Quoted in Boryczka and Cary, *No Strength Without Union,* 193.

12. Ruth McKenney, *Industrial Valley* (New York: Harcourt, Brace, 1939), 98, 100, 135.

13. Quoted in Nelson, *American Rubber Workers,* 181.

14. McKenney, *Industrial Valley,* 164, 173.

15. Ibid., 261–62.

16. Quoted in Phillips, *AlabamaNorth,* 192.

17. Quoted in ibid., 192, 223.

18. Quoted in James T. Patterson, *Mr. Republican: A Biography of Robert A. Taft* (New York: Houghton Mifflin, 1972), 10.

19. Quoted in ibid., 14.

20. Taft to Horace D. Taft, May 2, 1923, in Clarence E. Wunderlin, ed., *The Papers of Robert A. Taft, Volume 1, 1889–1939* (KSUP, 1997), 277.

21. Taft, "The New Deal: Recovery, Reform and Revolution," [Speech to the Chamber of Commerce], [April 9, 1935], Warren, Ohio; Taft, "Radio Address on the Constitution," [September 17, 1938], in ibid., 480–90, 587.

22. Quoted in Richard O. Davies, *Defender of the Old Guard: John Bricker and American Politics* (OSUP, 1993), 42, 43.

23. Quoted in ibid., 51, 53.

24. Taft to John M. Ewen Jr., December 1, 1938; Taft, "Radio Address," December 25, [1938], in Wunderlin, ed., *Papers of Robert A. Taft*, 596, 602.

25. Quoted in Phillips, *AlabamaNorth*, 252; Trotter, *River Jordan*, 143, 147.

26. Quoted in Davies, *Defender of the Old Guard*, 201.

27. Quoted in Kenneth L. Ames, "Of Times, Places, and Old Houses," in Nannette V. Maciejunes and Michael D. Hall, eds., *The Paintings of Charles Burchfield, North by Midwest* (New York: Harry N. Abrams; Columbus: Columbus Museum of Art, 1977), 61.

28. J. Benjamin Townsend, ed., *Charles Burchfield's Journals: The Poverty of Place* (Albany: State University of New York Press, 1993), 157.

29. Ibid., 465.

30. Bromfield, "Fifteen Years After," in Little, ed., *Louis Bromfield at Malabar Farm*, 222–23.

CHAPTER 11

1. Quoted in Mark Shaw, *Nicklaus* (Dallas: Taylor Publishing, 1997), 169, 173.

2. Quoted in Robert A. Burnham, "The Cincinnati Charter Revolt of 1924: Creating City Government for a Pluralistic Society," in Henry D. Shapiro and Jonathan D. Sarna, eds., *Ethnic Diversity and Civic Identity: Patterns of Conflict and Cohesion in Cincinnati Since 1820* (UIP, 1992), 207, 210.

3. Kenneth Rexroth, *An Autobiographical Novel* (Garden City, N.Y.: Doubleday, 1966), 83, 84; Wil Haygood, *The Haygoods of Columbus: A Love Story* (Boston: Houghton Mifflin, 1997), 239–40.

4. Michael DeCapite, *Maria, A Novel* (New York: John Day, 1943), 50, 80.

5. Ibid., 83, 171, 187, 248.

6. Michael DeCapite, *No Bright Banner* (New York: John Day, 1944), 87, 291.

7. Raymond DeCapite, *The Coming of Fabrizze* (New York: David McKay, 1960), 17.

8. Ibid., 122, 152, 161.

9. Ibid., 200, 208.

10. Raymond DeCapite, *A Lost King* (New York: David McKay, 1961), 8, 9, 21, 51, 76.

11. Ibid., 213.

12. Jo Sinclair [Ruth Seid], *The Changelings* (New York: McGraw Hill, 1955), 40, 42, 99.

13. Ibid., 135.

14. Watkins, *Dancing With Strangers: A Memoir* (New York: Simon and Schuster, 1998), 12.

15. Ibid., 24.

16. Ibid., 41.

17. Ibid., 58–59, 127–29, 131, 142, 144, 302.

18. Haygood, *Haygoods of Columbus*, 347, 359, 76, 262.

19. Ibid., 45.

20. Ibid., 94, 168, 173, 174.

21. Ibid., 4.

22. Quoted in Richard O. Davies, *Main Street Blues: The Decline of Small-Town America* (OSUP, 1998), 87.

23. Quoted in ibid., 185.

24. Baskin, *New Burlington: The Life and Death of an American Village* (New York: Norton, 1976), 12.

25. Quoted in ibid., 44, 53, 98, 105, 116, 117.

26. Quoted in ibid., 157, 255.

27. Andrew Wiese, "The Other Suburbanites: African American Suburbanization in the North Before 1950," *Journal of American History* 85 (1999): 1519.

28. Zane L. Miller, *Suburb: Neighborhood and Community in Forest Park, Ohio, 1935–1976* (Knoxville: University of Tennessee Press, 1981), 178.

29. Gold, *My Last Two Thousand Years* (New York: Random House, 1972), 7, 10, 11, 14, 15, 113, 114.

30. Greene, *Be True to Your School: A Diary of 1964* (New York: Atheneum, 1987), 21–22, 67–68, 93, 212.

31. Quoted in Geoffrey C. Ward, *Baseball: An Illustrated History* (New York: Knopf, 1994), 67, 144.

32. Quoted in William J. Baker, *Jesse Owens: An American Life* (New York: Free Press, 1986), 125, 237; Owens, *Blackthink: My Life as Black Man and White Man* (New York: William Morrow, 1970), 27.

33. Quoted in Paul Brown with Jack Clary, *PB: The Paul Brown Story* (New York: Atheneum, 1980), 6, 7, 11–12.

34. Jimmy Brown with Myron Cope, *Off My Chest* (Garden City, N.Y.: Doubleday, 1964), 5; Brown, *PB*, 21, 24.

35. Paul Hornung, *Woody Hayes: A Reflection* (Champaign, Ill.: Sagamore Publishing, 1991), 27, 80, 276, 281.

36. Quoted in Archie Griffin with Dave Diles, *Archie: The Archie Griffin Story* (Garden City, N.Y.: Doubleday, 1977), 84.

37. Quoted in John Feinstein, *A Season on the Brink: A Year with Bob Knight and the Indiana Hoosiers* (New York: Macmillan, 1986), 3.

CHAPTER 12

1. Quoted in Scott L. Bills, "Introduction: The Past in the Present," in Scott L. Bills, ed., *Kent State/May 4: Echoes Through a Decade* (KSUP, 1988 [1982]), 14.

2. Quoted in ibid., 66, 70, 72, 118, 121.

3. Quoted in ibid., 119, 120, 122.

4. Quoted in ibid., 84, 86, 91.

5. Quoted in ibid., xi.

6. Richard T. Cooper, "A Town Turns on Its Children: The Culture of Kent," *Nation* (November 23, 1970), 517, 518.

7. Bill Roorbach, "Song of the Olentangy," *Harper's Magazine* (April 2000), 34–37; Chrissie Hynde, "My City Was Gone," www.pretenders.org/lymy.htm.

8. See Susan Faludi, "A Good Dawg Will Always Remain Loyal: The Cleveland Browns Skip Town," in *Stiffed: The Betrayal of the American Man* (New York: William Morrow, 1999), 153–223.

9. Quoted in Raymond Boryczka and Lorin Lee Cary, *No Strength Without Union: An Illustrated History of Ohio Workers* (OHS, 1982), 259.

10. Russell Salamon quoted in Mike Golden, ed., *The Buddhist Third Class Junkmail Oracle: The selected poetry and art of d. a. levy* (New York: Seven Stories Press, 1999), 36.

11. Levy, *Cleveland Undercovers* (Cleveland: 7 Flowers Press, 1966) and "Suburban Monastery Death Poem" (1968), in ibid., 175, 176, 186, 257, 258.

12. Quoted in Bob Greene, *Duty: A Father, His Son, and the Man Who Won the War* (New York: Harper Collins, 2000), 141, 184.

13. Mike Henson, *Ransack* (Cambridge, Mass.: West End Press, 1980), 13, 27, 52, 60, 151.

14. Anne Wright, "Many Waters," in Frank Graziano and Peter Stitt, eds., *James Wright: A Profile* (Durango, Colo.: Logbridge-Rhodes, 1988), 111; Dave Smith, "James Wright: The Pure, Clear Word, an Interview," in Smith, ed., *The Pure Clear Word: Essays on the Poetry of James Wright* (UIP, 1982), 5, 6, 7, 9, 10.

15. Wright, "A Secret Gratitude"; "Many of Our Waters: Variations on a Poem by a Black Child," in Wright, *Collected Poems* (Middletown, Conn.: Wesleyan University Press, 1971), 184, 207; Wright, *Two Citizens,* ed. Anne Wright (Fredonia, N.Y.: White Pine Press, 1987), 4; Wright "Ars Poetica: Some Recent Criticism," "Prayer to the Good Poet," "Ohio Valley Swains," "The Old WPA Swimming Pool in Martins Ferry, Ohio," "At the Grave," in *Two Citizens,* 6, 10, 11, 20, 23, 25.

16. Wright, "To the Creature of the Creation," in *Two Citizens,* 46; Wright, "One Last Look at the Adige: Verona in the Rain," "Beautiful Ohio," in Wright, *To a Blossoming Pear Tree* (New York: Farrar, Straus, and Giroux, 1977), 5, 62.

17. Quoted in Louis H. Masotti and Jerome R. Coral, *Shoot-Out in Cleveland: Black Militants and the Police* (New York: Frederick A. Praeger, 1969), 125.

18. Stokes, *Promises of Power: A Political Autobiography* (New York: Simon and Schuster, 1973), 252.

19. Carolyn M. Morris, "Black Elected Officials in Ohio, 1978: Characteristics and Perceptions," *OH* 88 (1979): 291–309.

20. Joseph Watras, *Politics, Race, and Schools: Racial Integration, 1954–1994* (New York: Garland Publishing, 1997).

21. Gregory S. Jacobs, *Getting Around Brown: Desegregation, Development, and the Columbus Public Schools* (OSUP, 1998), 119.

22. Quoted in Zane L. Miller and Bruce Tucker, *Changing Plans for America's Inner Cities: Cincinnati's Over-the-Rhine and Twentieth-Century Urbanism* (OSUP, 1998), xviii, 112, 141.

23. Quoted in Boryczka and Cary, *No Strength Without Union,* 259. See Peter Davis, *Hometown* (New York: Simon and Schuster, 1982).

24. Richard G. Zimmerman, "Rhodes's First Eight Years, 1963–1971," in Alexander P. Lamis, ed., *Ohio Politics* (KSUP, 1994), 64.

25. James A. Rhodes, *Alternative to a Decadent Society* (Indianapolis: Howard W. Sams, 1969), 10, 58, 59, 96, 108.

26. Quoted in Sydney Ladensohn Stern, *Gloria Steinem: Her Passions, Politics, and Mystique* (Secaucus, N.J.: Birch Lane Press, 1997), 227.

27. Helen Hooven Santmyer, ". . . *And Ladies of the Club"* (New York: G. P. Putnam's Sons, 1984 [1982]), 1425.

28. Ian Frazier, "Home Town Anonymous," *Atlantic Monthly* (October 1994), 96–106.

29. Quoted in James Reston Jr., *Collision at Home Plate: The Lives of Pete Rose and Bart Giamatti* (New York: HarperCollins, 1991), 100.

30. Quoted in ibid., 139–40.

31. Michael Y. Sokolove, *Hustle: The Myth, Life, and Lies of Pete Rose* (New York: Simon and Schuster, 1990), 101.

32. Quoted in "Marge: The Deposition," in Mike Bass, *Marge Schott Unleashed* (Champaign, Ill.: Sagamore Publishing, 1993), 212, 216, 219, 231, 287.

33. Kevin Walzer, "Cincinnati: A Note from the Province," in John Moor and Larry Smith, eds., *In Buckeye Country: Photos and Essays of Ohio Life* (Huron, Ohio: Bottom Dog Press, 1994), 157.

EPILOGUE

1. Quoted in Jeff Robinson and Brian Adams, "As Seen on TV," *Ohio Magazine* 22, no. 8 (November 2000): 65, 63.

2. Quoted in ibid., 65.

3. Ibid.

4. Terry Ryan, *The Prize Winner of Defiance, Ohio: How My Mother Raised 10 Kids on 25 Words or Less* (New York: Simon and Schuster, 2001).

5. Rita Dove, *Through the Ivory Gate* (New York: Vintage, 1992), 135.

6. Http://quickfacts.census.gov/qfd/states and http://oh.profiles.iastate.edu.

7. John Baskin, "Foreword," in Randy McNutt, *Ghosts: Ohio's Haunted Landscapes, Lost Arts and Forgotten Places* (Wilmington, Ohio: Orange Fraser Press, 1996), xiv.

8. McNutt, *Ghosts,* 7.

9. Merrill C. Gilfillan, *Moods of the Ohio Moons: An Outdoorsman's Almanac* (KSUP, 1991), 97–98, 137.

10. Scott Russell Sanders, "The Buckeyes: An Introduction," in *In Buckeye Country: Photos and Essays of Ohio Life,* ed. John Moor and Larry Smith (Huron, Ohio: Bottom Dog Press, 1994), 9, 10.

11. "Maya Lin—Garden," in *Illusions of Eden: Visions of the American Heartland,* ed. Robert Stearns (Minneapolis: Arts Midwest and the Ohio Arts Council, 2000), 208, 212.

12. David Citino, "My State of the State/Address," in *In Buckeye Country,* ed. Moor and Smith, 51, 54.

13. Jeffrey Hammond, "Ohio States," *The American Scholar* 70, no. 3 (Summer 2001), 35, 37, 38, 39, 43, 46.

14. Constance Pierce, "On Being Landlocked," in *In Buckeye Country,* ed. Moor and Smith, 161, 167, 168.

Selected Bibliography

⌐━

Abbreviations follow the same format as in the Notes, with the addition of Cin. for Cincinnati, Cle. for Cleveland, and Col. for Columbus.

PRIMARY SOURCES

Address to the Constitutional Convention of Ohio, from the State Convention of Colored Men. [Col.]: E. Glover, 1851.

Anderson, Sherwood. *Poor White.* 1920; reprint, London: Jonathan Cape, 1920.

———. *Tar: A Midwest Childhood: A Critical Text.* Edited by Ray Lewis White. Cle.: Case Western Reserve University, 1969.

———. *Winesburg, Ohio.* 1919; reprint, New York: Viking, 1974.

Arms, George, et al. *Selected Letters, W. D. Howells.* Boston: Twayne, 1979–1983.

Atwater, Caleb. *A History of the State of Ohio, Natural and Civil.* 2d ed. Cin.: Glezen and Shepard, 1838.

Audretsch, Robert W., ed. *The Salem, Ohio, 1850 Women's Rights Convention Proceedings.* Salem: Salem Area Bicentennial Committee, 1976.

Balch, Emily Greene. *Our Fellow Slavic Citizens.* 1910; reprint, New York: Arno, 1969.

Barr, Lockwood, ed. "Letters from Dr. Joseph Strong to Captain John Pratt." *OH* 51 (1942): 236–42.

Baskin, John. *New Burlington: The Life and Death of an American Village.* New York: Norton, 1976.

Becker, Carl M., and Ritchie Thomas, eds. *Hearth and Knapsack: The Ladley Letters, 1857–1880.* OUP, 1988.

Bennett, Emerson. *Mike Fink.* 1852; reprint, Upper Saddle River, N.J.: Literature House, 1970.

Bills, Scott L., ed. *Kent State/May 4: Echoes Through a Decade.* 2d ed. KSUP, 1990.

Birch, Brian P. "A British View of the Ohio Backwoods: The Letters of James Martin, 1821–1836." *OH* 94 (1985): 139–57.

Black, Wilfred W., ed. "Civil War Letters of George M. Wise." *OHQ* 65 (1956): 53–81.

———, ed. "Marching Through South Carolina: Another Civil War Letter of Lieutenant George M. Wise." *OHQ* 66 (1957): 187–95.

———, ed. "Orson Brainard: A Soldier in the Ranks." *OH* 76 (1967): 54–72.

Blocker, Jack S., Jr. "Annie Wittenmyer and the Women's Crusade." *OH* 88 (1979): 419–22.

Boyd, Thomas A., ed. *Prophet of Progress: The Speeches of Charles F. Kettering.* New York: E. P. Dutton, 1961.

Braxton, Joanne, ed. *The Collected Poetry of Paul Lawrence Dunbar.* Charlottesville: University Press of Virginia, 1993.

Brodhead, Richard H., ed. *The Journals of Charles W. Chestnutt.* Durham, N.C.: Duke University Press, 1993.

Bromfield, Louis. *The Farm.* New York: Harper and Brothers, 1933.

Brown, Jimmy, with Myron Cope. *Off My Chest.* Garden City, N.Y.: Doubleday, 1964.

Brown, Paul, with Jack Clary. *PB: The Paul Brown Story.* New York: Atheneum, 1980.

Cady, Edwin H., and Norma W. Cady, eds. *Critical Essays on W. D. Howells, 1866–1920.* Boston: G. K. Hall, 1983.

Carpenter, Matilda Gilruth. *The Crusade: Its Origin and Development at Washington Court House and Its Results.* Col.: W. G. Hubbard, 1893.

Chase, Salmon P., ed. *The Statues of Ohio and of the Northwestern Territory.* Cin.: Corey and Fairbank, 1833–35.

Catherwood, Mary Hartwell. *Craque-O'Doom.* 1881; reprint, New York: Street and Smith, 1902.

———. *A Woman in Armor.* New York: Carleton, 1895.

Chestnutt, Charles W. *Conjure Tales and Stories of the Color Line.* Edited by William L. Andrews. New York: Penguin, 1992.

———. *The Wife of His Youth and Other Stories of the Color Line.* 1899; reprint, Ann Arbor: University of Michigan Press, 1968.

Chevalier, Michel. *Society, Manners, and Politics in the United States, Letters on North America.* 1831; reprint, Gloucester, Mass.: Peter Smith, 1967.

Coggeshall, William T. *The Poems and Poetry of the West: With Biographical and Critical Notices.* Col.: Follett, Foster, 1860.

Conrad, Ethel, ed. "Touring Ohio in 1811: The Journal of Charity Rotch." *OH* 99 (1990): 135–65.

Cooper, Richard T. "A Town Turns on Its Children: The Culture of Kent." *Nation,* November 23, 1970, 517–19.

Davis, Peter. *Hometown.* New York: Simon and Schuster, 1982.

"Dear Julia: Letter from Cincinnati, written in 1870." *BCHS* 18 (1960): 105–15.

DeCapite, Michael. *Maria, A Novel.* New York: John Day, 1943.

———. *No Bright Banner.* New York: John Day, 1944.

DeCapite, Raymond. *The Coming of Fabrizze.* New York: David McKay, 1960.

———. *A Lost King.* New York: David McKay, 1961.

Dillon, Merton L., ed. "A Visit to the Ohio State Prison in 1837." *OH* 69 (1960): 69–72.

Donald, David, ed. "The Autobiography of James Hall, Western Literary Pioneer." *OH* 56 (1947): 295–304.

Dove, Rita. *Fifth Sunday: Stories.* UPK, 1985.

———. *Selected Poems.* New York: Pantheon, 1993.

———. *Thomas and Beulah: Poems.* Pittsburgh: Carnegie-Mellon Press, 1986.

———. *Through the Ivory Gate.* New York: Pantheon, 1992.

Drake, B[enjamin], and E. D. Mansfield. *Cincinnati in 1826.* Cin.: Morgan, Lodge, and Fisher, 1827.

Dumont, Julia L. *Life Sketches from Common Paths: A Series of American Tales.* New York: D. Appleton, 1856.

———. *"Tecumseh" and Other Stories of the Ohio River Valley.* Edited by Sandra Parker. BGSUPP, 2000.

Duveneck, Josephine W. *Frank Duveneck, Painter-Teacher.* San Francisco: John Howell Books, 1920.

Dwight, Margaret Van Horn. *A Journey to Ohio in 1810.* Edited by Max Farrand and Jay Gitlin. 1913; reprint, Lincoln: University of Nebraska Press, 1991.

Ellsworth, Henry Leavitt. *A Tour to New Connecticut in 1811.* Edited by Phillip R. Shriver. WRHS, 1985.

England, J. Merton, ed. *Buckeye Schoolmaster: A Chronicle of Midwestern Rural Life, 1853–1865.* BGSUPP, 1996.

Fetterley, Judith, ed. *Clovernook Sketches and Other Stories.* New Brunswick, N.J.: Rutgers University Press, 1987.

Filler, Louis, ed. "Waiting for the War's End: The Letter of an Ohio Soldier in Alabama after Learning of Lincoln's Death." *OH* 74 (1965): 55–62.

Finley, James B. *Memorials of Prison Life.* 1850; reprint, Cin.: L. Swormstedt and J. H. Power, 1851.

———. *Sketches of Western Methodism.* Cin.: R. P. Thompson, 1854.

Flint, Timothy. *Recollections of the Last Ten Years.* Boston: Cummings, Hilliard, 1826.

Folmar, John Kent, ed. "Pre–Civil War Sentiment from Belmont County: Correspondence of Hugh Anderson." *OH* 78 (1969): 202–10.

Foner, Philip S., and Herbert Shapiro, eds. *Northern Labor and Antislavery: A Documentary History.* Westport, Conn.: Greenwood Press, 1994.

Foner, Philip S. and George E. Walker, eds. *Proceedings of the Black State Conventions, 1840–1865: Volume I: New York, Pennsylvania, Indiana, Michigan, Ohio.* Philadelphia: Temple University Press, 1979.

Foraker, Joseph Benson. *Notes of a Busy Life.* Cin.: Stewart and Kidd, 1916.

Foraker, Julia Bundy. *I Would Live It Again: Memories of a Vivid Life.* New York: Harper, 1932.

Ford, Harvey S., ed. "The Diary of John Beatt, January–June, 1884." *OH* 58 (1949): 119–52, 390–427; 59 (1950): 58–91, 165–95.

Frazier, Ian. "Home Town Anonymous." *Atlantic Monthly* 274, no. 4 (October 1994): 96–106.

Gallagher, William Davis. *Facts and Conditions of Progress in the North-West.* Cin.: H. W. Derby, 1850.

Garland, Hamlin. "Provincialism." In *Crumbling Idol: Twelve Essays on Art Dealing Chiefly with Literature, Painting, and the Drama,* edited by Jane Johnson. 1894; reprint, Cambridge, Mass.: Harvard University Press, 1960.

————. *Roadside Meetings.* New York: Macmillan, 1930.

Garraty, John A., ed. *The Barber and the Historian: The Correspondence of George A. Myers and James Ford Rhodes, 1910–1923.* Col.: OHS, 1956.

Gilfillan, Merrill C. *Moods of the Ohio Moons: An Outdoorsman's Almanac.* KSUP, 1991.

Gladden, Washington. *The Cosmopolis City Club.* New York: Century, 1893.

————. *Recollections.* Boston: Houghton Mifflin, 1909.

Gold, Herbert. *My Last Two Thousand Years.* New York: Random House, 1972.

Golden, Mike, ed. *The Buddhist Third Class Junkmail Oracle: The Selected Poetry and Art of d. a. levy.* New York: Seven Stories Press, 1999.

Good, Howard E. *Black Swamp Farm.* OSUP, 1967.

Goodwin, Frank P. *The Growth of Ohio: A Manual of State and Local History for the Schools of Southwestern Ohio.* Cin.: University of Cincinnati, 1906.

Gordon, Mary. *The Shadow Man: A Daughter's Search for Her Father.* New York: Random House, 1996.

Graf, Leroy P., ed., "The Journal of a Vermont Man in Ohio, 1836–1842." *OH* 60 (1951): 175–99.

Graybar, Lloyd J., ed. "The Whiskey War at Paddy's Run: Excerpts from a Diary of Albert Shaw." *OH* 75 (1966): 48–54.

Greene, Bob. *Be True to Your School: A Diary of 1964.* New York: Atheneum, 1987.

————. *Duty: A Father, His Son, and the Man Who Won the War.* New York: Harper Collins, 2000.

Griffin, Archie, with Dave Diles. *Archie: The Archie Griffin Story.* Garden City, N.Y.: Doubleday, 1977.

Hall, James. *The West: Its Commerce and Navigation.* Cin.: H. W. Derby, 1848.

Hammond, Jeffrey. "Ohio States." *The American Scholar* 70, no. 3 (Summer 2001): 33–48.

Hatton, Robert W. "Just a Little of Bit of the Civil War, As Seen by W. J. Smith, Company M, 2nd O. V. Cavalry—Part I." *OH* 84 (1975): 101–26, 222–48.

Haygood, Wil. *The Haygoods of Columbus: A Love Story.* Boston: Houghton Mifflin, 1997.

Hensen, Mike. *Ransack.* Cambridge, Mass.: West End Press, 1980.

Hildreth, Samuel Prescott. *Biographical and Historical Memoirs of the Early Pioneer Settlers of Ohio.* Cin.: H. W. Derby, 1852.

————. *Pioneer History: Being an Account of the First Examinations of the Ohio Valley, and the Early Pioneer Settlement of the Northwest Territory.* Cin.: H. W. Derby, 1848.

Himes, Chester. *The Quality of Hurt: The Autobiography of Chester Himes.* New York: Paragon House, 1971.

Holman, Winifred Lovering, ed. "Diary of the Rev. James-Hanmer Francis, 1837–1838." *OH* 51 (1942): 41–61.

Hornung, Paul. *Woody Hayes: A Reflection.* Champaign, Ill.: Sagamore Publishing, 1991.

Howe, Frederick C. *Confessions of a Reformer.* New York: Charles Scribner's Sons, 1925.

Howe, Henry. *Historical Collections of Ohio.* Cin.: E. Morgan, 1852.

Howells, William Cooper. *Recollections of Life in Ohio from 1813 to 1840.* Edited by Edwin H. Cady. 1895; facsimile reprint, Gainesville, Fla.: Scholars' Facsimiles and Reprints, 1963.

Howells, William Dean. *A Boy's Life.* In *Selected Writings of William Dean Howells.* Edited by Henry Steele Commager. New York: Random House, 1950.

———. *Sketch of the Life and Character of Rutherford B. Hayes.* New York: Hurd and Houghton, 1876.

———. *Stories of Ohio.* New York: American Book Company, 1897.

———. *Years of My Youth and Three Essays.* IUP, 1975.

Hughes, Langston. *The Big Sea: An Autobiography.* New York: Knopf, 1945.

Hyatt, Hudson, ed. "Captain Hyatt: Being the Letters Written during the Years 1863–1864, to His Wife, Mary, by Captain T. J. Hyatt, 126th Ohio Volunteer Infantry." *OH* 53 (1944): 166–83.

Hynde, Chrissie. "My City Was Gone." www.pretenders.org/lymy.htm.

Johnson, Tom. *My Story.* Edited by Elizabeth J. Hauer. New York: E. W. Huebsch, 1911.

Jones, Daryl E. and James W. Pickering, eds. "A Young Woman in the Midwest: The Journal of Mary Sears, 1859–1860." *OH* 82 (1973): 235–42.

Jones, Robert Leslie, ed. "Flatboating Down the Ohio and Mississippi, 1867–1873: Correspondence and Diaries of the William Dudley Devol Family of Marietta, Ohio." *OH* 59 (1950): 287–309, 385–418.

Jones, Samuel M. *The New Right: A Plea for Fair Play Through a More Just Social Order.* New York: Eastern Book Concern, 1899.

Joyce, Rosemary O. *A Woman's Place: The Life History of a Rural Ohio Grandmother.* OSUP, 1983.

Kilbourn, John, ed. *Public Documents Concerning the Ohio Canals.* Col.: I. N. Whiting, 1832.

King, Sarah Ann Worthington. *A Private Memoir of Thomas Worthington.* Cin.: Robert Clarke, 1882.

Klement, Frank L., ed. "I Whipped Six Texans: A Civil War Letter of an Ohio Soldier." *OH* 73 (1964): 180–82.

Kline, David, ed. *Great Possessions: An Amish Farmer's Journal.* San Francisco: North Point Press, 1990.

Langston, John Mercer. *Freedom and Citizenship: Selected Letters and Addresses.* 1883; facsimile reprint, Miami, Fla.: Mnemosyne, 1969.

———. *From the Virginia Plantation to the National Capitol.* 1894; facsimile reprint, New York.: Arno, 1969.

Lasser, Carole and Marlene Deahl Merrill, eds. *Friends and Sisters: Letters Between Lucy Stone and Antoinette Brown Blackwell, 1846–1893.* UIP, 1987.

"Letters from the Samuel Huntington Correspondence, 1800–1812." in *Tracts* 95 (WRHS, 1915): 55–163.

Levstik, Frank P., ed. "Life Among the Lowly: An Early View of an Ohio Poor House." *OH* 88 (1979): 84–88.

levy, d. a. *Cleveland Undercovers.* Cle.: 7 Flowers Press, 1966.

Lewis, Samuel. *First Annual Report of the Superintendent of Common Schools, Made to the Thirty-Sixth General Assembly of Ohio.* 3 vols. Col.: S. Medary, 1838–39.

Little, Charles E., ed. *Louis Bromfield at Malabar: Writings on Farming and Country Life.* Baltimore, Md.: Johns Hopkins University Press, 1988.

Lynd, Robert S., and Helen Merrell Lynd. *Middletown: A Study in American Culture.* New York: Harcourt, Brace, 1929.

McFarland, Marvin W., ed. *The Papers of Wilbur and Orville Wright.* 2 vols. New York: McGraw-Hill, 1953.

McKenney, Ruth. *Industrial Valley.* New York: Harcourt, Brace, 1939.

McMillen, Wheeler. *Ohio Farm.* OSUP, 1974.

McNutt, Randy. *Ghosts: Ohio's Haunted Landscapes, Lost Arts, and Forgotten Places.* Wilmington, Ohio: Orange Frazer Press, 1996.

Malvin, John. *The Autobiography of John Malvin, Free Negro, 1795–1880.* Edited by Allan Peskin. KSUP, 1988.

Marks, Bayley Ellen, ed. "Correspondence of Anna Briggs Bentley from Columbiana County, 1826." *OH* 78 (1969): 38–45.

Martin, Jay and Grossie H. Hudson, eds. *The Paul Dunbar Reader.* New York: Dodd, Mead, 1975.

Mayer, Mabel Watkins, ed. "Into the Breach: Civil War Letters of Wallace W. Chadwick." *OH* 51 (1942): 158–80.

Middleton, Stephen. *The Black Laws in the Old Northwest: A Documentary History.* Westport, Conn.: Greenwood Press, 1993.

Moor, John, and Larry Smith, eds. *In Buckeye Country: Photos and Essays of Ohio Life.* Huron, Ohio: Bottom Dog Press, 1994.

Morgan, H. Wayne, ed. "A Civil War Diary of William McKinley." *OH* 69 (1960): 272–90.

Morris, Thomas. "Speech on Slavery." *Congressional Globe.* VII, 25th Congress, 3d Session, February 9, 1839, 167–75.

Morrison, Toni. *Beloved.* New York: Knopf, 1987.

———. *The Bluest Eye.* New York: Holt, Rinehart, and Winston, 1970.

———. *Jazz.* New York: Knopf, 1992.

———. *Paradise.* New York: Knopf, 1998.

———. *Song of Solomon.* New York: Knopf, 1977.

———. *Sula.* New York: Knopf, 1973.

———. *Tar Baby.* New York: Knopf, 1981.

Myers, Allen O. *Bosses and Boodle in Ohio Politics: Some Plain Truths for Honest People.* Cin.: Lyceum Publishing, 1895.

Naylor, James Ball. *In the Days of St. Clair: A Romance of the Muskingum Valley.* Akron: Saalfield Publishing, 1902.

———. *The Kentuckian: A Thrilling Tale of Ohio Life in the Early Sixties.* Boston: C. M. Clark and Publishing, 1905.

———. *Ralph Marlowe, A Novel.* Akron: Saalfield Publshing, 1901.

———. *Under Mad Anthony's Banner.* Akron: Saalfield Publishing, 1903.

Norris, James D., and James K. Martin, ed. "Three Civil War Letters of James A. Garfield." *OH* 74 (1965): 247–52.

Owens, Jessie. *Blackthink: My Life as Black Man and White Man.* New York: William Morrow, 1970.

Oxford Addresses. Hanover, Ind.: J. C. Monfort, 1835.

Parker, John P. *His Promised Land: The Autobiography of John P. Parker, Former Slave and Conductor on the Underground Railroad.* Edited by Stuart Seely Sprague. New York: Norton, 1996.

Parker, Sandra, ed. *Home Material: Ohio's Nineteenth-Century Regional Women's Fiction.* BGSUPP, 1998.

Patterson, Isaac Franklin. *The Constitutions of Ohio.* Cle.: Arthur H. Clarke, 1912.

Pogel, Dan, ed. *Early Mormon Documents.* Salt Lake City: Signature Books, 1996.

Randall, E. O., ed. *Ohio Centennial Anniversary Celebration at Chillicothe.* Col.: Fred J. Heer, 1903.

Ratcliffe, Donald, ed. "The Autobiography of Benjamin Tappan." *OH* 85 (1976): 109–57.

Reports on Appalachians in Akron, Cleveland, Columbus, Dayton, Toledo. Cin.: Ohio Awareness Project, 1978.

Rexroth, Kenneth. *An Autobiographical Novel.* Garden City, N.Y.: Doubleday, 1966.

Rhodes, James A. *Alternative to a Decadent Society.* Indianapolis: Howard W. Sams, 1969.

Roorbach, Bill. "Song of the Olentangy." *Harper's Magazine* 300, no. 1799 (April 2000): 34–47.

Rose, Pete, and Roger Kahn. *My Story.* New York: Macmillan, 1989.

Rowan, Steven, trans. *Cleveland and Its Germans.* 1907; reprint, WRHS, 1998.

Ryan, Terry. *The Prize Winner of Defiance, Ohio: How My Mother Raised 10 Kids on 25 Words or Less.* New York: Simon and Schuster, 2001.

Sanford, Charles L., ed. "'A New Home—Who'll Follow?' Letters of a New England Emigrant Family in Ohio, 1831–1842." *OH* 65 (1956): 152–66.

Santmyer, Helen Hooven. *". . . And Ladies of the Club".* 1982; reprint, New York: G. P. Putnam's Sons, 1984.

———. *Ohio Town.* 1962; reprint, New York: Harper and Row, 1984.

Schultz, Charles, ed. "Glimpses into Cincinnati's Past: The Gest Letters, 1834–1842." *OH* 73 (1964): 157–79.

Shankman, Arnold, ed. "Vallandigham's Arrest and the 1863 Dayton Riot—Two Letters." *OH* 79 (1970): 119–23.

Shapiro, Henry D., and Zane L. Miller, eds. *Physician to the West: Selected Writings of Daniel Drake on Science and Society.* UPK, 1970.

Shriver, Phillip R. and Clarence E. Wunderlin, Jr., eds. *The Documentary Heritage of Ohio.* OUP, 2000.

Simon, John Y., ed. "Hannah Fancher's Notes on Ohio Speech in 1824." *OH* 73 (1964): 34–38.

———, ed. "Reminiscences of Isaac Jackson Allen." *OH* 73 (1964): 207–38.

Sinclair, Jo [Ruth Seid]. *Anna Teller.* New York: D. McKay, 1960.

———. *The Changelings.* New York: McGraw Hill, 1955.

———. *The Seasons: Death and Transfiguration: A Memoir.* New York: Feminist Press at the City University of New York, 1993.

———. *Wasteland, A Novel.* New York: Harper, 1946.

Smith, Dwight L., ed. "Nine Letters of Nathaniel Dike on the Western Country, 1816–1818." *OH* 67 (1958): 189–220.

Smith, J. V., ed. *Report of the Debates and Proceedings of the Convention for the Revision of the Constitution of the State of Ohio, 1850–1851.* 2 vols. Col.: S. Medary, 1851.

Smith, Thomas H., ed. *An Ohio Reader.* 2 vols. Grand Rapids, Mich.: Eerdmans, [1975].

Smith, William C. *Queen City Yesterdays: Sketches of Cincinnati in the Eighties.* Crawfordsville, Ind.: R. E. Banta, 1959.

Smith, William Henry. *The St. Clair Papers: The Life and Public Services of Arthur St. Clair.* 2 vols. Cin.: R. Clarke, 1882.

Speer, Michael, ed. "Autobiography of Adam Lowry Rankin." *OH* 79 (1970): 18–55.

Steen, Ivan D. "Cincinnati in the 1850s: As Described by British Travelers." *BCHS* 26 (1968): 254–75.

Steffens, Lincoln. "Ohio, A Tale of Two Cities." *McClure's Magazine* (July 1905): 293–311.

Stewart, Mother. *Memories of the Crusade.* Col.: William G. Hubbard, 1888.

Stokes, Carl B. *Promises of Power: A Political Autobiography.* New York: Simon and Schuster, 1973.

Stowe, Harriet Beecher. *Uncle Tom's Cabin.* 1851–1852; reprint, New York: Signet, 1981.

Sweet, William Warren, ed. "The Edward Dromgoole Letters, 1778–1812." In *Religion on the American Frontier, 1783–1840.* 4 vols. UCP, 1946. 4: 123–201.

Taylor-Guthrie, Danille, ed. *Conversations with Toni Morrison.* Jackson: University of Mississippi Press., 1994.

Thurber, James. *My Life and Hard Times.* 1933; reprint, New York: Harper and Row, 1971.

Tiffin, Edward. *Anniversary Long Talk, Delivered Before the Tammany Society or Columbian Order.* Chillicothe: J. S. Collins, 1811.

Tocqueville, Alexis de. *Democracy in America.* Edited by J. P. Mayer and translated by George Lawrence. 1841; reprint, Garden City, N.Y.: Doubleday, 1969.

Tolzmann, Don Heinrich, ed. *Cincinnati, or The Mysteries of the West: Emil Klauprecht's German-American Novel.* Translated by Steven Rowan. 1854–55; reprint, New York: Peter Lang, 1996.

Townsend, J. Benjamin, ed. *Charles Burchfield's Journals: The Poverty of Place.* Albany: State University of New York Press, 1993.

Trautmann, Frederick. "Cincinnati and Southwestern Ohio through a German's Eye: 1846–1847." *QCH* 45 (Summer 1987): 21–30.

Trollope, Frances. *Domestic Manners of the Americans.* Edited by Richard Mullen. 1839; reprint, New York: Oxford University Press, 1984.

Venable, W. H. *Beginnings of Literary Culture in the Ohio Valley.* Cin.: Robert Clarke, 1891.

Walker, Joseph E., ed. "Plowshares and Pruning Hooks for the Miami and Potowatomi: The Journal of Gerald T. Hopkins, 1804." *OH* 88 (1979): 361–407.

———, ed. "The Travel Notes of Joseph Gibbons, 1804." *OH* 92 (1983): 96–146.

Walker, Timothy. *Annual Discourse Delivered Before the Ohio Historical and Philosophical Society . . . 1837.* Cin.: A. Flash, 1838.

Wallace, Paul A. W., ed. *The Travels of John Heckewelder in Frontier America.* 1958; reprint, Pittsburgh: University of Pittsburgh Press, 1985.

Watkins, Mel. *Dancing With Strangers: A Memoir.* New York: Simon and Schuster, 1998.

Weatherford, John., ed. "School and Other Days, 1859: Selections from the Diaries of Robert and Sylvester Bishop." *OH* 70 (1961): 58–63.

White, Mary. "Mary White: Autobiography of an Ohio First Lady." *OH* 82 (1973): 63–87.

Whitlock, Brand. *Brand Whitlock's The Buckeyes: Politics and Abolitionism in an Ohio Town, 1836–1845.* Edited by Paul W. Miller. OUP, 1977.

———. *Forty Years of It.* New York: D. Appleton, 1914.

———. *The Letters and Journal of Brand Whitlock.* Edited by Allan Nevins. New York: D. Appleton-Century, 1936.

———. *The Thirteenth District: A Story of a Candidate.* Indianapolis: Bowen-Merrill, 1902.

———. *The Turn of the Balance.* New York: Grosset and Dunlap, 1907.

———. *Uprooted.* New York: D. Appleton, 1926.

Willard, Frances E. *Women and Temperance: or, The Work and Workers of The Women's Christian Temperance Union.* 1883; reprint, New York: Arno, 1972.

Williams, Charles R., ed. *Diary and Letters of Rutherford Birchard Hayes.* 5 vols. OSAHS, 1922–26.

Wise, Isaac. *Reminiscences.* Translated and edited by David Philipson. Cin.: L. Wise, 1901.

Woolson, Constance Fenimore. *Castle Nowhere: Lake-Country Sketches.* New York: Harper and Brothers, 1875.

Wortham, Thomas, ed. *The Early Prose Writings of William Dean Howells, 1853–1861.* OUP, 1990.

Wright, James. *Collected Poems.* Middletown, Conn.: Wesleyan University Press, 1971.

———. *To a Blossoming Pear Tree.* New York: Farrar, Strauss, and Giroux, 1977.

———. *Two Citizens.* Edited by Anne Wright. Fredonia, N.Y.: White Pine Press, 1987.

Wunderlin, Clarence E., ed. *The Papers of Robert A. Taft.* 2 vols. to date. KSUP, 1997– .

SECONDARY SOURCES

General

Adler, Jeffrey S. *Yankee Merchants and the Making of the Urban West: The Rise and Fall of Antebellum St. Louis.* CUP, 1991.

Allen, Michael. *Western Rivermen, 1763–1861: Ohio and Mississippi Boatmen and the Myth of the Alligator Horse.* Baton Rouge: Louisiana State University Press, 1990.

Anderson, Benedict. *Imagined Communities: Reflections on the Origin and Spread of Nationalism.* Rev. ed. London: Verso, 1991.

Appleby, Joyce. *Inheriting the Revolution: The First Generation of Americans.* Cambridge, Mass.: Harvard University Press, 2000.

Aron, Stephen. *How the West Was Lost: The Transformation of Kentucky from Daniel Boone to Henry Clay.* Baltimore, Md.: Johns Hopkins University Press, 1996.

Atherton, Lewis. *Main Street on the Middle Border.* IUP, 1984.

Ayers, Edward, et al. *All Over the Map: Rethinking American Regions.* Baltimore, Md.: Johns Hopkins University Press, 1996.

———. *The Promise of the New South: Life after Reconstruction.* New York: Oxford University Press, 1992.

Bailey, Beth. *From Front Porch to Back Seat: Courtship in Twentieth-Century America.* Baltimore, Md.: Johns Hopkins University Press, 1988.

———. *Sex in the Heartland.* Baltimore, Md.: Johns Hopkins University Press, 1999.

Barnhart, John D. *Valley of Democracy: The Frontier versus the Plantation in the Ohio Valley, 1775–1818.* IUP, 1953.

Basso, Keith H. *Wisdom Sits in Place: Landscape and Language among the Western Apache.* Albuquerque: University of New Mexico Press, 1996.

Berry, Chad. *Southern Migrants and Northern Exiles.* UIP, 2000.

Berwanger, Eugene H. *The Frontier Against Slavery: Western Anti-Negro Prejudice and the Slavery Extension Controversy.* UIP, 1967.

Blumin, Stuart M. *The Emergence of the Middle Class: Social Experience in the American City, 1760–1900.* CUP, 1989.

Buley, R. Carlyle. *The Old Northwest: Pioneer Period, 1815–1840.* 2 vols. IUP, 1950.

Cayton, Andrew R. L. *Frontier Indiana.* IUP, 1996.

Cayton, Andrew R. L., and Susan E. Gray, eds. *The American Midwest: Essays on Regional History.* IUP, 2001.

Cayton, Andrew R. L., and Peter S. Onuf. *The Midwest and the Nation: Rethinking the History of an American Region.* IUP, 1990.

Cayton, Mary Kupiec. "The Making of an American Prophet: Emerson, His Audiences, and the Rise of the Culture Industry in America." *American Historical Review* 92 (1987): 597–620.

Cohen, Lizabeth. "Citizens and Consumers in the United States in the Century of Mass Consumption." In *The Politics of Consumption: Material and Citizenship in Europe and America,* edited by Martin Daunton and Matthew Hinton, 203–22. New York: Berg, 2001.

———. "From Town Center to Shopping Center: The Reconfiguration of Community Marketplaces in Postwar America." In *His and Her: Gender, Consumption, and Technology,* edited by Roger Horowitz and Arwen Mohun, 189–234. Charlottesville: University Press of Virginia, 1998.

———. *Making a New Deal: Industrial Workers in Chicago, 1919–1939.* CUP, 1990.

Conzen, Kathleen Neils. *Immigrant Milwaukee, 1836–1860: Accommodation and Community in a Frontier City.* Cambridge, Mass.: Harvard University Press, 1976.

Coontz, Stephanie. *The Way We Never Were: American Families and the Nostalgia Trap*. New York: Basic Books, 1992.

———. *The Way We Really Are: Coming to Terms with America's Changing Families*. New York: Basic Books, 1997.

Cronon, William. *Nature's Metropolis: Chicago and the Great West*. New York: Norton, 1991.

Doyle, Don Harrison. *The Social Order of a Frontier Community: Jacksonville, Illinois, 1825–1870*. UIP, 1978.

Dumenil, Lynn. *Modern Temper: American Culture and Society in the 1920s*. New York: Hill and Wang, 1995.

Elkins, Stanley, and Eric McKitrick. "A Meaning for Turner's Frontier: Democracy in the Old Northwest." *Political Science Quarterly* 69 (1954): 321–54.

Epstein, Barbara Leslie. *The Politics of Domesticity: Women, Evangelism, and Temperance in Nineteenth-Century America*. Middletown, Conn.: Wesleyan University Press, 1981.

Etcheson, Nicole. *The Emerging Midwest: Upland Southerners and the Political Culture of the Old Northwest, 1787–1861*. IUP, 1996.

Faragher, John Mack. *Sugar Creek: Life on the Illinois Prairie*. YUP, 1986.

Farrell, James J. *The Spirit of the Sixties: Making Postwar Radicalism*. New York: Routledge, 1997.

Fink, Leon. *Workingmen's Democracy: The Knights of Labor and American Politics*. UIP, 1983.

Foner, Eric. *Free Soil, Free Labor, Free Men: The Ideology of the Republican Party Before the Civil War*. New York: Oxford University Press, 1970.

———. *Reconstruction: America's Unfinished Revolution, 1863–1877*. New York: Harper and Row, 1988.

Fox, Richard Wrightman, and T. J. Jackson Lears, eds. *The Culture of Consumption: Critical Essays in American History*. New York: Pantheon, 1983.

Frank, Thomas. *The Conquest of Cool: Business Culture, Counterculture, and the Rise of Hip Consumerism*. UCP, 1997.

Fuller, Wayne E. *The Old Country School*. UCP, 1982.

Gay, Peter. *The Bourgeois Experience*. 5 vols. New York: Oxford University Press and Norton, 1984–98.

Gienapp, William E. *The Origins of the Republican Party, 1852–1856*. New York: Oxford University Press, 1987.

Gilje, Paul., ed. *Wages of Independence: Capitalism in the Early American Republic*. Madison, Wis.: Madison House, 1997.

Gilkeson, John S., Jr. *Middle-Class Providence, 1820–1920*. Princeton, N.J.: Princeton University Press, 1986.

Gjerde, Jon. *The Minds of the West: Ethnocultural Evolution in the Rural Middle West, 1830–1917*. UNCP, 1997.

Goodwyn, Lawrence. *The Populist Moment: A Short History of the Agrarian Revolt in America*. New York: Oxford University Press, 1978.

Gordon-Reed, Annette. *Thomas Jefferson and Sally Hemings: An American Controversy*. Charlottesville: University Press of Virginia, 1997.

Gorn, Elliott J. *The Manly Art: Bare-Knuckle Prize Fighting in America*. Ithaca, N.Y.: Cornell University Press, 1986.

———. *Mother Jones: The Most Dangerous Woman in America*. New York: Hill and Wang, 2001.

Gray, Susan E. *The Yankee West: Community Life on the Michigan Frontier*. UNCP, 1996.

Grossman, James R. *Land of Hope: Chicago, Black Southerners, and the Great Migration*. UCP, 1989.

Guterl, Matthew Pratt. *The Color of Race in America, 1900–1940*. Cambridge, Mass.: Harvard University Press, 2001.

Gutman, Hebert G. *Work, Culture, and Society in Industrializing America: Essays in American Working-Class and Social History*. New York: Knopf, 1976.

Halttunen, Karen. *Confidence Men and Painted Women: A Study of Middle-Class Culture in America, 1830–1870*. YUP, 1982.

Hatch, Nathan O. *The Democratization of American Christianity*. YUP, 1989.

Hedrick, Joan D. *Harriet Beecher Stowe, A Life*. New York: Oxford University Press, 1994.

Hewett, Nancy A. *Women's Activism and Social Change: Rochester, New York, 1822–1872*. Ithaca, N.Y.: Cornell University Press, 1984.

Hinderaker, Eric. *Elusive Empires: Constructing Colonialism in the Ohio Valley, 1673–1800*. CUP, 1997.

Holt, Michael F. *The Political Crisis of the 1850s*. New York: John Wiley, 1978.

———. *The Rise and Fall of the American Whig Party: Jacksonian Politics and the Onset of the Civil War*. New York: Oxford University Press, 1999.

Hudson, John C. *Making the Corn Belt: A Geographical History of Middle-Western Agriculture*. IUP, 1994.

Isenberg, Nancy. *Sex and Citizenship in Antebellum America*. UNCP, 1998.

Jackson, Kenneth T. *Crabgrass Frontier: The Suburbanization of the United States*. New York: Oxford University Press, 1985.

Jacobson, Matthew Frye. *Whiteness of a Different Color: European Immigrants and the Alchemy of Race*. Cambridge, Mass.: Harvard University Press, 1998.

Jensen, Richard J. *The Winning of the Midwest: Social and Political Conflict, 1888–1896*. UCP, 1971.

Johannsen, Robert W. *To the Halls of the Montezumas: The Mexican War in the American Imagination*. New York: Oxford University Press, 1985.

John, Richard R. *Spreading the News: The American Postal System from Franklin to Morse*. Cambridge, Mass.: Harvard University Press, 1995.

Jones, Jacqueline. *The Dispossessed: America's Underclass from the Civil War to the Present*. New York: Basic Books, 1992.

Kaestle, Carl F. *Pillars of the Republic: Common Schools and American Society, 1780–1860*. New York: Hill and Wang, 1983.

Kennedy, David M. *Freedom from Fear: The American People in Depression and War, 1929–1945*. New York: Oxford University Press, 1999.

Kerber, Linda K. *Toward an Intellectual History of Women: Essays*. UNCP, 1997.

Kerr, K. Austin. *Organized for Prohibition: A New History of the Anti-Saloon League.* YUP, 1985.

Kimball, Roger. *The Long March: How the Cultural Revolution of the 1960s Changed America.* San Francisco: Encounter Books, 2000.

King, Desmond S. *Making Americans: Immigration, Race, and the Origins of the Diverse Democracy.* Cambridge, Mass.: Harvard University Press, 2000.

Kirby, Jack Temple. *The Countercultural South.* Athens: University of Georgia Press, 1995.

———. *Rural Worlds Lost: The American South, 1920–1960.* Baton Rouge: Louisiana State University Press, 1987.

———. "The Southern Exodus, 1910–1960: A Primer for Historians." *Journal of Southern History* 49 (1983): 585–600.

Kleppner, Paul. *The Cross of Culture: A Social Analysis of Midwestern Politics, 1850–1900.* New York: Free Press, 1970.

Larson, John Lauritz. *Internal Improvement: National Public Works and the Promise of Popular Government in the Early United States.* UNCP, 2001.

Levine, Bruce. *Half Slave and Half Free: The Roots of Civil War.* New York: Hill and Wang, 1992.

McPherson, James. *Battle Cry of Freedom: The Civil War Era.* New York: Oxford University Press, 1988.

———. *What They Fought For, 1861–1865.* New York: Doubleday, 1995.

Madison, James H. *A Lynching in the Heartland: Race and Memory in America.* New York: Palgrave for St. Martin's Press, 2001.

Mahoney, Timothy R. *Provincial Lives: Middle-Class Experience in the Antebellum Middle West.* CUP, 1999.

———. *River Towns in the Great West: The Structure of Provincial Urbanization in the American Midwest, 1820–1870.* CUP, 1990.

Marx, Anthony W. *Making Race and Nation: A Comparison of the United States, South Africa, and Brazil.* CUP, 1998.

Mattingly, Paul H., and Edward W. Stevens, Jr., ed. *"Schools and the Means of Education Shall Forever be Encouraged": A History of Education in the Old Northwest, 1787–1880.* Athens: Ohio University Libraries, 1987.

Matusow, Allen J. *The Unraveling of America: A History of Liberalism in the 1960s.* New York: Harper and Row, 1984.

May, Elaine Tyler. *Homeward Bound: American Families in the Cold War Era.* New York: Basic Books, 1988.

Meinig, D. W. *Continental America, 1800–1867.* YUP, 1993.

———. *Transcontinental America, 1850–1915.* YUP, 1998.

Montgomery, David. *The Fall of the House of Labor: The Workplace, the State, and American Labor Activism, 1865–1925.* CUP, 1987.

Morrison, Toni. *Playing in the Dark: Whiteness and the Literary Imagination.* Cambridge, Mass.: Harvard University Press, 1992.

Nelson, Daniel. *American Rubber Workers and Organized Labor, 1900–1941.* Princeton, N.J.: Princeton University Press, 1988.

Novick, Peter. *That Noble Dream: The "Objectivity Question" and the American Historical Profession.* CUP, 1988.

O'Brien, Michael. *The Idea of the American South 1920–1941.* Baltimore, Md.: Johns Hopkins University Press, 1979.

——. *Rethinking the South: Essays in Intellectual History.* Baltimore, Md.: Johns Hopkins University Press, 1988.

Onuf, Peter S. *Statehood and Union: A History of the Northwest Ordinance.* IUP, 1987.

Patterson, James T. *Grand Expectations: The United States, 1945–1974.* New York: Oxford University Press, 1996.

Pederson, Jane Marie. *Between Memory and Reality: Family and Community in Rural Wisconsin, 1870–1970.* Madison: University of Wisconsin Press, 1992.

Peiss, Kathy. *Cheap Amusements: Working Women and Leisure in Turn-of-the-Century New York.* Philadelphia: Temple University Press, 1986.

Perkins, Elizabeth A. *Border Life: Experience and Memory in the Revolutionary Ohio Valley.* UNCP, 1998.

Philliber, William W. *Appalachian Migrants in Urban America: Cultural Conflict or Ethnic Group Formation?* New York: Praeger, 1981.

Philliber, William W., and Clyde B. McCoy, eds. *The Invisible Minority: Urban Appalachians.* UPK, 1981.

Power, Richard Lyle. *Planting Corn Belt Culture: The Impress of the Upland Southerner and Yankee in the Old Northwest.* Indianapolis: Indiana Historical Society, 1953.

Reiss, Steven A. *Touching Base: Professional Baseball and American Culture in the Progressive Era.* UIP, 1999.

Richards, Leonard L. *"Gentlemen of Property and Standing": Anti-Abolition Mobs in Jacksonian America.* New York: Oxford University Press, 1970.

Rodgers, Daniel T. *Atlantic Crossings: Social Politics in a Progressive Age.* Cambridge, Mass.: Harvard University Press, 1998.

Roediger, David R. *The Wages of Whiteness: Race and the Making of the American Working Class.* 1991; revised edition, London: Verso, 1999.

Rohrbough, Malcolm J. *The Land Office Business: The Settlement and Administration of American Public Lands, 1789–1837.* New York: Oxford University Press, 1968.

——. *The Trans-Appalachian Frontier: People, Societies, and Institutions, 1775–1850.* New York: Oxford University Press, 1978.

Rorabaugh, W. J. *The Alcoholic Republic: An American Tradition.* New York: Oxford University Press, 1979.

Rosenberg, Charles E. *The Cholera Years: The United States in 1832, 1849, and 1866.* UCP, 1962.

Rosenzweig, Roy. *Eight Hours for What We Will: Workers and Leisure in An Industrial City, 1870–1920.* CUP, 1983.

Rothman, David J. *The Discovery of the Asylum: Social Order and Disorder in the New Republic.* Boston: Little, Brown, 1971.

Royster, Charles. *The Destructive War: William Tecumseh Sherman, Stonewall Jackson, and the Americans.* New York: Knopf, 1991.

Rugh, Susan Sessions. *Our Common Country: Family Farming, Culture, and Community in the Nineteenth-Century Midwest.* IUP, 2001.

Ryan, Mary P. *Civic Wars: Democracy and Public Life in the American City During the Nineteenth Century.* Berkeley: University of California Press, 1997.

————. *Cradle of the Middle Class: The Family in Oneida County, New York, 1790–1865.* CUP, 1981.

————. *Women in Public: Between Banners and Ballots, 1825–1880.* Baltimore, Md.: Johns Hopkins University Press, 1990.

Sheehan, Bernard W., ed. "The Northwest Ordinance: A Special Issue." *Indiana Magazine of History* 84 (March 1988).

Shortridge, James R. *The Middle West: Its Meaning in American Culture.* Lawrence: University Press of Kansas, 1989.

Sklar, Kathryn Kish. *Catharine Beecher: A Study in Domesticity.* YUP, 1973.

Smith, Rogers M. *Civic Ideals: Conflicting Visions of Citizenship in U.S. History.* YUP, 1997.

Sollors, Werner, ed. *Interracialism: Black-White Intermarriage in American History, Literature, and Law.* New York: Oxford University Press, 2000.

Stein, Stephen J. *The Shaker Experience in America: A History of the United Society of Believers.* YUP, 1992.

Stokes, Melvyn and Stephen Conway, eds., *The Market Revolution in America: Social, Political, and Religious Expressions, 1800–1880.* Charlottesville: University Press of Virginia, 1996.

Sugrue, Thomas J. *The Origins of the Urban Crisis: Race and Inequality in Postwar Detroit.* Princeton, N.J.: Princeton University Press, 1996.

Teaford, Jon. *Cities of the Heartland: The Rise and Fall of the Industrial Midwest.* IUP, 1993.

Thelen, David. *Paths of Resistance: Tradition and Dignity in Industrializing Missouri.* New York: Oxford University Press, 1986.

Thomas, John L. *Alternative America: Henry George, Edward Bellamy, Henry Demarest Lloyd and the Adversary Tradition.* Cambridge, Mass.: Harvard University Press, 1983.

Trachtenberg, Alan. *The Incorporation of America: Culture and Society in the Gilded Age.* New York: Hill and Wang, 1982.

Trotter, Joe William, Jr., ed. *The Great Migration in Historical Perspective: A New Dimension of Race, Class, and Gender.* IUP, 1991.

————. *River Jordan: African American Urban Life in the Ohio Valley.* UPK, 1998.

Van Slyck, Abigail A. *Free to All: Carnegie Libraries and American Culture, 1890–1920.* UCP, 1995.

Vincent, Stephen A. *Southern Seed, Northern Soil: African-American Farm Communities in the Midwest, 1765–1900.* IUP, 1999.

Voegeli, V. Jacque. *Free But Not Equal: The Midwest and the Negro During the Civil War.* UCP, 1967.

Wade, Richard C. *The Urban Frontier: Pioneer Life in Early Pittsburgh, Cincinnati, Lexington, Louisville, and St. Louis.* 1959; reprint, UCP, 1972.

Waldstreicher, David. *In the Midst of Perpetual Fetes: The Making of American Nationalism, 1776–1820.* UNCP for the Omohundro Institute of Early American History and Culture, 1997.

Walker, Juliet E. K. *Free Frank: A Black Pioneer on the Antebellum Frontier.* UPK, 1983.

Ward, Geoffrey C. *Baseball: An Illustrated History.* New York: Knopf, 1994.

Way, Peter. *Common Labour: Workers and the Digging of North American Canals, 1780–1860.* CUP, 1993.

Weber, Ronald. *The Midwestern Ascendancy in American Writing.* IUP, 1992.

Wood, Gordon S. *The Radicalism of the American Revolution.* New York: Knopf, 1992.

Specific to Ohio

Aaron, Daniel. *Cincinnati, Queen City of the West.* OSUP, 1992.

Anderson, David D. *Louis Bromfield.* New York: Twayne, 1964.

———. "The Odyssey of Petroleum Vesuvius Nasby." *OH* 74 (1965): 232–46.

———. *Sherwood Anderson: An Introduction and Interpretation.* New York: Holt, Rinehart, and Winston, 1967.

Andrews, William L. *The Literary Career of Charles W. Chestnutt.* Baton Rouge: Louisiana State University Press, 1980.

Baker, William J. *Jesse Owens: An American Life.* New York: Free Press, 1986.

Baldwin, Neil. *Edison: Inventing the Century.* New York: Hyperion, 1995.

Barton, Josef J. *Peasants and Strangers: Italians, Rumanians, and Slovaks in an American City, 1890–1950.* Cambridge, Mass.: Harvard University Press, 1975.

Bass, Mike. *Marge Schott Unleashed.* Champaign, Ill.: Sagamore Publishing, 1993.

Baur, John I. H. *The Inlander: Life and Work of Charles Burchfield, 1893–1967.* Newark: University of Delaware Press, 1982.

Becker, Carl M., and Richard H. Grisgby. "Baseball in the Small Ohio Community, 1865–1900." In *Sport in America: New Historical Perspectives,* edited by Donald Spivey, 77–94. Westport, Conn.: Greenwood Press, 1985.

Blackford, Mansel G., and K. Austin Kerr. *BF Goodrich: Tradition and Transformation, 1870–1995.* OSUP, 1996.

Blocker, Jack S., Jr. *"Give to the Winds Thy Fears": The Women's Temperance Crusade, 1873–1874.* Westport, Conn.: Greenwood Press, 1985.

———. "Market Integration, Urban Growth and Economic Change in an Ohio County, 1850–1880." *OH* 90 (1981): 298–316.

Blue, Frederick J. *Salmon P. Chase: A Life in Politics.* KSUP, 1987.

Bonadio, Felice A. *North of Reconstruction: Ohio Politics, 1865–1870.* New York: New York University Press, 1970.

Bond, Beverley W., Jr. *The Foundations of Ohio.* OSAHS, 1941.

Bordin, Ruth. "'A Baptism of Power and Liberty': The Women's Crusade of 1873–1874." *OH* 87 (1978): 393–404.

———. *Women and Temperance: The Quest for Power and Liberty, 1873–1800.* Philadelphia: Temple University Press, 1981.

Boryczka, Raymond and Lorin Lee Cary. *No Strength Without Union: An Illustrated History of Ohio Workers, 1803–1980.* Col.: OHS, 1982.

Boyle, Richard J. *John Henry Twachtman.* New York: Watson Guptill, 1979.

Boynton, Virginia R. "Contested Terrain: The Struggle Over Gender Norms for Black Working-Class Women in Cleveland's Phillis Wheatley Association, 1920–1950." *OH* 103 (1994): 5–22.

Brandt, Nat. *The Town That Started the Civil War.* Syracuse, N.Y.: Syracuse University Press, 1990.

Brown, Jeffrey P. "Chillicothe's Elite: Leadership in a Frontier Community." *OH* 96 (1987): 140–56.

———. "Frontier Politics: The Evolution of a Political Society in Ohio, 1788–1814." Ph.D. diss., University of Illinois, 1979.

———. "Samuel Huntington: A Connecticut Aristocrat on the Ohio Frontier." *OH* 89 (1980): 420–38.

Brown, Jeffrey P., and Andrew R. L. Cayton, eds. *The Pursuit of Public Power: Political Culture in Ohio, 1787–1861.* KSUP, 1994.

Burke, Mary Alice Heekin. *Elizabeth Nourse, 1859–1938: A Salon Career.* Washington, D.C.: Smithsonian Institution Press, 1983.

Cady, Edwin Harrison. *The Road to Realism: The Early Years, 1837–1885, of William Dean Howells.* Syracuse, N.Y.: Syracuse University Press, 1956.

Campbell, Thomas F., and Edward M. Miggins, eds. *The Birth of Modern Cleveland.* WRHS, 1988.

Cayton, Andrew R. L. *The Frontier Republic: Ideology and Politics in the Ohio Country, 1780–1825.* KSUP, 1986.

Cebula, James E. "The New City and the New Journalism: The Case of Dayton, Ohio." *OH* 88 (1979): 277–90.

Cheek, William F., and Aimee Lee Cheek. *John Mercer Langston and the Fight for Black Freedom, 1829–1865.* UIP, 1989.

Chernow, Ron. *Titan: The Life of John D. Rockefeller, Sr.* New York: Random House, 1998.

Cole, Charles C., Jr. *A Fragile Capital: Identity and the Early Years of Columbus, Ohio.* OSUP, 2001.

Contosta, David R. *Lancaster, Ohio, 1800–2000: Frontier Town to Edge City.* OSUP, 1999.

Cotkin, George B. "Strikebreakers, Evictions and Violence: Industrial Conflict in the Hocking Valley, 1884–1885." *OH* 87 (1978): 140–50.

Cramer, C. H. *Newton D. Baker: A Biography.* Cle.: World, 1961.

Crouch, Tom D. *The Bishop's Boys: A Life of Wilbur and Orville Wright.* New York: Norton, 1989.

Crowley, John William. *The Black Heart's Truth: The Early Career of W. D. Howells.* UNCP, 1985.

Dannenbaum, Jed. *Drink and Disorder: Temperance Reform in Cincinnati from the Washingtonian Revival to the WCTU.* UIP, 1984.

———. "The Origins of Temperance Activism and Militancy Among American Women." *Journal of Social History* 15, no. 2 (1981): 235–52.

David, J. Ridgway. "A Century of Voting in Three Ohio Counties." *OH* 69 (1960): 121–56.

Davies, Richard O. *Defender of the Old Guard: John Bricker and American Politics.* OSUP, 1993.

———. *Main Street Blues: The Decline of Small-Town America.* OSUP, 1998.

DeMatteo, Arthur E. "The Downfall of a Progressive: Mayor Tom L. Johnson and the Cleveland Streetcar Strike of 1908." *OH* 104 (1995): 24–41.

Dillon, Kathleen M. "Painters and Patrons: The Fine Arts in Cincinnati, 1820–1860." *OH* 96 (1987): 7–32.

Dobbert, Guido Andre. *The Disintegration of an Immigrant Community: The Cincinnati Germans, 1870–1920.* New York: Arno, 1980.

Doezema, Marianne. *George Bellows and Urban America.* YUP, 1992.

Dorn, Jacob Henry. *Washington Gladden, Prophet of the Social Gospel.* OSUP, 1968.

Dunlop, M. H. "Curiosities Too Numerous to Mention: Early Regionalism and Cincinnati's Western Museum." *American Quarterly* 26 (1984): 524–48.

Erickson, Leonard. "Politics and Repeal of Ohio's Black Laws, 1837–1849." *OH* 82 (1973): 154–75.

Faludi, Susan. "A Good Dawg Will Always Remain Loyal: The Cleveland Browns Skip Town." In *Stiffed: The Betrayal of the American Man.* New York: William Morrow, 1999, 153–223.

Feather, Carl E. *Mountain People in a Flat Land: A Popular History of Appalachian Migrants to Northeast Ohio, 1940–1965.* OUP, 1998.

Feinstein, John. *A Season on the Brink: A Year with Bob Knight and the Indiana Hoosiers.* New York: Macmillan, 1986.

Filler, Louis, ed. *An Ohio Schoolmistress: The Memoirs of Irene Hardy.* KSUP, 1980.

Fine, Sydney. "The Toledo Chevrolet Strike of 1935." *OH* 67 (1958): 326–56.

Finegold, Kenneth. *Experts and Politicians: Reform Challenges to Machine Politics in New York, Cleveland, and Chicago.* Princeton, N.J.: Princeton University Press, 1995.

Fisk, William L., Jr. "The Scotch-Irish in Central Ohio." *OH* 57 (1948): 111–25.

Fones-Wolf, Elizabeth, and Kenneth Fones-Wolf. "The War at Mingo Junction: The Autonomous Workman and the Decline of the Knights of Labor." *OH* 92 (1983): 37–51.

Fruehling, Byron D. and Robert H. Smith. "Subterranean Hideaways of the Underground Railroad in Ohio: An Architectural, Archaeological and Historical Critique of Local Traditions." *OH* 102 (1993): 98–117.

Fry, C. George. "Washington Gladden: First Citizen of Columbus." *OH* 73 (1964): 90–99.

Gara, Larry. *The Liberty Line: The Legend of the Underground Railroad.* 1961; reprint, UPK, 1996.

Gartner, Lloyd P. *History of the Jews of Cleveland.* Cle.: WRHS and the Jewish Theological Seminary of America, 1978.

Geary, Linda L. *Balanced in the Wind: A Biography of Betsey Mix Cowles.* Lewisburg, Pa.: Bucknell University Press for the WRHS, 1989.

Geer, Emily Apt. *First Lady: The Life of Lucy Webb Hayes.* KSUP, 1984.

Gerber, David A. *Black Ohio and the Color Line, 1860–1915.* UIP, 1976.

Ginzberg, Lori D. "Women in an Evangelical Community: Oberlin, 1835–1850." *OH* 89 (1980): 78–88.

Glazer, Walter. *Cincinnati in 1840: The Social and Functional Organization of an Urban Community During the Pre–Civil War Period.* OSUP, 1999.

Grabowski, John J. "From Progressive to Patrician: George Bellamy and Hiram House: Social Settlement, 1896–1914." *OH* 87 (1978): 37–52.

Graziano, Frank and Peter Stitt, eds. *James Wright: A Profile.* Durango, Colo.: Logbridge-Rhodes, 1988.

Green, Jay D. "'Nothing to Advertise Except God': Christian Radio and the Creation of an Evangelical Subculture in Northeast Ohio, 1958–1972." *OH* 106 (1997): 171–91.

Greenberg, Gerald S. "Literary Bequests in Early Ohio Wills." *OH* 102 (1993): 20–34.

Griffin, William. "Black Insurgency in the Republican Party of Ohio, 1920–1932." *OH* 82 (1973): 25–46.

Groseclose, Barbara. "Itinerant Painting in Ohio: Origins and Implications." *OH* 90 (1981): 129–40.

Gruenwald, Kim. *River of Enterprise: The Commercial Origins of Regional Identity in the Ohio Valley, 1790–1850.* IUP, 2002.

Guschow, Stephen D. *The Red Stockings of Cincinnati: Baseball's First All-Professional Team and Its Historic 1869 and 1870 Seasons.* Jefferson, N.C.: McFarland, 1998.

Gutman, Herbert G. "An Iron Workers' Strike in the Ohio Valley, 1873–1874." *OH* 68 (1959): 353–70.

Harper, Robert S. *The Ohio Press in the Civil War.* OSUP, 1962.

Harris, Marc L. "The Process of Voluntary Association: Organizing the Ravenna Temperance Society, 1830." *OH* 94 (1985): 158–70.

Harrold, Stanley. *Gamaliel Bailey and Antislavery Union.* KSUP, 1986.

Harte, Brian. "Land in the Old Northwest: A Study of Speculation, Sales, and Settlement on the Connecticut Western Reserve." *OH* 101 (1992): 114–39.

Havighurst, Walter. *The Miami Years, 1809–1984.* New York: Putnam, 1984.

Hill, Leonard U. "John Randolph's Freed Slaves Settle in Western Ohio." *BCHS* 23 (1965): 179–87.

Hines, Thomas F. "The Paradox of Progressive Architecture: Urban Planning and Public Building in Tom Johnson's Cleveland." *American Quarterly* 25 (1973): 426–48.

Holli, Melvin G. "Toledo's Golden Ruler: Samuel P. Jones." *Timeline* 17, no. 4 (July–August 2000): 40–51.

Hoogenboom, Ari. *Rutherford B. Hayes: Warrior and President.* Lawrence: University Press of Kansas, 1995.

Hough, Leslie S. *The Turbulent Spirit: Cleveland, Ohio and Its Workers, 1877–1899.* New York: Garland, 1991.

Hough, Robert Lee. *The Quiet Rebel: William Dean Howells as Social Commentator.* Lincoln: University of Nebraska Press, 1959.

Howard, Fred. *Wilbur and Orville: A Biography of the Wright Brothers.* New York: Knopf, 1987.

Huber, Donald L. "The Prophet Joseph in Ohio." *Timeline* 16, no. 6 (November–December 1999): 2–17.

Hunker, Henry L. *Columbus, Ohio: A Personal Geography.* OSUP, 2000.

Hurt, R. Douglas. *The Ohio Frontier: Crucible of the Old Northwest, 1720–1830.* IUP, 1996.

———. "Ohio: Gateway to the Midwest." In *Heartland: Comparative Histories of the Midwestern States,* edited by James H. Madison, 206–25. IUP, 1988.

Hutslar, Donald A. *The Architecture of Migration: Log Construction in the Ohio Country, 1750–1850.* OUP, 1986.

Irrmann, Robert H. "The Library of an Early Ohio Farmer." *OH* 57 (1948): 185–93.

Jacobs, Gregory S. *Getting Around Brown: Desegregation, Development, and the Columbus Public Schools.* OSUP, 1998.

Jenkins, William D. *Steel Valley Klan: The Ku Klux Klan in Ohio's Mahoning Valley.* KSUP, 1990.

Johnson, Ronald M. "Politics and Pedagogy: The 1892 Cleveland School Reform." *OH* 84 (1975): 196–206.

Jones, Marnie. *Holy Toledo: Religion and Politics in the Life of "GOLDEN RULE" Jones.* UPK, 1998.

Jones, Robert Leslie. *History of Agriculture in Ohio To 1880.* KSUP, 1983.

Jordan, Philip D. *Ohio Comes of Age, 1873–1900.* OSAHS, 1943.

Kessler, John S., and Donald B. Ball. *North from the Mountains: A Folk History of the Carmel Melungeon Settlement, Highland, County, Ohio.* Macon, Ga.: Mercer University Press, 2001.

Ketner, Joseph D. *The Emergence of the African-American Artist: Robert S. Duncanson, 1821–1872.* Columbia: University of Missouri Press, 1993.

Klement, Frank L. *The Copperheads in the Middle West.* Gloucester, Mass.: P. Smith, 1970.

———. *The Limits of Dissent: Clement L. Vallandigham and the Civil War.* UPK, 1970.

Klingaman, David C., and Richard K. Vedder, eds. *Essays on the Economy of the Old Northwest.* OUP, 1987.

———, eds. *Essays in Nineteenth Century Economic History: The Old Northwest.* OUP, 1975.

Knepper, George W. *Ohio and Its People.* 2d ed. KSUP, 1997.

Knowles, Anne Kelley. *Calvinists Incorporated: Welsh Immigrants on Ohio's Industrial Frontier.* UCP, 1997.

Kozlowski, L. J. "A Painter's Struggle: Sala Bosworth." *Timeline* 16, no. 6 (November–December 1999): 22–35.

Kusmer, Kenneth L. *A Black Ghetto Takes Shape: Black Cleveland, 1870–1930.* UIP, 1976.

Lamis, Alexander P., ed. *Ohio Politics.* KSUP, 1994.

Laughlin, Kathleen A. "Sisterhood, Inc.: The Status of Women Commission Movement and the Rise of Feminist Coalition Politics in Ohio, 1964–1974." *OH* 108 (1999): 39–60.

Leonard, Henry B. "Ethnic Cleavage and Industrial Conflict in Late Nineteenth Century America: The Cleveland Rolling Mill Company Strikes of 1882 and 1885." *Labor History* 20 (1979): 524–48.

Lesick, Lawrence Thomas. *The Lane Rebels: Evangelicalism and Antislavery in Antebellum America.* Metuchen, N.J.: Scarecrow Press, 1980.

Leslie, Stuart W. *Boss Kettering.* New York: Columbia University Press, 1983.

Lindenmeyer, Kriste. "Saving Mothers and Babies: The Sheppard-Towner Act in Ohio, 1921–1929." *OH* 99 (1990): 105–34.

Linden-Ward, Blanche. "The Greening of Cincinnati: Adolph Strauch's Legacy in Park Design." *QCH* 51 (Spring 1993): 20–39.

Linn, Brian M. "'Pretty Scaly Times': The Ohio National Guard and the Railroad Strike of 1877." *OH* 94 (1985): 171–81.

Lupold, Harry F. and Gladys Haddad, eds. *Ohio's Western Reserve: A Regional Reader.* KSUP, 1988.

Lynn, Kenneth Schuyler. *William Dean Howells: An American Life.* New York: Harcourt, Brace, Jovanovich, 1971.

McCormick, Edgar L. *Brimfield and Its People: Life in a Western Reserve Township, 1816–1941.* Grantham, N.H.: Tompson and Rutter, 1988.

McCormick, Virginia E., "Butter and Egg Business: Implications from the Records of a Nineteenth-Century Farm Wife." *OH* 100 (1991): 57–67.

————. *Educational Architecture in Ohio: From One-Room Schools and Carnegie Libraries to Community Education Villages.* KSUP, 2001.

McCormick, Virginia E. and Robert W. McCormick, *New Englanders on the Ohio Frontier: Migration and Settlement of Worthington, Ohio.* KSUP, 1998.

McGerr, Michael. "The Meaning of Liberal Republicanism: The Case of Ohio." *Civil War History* 28 (1982): 307–23.

McGroarty, William Buckner. "Exploration in Mass Migration." *William and Mary College Quarterly Historical Magazine* 21 (2nd ser., July 1941): 208–26.

McTighe, Michael J. *A Measure of Success: Protestants and Public Culture in Antebellum Cleveland.* Albany: State University Press of New York, 1994.

Mach, Thomas S. "George Hunt Pendleton, The Ohio Idea and Political Continuity in Reconstruction America." *OH* 108 (1999): 125–44.

Maciejunes, Nannette V., and Michael D. Hall, eds. *The Paintings of Charles Burchfield, North by Midwest.* New York: Harry N. Abrams and Col.: Columbus Museum of Art, 1977.

Maizlish, Stephen E. *The Triumph of Sectionalism: The Transformation of Ohio Politics, 1844–1856.* KSUP, 1983.

Marcus, Alan I. *Plague of Strangers: Social Groups and the Origins of City Services in Cincinnati, 1819–1870.* OSUP, 1991.

Masotti, Louis H., and Jerome R. Coral. *Shoot-Out in Cleveland: Black Militants and the Police.* New York: Praeger, 1969.

Miller, Janet A. "Urban Education and the New City: Cincinnati's Elementary Schools, 1870 to 1914." *OH* 88 (1979): 152–72.

Miller, Zane L. *Boss Cox's Cincinnati: Urban Politics in the Progressive Era.* UCP, 1968.

———. *Suburb: Neighborhood and Community in Forest Park, Ohio, 1935–1876.* Knoxville: University of Tennessee Press, 1981.

———. *Visions of Place: The City, Neighborhoods, Suburbs, and Cincinnati's Clifton, 1850–2000.* OSUP, 2001.

Miller, Zane L., and Bruce Tucker. *Changing Plans for America's Inner Cities: Cincinnati's Over-the-Rhine and Twentieth-Century Urbanism.* OSUP, 1998.

Millette, Stephen M. "Charles E. Ruthenberg: The Development of an American Communist, 1909–1927." *OH* 81 (1972): 193–209.

Morgan, Charles H. *George Bellows: Painter of America.* New York: Reynal, 1965.

Morris, Carolyn M. "Black Elected Officials in Ohio, 1978: Characteristics and Perceptions." *OH* 88 (1979): 291–309.

Morton, Marian J. "'Go and Sin No More': Maternity Houses in Cleveland, 1869–1936." *OH* 93 (1984): 117–46.

Mulder, John C. "The Heavenly City and Human Cities: Washington Gladden and Urban Reform." *OH* 87 (1978): 151–74.

Murdock, Eugene C. "Life of Tom L. Johnson." Ph.D. diss., Columbia University, 1951.

Neuhaus, Robert. *Unsuspected Genius: The Art and Life of Frank Duveneck.* San Francisco: Bedford Press, 1987.

Niven, John. *Salmon P. Chase: A Biography.* New York: Oxford University Press, 1995.

Obermiller, Phillip J. *Down Home, Downtown: Urban Appalachians Today.* Dubuque, Iowa: Kendall/Hunt Publishing, 1996.

Obermiller, Phillip J., and William W. Philliber, eds. *Two Few Tomorrows: Urban Appalachians in the 1980s.* Boone, N.C.: Appalachian Consortium Press, 1987.

Patterson, James T. *Mr. Republican: A Biography of Robert A. Taft.* New York: Houghton Mifflin, 1972.

Payne, Phillip Gene. "Modernity Lost: Ironton, Ohio, in Industrial and Post-Industrial America." Ph.D. diss., The Ohio State University, 1994.

Peacefull, Leonard, ed. *A Geography of Ohio.* KSUP, 1996.

Perlman, Bennard B. *Robert Henri: His Life and Art.* 1919; reprint, New York: Viking, 1974.

Peskin, Allan. *Garfield, A Biography.* KSUP, 1978.

Phillips, Kimberley L. *AlabamaNorth: African-American Migrants, Community, and Working-Class Activism in Cleveland, 1915–1945.* UIP, 1999.

Pierce, Michael. "Farmers and the Failure of Populism in Ohio, 1890–1891." *Agricultural History* 74 (2000): 58–85.

———. "The Populist President of the American Federation of Labor: The Career of John McBride, 1880–1895." *Labor History* 41 (2000): 5–24.

Pocock, Emil. "Evangelical Frontier: Dayton, Ohio 1796–1839." Ph.D. diss., Indiana University, 1984.

Preston, Daniel. "Market and Mill Town: Hamilton, Ohio, 1795–1860." Ph.D. diss., University of Maryland, 1987.

———. "Thomas Kelsey, Hardluck Entrepreneur." *OH* 104 (1995): 127–41.

Quay, Joyce Crosby. *Early Promise, Late Reward: A Biography of Helen Hooven Santmyer.* Manchester, Conn.: Knowledge, Ideas, and Trends, 1995.

Quick, Michael. *An American Painter Abroad: Frank Duveneck's European Years.* Cin.: Cincinnati Museum of Art, 1987.

Raphael, Marc Lee. *Jews and Judaism in a Midwestern Community: Columbus, Ohio, 1840–1875.* Col.: OHS, 1979.

Rarick, Molly M. *Progressive Vision: The Planning of Downtown Cleveland, 1903–1930.* Cle.: Cleveland Museum of Art, 1986.

Ratcliffe, Donald J. *Party Spirit in a Frontier Republic: Democratic Politics in Ohio, 1793–1821.* OSUP, 1998.

———. *The Politics of Long Division: The Birth of the Second Party System in Ohio, 1818–1828.* OSUP, 2000.

Reid, Robert L., ed. *Always a River: The Ohio River and the American Experience.* IUP, 1991.

Reston, James. *Collision at Home Plate: The Lives of Pete Rose and Bart Giamatti.* New York: Harper Collins, 1991.

Rideout, Walter Bates. *Sherwood Anderson: A Collection of Critical Essays.* Englewood Cliffs, N.J.: Prentice-Hall, 1974.

Rippley, La Vern J. "The Chillicothe Germans." *OH* 75 (1966): 212–25.

Robinson, Jeff, and Brian Adams. "As Seen on TV." *Ohio Magazine* 22, no. 8 (Nov. 2000): 62–65.

Rolt-Wheeler, Francis. *Thomas Alva Edison.* New York: Book League of America, 1990.

Roseboom, Eugene H. *The Civil War Era, 1850–1873.* OSAHS, 1944.

Ross, Steven J. *Workers on the Edge: Work, Leisure, and Politics in Industrializing Cincinnati, 1788–1890.* New York: Columbia University Press, 1985.

Russell, Francis. *The Shadow of Blooming Grove: Warren G. Harding in His Times.* New York: McGraw-Hill, 1968.

Sarna, Jonathan, and Nancy H. Klein. *The Jews of Cincinnati.* Cin.: Center for the Study of the American Jewish Experience, 1989.

Sawrey, Robert D. *Dubious Victory: The Reconstruction Debate in Ohio.* UPK, 1992.

Scharf, Lois. "'I Would Go Wherever Fortune Would Direct': Hannah Huntington and the Frontier of the Western Reserve." *OH* 97 (1988): 5–28.

Scheiber, Harry N. "Alfred Kelley and the Ohio Business Elite, 1822–1859." *OH* 87 (1978): 365–92.

———. *Ohio Canal Era: A Case Study of Government and the Economy, 1820–1861.* OUP, 1969.

Scheurman, William E. "Canton and the Great Steel Strike of 1919: A Marriage of Nativism and Politics." *OH* 93 (1984): 68–87.

Schmidlin, Thomas W., and Jeanne Appelhans Schmidlin. *Thunder in the Heartland: A Chronicle of Outstanding Weather Events in Ohio.* KSUP, 1996.

Sears, Alfred Byron. *Thomas Worthington, Father of Ohio Statehood.* Col.: OSUP for the OHS, 1958.

Shade, William Gerald. *Banks or No Banks: The Money Issue in Western Politics, 1832–1865.* Detroit: Wayne State University Press, 1972.

Shapiro, Henry D. and Jonathan D. Sarna, eds. *Ethnic Diversity and Civic Identity: Patterns of Conflict and Cohesion in Cincinnati Since 1820.* UIP, 1992.

Sharp, James Roger. *The Jacksonians versus the Banks: Politics in the States After the Panic of 1837.* New York: Columbia University Press, 1970.

Shaw, Mark. *Nicklaus.* Dallas: Taylor Publishing, 1997.

Smith, Dave, ed. *The Pure Clear Word: Essays on the Poetry of James Wright.* UIP, 1982.

Smith, Thomas H. "Crawford County 'Ez Trooly Dimecratic': A Study of Midwestern Copperheadism." *OH* 76 (1967): 33–53.

Sokolove, Michael Y. Hustle. *The Myth, Life and Lies of Pete Rose.* New York: Simon and Schuster, 1990.

Sollors, Werner, "Emil Klauprecht's *Cincinnati, Oder Geheimnisse Des Westens* and the Beginnings of Urban Realism in America." *QCH* 42 (Fall 1984): 40–48.

Soltow, Lee. "Inequality Amidst Abundance: Land Ownership in Early Nineteenth-Century Ohio." *OH* 88 (1979): 133–51.

Sponholtz, Lloyd. "The Politics of Temperance in Ohio, 1880–1912." *OH* 85 (1976): 4–27.

Stearns, Robert, ed. *Illusions of Eden: Visions of the American Heartland.* Minneapolis: Arts Midwest and Col.: Columbus Museum of Art, 2000.

Stern, Joseph S., Jr. "It Was the Best of Times; It Was the Worst of Times." *QCH* 42 (Spring 1984): 3–12.

Stern, Sydney Ladensohn. *Gloria Steinem: Her Passions, Politics, and Mystique.* Secaucus, N.J.: Birch Lane Press, 1997.

Stevens, Harry R. *The Early Jackson Party in Ohio.* Durham, N.C.: Duke University Press, 1957.

———. "Folk Music on the Midwestern Frontier, 1788–1825." *OH* 57 (1948): 126–46.

Stewart, James Brewer. *Joshua R. Giddings and the Tactics of Radical Politics.* Cle: Press of Case Western Reserve University, 1970.

Tague, James A. "William D. Gallagher, Champion of Western Literary Periodicals." *OH* 69 (1960): 257–71.

Tamburro, Samuel J. "Frances Jennings Casement and the Equal Rights Association of Painesville, Ohio: The Fight for Women's Suffrage, 1883–1889." *OH* 108 (1999): 162–76.

Taylor, Henry C. "On Slavery's Fringe: City-Building and Black Community Development in Cincinnati, 1800–1850." *OH* 95 (1986): 5–33.

Taylor, Henry Louis, ed. *Race and the City: Work, Community, and Protest in Cincinnati, 1820–1970.* UIP, 1993.

Terzian, Barbara A. "'Effusions of Folly and Fanaticism': Race, Gender, and Constitution Making in Ohio, 1802–1923." Ph.D. diss., The Ohio State University, 2000.

Tolzmann, Don Heinrich. *The Cincinnati Germans After the Great War.* New York: Peter Lang, 1987.

———. *Cincinnati's German Heritage.* Bowie, Md.: Heritage Books, 1994.

———. *Das Ohiotal—The Ohio Valley: The German Dimension.* New York: Peter Lang, 1993.

Torsney, Cheryl B. *Constance Fenimore Woolson: The Grief of Artistry.* Athens: University of Georgia Press, 1989.

Tracy, Steven C. *Going to Cincinnati: A History of the Blues in the Queen City.* UIP, 1993.

Trolander, Judith A. "Twenty Years at Hiram House." *OH* 78 (1969): 25–37.

Utter, William T. *The Frontier State, 1803–1825.* OSAHS, 1942.

Van Tassell, David D., and John J. Grabowski, eds. *Cleveland—A Tradition of Reform.* KSUP, 1986.

Van Tine, Warren, et al. *In the Worker's Interest: A History of the Ohio AFL-CIO, 1958–1998.* Col.: Center for Labor Research, 1998.

Vazzano, Frank P. "Harry Hopkins and Martin Davey: Federal Relief and Ohio Politics During the Great Depression." *OH* 96 (1987): 124–39.

Vitz, Robert C. *The Queen and the Arts: Cultural Life in Nineteenth-Century Cincinnati.* KSUP, 1989.

Wachhorst, Wyn. *Thomas Alva Edison: An American Myth.* Cambridge, Mass.: MIT Press, 1981.

Warner, Hoyt Landon. *Progressivism in Ohio, 1897–1917.* OSUP, 1964.

Watras, Joseph. *Politics, Race, and Schools: Racial Integration, 1954–1994.* New York: Garland, 1997.

Weisenburger, Francis P. *The Passing of the Frontier, 1825–1850.* OSAHS, 1941.

Wheeler, Kenneth. "The Antebellum College in the Old Northwest: Higher Education and the Defining of the Midwest." Ph.D. diss., The Ohio State University, 1999.

Wheeler, Robert A. "Land and Community in Rural Nineteenth Century America: Claridon Township, 1810–1870." *OH* 97 (1988): 101–21.

Wienberg, Daniel E. "Ethnic Identity in Industrial Cleveland: The Hungarians, 1900–1920." *OH* 86 (1977): 171–86.

Wiese, Andrew. "The Other Suburbanites: African American Suburbanization in the North Before 1950." *Journal of American History* 85 (1999): 1495–1524.

Williams, Lee. "Newcomers to the City: A Study of Black Population Growth in Toledo, Ohio, 1910–1930." *OH* 89 (1980): 5–24.

Williams, T. Harry. *Hayes of the Twenty-Third: The Civil War Volunteer Officer.* New York: Knopf, 1965.

Winkle, Kenneth J. *The Politics of Community: Migration and Politics in Antebellum Ohio.* CUP, 1988.

Wintz, Cary D. "Race and Realism in the Fiction of Charles W. Chestnutt." *OH* 81 (1972): 122–30.

Wittke, Carl. "Ohio's Germans, 1840–1875." *OH* 66 (1957): 339–54.

Acknowledgments

It was Charlotte Dihoff and Barbara Lyon's idea to have The Ohio State University Press commission a history of Ohio for publication in conjunction with the bicentennial anniversary of the state in 2003. It was Zane Miller at the University of Cincinnati who recommended me as a potential author. And it was Barbara Hanrahan who would not accept my initial refusal to undertake such a project. I am happy to offer sincere thanks to all these people, for the book I dreaded doing quickly became a richly rewarding experience.

Many friends have had to listen to me talk, or rather fret, about this project. I am grateful in particular for the wisdom and support of Susan Gray and Fred Anderson. Others who offered advice and encouragement, even when they did not know they were doing so, include Richard Aquila, Renee Baernstein, Dan Goffman, Charlotte Newman Goldy, Matthew Gordon, Jack Kirby, John Larson, Jim Madison, Dan Nathan, Bill Owen, Constance Pierce, Barbara Terzian, Fredrika Teute, Bob Thurston, Peter Williams, Allan Winkler, and Gretchen Ziolkowski. A conversation with John Kulewicz, and David Kyvig convinced me to attempt a history of Ohio. And the assistance of Jeri Schaner and Liz Smith in the history department at Miami University was invaluable in making it a reality. No one was more helpful than my expert fellow readers and wonderful friends, Irene Kleiman and Marj Nadler.

Malcolm Litchfield, Director of The Ohio State University Press, guided a mammoth manuscript into a much shorter book. Paul Boyer, Austin Kerr, and Fred Blue were model reviewers, combining encouragement with constructive suggestions. Warren Van Tine's penetrating criticism of my original proposal inspired a major revision of the last third of the manuscript. Lynne Bonenberger proved to be an ideal copyeditor. My good friends at the *Encyclopedia of the Midwest* project at The Ohio State University, Dick Sisson and Chris Zacher, have been very supportive. In one of life's delicious ironies, I got to know Charlotte Dihoff while we were working on the encyclopedia. When Char came up with the idea for a history of Ohio, she never dreamed that she would have to hold the hand of the author while he wrote it. But that is exactly what happened. I and the book are much better because of it.

In spring 1999, I was fortunate to serve as the John Adams Visiting Professor of American Studies at Leiden University in the Netherlands. During the term, I attended a weekly series of lectures entitled "The African American Century." The presentations and conversations with scholars helped shape the content of this book. In Leiden, Joke Kardux and Eduard Van de Bilt moved from gracious hosts into fast friends while George Strong, a European historian at the College of William and Mary also teaching at Leiden, accompanied me on more than one memorable trip across Holland, Belgium, and Italy.

Over the years, I have enjoyed teaching United States history to thousands of students at Miami University, most of whom are natives of Ohio. The fifty students enrolled in HST 261 (The History of Ohio) in the fall of 1998 gave me the confidence to abandon a more traditional framework and try something different. As is always true with good classes, they taught me much more than I taught them. Rebecca Wanzo, one of my students and teachers with whom I share the joys of middlebrow reading, will find her influence on nearly every page. Rebecca was my ideal reader; I wrote this book to her.

No matter how long Mary Kupiec Cayton lives in Ohio, she will never be an Ohioan. She would rather be closer to her real home in northern Virginia. Nevertheless, she chose to make a life with me in a place far away from the Potomac River. I will be forever grateful for that decision and the many things we have enjoyed together, none of which we treasure more than those exemplary Buckeyes, Elizabeth Renanne Cayton and Hannah Kupiec Cayton.

Index